Foreigners, minorities and integration

Manchester University Press

Foreigners, minorities and integration

The Muslim immigrant experience in Britain and Germany

Sarah Hackett

Manchester University Press

Copyright © Sarah Hackett 2013

The right of Sarah Hackett to be identified as the author of this work has been asserted by her in accordance with the Copyright, Designs and Patents Act 1988.

Published by Manchester University Press
Altrincham Street, Manchester M1 7JA, UK
www.manchesteruniversitypress.co.uk

British Library Cataloguing-in-Publication Data is available

Library of Congress Cataloging-in-Publication Data is available

ISBN 978 1 7849 9281 1 *paperback*

First published by Manchester University Press in hardback 2013

This paperback edition first published 2016

The publisher has no responsibility for the persistence or accuracy of URLs for any external or third-party internet websites referred to in this book, and does not guarantee that any content on such websites is, or will remain, accurate or appropriate.

Printed by Lightning Source

Contents

List of tables	*page* vii
Preface and acknowledgements	ix
Introduction A history of immigration to modern Britain and Germany: national and local perspectives	1
1 Self-preservation to determination: the employment sector	27
2 Neighbourhood which? The housing sector: owner-occupation and ethnic neighbourhoods	87
3 The education sector: the three Rs – race, relations and arithmetic	149
4 Conclusion: comparing communities, challenging conceptions	217
Bibliography	229
Index	279

Tables

1.1	Types of harassment suffered by Asian traders and their families in Newcastle according to a study undertaken between July 1995 and January 1996	page 49
1.2	Types of harassment suffered by Asian traders in the East End of Newcastle according to interviews carried out in December 1997 and January 1998	50
1.3	The ethnic origin of 449 ethnic minority businessmen in Newcastle, 1997	53
1.4	Unemployment rate amongst the State of Bremen's entire workforce and foreign workforce, 1974–78	69
1.5	Reasons given for becoming self-employed by 102 Turkish businessmen in Bremen and Bremerhaven in 2001	76
1.6	The employment sectors occupied by 102 Turkish businessmen in Bremen and Bremerhaven in 2001	77
2.1	Characteristics and issues relating to council housing in Newcastle amongst whites, Chinese, South Asians and Afro-Caribbeans, 1986	115
2.2	Districts in Bremen in which the ethnic minority population constituted a minimum of 6 per cent, April 1977	134
2.3	The seven districts in Bremen with the highest ethnic minority population constitutions, February 1980	138
2.4	The seven districts in Bremen with the highest ethnic minority constitutions, January 1993	142
2.5	The seven sub-districts in Bremen with the highest ethnic minority constitutions, December 1992	142
3.1	The seven districts in Bremen with the highest numbers of ethnic minority pupils, 1980–81	206
3.2	The seven districts in Bremen with the highest constitutions of ethnic minority primary school-aged children, January 1993	206

Preface and acknowledgements

This book is a study of two post-war Muslim ethnic minority communities that have seldom featured in the academic literature or the public debate on migration to Britain and Germany: those of Newcastle upon Tyne and Bremen. It is the first work to offer a comparative assessment of the experiences of Muslims at a local level in these two countries. Its focus on the employment, housing and education sectors is a novel approach that exposes both the manner in which migrants have negotiated their local host surroundings and the role played by minority agency. The conclusions transgress geographical and chronological frameworks, and offer a critical reassessment of ethnic minority integration and the role played by Islam in the migration process. The use of Newcastle and Bremen as case studies as well as the comparative nature allow for an in-depth level of detail and analysis, and for a comprehensive assessment of both Muslim migrant communities from their arrival during the 1960s through to their emergence as fixed attributes on the cities' landscapes at the turn of the millennium.

This book began as a PhD thesis at the University of Durham in 2004, and stemmed from undergraduate and MA level work that addressed Muslim migrant populations in other European countries, including France and Spain. On an academic level, it was my interest in the particulars of Britain and Germany's immigration histories and frameworks, and the intricacies of ethnic minority integration, that initially formed the basis of this study. I was further intrigued by the ever-increasing importance awarded to the terms 'Muslim' and 'Islam' in both academic and political debates. This project was also driven by a personal interest in the relationships and interactions between people of different backgrounds, ethnicities and cultures that developed during my time as an American growing up in a number of European countries.

My curiosity and enthusiasm were further heightened by the fact that Muslim migration was a topic that seemed to be gaining momentum and prominence on almost a daily basis in the immediate post-9/11 world. This was reinforced by both past and unfolding events across Europe, such as France's headscarf affair, the rise of far-right parties, the Madrid bombings, the murder of Theo van Gogh in the Netherlands and Denmark's cartoon scandal. These were complemented by events closer to home in both Britain and Germany, including the Rushdie Affair,[1] the London bombings of July 2005, Islamic fundamentalist terrorism, and disputes regarding single faith schools, religious instruction, religious discrimination legislation, the wearing of headscarves amongst teachers and the building of mosques. More recently, Angela Merkel and David Cameron's claims that multiculturalism has failed have further triggered debate about Britain and Germany's Muslim ethnic minority communities.

This climate of political and academic frenzy certainly made researching and writing about Muslims a somewhat daunting task, yet it also appeared to be a pertinent time at which to conduct an investigation into the history of two often forgotten Muslim migrant populations. It seemed logical to assume that the exposure of these communities' settlement patterns and practices, as well as a survey of their respective local governments' policies and measures, might help contextualise and provide a framework for these increasingly heated debates. It was also hoped that a study of numerically smaller Muslim ethnic minority communities that had largely escaped the limelight would constitute an additional branch to the existing literature. Furthermore, this book has developed from an ambition to shift attention away from the often too imposing overarching crises towards an understanding of the 'everyday' lives of British and German Muslims.

Yet a study of Muslim migrant communities in Britain and Germany during the post-war period is not without its difficulties, and is prone to certain generalisations and prioritisations. I am conscious, for example, that Muslim ethnic minorities in neither Newcastle nor Bremen constitute one homogenous group, despite the term 'community' suggesting otherwise. Furthermore, in choosing to focus on Muslims, a study is almost undoubtedly prioritising religious

---

[1] The Rushdie Affair was the reaction amongst some Muslims to the publication of Salman Rushdie's 1988 novel *The Satanic Verses*. Arguing that the book was blasphemous, British Muslims tried to prevent its publication and burned a copy of the novel during a 1989 protest march in Bradford.

identity over other factors, such as ethnicity, class and gender. Attempts have been made to avoid such pitfalls whenever possible and differences between Muslims of different ethnic backgrounds are acknowledged as are numerous markers of identity.

An additional difficulty is that this book investigates Muslim ethnic minorities before Islam was considered at an official level and deemed an influential factor in the migration experience. As a result, the sources drawn upon are overwhelmingly compiled along ethnic lines. Whilst this is the case for any study adopting a historical approach to Muslim migrants in Britain and Germany, I feel that it should nevertheless be openly recognised. Lastly, this book is a keen advocate of ethnic minority self-determination and independence, and stresses the role that migrant agency has played in the integration process in both Newcastle and Bremen. Yet whilst it exposes the 'winners' of migration, I am keen to avoid generalisation and accept that there have most certainly also been 'losers'. Despite its limitations however, I am hopeful that the final product will make a small contribution to the ever-growing body of literature on Muslim migrants in both Britain and Germany.

I received a great deal of help and support with this project from the very beginning. I am thankful for a PhD bursary from the University of Durham, as well as for grants received from the German History Society, the Deutscher Akademischer Austauschdienst (DAAD) and the German Historical Institute London (GHIL), all of which enabled me to carry out the necessary research during my time as a PhD student. Yet the book has moved on from the PhD thesis and I am thankful for the financial support that I received from the Culture and Regional Studies Research Beacon at the University of Sunderland, which allowed me to conduct further research in Bremen during the summer of 2010, and attend numerous conferences where I was able to test some of my ideas and arguments.

I was very fortunate to have Professor Lawrence Black and Dr Kay Schiller as supervisors for my PhD. I am extremely grateful for their guidance and advice, and for the generous amount of time, interest and patience that they granted to my project. I have also benefited from the help, direction and encouragement of many others, both within and outside the field of migration studies and I owe special thanks in particular to Professor Robert Colls, Professor Jo Fox, Professor David Moon, Dr Andrzej Olechnowicz, Professor Panikos Panayi and Professor Ceri Peach. I would also like to thank my colleagues at the University of Sunderland for their continued support, especially Dr

Delphine Doucet, Dr Kathleen Kerr-Koch, Dr Susan Mandala, Dr Geoffrey Nash, Professor Peter Rushton and Dr Kevin Yuill. I am extremely grateful to Dr Dieter K. Buse for his suggested reading on identity in Bremen, and to Nadeem Ahmad for going out of his way to respond to my queries and provide me with information on Newcastle.

Special thanks to all those in Newcastle and Bremen who took the time to help me gain an insight into local policies and the cities' Muslim communities. This book also benefited from the assistance received from the staffs at the Bremische Bürgerschaft library, the Statistisches Landesamt Bremen, Staatsarchiv Bremen, Tyne & Wear Archives and the Local Studies Collection at Newcastle City Library. Many thanks also to Manchester University Press for their time and patience in getting this book ready for publication, and to the anonymous reviewer for very helpful comments and suggestions. For any errors, inadequacies or shortcomings that remain, I am of course solely responsible.

I am deeply grateful to my parents and brothers who have supported this project from the beginning. Thank you for believing in me. I would like to express my gratitude to my friends for the welcome distractions and for keeping me sane throughout. Many thanks also to my students at the University of Sunderland who have brought much joy to the early stage of my career, and made the time during which I was researching and writing this book much more pleasurable. Lastly, my greatest debt of gratitude is to my husband, Matthew. He has lived with this project for almost as long as I have, and has provided advice and guidance throughout. Without his support and encouragement, it simply would not have been possible. For making it all worthwhile, I dedicate this book to him.

At a time at which Islam continues to be perceived as a barrier to integration and harmony in Europe, this book demonstrates that this need not be the case.

Introduction
A history of immigration to modern Britain and Germany: national and local perspectives

The national contexts

The history of immigration to Britain and West Germany in the post-war period has traditionally been seen as one of contrasts.[1] The reasons for this were not new to the post-1945 era, but rather were entrenched in both countries' histories. Britain has often been perceived as a country with a long tradition of migration and one that was perhaps destined to become multi-racial. The black soldiers who fought in the Roman armies that invaded Britain, the migrants who arrived from the Indian subcontinent during the 1600s and 1700s, and the Yemeni seamen who settled in dockland areas from the mid-nineteenth century act as testimony to this.[2] Furthermore, the British Empire ensured that people from all corners of the globe felt a connection with the 'mother country'. Indeed Britain's role as the imperial hub for a quarter of the world's surface guaranteed a widespread familiarity with the British language, education system and way of life.[3] Germany, by contrast, is a

---

[1] 'Germany' will be used from this point onwards.
[2] See Fred Halliday, *Arabs in Exile: Yemeni Migrants in Urban Britain* (London, 1992); Ian Spencer, *British Immigration Policy since 1939: The Making of Multi-Racial Britain* (London, 1997), p. 1; and Rozina Visram, *Asians in Britain: 400 Years of History* (London, 2002).
[3] See Zig Layton-Henry, *The Politics of Immigration: Immigration, 'Race' and 'Race' Relations in Post-war Britain* (Oxford, 1992), p. 9; and Joanna Herbert, *Negotiating Boundaries in the City: Migration, Ethnicity, and Gender in Britain* (Aldershot, 2008).

young country that, following its unification in 1871, displayed both nationalistic and racial ideology. In its short history, the notions of race and minority groups have never been far from its political agenda, whether in the form of racial hierarchy, exclusion and persecution, or xenophobia and discrimination.[4]

Other contrasts between Britain and Germany's immigration histories also exist and have been well documented in the historiography. Starting with its unification, Germany implemented a policy of Germanisation, the legacy of which lasted throughout the twentieth century. Furthermore, its *völkisch* ethno-cultural nationhood arguably shaped a national identity that limited the recognition of foreigners in the country. This was further accentuated by its status as the only major European immigration country with a pure *jus sanguinis* notion of citizenship. Britain's imperial policy, on the contrary, whilst undoubtedly based on a racial hierarchy to some extent, never widely consisted of overt racial persecution. Furthermore, British citizenship was comparably more accessible as a result of the concept of *jus soli*, allowing immigrants to become integrated. In essence, by the second half of the twentieth century, Britain had a strong multi-ethnic tradition to act as the foundation for post-1945 immigration whilst Germany did not.[5]

A further key contrast is revealed in the differences between Britain's colonial immigration and Germany's policy of labour importation. Immigration to Britain from the colonies has historically taken place within a largely unofficial framework with migrants moving as independent agents.[6] In contrast, Germany has a history of recruiting foreign workers in times of labour shortage. The result was a privately

---

[4] See Michael Burleigh and Wolfgang Wippermann, *The Racial State: Germany 1933–1945* (Cambridge, 1991); and Panikos Panayi, *Ethnic Minorities in Nineteenth and Twentieth Century Germany: Jews, Gypsies, Poles, Turks and Others* (Harlow, 2000), pp. 1–25.

[5] See Christian Joppke, *Immigration and the Nation-State: The United States, Germany, and Great Britain* (Oxford, 1999); and Panikos Panayi, 'The evolution of multiculturalism in Britain and Germany: An historical survey', *Journal of Multilingual and Multicultural Development*, 25:5–6 (2004), pp. 467–8. See also Rogers Brubaker, *Citizenship and Nationhood in France and Germany* (Cambridge MA, 1992).

[6] See Kathleen Paul, *Whitewashing Britain: Race and Citizenship in the Postwar Era* (Ithaca NY, 1997); and Randall Hansen, *Citizenship and Immigration in Post-war Britain: The Institutional Origins of a Multicultural Nation* (Oxford, 2000).

negotiated economic immigration that by its very nature was meant to be a temporary phenomenon.[7] It has also been argued that these differing post-war immigration paradigms have shaped what have been two distinct approaches to integration. Britain was home to the race relations model through which migrant communities were urged to maintain their own ethnic identities, and the Race Relations Acts of 1965, 1968 and 1976 advocated tolerance. Overall, whilst post-war Commonwealth immigration to Britain was almost entirely unwanted and numerous attempts were made to restrict it, Britain has nevertheless been more accepting of its position as a country of immigration than Germany. Germany's immigration and integration policy, however, has often been summarised by the statement '*Deutschland ist kein Einwanderungsland*' or 'Germany is not a country of immigration'. This line was maintained even once it became clear that many guest-workers (*Gastarbeiter*) were settling in Germany permanently and family reunification was taking place.[8]

It is these differences between Britain and Germany's immigration histories in the post-war era that form the basis of this book. It offers a long-term assessment of Britain's relatively liberal (albeit constrained after 1962) immigration policy and Germany's rigid guest-worker rotation system at a local level between two comparable cities, Newcastle upon Tyne and Bremen.[9] It concentrates specifically on Newcastle's South Asian Muslims and Bremen's Turkish Muslims, and measures their overall levels of integration through an assessment of the employment, housing and education sectors from the 1960s to the 1990s. It considers the effect that post-war immigration histories and paradigms had on these migrants' performances and behaviour in all three areas, and suggests that whilst Britain and Germany's immigration frameworks were indeed distinct, an increasing convergence of

[7] See Ulrich Herbert, *A History of Foreign Labor in Germany, 1880–1980: Seasonal Workers/Forced Laborers/Guest Workers*, trans. William Temple (Ann Arbor, 1990); and Stephen Castles, 'Migrants and minorities in post-Keynesian capitalism: The German case', in Malcolm Cross (ed.), *Ethnic Minorities and Industrial Change in Europe and North America* (Cambridge, 1992), pp. 36–54.

[8] See Simon Green, 'Divergent traditions, converging responses: Immigration and integration policy in the UK and Germany', *German Politics*, 16:1 (2007), p. 98.

[9] Under the rotation system, guest-workers were initially granted a one-year work permit, which could then be renewed. However, rotation was not strictly enforced, and many guest-workers and their families became long-term residents.

conduct and practices has been witnessed amongst both cities' Muslim migrants.

There exists an abundant historiography on both Britain and Germany's post-1945 immigration histories and there is certainly no need to offer more than a short summary here. In Britain, it was the arrival of 492 Jamaican men at Tilbury Docks in London on board the *Empire Windrush* on 22 June 1948 that has come to signal the start of a new chapter in the country's immigration history. New Commonwealth immigration began because post-war reconstruction and the expanding economy created labour positions that could not be filled by British workers. Both West Indian immigrants that began arriving in the late 1940s and those from the Indian subcontinent who followed during the 1950s and 1960s played a key role in Britain's labour market, filling vacancies in numerous sectors including those offered by transport providers, the British Hotels and Restaurants Association, the Ministry of Health and northern textile companies.[10]

The Second World War acted as a catalyst for immediate post-war migration, with many migrants, especially those of Jamaican origin, migrating to Britain having served in the RAF or in the munitions factories. Many had experienced the British way of life and identified long-term employment opportunities there, and many others followed them to the 'mother country'. South Asian communities in Britain have been shaped by four distinct phases of migration in the post-war period, with the single male workers of the late 1950s and early 1960s soon being joined by a chain migration of other unskilled male workers, wives and families, and eventually the appearance of a British-born generation.[11] Indeed there exists a well-established and still evolving historiography on the development of both West Indian and South Asian communities in post-1945 Britain.[12]

---

[10] For an insight into post-war colonial immigration to Britain, see Paul, *Whitewashing Britain*; and Leo Lucassen, *The Immigrant Threat: The Integration of Old and New Migrants in Western Europe since 1850* (Chicago, 2005), pp. 113–43.

[11] See Spencer, *British Immigration Policy since 1939*, pp. 18–19; and Philip Lewis, *Islamic Britain: Religion, Politics and Identity among British Muslims* (London, 2002), pp. 16–18.

[12] See Ceri Peach, *West Indian Migration to Britain: A Social Geography* (London, 1968); Colin Holmes, *John Bull's Island: Immigration and British Society, 1871–1971* (Basingstoke, 1988); and Panikos Panayi, *An Immigration History of Britain: Multicultural Racism since 1800* (Harlow, 2010).

There is also an abundant body of literature detailing the features of Germany's post-war guest-worker system and the initial experiences of foreign workers.[13] Guest-workers began arriving in Germany in 1955 when a foreign labour recruitment agreement was signed with Italy. This was followed by agreements with Spain and Greece (1960), Turkey (1961), Morocco (1963), Portugal (1964), Tunisia (1965) and Yugoslavia (1968). This foreign workforce was the result of Germany's economic miracle of the 1950s and arrived as nothing short of economic pawns in the country's prospering economy, constituting what Ulrich Herbert famously termed 'a reserve labor army'.[14] These guest-workers were recruited by means of an estimated 400 recruitment offices in the countries concerned, the aim of which was to find workers to fill vacancies in firms and companies in Germany. Before a guest-worker arrived, he had to have been interviewed, medically examined and screened for a criminal record. Furthermore, a contract had to be signed and his transport was arranged for him.

Whilst the recruitment of foreign labour was slow during the initial stages, by 1964, Germany was welcoming its one-millionth guest-worker. On the whole, it appeared as though the recruitment system would benefit every party concerned. The recruiters deemed it as one that would provide the opportunity to expand the German economy without the burden of excessive financial investment and social costs. The policymakers in the countries providing the workers believed that this system would remove many of their unskilled and unemployed workers who would bring in foreign currency and eventually return having undergone training. The workers themselves were to earn more in Germany than they would in their respective home countries and this would, in turn, allow them to provide for their families and enhance their economic status upon returning home. Furthermore, it provided German workers with an opportunity for upward mobility.

Yet there is no doubt that what originally appeared to be merely another phase in Germany's history of labour recruitment has increasingly developed into a multifaceted paradigm that has entertained politicians and academics alike for decades. Germany's 'reserve labor

---

[13] See Herbert, *A History of Foreign Labor in Germany*; Deniz Göktürk, David Gramling and Anton Kaes (eds), *Germany in Transit: Nation and Migration, 1955–2005* (Berkeley CA, 2007); Rita Chin, *The Guest Worker Question in Postwar Germany* (Cambridge, 2007); and Nermin Abadan-Unat, *Turks in Europe: From Guest Worker to Transnational Citizen* (Oxford, 2011).

[14] Herbert, *A History of Foreign Labor in Germany*, p. 211.

army' has certainly been transformed into something far more complex than ever envisaged. Whether it was due to the lack of a comprehensive public debate on the topic or because of a desire to be seen as a newfound post-war liberal democracy, the situation that Germany found itself in by the 1970s with regard to its foreign population was one that was arguably almost entirely unforeseen. This transformation only intensified during the decades that followed and, by the turn of the century, an estimated 10 per cent of Germany's population was comprised of ethnic minority groups.[15]

There is no denying the fixed place that Muslim immigration has been awarded on Europe's political agenda. In recent decades, Europe has witnessed, amongst other events, France's headscarf affair, the rise of the far-right, the 2004 Madrid bombings and Denmark's cartoon scandal. Furthermore, there have been numerous recent incidents and issues in Britain and Germany specifically linked to post-war and guest-worker immigration that have resulted in an increase in the attention awarded to ethnic minorities in both the political and public debate. Britain has witnessed the catastrophe surrounding the investigation into the racially motivated murder of black teenager Stephen Lawrence, the Rushdie Affair and debates on single faith schools, and suffered the consequences of home-grown Islamic fundamentalism during the London bombings of July 2005. Germany has been home to the Islamic extremists connected with the 1993 bombing of the World Trade Center and 9/11, a Turkish community that is still feeling the effects of the guest-worker rotation system and its accompanying discriminatory practices, and is a country that has only recently admitted to being a nation of immigrants.

Furthermore, in October 2010, Angela Merkel gave a speech in which she stressed that German multiculturalism has failed and that ethnic minority communities needed to do more to become integrated, a claim that has reignited debate about the country's Muslim migrant population. A few months later, in February 2011, David Cameron heavily condemned state multiculturalism, claiming that Britain is in

[15] See Lucassen, *The Immigrant Threat*, p. 144; Triadafilos Triadafilopoulos and Karen Schönwälder, 'How the Federal Republic became an immigration country: Norms, politics and the failure of West Germany's guest worker system', *German Politics and Society*, 24:3 (2006), pp. 1–19; and Karen Schönwälder, 'West German society and foreigners in the 1960s', in Philipp Gassert and Alan E. Steinweis (eds), *Coping with the Nazi Past: West German Debates on Nazism and Generational Conflict, 1955–1975* (Oxford, 2006), pp. 113–27.

need of a much stronger national identity, and making reference to Islamic extremism and young Muslims in Britain specifically.

This enhanced focus on Muslim migrants in Britain and Germany has been reflected in the academic literature. In Britain, there has been an increase in the number of studies addressing Muslim ethnic minorities, particularly since the 1990s. These have included the works of Philip Lewis, Humayun Ansari, Tahir Abbas, Tariq Modood, Serena Hussain and Sophie Gilliat-Ray.[16] There are also many works that have focused on Muslim migrants of particular ethnicities and others that have recognised the importance of Islam in the debate on migrant communities in Britain without focusing on Muslim ethnic minorities exclusively.[17] Whilst a number of these works do go some way to addressing the employment, housing and education sectors together, they do so largely from a national perspective. Despite these three areas having been traditionally awarded a central position in the debate on migrant communities in Britain, they have overwhelmingly been assessed at a local level on an individual rather than collective basis.[18] Yet their importance remains assured because, as will be discussed, it is being increasingly argued that Islam plays a role in shaping migrants' experiences in all three.

In Germany, there has been an absence of research that has clearly distinguished between Muslim and non-Muslim migrants with regard to employment, housing and education, and levels of ethnic minority integration more widely. The prime exception is the 2009 Federal

[16] Lewis, *Islamic Britain*; Humayun Ansari, *'The Infidel Within': Muslims in Britain since 1800* (London, 2004); Tahir Abbas (ed.), *Muslim Britain: Communities under Pressure* (London, 2005); Tariq Modood, *Multicultural Politics: Racism, Ethnicity and Muslims in Britain* (Edinburgh, 2005); Serena Hussain, *Muslims on the Map: A National Survey of Social Trends in Britain* (London, 2008); and Sophie Gilliat-Ray, *Muslims in Britain: An Introduction* (Cambridge, 2010).

[17] See John Eade, 'Identity, nation and religion: Educated young Bangladeshi Muslims in London's 'East End'', *International Sociology*, 9:3 (1994), pp. 377–94; Tariq Modood, Richard Berthoud, Jane Lakey, James Nazroo, Patten Smith, Satnam Virdee and Sharon Beishon (eds), *Ethnic Minorities in Britain: Diversity and Disadvantage* (London, 1997); Alison Shaw, *Kinship and Continuity: Pakistani Families in Britain* (Amsterdam, 2000); and Pnina Werbner, *Imagined Diasporas among Manchester's Muslims: The Public Performance of Pakistani Transnational Identity Politics* (Oxford, 2002).

[18] For exceptions, see John Rex and Sally Tomlinson, *Colonial Immigrants in a British City: A Class Analysis* (London, 1979); and Herbert, *Negotiating Boundaries in the City*.

Office for Migration and Refugees study, which was the first to offer a comprehensive insight into Muslim life in Germany.[19] It exposes employment, housing and education patterns and behaviour as well as revealing the socio-demographic characteristics and religious practices of Muslims. Whilst there are some other works on Muslims in Germany, these tend to discuss 'Muslim specific' issues, such as the headscarf debate, the building of mosques and the development of Islam.[20] Instead, whilst there exists a vast historiography on ethnic minorities' performances in the employment, housing and education sectors, it is the Turkish rather than the Muslim community that has traditionally received the most attention, and continues to do so. Furthermore, studies have tended to assess these areas individually.[21] Those that do examine more than one of them generally do so from a national perspective.[22] On the whole, an examination of Muslim migrants' performances and experiences in all three sectors in Britain and Germany in comparative perspective constitutes an entirely novel approach.

Aims of the book

This book aims to make a contribution to five historiographical voids. Firstly, it is the first to offer a long-term assessment of Britain and Germany's post-war immigration frameworks at a local level in two cities. Whilst both countries' immigration policies have been assessed from a comparative perspective, there is a distinct lack of research on

---

[19] Federal Office for Migration and Refugees, *Muslim Life in Germany. A Study Conducted on Behalf of the German Conference on Islam* (Nuremberg, 2009).

[20] See Kornelia Sammet, 'Religion oder Kultur? Positionierungen zum Islam in Gruppendiskussionen über Moscheebauten', in Monika Wohlrab-Sahr and Levent Tezcan (eds), 'Konfliktfeld Islam in Europa', *Soziale Welt*, 17 (2007), pp. 179–198; and Ala Al-Hamarneh and Jörn Thielmann (eds), *Islam and Muslims in Germany* (Leiden, 2008).

[21] See Jens Dangschat, 'Concentration of poverty in the landscapes of 'boomtown' Hamburg: The creation of a new urban underclass?', *Urban Studies*, 31:7 (1994), pp. 1133–47; Susanne Worbs, 'The second generation in Germany: Between school and labor market', *International Migration Review*, 37:4 (2003), pp. 1011–38; and Frank Kalter, 'Ethnische Kapitalien und der Arbeitsmarkterfolg Jugendlicher türkischer Herkunft', in Monika Wohlrab-Sahr and Levent Tezcan (eds), 'Konfliktfeld Islam in Europa', *Soziale Welt*, 17 (2007), pp. 393–417.

[22] See Lucassen, *The Immigrant Threat*, pp. 144–70.

the manner in which this procedure and legislation has impacted ethnic minority integration at a grassroots level, especially of a comparative nature.[23] Secondly, in assessing the employment, housing and education sectors, this work aims to bridge the gap between what are well-developed, yet overwhelmingly separate, bodies of literature, particularly at a local level. Thirdly, its focus on the performance and behaviour of Muslim immigrants in these three capacities furthers what is an ever-growing historiography in Britain and an emerging area of research in Germany. Fourthly, by using Newcastle and Bremen as case studies, this investigation examines established Muslim migrant communities that have been overwhelmingly neglected in the academic literature. Fifthly, by drawing upon both government documents and secondary literature, it allows the settlement and development of both cities' Muslim ethnic minorities to be assessed from the viewpoints of the local authorities and those of the migrants themselves.

This ambitious study is novel in approach, but also in content. There are six key arguments and themes that run throughout this work. Firstly, in assessing the impact that Britain and Germany's differing post-war immigration frameworks had on the long-term integration of Muslim migrants, it challenges the notion that these histories should be seen as contrasting. Instead it exposes the manner in which Newcastle and Bremen's Muslim ethnic minority populations demonstrated a growing similarity in behaviour, performance and attitude in employment, housing and education over time. Whilst this convergence has previously been recognised with regard to immigration policy and the evolution of multiculturalism, it has yet to be considered from the viewpoint of migrant experiences and practices.[24]

Furthermore, this work builds upon this existing literature and, in offering an assessment of local policies from the 1960s to the 1990s, it reveals the extent to which similarities have existed between Newcastle and Bremen's immigration and integration policies. Moreover,

[23] See James F. Hollifield, *Immigrants, Markets, and States: The Political Economy of Postwar Europe* (Cambridge MA, 1992); Karen Schönwälder, *Einwanderung und ethnische Pluralität: politische Entscheidungen und öffentliche Debatten in Grossbritannien und der Bundesrepublik von den 1950er bis zu den 1970er Jahren* (Essen, 2001); Andrew Geddes, *The Politics of Migration and Immigration in Europe* (London, 2003); and Martin Schain, *The Politics of Immigration in France, Britain, and the United States: A Comparative Study* (Basingstoke, 2008).
[24] See Panayi, 'The evolution of multiculturalism in Britain and Germany'; and Green, 'Divergent traditions, converging responses'.

Bremen's commitment to the integration of its migrant population as early as the 1960s was a far cry from an approach that Ulrich Herbert termed '*zukunftsblind*' or 'blind to the future'.[25] Instead Bremen's policies during the early guest-worker years support the thesis that the traditional view of settlement only becoming a political issue after the 1973 halt in recruitment is in need of revision, revealing that a conscious decision not to enforce the rotation principle was made, and that *Gastarbeiter* and their families were being integrated into the German welfare state from the outset.[26]

Secondly, this study assesses the role of Islam in determining the performances and behaviour of Muslim ethnic minorities in employment, housing and education, and in their overall levels of integration. This is especially important at a time at which the academic literature is increasingly calling for the role of Islam to be recognised in all three sectors, and Europe has been accused of failing to address Islamic fundamentalism and integrate its Muslims.[27] Yet the findings of this research suggest that Islam has had little impact on the conduct and levels of integration of Muslim immigrants in Newcastle and Bremen. Moreover, they propose that Muslim ethnic minorities in both cities have often traditionally adhered to patterns and traits displayed by Muslim and non-Muslim migrant communities alike in Britain, Germany, Europe and across the Western world.

Thirdly, this study seeks to overturn the conventional wisdom of the established historiography on ethnic minority populations in Britain

---

[25] Ulrich Herbert, *Geschichte der Ausländerbeschäftigung in Deutschland 1880 bis 1980. Saisonarbeiter, Zwangsarbeiter, Gastarbeiter* (Bonn, 1986), pp. 232, 234. See also Karen Schönwälder, 'Zukunftsblindheit oder Steuerungsversagen? Zur Ausländerpolitik der Bundesregierungen der 1960er und frühen 1970er Jahre', in Jochen Oltmer (ed.), *Migration steuern und verwalten. Deutschland vom späten 19. Jahrhundert bis zur Gegenwart* (Göttingen, 2003), pp. 123–44.

[26] See Klaus J. Bade, *Europa in Bewegung: Migration vom späten 18. Jahrhundert bis zur Gegenwart* (Munich, 2000), pp. 166–7; and Triadafilopoulos and Schönwälder, 'How the Federal Republic became an immigration country'.

[27] See Zachary Shore, *Breeding Bin Ladens: America, Islam, and the Future of Europe* (Baltimore MD, 2006); and Bruce Bawer, *While Europe Slept: How Radical Islam is Destroying the West from Within* (London, 2006). For an insight into the relationship between Islam and Europe more widely, see Bernard Lewis, *Islam and the West* (Oxford, 1993); and Iftikhar H. Malik, *Islam and Modernity: Muslims in Europe and the United States* (London, 2004).

and Germany. A large proportion of the academic literature has long revelled in claims of isolated and exploited migrant communities whose employment, housing and education experiences are dominated by discrimination, segregation, underachievement and a lack of opportunities. On the contrary, this work argues for the triumph of minority agency over institutional and non-institutional constraints. In both Newcastle and Bremen, migrant success has been witnessed in their pursuit of independence and self-determination in the employment and housing sectors in the shape of self-employment and owner-occupation, and in education in the form of above-average achievements and experiences. Rather than perceive this self-sufficiency as a failure to integrate, this study exposes the manner in which Muslim migrants have succeeded in engaging with and manoeuvring their local surroundings in order to achieve their aims.

The remaining three arguments and themes are secondary to those discussed above, but still play a role. The first is regarding the impact that the size of an ethnic minority community can have on its overall levels of integration. Whilst certainly being controversial, there is no doubt that Newcastle's Muslim migrant population has benefited from being a smaller and more close-knit community than those of many other British cities. This has benefited both the migrants' performances in and the local authority's policies regarding the employment, housing and education sectors. This was also the case for Bremen although not to the same extent as, after a late start, the city's Muslim ethnic minority population eventually grew to be much larger than that of Newcastle. The second theme concerns the breach that existed between local immigration policies and the will of the migrants themselves. This study does not argue that either city's government's policies and measures have been misdirected or impractical, rather that Muslim migrants in both have often proceeded and achieved success despite them. The third involves the manner in which regional patriotism acts as a regulator or barrier to integration. Both Newcastle and Bremen are cities which it has often been argued have strong regional identities that impact the way ethnic minority communities are treated. As well as being one of the reasons these two cities were chosen for investigation, the validity of this claim will be assessed.

The employment, housing and education sectors have been chosen for this study for three reasons. Firstly, whilst there are certainly alternative indicators of integration, such as the political participation and health of ethnic minorities, the three selected areas permit a genuine long-term analysis of both Newcastle and Bremen's Muslim migrant populations. Regardless of time of arrival or citizenship, these were three sectors that Muslim immigrants in both cities engaged with. Secondly, the importance of these three spheres continues to dominate both political and academic debate. All three had a role to play in the UK's 2007 Commission on Integration and Cohesion report, *Our Shared Future*, and in Germany's 2007 National Integration Plan. Furthermore, all three areas continue to play a role in studies that address ethnic minority integration.[28] Thirdly, there is a readily available amount of archival material pertaining to both Newcastle and Bremen for all three sectors about which further details will now be provided.

Sources

It proves difficult to conduct an investigation into post-war Muslim immigrant communities in Britain and Germany. In Britain, this is because until the 2001 Census which included a question on religious affiliation for the first time, official documents approached migrant communities along ethnic rather than religious lines. Therefore, studies on Muslim ethnic minorities had to rely on Labour Force Surveys and PSI data, the information in which tended to be based on ethnic origin or country of birth. For many South Asians, it was largely safe to assume that the migrants in question were indeed Muslim as most Pakistanis and Bangladeshis were. However, for immigrants from countries like India, Turkey or Malaysia, it proved more difficult as they were not overwhelmingly Muslim. As a result, attempts to provide either the total number of Muslim migrants in Britain or figures for individual Muslim ethnic minority populations were no more than approximations, with some undoubtedly being more accurate than others.[29] A more certain estimate of the British Muslim population emerged from the 2001 Census, which put the figure at just under 1.6

[28] See Friedrich Heckmann and Dominique Schnapper (eds), *The Integration of Immigrants in European Societies: National Differences and Trends of Convergence* (Stuttgart, 2003); Deborah Phillips, 'Minority ethnic segregation, integration and citizenship: A European perspective', *Journal of Ethnic and Migration Studies*, 36:2 (2010), pp. 209–25; and Yann Algan, Christian Dustmann, Albrecht Glitz and Alan Manning, 'The economic situation of first and second-generation immigrants in France, Germany and the United Kingdom', *The Economic Journal*, 120:542 (2010), pp. F4–F30.

[29] See Ceri Peach, 'The Muslim population of Great Britain', *Ethnic and Racial Studies*, 13:3 (1990), pp. 414–19.

million although, as a result of asylum-seeking and undocumented Muslims, it is thought to be closer to 2 million.[30]

The study of Muslim migrants in Germany has posed similar problems. As in Britain before 2001, there is no official register of Muslims in Germany. Data secured through the German Socio-Economic Panel (GSOEP) and the Micro-census did not include Islamic affiliation and, therefore, figures on Muslims in Germany have historically been approximations.[31] Some studies suggest that there are around 3.2 million Muslims in Germany.[32] Yet in 2009, the Federal Office for Migration and Refugees estimated the number of Muslims to be anywhere between 3.8 and 4.3 million, of which between 2.5 and 2.7 million were of Turkish descent.[33] As a result of this lack of official data on Muslims in Germany, studies continue to focus primarily on Turkish migrants without differentiating between Muslims and non-Muslims.[34]

Similarly, this work aims to investigate the employment, housing and education performances and experiences of Muslim ethnic minorities in Newcastle and Bremen before Islam was considered at an official level and deemed an influential factor. This is reflected in the archival documents that are made use of throughout. For Newcastle, data is primarily drawn from various local government committees, which addressed different aspects of the city's ethnic minority communities' lives from the 1960s onwards. These include the Racial Equality Sub-Committee, the Economic Development Committee, the Housing Committee and the Education Committee. The available information comes overwhelmingly in the form of reports that document either

[30] See Ansari, *'The Infidel Within'*, p. 172.
[31] See Gerhard Robbers, 'Germany', in Jorgen S. Nielsen, Samim Akgönül, Ahmet Alibašić, Brigitte Maréchal and Christian Moe, *Yearbook of Muslims in Europe* (Leiden, 2009), p. 141; and Federal Office for Migration and Refugees, *Muslim Life in Germany*, p. 25.
[32] See Melanie Kamp, 'Prayer leader, counsellor, teacher, social worker, and public relations officer – on the roles and functions of imams in Germany', in Ala Al-Hamarneh and Jörn Thielmann (eds), *Islam and Muslims in Germany* (Leiden, 2008), p. 138.
[33] See Federal Office for Migration and Refugees, *Muslim Life in Germany*, pp. 11–12.
[34] See Nadia Granato and Frank Kalter, 'Die Persistenz ethnischer Ungleichheit auf dem deutschen Arbeitsmarkt. Diskriminierung oder Unterinvestition in Humankapital?', *Kölner Zeitschrift für Soziologie und Sozialpsychologie*, 53:3 (2001), pp. 497–520; and Ruth Mandel, *Cosmopolitan Anxieties: Turkish Challenges to Citizenship and Belonging in Germany* (Durham NC, 2008).

local policies and initiatives or the city's migrant population's experiences, and concentrates largely upon immigrants of South Asian origin.

The available material for Bremen is also compiled along ethnic lines and there is a noticeable focus on the Turkish community. There is a greater variety and quantity of information for Bremen than for Newcastle for two key reasons. Firstly, because of Germany's federal structure and Bremen's position as a city-state, it is home to its own *Bürgerschaft* (citizens' assembly) both at a state and a city level. In Germany, individual states have been able to play a prominent role in devising their own integration policies and have direction over various aspects of their ethnic minority communities' lives, most notably in education. As a result, whilst Newcastle's local authority often adhered to national mandate, there was much more extensive documentation of policies and measures produced in Bremen.

The second reason is the nature of Germany's guest-worker system in that there exists evidence of what was a privately negotiated economic immigration, such as company reports on immigrants' working and housing conditions. Because of the different nature of post-war immigration to Britain, this type of documentation is absent for Newcastle. The data used in this study for Bremen includes government correspondence, company guest-worker barrack blueprints, and reports compiled by the *Statistisches Landesamt Bremen* (Bremen's Statistical Land Office) and the *Bürgerschaft*. Personal accounts and experiences provided by the existing historiography and government documents pertaining to both cities have also been drawn upon. The following section introduces the Muslim ethnic minority communities of Newcastle and Bremen, and provides a rationale for choosing these two cities as case studies.

Newcastle and Bremen: a tale of two cities – industry and identity

This comparative study between Newcastle and Bremen offers a deeper analysis of Muslim immigration and integration at a local level. It provides a comparison between the Muslim ethnic minority populations of both cities, as well as between migrant communities and their white counterparts.[35] Furthermore, the experiences and behaviour of Muslims in Newcastle and Bremen are situated within the wider British

---

[35] The term 'white' is used to refer to a native British or German person of white descent.

and German contexts. It is an impartial and unbiased study that presupposes that non-conformity by migrant communities does not necessarily equate to a lack of integration. It is equally revealing and valuable regarding the daily experiences of Muslim immigrants as studies addressing larger ethnic minority hubs like Bradford and Berlin, and offers a significant regional variation within national historiographical frameworks. This work proposes both a politicised and personalised study of immigration, shedding light on previously neglected migrant populations. In doing so, it offers an additional branch to the existing literature.

Whilst the historiography addressing immigration to Britain and Germany is bountiful, studies of individual cities have been less abundant. Moreover, it has tended to be cities with large and well-established ethnic minorities, such as Birmingham and Bradford in Britain and Berlin and Frankfurt in Germany, that have been awarded the most attention.[36] Furthermore, few works have involved comparisons between cities. One exception is Roger Boyes and Dorte Huneke's 2004 study addressing Turks in Berlin and Pakistanis in Bradford which, although a valuable contribution to the field, is nevertheless a comparison between two cities that have little more in common than their large ethnic minority communities.[37] This book, however, proposes a historical comparative analysis between Newcastle and Bremen, two cities that share historical, economic and social characteristics. Whilst Bremen certainly has more experience of migration than Newcastle as a result of its history of receiving foreign labour during the *Kaiserreich* and the Second World War, both cities remain largely unexplored with regard to their post-war Muslim migrant populations.[38]

---

[36] See Tahir Abbas, 'Teacher perceptions of South Asians in Birmingham schools and colleges', *Oxford Review of Education*, 28:4 (2002), pp. 447–71; Brett Klopp, *German Multiculturalism: Immigrant Integration and the Transformation of Citizenship* (Westport CT, 2002); Wolfgang Kil and Hilary Silver, 'From Kreuzberg to Marzahn: New migrant communities in Berlin', *German Politics & Society*, 24:4 (2006), pp. 95–121; and Deborah Phillips, Cathy Davis and Peter Ratcliffe, 'British Asian narratives of urban space', *Transactions of the Institute of British Geographers*, 32:2 (2007), pp. 217–34.

[37] Roger Boyes and Dorte Huneke, *Is it Easier to be a Turk in Berlin or a Pakistani in Bradford?* (London, 2004).

[38] See Diethelm Knauf and Helga Schröder (eds), *Fremde in Bremen – Auswanderer, Zuwanderer, Zwangsarbeiter* (Bremen, 1993); and Panayi, *Ethnic Minorities in Nineteenth and Twentieth Century Germany*, pp. 113–14, 185–6.

Both Newcastle and Bremen acted as major European ports, were home to economies dominated by the primary sector and dedicated to basic manufacturing, and both have since become post-industrial landscapes struggling with economic readjustment. There is no doubt that Tyneside's identity has been shaped by coalmining, shipping, shipbuilding, iron production and heavy engineering, industries that dominated the region's economy from the seventeenth century until their decline and eventual collapse in the 1970s and 1980s.[39] Similarly, Bremen has been an industrial centre since the mid-seventeenth century and has been home to an active port and a wide variety of industries including steel, wool textile, craft and food production, tobacco and cigar manufacturing and ship construction.[40] Perhaps more importantly, it has been argued that both cities have a strong sense of regional identity that has potentially influenced the experiences of their respective immigrant communities. Regarding Newcastle, the literature suggests that this city sits at the centre of a region that prides itself on being a welcoming host. In contrast, Bremen's regional patriotism has been founded on a unique identity derived from its political and economic distinctiveness.

The existing historiography offers many examples of the North East acting in a welcoming manner. Whilst acknowledging that racism has played a role in the region, Anoop Nayak stresses the extent to which anti-racist activism has been witnessed. He provides numerous examples, including the concern expressed during the 1790s over using sugar in tea due to the human exploitation involved in its production, the campaigning against slavery that took place during the 1820s and 1830s, the public condemnation of Nazi anti-Semitism, and the protest march against Enoch Powell's infamous 1968 'Rivers of Blood' speech.[41] Examples have also been provided concerning minorities in

---

[39] See David Levine and Keith Wrightson, *The Making of an Industrial Society: Whickham, 1560–1765* (Oxford, 1991); and Elaine Knox, '"Keep your feet still, Geordie hinnie": Women and work on Tyneside', in Robert Colls and Bill Lancaster (eds), *Geordies: Roots of Regionalism* (Newcastle, 2005), p. 93.

[40] See Volkmar Leohold, *Die Kämmeristen. Arbeitsleben auf der Bremer Woll-Kämmerei* (Hamburg, 1986); and Anne Power, Jörg Plöger and Astrid Winkler, *Phoenix Cities: The Fall and Rise of Great Industrial Cities* (Bristol, 2010).

[41] Anoop Nayak, *Race, Place and Globalization: Youth Cultures in a Changing World* (Oxford, 2003), p. 45; and Anoop Nayak, 'Young people's geographies of racism and anti-racism: The case of North East England', in Claire Dwyer and Caroline Bressey (eds), *New Geographies of Race and Racism* (Aldershot, 2008), pp. 274–5.

the region. In a work addressing black people on Tyneside, Nigel Todd reveals how, in 1863, two Confederates were told 'not to try it on in Newcastle where a Negro is treated as a man and a brother'.[42] Others have stressed the manner in which the North East successfully integrated the Irish immigrants who settled during the 1800s and lacked any real hostility towards them.[43]

Other examples relate directly to the post-war period. Sydney Collins's 1957 study on the port cities of Cardiff, Liverpool and Newcastle argued that whilst Newcastle did show some signs of racial discrimination, it was comparatively a more promising location for immigrants.[44] Brian Ward explains how when Martin Luther King, Jr. arrived in Newcastle in November 1967 to receive an honorary degree from the city's university, he encountered a city that prided itself on its reputation for positive race relations.[45] Indeed, earlier that year, the Tyneside branch of CARD (Campaign Against Racial Discrimination) had published a report on immigrant communities in Newcastle and concluded that racial discrimination was not a widespread problem in the city.[46] Writing during the early 1990s, Barry Carr suggested that the history of South Shields, a town eleven miles from Newcastle that has been home to a sizeable Arab community since the late 1800s, made the future of race relations in the North East look promising.[47]

Yet there are certainly many weaknesses that can be provided regarding the North East's 'welcoming host' hypothesis.[48] It neglects

[42] Nigel Todd, 'Black-on-Tyne: The black presence on Tyneside in the 1860s', *North East Labour History Society Bulletin*, 21 (1987), p. 23.
[43] Roger Cooter, *When Paddy Met Geordie: The Irish in County Durham and Newcastle, 1840–1880* (Sunderland, 2005); and David Byrne, 'Immigrants and the formation of the North Eastern industrial working class', *North East Labour History Society Bulletin*, 30 (1996), p. 31.
[44] Sydney Collins, *Coloured Minorities in Britain: Studies in British Race Relations Based on African, West Indian and Asiatic Immigrants* (London, 1957).
[45] Brian Ward, 'A king in Newcastle: Martin Luther King, Jr. and British race relations, 1967–1968', *The Georgia Historical Quarterly*, 79:3 (1995), pp. 599–632.
[46] Tyneside Campaign Against Racial Discrimination, *Colour Discrimination in Newcastle upon Tyne* (Newcastle, 1967).
[47] Barry Carr, 'Black Geordies', in Robert Colls and Bill Lancaster (eds), *Geordies: Roots of Regionalism* (Newcastle upon Tyne, 2005), p. 148.
[48] See also Sarah E. Hackett, 'The Asian of the north: Immigrant experiences and the importance of regional identity in Newcastle upon Tyne during the 1980s', *Northern History*, 46:2 (2009), pp. 293–311.

the overcrowded living conditions and instances of hostility suffered by the Irish in the city during the 1800s; the cases of abuse, discrimination and segregation encountered by Arab seamen during the early 1900s; and race riots throughout the twentieth century, including those in South Shields in 1919 and 1930 and the Cannon Street Riots in Middlesbrough in 1961.[49] Furthermore, it fails to recognise the differences between migration patterns, with the white Catholic Irish immigration of the nineteenth century undoubtedly having been very dissimilar to post-war South Asian Muslim migration, as well as the immigration histories of different cities and towns. Yet regardless of its flaws and ambiguities, what is interesting about this identity is that, in some shape and form, it exists and has been recognised.[50] Furthermore, despite continuing to attract academic attention, it has never been comprehensively assessed with regard to Newcastle's post-war Muslim ethnic minority communities.

It has also been argued that Bremen has historically been home to a strong regional identity, albeit one that has not been so closely associated with minority groups, but rather with its political and economic individuality. Dieter K. Buse highlights how, before the 1860s, Bremers lived in 'a special urban world', maintaining that it was a city that stood out as a result of its particular appearance, political system, specialised economy, lifestyle and even its high level of home ownership and its unique 'Bremer' houses. It was a city in which local patriotism prevailed and where, despite its position as an international shipping and trading centre, there was a general suspicion of strangers.[51] In his assessment of federalism and identity in Bremen during the post-war period, Buse stresses how it was seen to be different from the other German cities captured by the Allies. Furthermore, the war had caused a reassessment of who a Bremer was and the immediate post-1945

---

[49] See Panikos Panayi, 'Middlesbrough 1961: A British race riot of the 1960s?', *Social History*, 16:2 (1991), pp. 139–53; Richard Lawless, *From Ta'izz to Tyneside. An Arab Community in the North-East of England during the Early Twentieth Century* (Exeter, 1995); and Joan Allen and Richard C. Allen, 'Competing identities: Irish and Welsh migration and the North East of England, 1851–1980', in Adrian Green and A.J. Pollard (eds), *Regional Identities in North-East England, 1300–2000* (Woodbridge, 2007), pp. 133–59.

[50] See also 'Give the Coloured Bus Crews a Chance: Let's Show TRUE Geordie Spirit' (letter to the editor), *Evening Chronicle* (27 February 1958).

[51] Dieter K. Buse, 'Urban and national identity: Bremen, 1860–1920', *Journal of Social History*, 26:3 (1993), pp. 524–6.

period saw a clear attempt in the city to construct an identity for its people. This local identity was key to the city's recovery process and played a vital role in Bremen's crusade to preserve its political and economic distinctness, and be restored as an 'independent, free and Hanseatic' city.[52] Similarly, Bernd Ulrich writes about a special identity that was inherently linked to the history and traditions of Bremen which, having survived both late nineteenth-century German nationalism and the Nazi period, acted as a source of strength and reassurance following the Second World War.[53] Overall, it has been suggested that 'strictly one cannot become a Bremer. One is Bremer (or not)'.[54]

Whilst it might be imagined that an identity that revels in distinctiveness may lead to the exclusion and marginalisation of immigrant communities, this does not appear to have been the case in Bremen. In fact, drawing on a history of centuries of immigration in the form of Czechs, Poles, Russians and Slovaks who travelled to the city to work in local industries, Bremen has without a doubt pursued a policy of integration throughout the post-war period.[55] Despite being a city that has been plagued by economic crises and high unemployment rates for much of the second half of the twentieth century, Bremen's local authority portrayed a clear commitment to cater for its guest-worker community's employment, housing and education needs. This was probably most clearly demonstrated in the 1979 *Konzeption zur Integration der ausländischen Arbeitnehmer und ihrer Familienangehörigen im Lande Bremen* (Concept of the Integration of Foreign Workers and their Family Members in the State of Bremen), which documented a ground-breaking series of policies and measures catering for the integration of its immigrant populations.[56] This dedication and individuality was witnessed in Bremen throughout the late twentieth

---

[52] Dieter K. Buse, 'Federalism and identity: Bremen, 1945–1960s', *Debatte: Journal of Contemporary Central and Eastern Europe*, 10:1 (2002), pp. 35–6, 45.

[53] Bernd Ulrich, 'The senator's tale: The development of Bremen's bourgeoisie in the post-1945 era', *Social History*, 28:3 (2003), pp. 303–20.

[54] See Buse, 'Federalism and identity', p. 33.

[55] See Knauf and Schröder (eds), *Fremde in Bremen*; and Karl Marten Barfuss, 'Foreign workers in and around Bremen, 1884–1918', in Dirk Hoerder and Jörg Nagler (eds), *People in Transit: German Migrations in Comparative Perspective, 1820–1930* (Cambridge, 1995), pp. 201–24.

[56] Der Senat der Freien Hansestadt Bremen, *Konzeption zur Integration der ausländischen Arbeitnehmer und ihrer Familienangehörigen im Lande Bremen* (June 1979).

and into the twenty-first century, and was recognised both within Bremen and further afield.[57] It was further reinforced by the city's mayor, Jens Böhrnsen, in his welcoming note to the city's 2010 *Integrationswoche* (Bremen Week of Integration) in which he stressed that Bremen is a city of 'diversity, tolerance and cosmopolitanism'.

As well as their economic histories and regional identities, Newcastle and Bremen share a further trait in that both cities' immigration histories have been somewhat overshadowed. Studies on immigrant communities in the North East of England have traditionally focused overwhelmingly on South Shields. It is perhaps no surprise that this town's Yemenis, who arrived in the region during the late 1800s and have been referred to as Britain's first Muslim community, should attract so much attention.[58] Yet this does not mean that Newcastle's immigration history has been entirely neglected in the academic literature. Nevertheless, existing studies have been few and sporadic. They have, however, reached original and intriguing conclusions that merit further investigation. Jon Gower Davies's 1972 work and J.H. Taylor's 1976 study on the employment, housing and education performances and patterns amongst South Asian migrants in the city argued forcefully against the more traditional claims of disadvantage, segregation and underachievement.[59] More recently, Stuart Cameron stressed that Newcastle's Bangladeshi community represents the city's economic future in that it largely works in the restaurant trade, the type of employment that has recently experienced the creation of new jobs.[60] Other works on ethnic minorities and Muslim migrants in Britain have

---

[57] See 'Großwerft ohne Gastarbeiterprobleme. Bremer Vulkan will die Ausländer nicht nur für ein Gastspiel gewinnen – Integration wird schon längst praktiziert', *Ostbremer Rundschau* (20 September 1973); 'Die soziale Zeitbombe tickt nicht überall. Bremens Schule an der Schmidtstraße als Modell für die Integration', *Stuttgarter Zeitung* (21 September 1979); and 'Bremen als Vorreiter? Initiative fordert kommunales Wahlrecht für Ausländer', *Frankfurter Rundschau* (9 May 1986).

[58] See Lawless, *From Ta'izz to Tyneside*; and Laura Tabili, *Global Migrants, Local Culture: Natives and Newcomers in Provincial England, 1841–1939* (Basingstoke, 2011).

[59] Jon Gower Davies, *The Evangelistic Bureaucrat. A Study of a Planning Exercise in Newcastle upon Tyne* (London, 1972); and J.H. Taylor, *The Half-Way Generation: A Study of Asian Youths in Newcastle upon Tyne* (Windsor, 1976).

[60] Stuart Cameron, 'Ethnic minority housing needs and diversity in an area of low housing demand', *Environment and Planning A*, 32:8 (2000), p. 1438.

periodically mentioned Newcastle, but not awarded much attention to the city.[61]

In a similar manner to which Newcastle's history of immigration has been partially marred by the experiences and reputation of South Shields, Bremen's has often been overshadowed by its role as an emigration port despite its history of experiencing foreign labour. Indeed there is no doubting the role that Bremen played in Europe's emigration history, with Bremen/Bremerhaven having acted as Germany's major emigration port, peaking during the late 1800s and early 1900s.[62] As with Newcastle, studies on Bremen's post-1945 immigrant communities have been scarce. As part of a larger study on migration to and from Bremen, Diethelm Knauf and Helga Schröder offered a small glimpse into the arrival and experiences of guest-workers and their families in one of the city's districts.[63] A 2001 investigation based on oral history interviews provided an insight into the city's Greek community, focusing particularly on their work and education experiences.[64] A 2003 work by Hasan Çil consisted of a collection of Turkish guest-workers' personal accounts detailing their arrival in Bremen, working experiences and the positive aspects and difficulties of life in Germany.[65] The two studies that have gone some way to exploring the integration of Bremen's Turkish community are Anne E. Dünzelmann's 2005 work which addressed factors such as the development of neighbourhoods, socio-cultural practices and political participation, and Andreas Farwick's 2011 assessment of ethnic residential segregation in the city.[66] It is upon these works that this study builds.

[61] See Ansari, 'The Infidel Within', p. 359; and Panayi, *An Immigration History of Britain*, pp. 24, 89–90, 293.
[62] See Arno Armgort, *Bremen, Bremerhaven, New York: Geschichte der europäischen Auswanderung über die bremischen Häfen* (Steintor, 1991); and Dirk Hoerder, 'The traffic of emigration via Bremen/Bremerhaven: Merchants' interests, protective legislation, and migrants' experiences', *Journal of American Ethnic History*, 13:1 (1993), pp. 68–101.
[63] Knauf and Schröder (eds), *Fremde in Bremen*.
[64] See Gregorios Panayotidis, *Griechen in Bremen. Bildung, Arbeit und soziale Integration einer ausländischen Bevölkerungsgruppe* (Münster, 2001).
[65] Hasan Çil (ed.), *Anfänge einer EPOCHE. Ehemalige türkische Gastarbeiter erzählen* (Berlin, 2003).
[66] Anne E. Dünzelmann, *Aneignung und Selbstbehauptung: Zum Prozess der Integration und Akkulturation von >GastarbeiterInnen< in Bremen* (Göttingen, 2005); and Andreas Farwick, 'The effect of ethnic segregation on the process of assimilation', in Matthias Wingens, Michael Windzio, Helga de Valk and Can Aybek (eds), *A Life-Course Perspective on Migration and Integration* (Dordrecht, 2011), pp. 239–58.

Newcastle and Bremen's Muslim ethnic minority communities

Newcastle has never been a major British ethnic minority hub. The 1961 Census recorded 832 Indians and 370 Pakistanis in the city; the total population was 269,678. The 1981 Census documented 1,380 Indians, 1,094 Pakistanis and 223 Bangladeshis out of a population of 272,922. However, because both sets of figures include only those people born in India, Pakistan and Bangladesh, and not any descendants born in Britain, the real numbers were undoubtedly much higher. According to the 2001 Census, the Indian, Pakistani and Bangladeshi populations of Newcastle, measured by ethnicity, stood at 3,093, 4,847 and 2,612 respectively.[67] Regarding the Muslim migrant community specifically, a 1986 article estimated its size to be circa 7,000 and the 2001 Census, the first to include a question on religious affiliation, recorded 9,430 Muslims in the city, which constituted 3.6 per cent of the total population of just under 260,000. In 2001, 92.3 per cent of Newcastle's Pakistanis were Muslim, as were 90.4 per cent of Bangladeshis and 3.36 per cent of Indians.[68]

Compared to Newcastle, Bremen has traditionally been home to a greater number of ethnic minority inhabitants. As a result of its postwar emergence as a renewed trade and industrial centre, its immigrant population went from constituting under 2 per cent of the total population in 1968 to 6 per cent in 1978 and almost 10 per cent in 1988.[69] In 1966, the city had 11,351 migrant residents of which 1,673 were Turkish. By 1976, these figures had increased to 32,723 and 16,535 respectively. By 2009, Bremen had a total of 150,626 residents with a migration background of which 36,406 were of Turkish origin and constituted by far the largest ethnic group. This was out of a total population of 547,685. Bremen is also home to a much more varied ethnic minority population than Newcastle and much smaller Muslim migrant communities in the city include Bangladeshis, Iranians, Moroccans and Tunisians.[70] Whilst there is no official data available on the number of Muslims in Germany, the

[67] These statistics were provided by the Office for National Statistics (ONS).
[68] See G.D. Qureshi, 'The Newcastle mosque and Muslim community centre', *Multicultural Teaching*, 4:3 (1986), p. 34; and 2001 Census.
[69] See Patrick Ireland, *Becoming Europe: Immigration, Integration, and the Welfare State* (Pittsburgh PA, 2004), p. 86.
[70] Figures provided by the *Statistisches Landesamt Bremen* (Bremen's Statistical Land Office).

figure for both Bremen and Bremerhaven was estimated to be just over 40,000 in 2002.[71]

The fact that Islam is overwhelmingly absent from the local authority documents that will be drawn upon in the following chapters does not mean that Muslim ethnic minorities in Newcastle and Bremen have constituted invisible communities. On the contrary, both cities have long had mosques, Muslim community centres and neighbourhoods, and shops and cafes that have acted as conduits of Islamic culture. Newcastle is home to the annual Mela festival that promotes South Asian culture, food, art, music and entertainment, and regularly hosts Muslim art festivals and multicultural writing and music events. Similarly, Bremen has held a number of *Islam-Wochen* (Islam Weeks) and *Integrationswochen* (Integration Weeks). Both types of event have promoted an understanding between Bremen and its Muslim ethnic minorities, and involved talks about Islam, mosque tours and visits, and Ramadan meals.

Yet despite the fact that this study addresses Muslim ethnic minorities in Newcastle and Bremen, it acknowledges that Muslims in neither city constitute one homogenous community. Indeed, concerning Britain as a whole, it has been recognised that Muslims originate from a wide variety of ethnic, social, cultural and linguistic backgrounds, and there exists an extensive debate regarding the extent to which their identities and everyday lives are influenced by Islam.[72] More pertinent to this study, it has also correctly been argued that disparities exist in Britain both between Muslims of different South Asian origins and amongst those of a singular common South Asian ethnicity. With regard to Indians, Pakistanis and Bangladeshis specifically, the majority of which are Sunnis, these have included regions of origin and their accompanying identities; differences in caste, levels of education and type of employment before migration; and the emergence of generational differences after settlement in Britain.[73]

---

[71] This was the figure given in Bremen's 2002 *Islam-Woche* (Islam Week) programme. Because Bremerhaven has a small ethnic minority population, the vast majority would certainly have been living in Bremen.

[72] See Kim Knott and Sajda Khokher, 'Religious and ethnic identity among young Muslim women in Bradford', *Journal of Ethnic and Migration Studies*, 19:4 (1993), pp. 593–610; John Rex and Tariq Modood, 'Muslim identity: Real or imagined? A discussion by John Rex and Tariq Modood', *Centre for the Study of Islam and Christian-Muslim Relations Papers*, 12 (Birmingham, 1994); and Ansari, 'The Infidel Within', pp. 6–14.

[73] See Shaw, *Kinship and Continuity*; Ansari, 'The Infidel Within', pp. 2–3;

Similarly, although not as extensive as that addressing Britain, the literature on Germany's Muslim population has also exposed its heterogeneity. Whilst the Turks constitute by far the country's largest Muslim ethnic group, Germany is also home to substantial south-eastern European, Middle Eastern and North African Muslim communities.[74] Furthermore, despite German public discourse having long perceived the country's Turkish population as one entity, there are a number of factors that suggest otherwise. The vast majority are Sunnis though some are Alevis; there are differences in their education levels, political affiliations and interpretations of Islam; and religious practices differ according to gender and generation.[75] Indeed the divisions within Islam generally are varied, with Muslims divided primarily along ethnic and sectarian lines. These have traditionally been reflected amongst Europe's Muslim communities despite academic and public discourse often referring to 'European Muslims' or 'European Islam'.[76]

Needless to say, South Asian Muslims in Newcastle and Turkish Muslims in Bremen stem from different Islamic traditions and backgrounds. Indian and Pakistani immigrants who arrived in Newcastle during the 1950s and 1960s were mainly from the Punjab and Kashmir, whilst the Bangladeshis who settled during the 1970s came primarily from the rural area of Sylhet.[77] A large proportion of the Turkish guestworkers who arrived to Bremen during the 1960s and early 1970s were from rural Anatolia, with many originating from the area around

---

Claire Alexander, 'Imagining the politics of BrAsian youth', in N. Ali, V.S. Kalra and S. Sayyid (eds), *A Postcolonial People: South Asians in Britain* (Cambridge, 2008), pp. 258–71; and Gilliat-Ray, *Muslims in Britain*, p. 45.

[74] See Federal Office for Migration and Refugees, *Muslim Life in Germany*, pp. 12–13.

[75] See Federal Office for Migration and Refugees, *Muslim Life in Germany*, p. 131; and Patricia Ehrkamp, 'Beyond the mosque: Turkish immigrants and the practice and politics of Islam in Duisburg-Marxloh, Germany', in Cara Aitchison, Peter Hopkins and Mei-Po Kwan (eds), *Geographies of Muslim Identities: Diaspora, Gender and Belonging* (Aldershot, 2007), pp. 11–28.

[76] See Bassam Tibi, 'Muslim migrants in Europe: Between Euro-Islam and ghettoization', in Nezar AlSayyad and Manuel Castells (eds), *Muslim Europe or Euro-Islam: Politics, Culture, and Citizenship in the Age of Globalization* (Lanham MD, 2002), p. 33; and Jacques Waardenburg, 'Diversity and unity of Islam in Europe: Some reflections', in Jamal Malik (ed.), *Muslims in Europe: From the Margin to the Centre* (Münster, 2004), pp. 21–34.

[77] See Taylor, *The Half-way Generation*, pp. 13–16; and Cameron, 'Ethnic minority housing needs and diversity in an area of low housing demand', pp. 1432, 1438.

Sivas.[78] Whilst this study is not directly concerned with either city's Muslims' religious beliefs or practices, it is nevertheless keen to avoid the common misconception that Muslims in Europe comprise one collective religious or cultural community.

Yet Muslims in Newcastle and Bremen have not been chosen for this study merely because they constitute large sections of both cities' ethnic minority populations. On the contrary, they have gradually displayed similarities that go beyond those in the employment, housing and education sectors that will be considered in subsequent chapters. Over the years, they have progressively succeeded in reproducing religious and cultural traditions and practices in their adopted British and German environments. As in cities across Britain and Germany, this has been portrayed through the building of mosques and Islamic community centres, the opening of halal butchers and specialist food stores, and traditions that convey a strong sense of attachment to their countries and regions of origin.

As is the case throughout Britain and Germany more widely, Newcastle and Bremen are home to both religiously active Muslims and those who have simply inherited their religion, but do not practise it. Some may have received official instruction in the Qur'an and become familiar with formal religious tradition, whilst others have not. Yet being Muslim often constitutes an important part of their identities irrespective of religious beliefs. As a result, even those who do not practise Islam may partake in Islamic cultural and social practices, such as the celebration of feast days and the wearing of Islamic dress, and display an allegiance to the customs and traditions they have learnt from their parents and the older generations of their respective migrant communities. Despite the fact that, as a result of the heterogeneity of Islam, the personal nature of religion and the possible development of a British and German Islam, it is impossible to produce a definition of what being Islamic constitutes, Newcastle and Bremen are nevertheless home to established and visible Muslim ethnic minorities. Furthermore, regardless of levels of religious belief and practice, Muslim migrants in both cities have demonstrated clear signs of loyalty and commitment to their communities. Whilst in many cases this may not have been a direct result of their religious affiliation, there is no doubt that their performances and experiences in Newcastle and Bremen's employment, housing and education sectors have traditionally often been shaped by their communities.

[78] See Dünzelmann, *Aneignung und Selbstbehauptung*, pp. 75, 95–6.

Yet behind these evident signs of modern diverse and multicultural societies lie two complex immigration histories, which the following three chapters on Muslim migrants' performances and behaviour in the employment, housing and education sectors go some way to exposing. It is through its comparative nature that this study facilitates a deeper understanding of Newcastle's South Asian and Bremen's Turkish Muslims, and achieves a more in-depth analysis of national and international trends and uniqueness. In both Newcastle and Bremen, initial overarching political frameworks soon made way to reveal the people underneath. What emerged were two local authorities and two Muslim immigrant communities trying to adapt to the new situation in which they found themselves.

1

Self-preservation to determination: the employment sector

Ethnic minorities in Britain and Germany's labour markets

There is no doubting the importance of the employment sector when assessing the experiences and integration of ethnic minority groups in Britain and Germany. Indeed this area has occupied a prominent position at the centre of political debate and academic research in both countries. Economic opportunities were often the main motivation for immigration to Britain and Germany in the first instance. In Britain, New Commonwealth immigrants began arriving in the late 1940s because both post-war reconstruction and the expanding economy created labour positions that could not be filled by British workers. Both West Indian immigrants and later those from the Indian subcontinent played a vital part in Britain's labour market.[1] It is essential to recognise the aforementioned connection that existed between Britain and her colonial immigrants, with many having a familiarity with the British way of life.

In Germany, the correlation between post-war immigration and labour has been even more clearly defined. Whilst immigrants who travelled to Britain largely did so independently and paid their own costs, Germany implemented a guest-worker rotation system that generated privately negotiated economic immigration and one that by its very nature was meant to be a temporary phenomenon. Guest-workers were defined and perceived by the work they carried out, were expendable and could be returned home should unemployment increase, and the West German authorities had the power to determine

---

[1] See Layton-Henry, *The Politics of Immigration*, pp. 12–13; Lewis, *Islamic Britain*, p. 54.

both their length of stay and their access to the labour market.[2] They filled jobs rejected by German workers, permitted an upwards shift amongst the German workforce, and appeared to allow the expansion of the economy without the burden of long-term financial investment and social costs.[3]

Whilst there is no need to offer an in-depth analysis of the well-documented features of the guest-worker rotation system, it is necessary to realise that this inherent difference between Britain as the recipient of permanent immigration and Germany's perception of itself as the receiver of temporary economic workers sets the context and the starting point for both the book and this chapter more specifically. Furthermore, although it is forcefully argued that the underlying social and cultural factors that accompanied the guest-worker recruitment scheme tended to be largely neglected, it is this group of immigrants which, whilst initially identified by their economic purpose, is largely responsible for Germany's ethnically diverse population at the beginning of the twenty-first century.

Not only were economic opportunities the reason why many Muslim immigrants arrived in Britain and Germany in the first instance, but these labour market experiences have also shaped their daily lives since. With regard to Britain, findings often cite the existence of an ethnic or Islamic penalty, asserting that ethnic minority communities, and particularly Muslims, suffer from discrimination in the employment sector, high rates of unemployment, low wages and poor working conditions. Such conclusions have largely dominated the historiography on the employment of post-war migrants in Britain, from the ground-breaking studies of the 1960s and 1970s right through to the most recent analyses of the 2000s.[4] Furthermore,

---

[2] See Ulrich Herbert and Karin Hunn, 'Guest workers and policy on guest workers in the Federal Republic: From the beginning of recruitment in 1955 until its halt in 1973', in Hanna Schissler (ed.), *The Miracle Years: A Cultural History of West Germany, 1949–1968* (Princeton NJ, 2001), pp. 194–7.

[3] See Herbert, *A History of Foreign Labor in Germany*, pp. 209–28.

[4] See William W. Daniel, *Racial Discrimination in England: Based on the PEP Report* (London, 1968); David J. Smith, *Racial Disadvantage in Britain: The PEP Report* (Harmondsworth, 1977); C. Brown, *Black and White Britain: The Third PSI Survey* (London, 1984); Tariq Modood, 'Employment', in Tariq Modood *et al.* (eds), *Ethnic Minorities in Britain: Diversity and Disadvantage* (London, 1997), pp. 83–149; and L. Simpson, K. Purdam, A. Tajar, E. Fieldhouse, V. Gavalas, M. Tranmer, J. Pritchard and D. Dorling, *Ethnic Minority Populations and the Labour Market: An Analysis of the 1991 and 2001 Census* (Leeds, 2006).

there has been an increasingly widespread concern that the second generation of Pakistani and Bangladeshi communities especially are experiencing the same patterns of disadvantage as the first and that Muslims in particular are suffering an inexplicable labour market penalty.[5]

Despite the inherent differences between Britain's colonial immigration and Germany's guest-worker rotation system, and the fact that guest-workers were perceived as temporary economic relief from the outset, ethnic minorities in both countries have experienced similar disadvantages and obstacles during the post-war period. Whilst the Pakistanis and Bangladeshis have been singled out as the most disadvantaged groups in Britain's employment sector, an overwhelming proportion of the literature on Germany focuses on the Turkish community. It has repeatedly highlighted long-term unemployment, a concentration in unskilled work, discriminatory practices and little opportunity for upward mobility.[6] As with that addressing Britain, it raises concerns about the second generation who, whilst enjoying better labour market prospects than their parents, still have a long way to go before matching those of their German counterparts.[7] Furthermore, although not as established and advanced as in Britain, the debate in Germany is also increasingly citing Islam as a defining feature in shaping these experiences. Muslim women, for example, are often discriminated against or criticised for wearing headscarves in the workplace, and a 2009 study conducted by the Federal Office for Migration and Refugees concluded that Muslim migrants in Germany endure higher unemployment rates than those of other religious affiliations, and continue to be disadvantaged by the close

---

[5] See The Commission on the Future of Multi-Ethnic Britain, *The Future of Multi-Ethnic Britain: The Parekh Report* (London, 2002), pp. 192–204; Muhammad Anwar, 'Muslims in Britain: Issues, policy and practice', in Tahir Abbas (ed.), *Muslim Britain: Communities under Pressure* (London, 2005), pp. 34–6; and Anthony Heath and Sin Yi Cheung, *Ethnic Penalties in the Labour Market: Employers and Discrimination* (Leeds, 2006).

[6] See Stefan Bender and Wolfgang Seifert, 'Zuwanderer auf dem Arbeitsmarkt: Nationalitäten- und geschlechtsspezifische Unterschiede', *Zeitschrift für Soziologie*, 25:6 (1996), pp. 473–95; and Frank Kalter, 'The second generation in the German labor market: Explaining the Turkish exception', in Richard Alba and Mary C. Waters (eds), *The Next Generation: Immigrant Youth in a Comparative Perspective* (New York, 2011), pp. 166–84.

[7] See Granato and Kalter, 'Die Persistenz ethnischer Ungleichheit auf dem deutschen Arbeitsmarkt'.

link between educational attainment and labour market performance.[8]

The employment sector is also a topic worthy of research in the study of ethnic minority communities because of the manner in which it continuously permeates other areas of migrants' lives. There is a clear link between the performance of ethnic minority populations in the British and German labour markets, and their experiences in the other two sectors investigated in this study, those of housing and education. Research has concluded that ethnic minorities in Britain who live largely in white neighbourhoods are economically advantaged compared those in more ethnically mixed areas.[9] Low educational attainment and a lack of qualifications are reasons repeatedly given for the difficulties faced by ethnic minorities in the British labour market.[10] In Germany, the correlation between the employment and education sectors is even more apparent, and is consistently reinforced by the fact that the German school system requires pupils to be streamed at an early age, a process that is argued to disadvantage youths of ethnic minority origin.[11] Regarding housing, not only did guest-workers largely initially live in barrack accommodation provided to them by their employers, but they have since often resided in inexpensive neighbourhoods and housing as a result of low wages, with some making a conscious economic decision to live in areas that can provide them with the necessary financial and social support for their business ventures. Furthermore, it has been argued that there is also a clear correlation between ethnic minority labour market performance and the economic and social exclusion of migrants and their children, the contribution

---

[8] See Joyce Marie Mushaben, 'Thinking globally, integrating locally: Gender, entrepreneurship and urban citizenship in Germany', *Citizenship Studies*, 10:2 (2006), p. 220; Rita Chin, 'Guest worker migration and the unexpected return of race', in Rita Chin, Heide Fehrenbach, Geoff Eley and Atina Grossmann (eds), *After the Nazi Racial State: Difference and Democracy in Germany and Europe* (Ann Arbor, 2009), pp. 97–8; and Federal Office for Migration and Refugees, *Muslim Life in Germany*, pp. 214–29.

[9] See Simpson *et al.*, *Ethnic Minority Populations and the Labour Market*, p. 9.

[10] See Nii Djan Tackey, Jo Casebourne, Jane Aston, Helen Ritchie, Alice Sinclair, Claire Tyers, Jennifer Hurstfield, Rebecca Willison and Rosie Page, *Barriers to Employment for Pakistanis and Bangladeshis in Britain* (Leeds, 2006).

[11] See Cornelia Kristen, 'Ethnic differences in educational placement: The transition from primary to secondary schooling', *Mannheimer Zentrum für Europäische Sozialforschung Working Paper*, 32 (2000); and Worbs, 'The second generation in Germany'.

they make to the economy, and the perception held of them by the host population.[12]

Muslim ethnic minorities in Britain and Germany's labour markets

It is perhaps surprising that despite the ever-increasing importance awarded to Islam in the study of Europe's migrant communities, the recognition of religion as an influential factor in the shaping of labour market experiences in both Britain and Germany has been a more recent phenomenon. In Britain, it was not until the 1990s that research of this type began to emerge in any volume, and there certainly existed a well-established and vibrant debate on Muslims in the British employment sector before the inclusion of a question regarding religious affiliation in the 2001 Census. The works of Kenneth Clark, Stephen Drinkwater and Ceri Peach, to name but a few, have pointed to higher unemployment rates and lower occupational profiles amongst Muslims, with Joanne Lindley referring to an 'Islamic penalty' within Britain's employment sector.[13] Kenneth Clark and Stephen Drinkwater go so far as to assert that there is a link between religions that values entrepreneurship, such as Islam, Hinduism and Sikhism, and higher levels of self-employment.[14] In his work that drew upon the 1994 National Survey of Ethnic Minorities, Mark S. Brown concluded that there was a higher proportion of Sikhs and Muslims amongst self-employed managers, employers and professionals, and argued that a religious classification could potentially

---

[12] See Algan, Dustmann, Glitz and Manning, 'The economic situation of first and second-generation immigrants in France, Germany and the United Kingdom', pp. F4–F5.

[13] Joanne Lindley, 'Race or religion? The impact of religion on the employment and earnings of Britain's ethnic minorities', *Journal of Ethnic and Migration Studies*, 28:3 (2002), pp. 427–42; Kenneth Clark and Stephen Drinkwater, 'Dynamic and diversity: Ethnic employment differences in England and Wales, 1991–2001', *IZA Discussion Paper*, 1698 (Bonn, 2005); and Ceri Peach, 'Muslims in the 2001 Census of England and Wales: Gender and economic disadvantage', *Ethnic and Racial Studies*, 29:4 (2006), pp. 629–55.

[14] Kenneth Clark and Stephen Drinkwater, 'Pushed in or pulled out? Self-employment among ethnic minorities in England and Wales', *Labour Economics*, 7:5 (2000), pp. 603–28. See also Stephen Drinkwater, 'Self-employment amongst ethnic and migrant groups in the United Kingdom', in OECD, *Open for Business: Migrant Entrepreneurship in OECD Countries* (Paris, 2010), p. 192.

offer a more in-depth insight into South Asian economic activity at a local level than an ethnic one.[15]

The literature addressing Germany has followed a different path to that regarding Britain. Apart from the aforementioned 2009 Federal Office for Migration and Refugees study, there has been an absence of research that has clearly distinguished between Muslim and non-Muslim migrants, not only with regard to the labour market, but also housing, education and ethnic minority levels of integration more widely. Instead, the primary focus of a large proportion of the historiography has been on the Turkish community in a Germany where *Türke* has become synonymous with *Ausländer*, and is often perceived as being politically, religiously and culturally at odds with German society.[16] It is not surprising that the Turkish community should receive so much attention. Firstly, Turks have steadily become the largest ethnic minority group, comprising approximately 2.5 to 2.7 million out of 3.8 to 4.3 million muslims living in Germany in 2009.[17] Secondly, much of the data drawn upon by the academic literature, such as the German Socio-Economic Panel (GSOEP) and the Micro-census, did not include information on Islamic affiliation, thus encouraging research along ethnic lines. Thirdly, the focus on the Turkish community has no doubt been reinforced by the conclusions reached, which often set Turks apart from other ethnic minority groups. Over recent decades, Turks have suffered the highest rates of unemployment, have been forced into unskilled work and have constituted the largest proportion of non-German self-employed workers.[18]

Yet there is no doubt that the religious affiliation of Muslim migrants is increasingly being recognised as an important factor when

---

[15] Mark S. Brown, 'Religion and economic activity in the South Asian population', *Ethnic and Racial Studies*, 23:6 (2000), pp. 1035–61.

[16] *Ausländer* can be literally translated as 'foreigner', although the term also carries negative connotations, inplying 'otherness' and not belonging. See Ruth Mandel, 'Turkish headscarves and the 'foreigner problem': Constructing difference through emblems of identity', *New German Critique*, 46 (1989), pp. 27–46; Mandel, *Cosmopolitan Anxieties*; and Abadan-Unat, *Turks in Europe*.

[17] Federal Office for Migration and Refugees, *Muslim Life in Germany*, pp. 11–12.

[18] See Antoine Pécoud, "Weltoffenheit schafft Jobs': Turkish entrepreneurship and multiculturalism in Berlin', *International Journal of Urban and Regional Research*, 26:3 (2002), pp. 494–507; and Irena Kogan, 'A study of immigrants' employment careers in West Germany using the sequence analysis technique', *Social Science Research*, 36:2 (2007), pp. 491–511.

studying and assessing their position in and approach to the German labour market, although it should be noted that this is largely the case amongst works of an international scope. Some Turkish Muslims in Berlin who took part in a 2008 study, for example, maintained that their religious and ethnic backgrounds had limited their career opportunities, and it has been argued that unemployment rates amongst Muslims in Germany are higher than those amongst non-Muslims.[19] Furthermore, a 2006 Pew Global Attitudes Project found that unemployment was one of the most popular concerns amongst Muslims in Germany as well as in Britain.[20] It is upon these previous studies on Muslim ethnic minorities in Britain and Germany that this work hopes to build.

Aims of the chapter

This chapter investigates and analyses the employment of Muslim ethnic minority communities in both Newcastle and Bremen from the 1960s to the 1990s from the perspective of both the migrants themselves and the cities' local governments. It highlights the extent to which not discrimination, but rather a desire for self-employment and economic independence, has determined their labour market performance and behaviour. Both cities witnessed some degree of economic integration taking place in that Muslim immigrants at one point worked alongside their indigenous counterparts as factory workers and transport drivers. Research reveals how these immigrants used training and capital-accumulation in these sectors in order to establish small businesses, indicating that perhaps not economic integration, but rather economic independence has been the long-term goal of Newcastle and Bremen's Muslim immigrants. The initial differences between the *Gastarbeiter* in Bremen who adhered to the stringent and restrictive patterns of the guest-worker rotation system through their work in the city's shipyards and steelworks, and Newcastle's colonial immigrants who enjoyed economic mobility and aspiration from the outset, are acknowledged and their long-term impacts on employment

---

[19] See Joachim Brüß, 'Experiences of discrimination reported by Turkish, Moroccan and Bangladeshi Muslims in three European cities', *Journal of Ethnic and Migration Studies*, 34:6 (2008), p. 887; and Pamela Irving Jackson and Peter Doerschler, *Benchmarking Muslim Well-Being in Europe: Reducing Disparities and Polarizations* (Bristol, 2012), pp. 132–3.

[20] The Pew Global Attitudes Project, *Muslims in Europe: Economic Worries Top Concerns about Religious and Cultural Identity* (Washington DC, 2006), p. 7.

patterns challenged. Accordingly, this chapter also seeks to investigate the extent to which Britain and Germany's immigration paradigms have shaped and moulded the economic position of Muslim migrants over time and across generations, and stresses the manner in which the legacies of and contrasts between these initial frameworks made way for grassroots employment aspirations and, in Germany's case, the comparatively delayed emergence of economic autonomy.

The chapter draws largely upon local government correspondence, minutes and reports, which provide details of local initiatives, as well as accounts of members of the migrant communities. As previously mentioned, it proves difficult to conduct an investigation into post-war Muslim immigrant communities in both Newcastle and Bremen because, for the most part, official documents approached migrant communities along ethnic rather than religious lines. In Britain, it was not until the 1990s that religion emerged as a recognised source of minority discrimination in the labour market and indeed further afield.[21] The study of Muslim migrant communities in Germany has posed similar problems. Data secured through the German Socio-Economic Panel (GSOEP) and the Micro-census did not include Islamic affiliation and, as in Britain, figures relating to Muslims in Germany have largely been estimates. Indeed, this project aims to investigate the employment patterns of Muslim migrants in Britain and Germany before religion and, in this case Islam, was officially considered a possible influential factor.

Whilst using previous research on Muslim ethnic minorities in Britain and Germany as a foundation, it is not the view of this study that Islam has acted as an overly determining factor. On the contrary, despite scholars increasingly calling for the role of religion to be considered and recognised in shaping labour market behaviour, Islam appears to have only played a minor and sporadic part in influencing employment choices and performances in both cities. Whilst Muslims' choice of businesses may often be determined by their religious affiliation and take the form of halal butchers and cloth stores, and their working days be partially shaped by prayer and dress requirements, their labour market behaviour and patterns have otherwise not been largely affected and have in fact adhered to those of non-Muslim ethnic minority groups in Britain, Germany and further afield.

[21] See Modood, 'Employment', pp. 133–4, 350, 352–3; and Runnymede Trust, *Islamophobia: A Challenge for Us All: Report of the Runnymede Trust Commission on British Muslims and Islamophobia* (London, 1997).

Furthermore, it is not the view of this study that the participation of Muslim immigrants in Britain and Germany's employment sectors should be perceived in terms of disadvantage and discrimination. The extent to which ethnic minority communities contribute to their host economies has after all been recognised, and Newcastle and Bremen are not exceptions. A 2003 Cabinet Office report, for example, stressed the importance of the ethnic minority population in Britain's labour market, suggesting that it would be responsible for half the growth of the working-age population between 1999 and 2009.[22] Studies have shown the extent to which British cities, and especially London, have come to depend upon migrant labour.[23] Similarly, regarding Germany, the manner in which migrant communities have contributed to the labour market was not confined to the economic miracle of the post-war years, but rather has continued throughout the decades that followed.[24] Increasingly, migrants in both countries are being recognised for the important role that ethnic businesses especially play in shaping local economies. Whilst migrant entrepreneurship has certainly undergone its fair share of criticism, this study hopes to build upon the more positive aspects and consequences of these businesses and their products, including enabling social and economic mobility and independence; promoting social stability, positive race relations and integration; tackling racism and disadvantage; and helping secure new labour standards.[25] Furthermore, with regard to the labour market performance of both cities' Muslim migrant communities more widely,

[22] Cabinet Office, *Ethnic Minorities and the Labour Market: Final Report* (London, 2003), p. 4.
[23] See Jon May, Jane Wills, Kavita Datta, Yara Evans, Joanna Herbert and Cathy McIlwaine, 'Keeping London working: Global cities, the British state, and London's new migrant division of labour', *Transactions of the Institute of British Geographers*, 32:2 (2007), pp. 151–67; and Jane Wills, Kavita Datta, Yara Evans, Joanna Herbert, Jon May and Cathy McIlwaine, *Global Cities at Work: New Migrant Divisions of Labour* (London, 2009).
[24] See Sarah Spencer (ed.), *Immigration as an Economic Asset: The German Experience* (Stoke on Trent, 1994).
[25] See Ansari, *'The Infidel Within'*, pp. 195–7; Antoine Pécoud, 'German-Turkish entrepreneurship and the economic dimension of multiculturalism', in Han Entzinger, Marco Martiniello and Catherine Wihtol de Wenden (eds), *Migration Between States and Markets* (Aldershot, 2004), pp. 119–29; and Ian Worthington, Monder Ram and Trevor Jones, 'Exploring corporate social responsibility in the U.K. Asian small business community', *Journal of Business Ethics*, 67:2 (2006), pp. 201–17.

this chapter argues that choice has triumphed over constraint in that employment patterns and behaviour have not been the result of discrimination and limitations, but rather conscious decisions taken by, and the economic aspirations of, the migrants themselves.

Newcastle

Although Newcastle and the North East more generally have been largely neglected in the study of ethnic minorities and Muslim communities in Britain, there is no doubt that these communities have played a role in the local economy. A 2006 Institute for Public Policy Research report offered an insight into the enormous contribution that they had made in recent years. Not only did they form a younger and more mobile workforce, but they were also more likely to be in higher level, managerial and professional occupations, have better qualifications than those born in the British Isles and their migrant counterparts across the UK, and fill vacancies that could otherwise remain empty. Overall, the report stressed the extent to which migration had the potential to help address the North East's long-term problems of a decreasing working-age population and out-migration.[26] A second 2006 report, this one issued by the Centre for Urban and Regional Development Studies, demonstrated the role played by ethnic minorities in certain professions and sectors, including hotels and restaurants; transport, storage and communications; wholesale and retail trade; and health and social work.[27] It also highlighted the extent to which self-employment had become a widespread practice amongst black and minority ethnic (BME) communities by the beginning of the 2000s. In Newcastle, BME members comprised 6.5 per cent of all of those employed yet made up 15.9 per cent of all people self-employed full-time. This figure was even higher amongst young people aged between 16 and 24, and stood at 34.3 per cent. Furthermore, entrepreneurship was by no means solely a male practice, with ethnic minority women more likely to be practising self-employment full-time than part-time.[28] As in cities and towns across Britain, ethnic minority businesses have

---

[26] Rachel Pillai, *Destination North East? Harnessing the Regional Potential of Migration* (London, 2006), pp. 6, 27–8, 34.
[27] Cheryl Conway, Mike Coombes and Lynne Humphrey, *Mapping Ethnicity in the North East Labour Market (Draft Report)* (Newcastle upon Tyne, 2006), p. 26.
[28] Ibid., p. 14.

earned themselves a firm place in Newcastle's post-war landscape, with Indian takeaways, Pakistani corner shops, Chinese restaurants and Bangladeshi clothing stores having long been common sights. These businesses have constituted a vital additional tier to the city's economy, and have introduced a diverse range of new ideas and products, provided job opportunities for members of their communities, and acted as a bridge between the migrant and white host populations, with many serving the local white population.

The labour market performance of Newcastle's ethnic minorities is also pertinent in other ways. A debate in both council documents and the local press about their employment started in the late 1950s and remains active, and has addressed issues from their early work on the buses to the performance of the city council as an employer of ethnic minorities and the idea of establishing an entrepreneurial 'Asian Town' in the West End.[29] Whether their employment involved working alongside their white counterparts or running small businesses, there is no doubting the manner in which the city's Muslim migrants have come to constitute an inherent part of the local economy. Stuart Cameron has gone so far as to argue that the Bangladeshi community, despite suffering from lower per capita income compared to other ethnic groups, represents the city's economic future in that Bangladeshis are largely employed in the restaurant trade, the type of employment that has recently experienced the creation of new jobs.[30] Moreover, the fact that the ethnic minority population is younger than the white population, thus meaning that its share of the local workforce will rise in the near future, further emphasises the importance of this topic.[31]

---

[29] See 'City Busmen Protest Over New Coloured Crews', *Evening Chronicle* (24 February 1958); 'Our City Busmen ... A Passenger Praises Coloured Workers', *Evening Chronicle* (1 February 1961); Tyne & Wear Archives Service (TWAS), Newcastle, MD.NC/162/3, Local Government and Racial Equality Sub-Committee of Corporate Joint Sub-Committee 6 August 1987–16 March 1988, Local Government and Racial Equality Sub-Committee, 'Recruitment of employees to the city council', 16 March 1988; and TWAS, MD.NC/358, Asian Traders Working Group 4 July 1996–17 April 1998, 'City of Newcastle upon Tyne Asian Traders Working Group', 17 April 1998.

[30] Cameron, 'Ethnic minority housing needs and diversity in an area of low housing demand', p. 1438.

[31] Conway, Coombes and Humphrey, *Mapping Ethnicity in the North East Labour Market*, p. 7.

The 1960s and 1970s

Whilst there is a distinct lack of extensive research on the labour market experiences of Newcastle's ethnic minorities, there is still nevertheless sufficient information to piece together their employment patterns of the 1960s and 1970s, from which emerges a fairly positive account. A 1967 report issued by the City of Newcastle upon Tyne based on interviews, questionnaires, observations and group activities offered a detailed insight into the city's migrant community.[32] During the 1950s and 1960s, many of Newcastle's ethnic minorities were employed in the public services as bus drivers, conductors and mechanics. Others worked as draughtsmen, clerks and technicians at Reyrolles in Hebburn and seamstresses at S. Levine & Co. in the West End. The largest employer of ethnic minorities was the Newcastle Corporation Transport Department, which employed 162 immigrants in 1967, many of whom were of Indian and Pakistani origin. They often began as bus conductors and were later promoted to bus drivers. The report stressed the manner in which these workers had trouble becoming integrated with their English colleagues.[33]

The migrant bus crews in Newcastle during the late 1950s and early 1960s certainly captured the attention of both the press and the public. The *Evening Chronicle* especially followed the friction that developed between the migrant and white workers.[34] Yet it also published articles praising Newcastle's Transport Authority for hiring members of ethnic minorities, and views of the public commending the quality of work carried out by the Indian and Pakistani drivers and conductors, and calling for Newcastle to show 'true Geordie spirit' and give these ethnic minority workers a chance.[35] Whilst this type of employment within the city's transport sector has previously been dismissed simply as work

---

[32] Sudha D. Telang (Newcastle upon Tyne City Planning Department), *The Coloured Immigrant in Newcastle upon Tyne* (Newcastle upon Tyne, 1967).

[33] Ibid., pp. 12–13.

[34] 'City Busmen Protest Over New Coloured Crews', *Evening Chronicle* (24 February 1958); 'Coloured Busmen Get No Special Treatment', *Evening Chronicle* (25 February 1958); and 'Bus Crews Say: 'No More Coloured Men'', *Evening Chronicle* (17 November 1958).

[35] 'Give the Coloured Bus Crews a Chance: Let's Show TRUE Geordie Spirit' (Letter to the editor), *Evening Chronicle* (27 February 1958); and 'Our City Busmen ... A Passenger Praises Coloured Workers', *Evening Chronicle* (1 February 1961).

that others did not want to do,[36] this argument really fails to situate these migrants' economic experiences within the wider context. The case that will be proposed here is that this work carried out during the late 1950s and into the 1960s served a long-term economic purpose in that it often acted as the financial foundation for the establishment of small businesses. In other words, it was this type of work, which many Muslim migrants completed on a temporary basis, that enabled a long-term sought-after entrepreneurialism. The 1967 City of Newcastle upon Tyne report also conveyed that whilst about half of the immigrants had encountered difficulties finding work, they were not suffering from high unemployment rates, with only 100 out of 41,100 unemployed men in the Northern Region being from Commonwealth countries in February 1967. Furthermore, there were only twenty-five unemployed Commonwealth immigrants within the three Newcastle Employment Exchange areas.[37]

J.H. Taylor's 1976 study of all Indian and Pakistani boys who reached leaving age in Newcastle's schools between 1962 and 1967 further exposed these migrant communities' positive employment experiences.[38] When comparing his respondents to their English counterparts, he discovered that similar proportions had secured apprenticeships or semi- and unskilled manual occupations. Furthermore, the South Asian youths actually performed better with regard to skilled manual employment and only seemed disadvantaged in non-manual work. The greatest difficulty facing Taylor's respondents seemed to be the time it took them to secure employment, with the English youths finding work much quicker after leaving school and after applying to fewer firms, both of which he put down to discrimination on occasions, but largely to insufficient English language skills.[39] Moreover, his South Asian respondents earned on average higher wages than their English counterparts, experienced low rates of unemployment and secured better jobs and higher levels of appreticeships than many ethnic minotiry youths in other areas of Britain.[40] Additionally, they achieved this despite a large proportion of them having arrived in Britain after the age of eleven.[41]

[36] See Dave Renton, *Colour Blind? Race and Migration in North East England since 1945* (Sunderland, 2007), p. 106.
[37] Telang, *The Coloured Immigrant in Newcastle upon Tyne*, p. 12.
[38] Taylor, *The Half-way Generation*.
[39] Ibid., pp. 176–9.
[40] Ibid., pp. 182–3.
[41] Ibid., pp. 179–86.

Taylor made an attempt to establish why South Asians in Newcastle performed better in the employment sector than those in other areas across Britain. Firstly, he suggested that Newcastle had a comparably smaller ethnic minority community, a feature that might have led to less discrimination taking place. He pointed out how, according to the 1971 Census, people born in the New Commonwealth countries constituted only 1.3 per cent and 0.6 per cent of Newcastle and Tyneside's populations respectively. These figures were indeed small when compared to those of cities such as Greater London (6.4 per cent), Huddersfield (6.6 per cent) and Birmingham (6.7 per cent).[42] Whilst it is certainly controversial to suggest that smaller ethnic minority communities are in any way more likely to succeed, the possibility that they potentially achieve higher levels of integration is one of the themes that runs throughout this study, not just with reference to the employment sector, but also housing and education, and in Bremen as well as in Newcastle.

Secondly, Taylor believed that Indian and Pakistani youths tried harder to attain apprenticeships than their English peers, who often gave up and were not as willing to pursue less skilled jobs. Thirdly, he argued that the youths' fathers' employment played a role in that those whose fathers were self-employed appeared to have a better chance of securing apprenticeships because they had a larger number of contacts and greater influence than those working, for example, in a factory or on the buses. Taylor believed that this was probably especially true of those youths who had fathers who worked as credit drapers, a profession that, as will be further discussed, involved a lot of travelling and interacting with many different communities. He interpreted the fact that 40 per cent of his employed South Asian respondents had secured employment through personal or family contacts as evidence of this.[43]

Indeed, as in towns and cities across Britain, self-employment was a widespread employment choice amongst Newcastle's Muslim ethnic minorities from the outset, with many owning small retail businesses, such as drapers, or working as landlords, thus making entrepreneurship the type of work that has been awarded the most attention in the existing historiography and local government documents. Taylor discovered that 57 per cent of his South Asian youths' fathers were self-employed, a figure that was not only higher than that of the indigenous

[42] Ibid., pp. 186–7.
[43] Ibid., pp. 188–91.

population, but also far greater than that of South Asian communities in other parts of Britain. As he pointed out, according to the Commonwealth Immigrant Tables provided by the 1966 Sample Census, the self-employment figure stood at only 3.5 per cent amongst Indians and 5.9 per cent amongst Pakistanis in Greater London, and 4.6 per cent and 3.3 per cent for Britain as a whole. The largest proportion of Newcastle's self-employed South Asians were credit drapers, travelling salesmen who sold pieces of clothing door-to-door, and who initially used the buses and later mostly upgraded to cars. The second largest group were the shopkeepers, who mainly ran tailors' shops and grocery stores. Taylor admits that self-employed males were over-represented amongst his respondents' fathers due to the fact that they belonged to the older proportion of Newcastle's South Asian community, which was most likely to be involved in the credit drapery trade. Yet there remains no doubt that this choice of entrepreneurship was more popular than in most other areas of Britain, even when compared to a region like Teesside which, although only 40 miles away, only had about a dozen South Asians employed in credit drapery.[44]

As well as the high levels of self-employment amongst Newcastle's South Asian communities, another remarkable factor about them is the extent to which their work involved a familiarity and consistent contact with the local white population, a characteristic that will also be discussed at a later point with regard to Muslim businesses in Bremen. Not only did credit drapers travel across the North East region and were their customers almost exclusively all members of the local working class, but they also carried out a type of work that was inherent to Britain and, more specifically, to Tyneside. Those South Asians who became credit drapers were adhering to an employment pattern that had long been practised in the region by both members of the local indigenous population and Jewish immigrants who had settled in Newcastle at the turn of the twentieth century. As Taylor explains, South Asians arriving in post-war Newcastle found more so than in most other areas across Britain, 'a ready-made entrepreneurial role'.[45] These post-war Muslim ethnic minorities were also conforming to a long-established regional entrepreneurialism, with South Shields

[44] Taylor, *The Half-way Generation*, pp. 48–50. One city in which South Asians showed similar entrepreneurial patterns to those of Newcastle was Manchester. See Pnina Werbner, 'What colour "success"? Distorting value in studies of ethnic entrepreneurship', *Sociological Review*, 47:3 (1999), pp. 548–79.
[45] Taylor, *The Half-way Generation*, pp. 49–50.

having been home to European and Arab migrant businessmen since the mid-1800s.[46]

In essence, this choice of employment was a direct consequence of the community in which these South Asians had settled rather than being in any way linked to their own history, ethnicity, culture or religion. Similarly, the majority of the shopkeepers, whilst selling some products specifically for Indian and Pakistani customers, catered primarily for an English market, a trait which Taylor argued distinguished them from the norm in other British towns and cities, and one that had been prevalent amongst some Arab businessmen in South Shields during the first half of the twentieth century.[47]

This pattern of self-employment amongst South Asians in Newcastle was confirmed by Jon Gower Davies in his 1972 work on the Rye Hill area of Newcastle's West End. He argued that this same pursuit of economic independence and ownership extended to cover the housing sector, with South Asians often purchasing houses to rent out.[48] Whilst this trait of home ownership is one that will be developed much further in the next chapter, it is essential to note here the role that it also played within South Asian immigrants' self-employment portfolios.

There are numerous reasons why self-employment might have played such a large role amongst Newcastle's South Asian Muslim community. Some might argue that the success of ethnic minority businesses has historically been the consequence of a North Eastern identity and the region's reputation as being welcoming. Perhaps it simply had a deeper-rooted entrepreneurial spirit than other areas of Britain. Businessmen were certainly capable of adapting to what could be considered traditional British working-class types of work, be it in the form of becoming door-to-door salesmen or owning corner shops. After all, Jewish immigrants who arrived on Tyneside at the end of the nineteenth and the beginning of the twentieth century also worked as credit drapers and, in the same way South Asian Muslim arrivals would during the post-1945 period, had many customers in the North East pit villages.[49] However, it is important to realise that these migrant entrepreneurial traits were not particular to Newcastle nor to the post-war

---

[46] See Tabili, *Global Migrants*, pp. 56–61, 63, 83–6, 93, 166–9, 212–15, 226.
[47] Taylor, *The Half-way Generation*, pp. 46–51; and Tabili, *Global Migrants*, p. 215.
[48] Davies, *The Evangelistic Bureaucrat*, pp. 33–41.
[49] Taylor, *The Half-way Generation*, p. 49.

period, with the existence of South Asian Muslim peddlers, many from the Punjab, in numerous large British cities, including London, Birmingham and Glasgow during the pre-war era being widely recognised in the historiography.[50]

This does not mean, however, that there was nothing particular about Newcastle's post-war Muslim peddlers. Much like Taylor argued during the mid-1970s, Humayun Ansari asserted that Muslim peddlers in the North East were potentially helped by the fact that tallying and check selling, where goods were sold on credit, were well-established practices in the region's pit villages, having previously been carried out by both English and Jewish salesmen. In other words, Muslim peddlers were successful because their customers were already familiar with this type of business.[51] This history of migrant entrepreneurship is similar to Pnina Werbner's description of that in Manchester. There also, not only did post-war South Asian communities, a significant proportion of which were Muslim, adhere to the entrepreneurial behaviour that had previously been established by Jews, but they also emerged as a new entrepreneurial group in what was otherwise a city suffering the process of industrial decline.[52]

Whatever the reason for this entrepreneurial success, there is no doubt that Newcastle's South Asian Muslim businessmen have advocated the triumph of minority agency. They have diverted from what is often thought to have been a widespread self-employment paradigm. Rather than entrepreneurship having been the undesired consequence of discrimination, racism or poor race relations, it appears as though it was the chosen employment path of many of the city's South Asian Muslims. Furthermore, it gradually grew from a hidden practice in the form of door-to-door peddlers and market stalls to a much more visible and complex phenomenon in the shape of shops, restaurants and business networks. It is not surprising that this ever-increasing entrepreneurialism had been awarded, by the early 1980s, a firm position in Newcastle's local government's debate on ethnic minority labour market performance.

---

[50] See Pnina Werbner, 'Renewing an industrial past: British Pakistani entrepreneurship in Manchester', in Judith M. Brown and Rosemary Foot (eds), *Migration: The Asian Experience* (Basingstoke, 1994), pp. 110–11; Visram, *Asians in Britain*, pp. 212–13; and Ansari, '*The Infidel Within*', pp. 47–50.
[51] Ansari, '*The Infidel Within*', p. 49.
[52] Werbner, 'Renewing an industrial past', pp. 104–30.

Entrepreneurialism: the 1980s and 1990s

The significance and volume of ethnic minority businesses in Britain is seen in that, certainly by the early 1980s, self-employment rates amongst the South Asian and Chinese communities had overtaken that of the white population.[53] It was at exactly this point that the compilation of several reports and committee documents addressing entrepreneurship amongst Newcastle's Indian, Pakistani and Bangladeshi communities began to emerge. Businesses owned and run by Britain's Muslim migrant community have often been perceived as either an extension or a consequence of a restrictive and unsuccessful employment scenario. It has frequently been argued that many of these businessmen have been pushed into self-employment, seeing it as a welcome alternative to either unemployment or low-skilled and poorly paid work caused by an often racist and discriminatory employment sector.[54] It has also been suggested that these businesses have often been established by individuals with very little experience and relying on personal savings, and that they are disadvantaged from the outset either because their owners' religion constrains the type of goods and services they can provide or as a result of the fact that they often cater for ethnic minority communities, thus situating themselves in deprived areas.[55]

Yet ethnic minority entrepreneurship was seen in a more positive light by some, especially outside of academic circles. During the 1980s, business ownership was thought to have the potential to help Afro-Caribbean and African communities overcome social segregation and

---

[53] Giles A. Barrett, Trevor P. Jones and David McEvoy, 'United Kingdom: Severely constrained entrepreneurialism', in Robert Kloosterman and Jan Rath (eds), *Immigrant Entrepreneurs: Venturing Abroad in the Age of Globalization* (Oxford, 2003), p. 101.

[54] See Kenneth Clark and Stephen Drinkwater, 'Ethnicity and self-employment in Britain', *Oxford Bulletin of Economics and Statistics*, 60:3 (1998), pp. 383–407; and Anuradha Basu, 'Ethnic minority entrepreneurship', in Mark Casson, Bernard Yeung, Anuradha Basu and Nigel Wadeson (eds), *The Oxford Handbook of Entrepreneurship* (Oxford, 2006), pp. 583–4.

[55] See Mohammed Rafiq, 'Ethnicity and enterprise: A comparison of Muslim and non-Muslim owned Asian businesses in Britain', *New Community*, 19:1 (1992), pp. 43–9; Ansari, *'The Infidel Within'*, pp. 196–200; David Smallbone, Monder Ram and David Deakins, 'Access to finance by ethnic minority entrepreneurs in the UK', in Léo-Paul Dana (ed.), *Handbook of Research on Ethnic Minority Entrepreneurship: A Co-evolutionary View on Resource Management* (Cheltenham, 2007), pp. 390–404.

the South Asian business community was often perceived as a success story, with the press boasting about the number of Asian millionaires in Britain and the Prince of Wales describing such success as an 'outstanding example' of 'hard work'.[56] Similarly, a mid-1980s Newcastle City Council report entitled 'Black business development project' quoted a Home Affairs Committee Report on Racial Disadvantage, which argued that entrepreneurship offered migrant businessmen an alternative source of income and helped fund the regeneration of ethnic minority neighbourhoods. It claimed that the participation of ethnic minorities in business should be enabled, and any barriers present in the founding and running of these businesses should be removed.[57]

The report highlighted the extent to which these ethnic minority communities in Newcastle did not become concentrated in the local economy's 'dirty sector', claiming that this was potentially because of the fact that the North East, even at the time of an economic boom, still experienced unemployment and thus also competition for low-end employment. Instead, it reinforced the notion that many of the city's ethnic minorities were employed by the Tyne & Wear Passenger Transport Executive as well as foundries and manufacturing companies, but that for many this type of employment was not perceived as long-term or permanent but, as previously mentioned, as a way in which to eventually fund self-employment. Many of the ethnic minority workers employed at the Passenger Transport Executive, for example, saved their earnings in order to purchase a retail business whilst others already had a family business that they hoped would ultimately act as their main source of income. The report reinforced the previously mentioned business and entrepreneurial patterns. As Taylor established, Indians and Pakistanis often worked in the drapery trade with the hope of eventually opening a market stall, a general dealers or an off-license shop. Bangladeshis found work in restaurants and started off as kitchen staff until their English had improved and they were promoted to floor staff. Many hoped to open their own takeaways and restaurants in time, and it was not unusual for these to be co-owned, thus constituting a community venture.[58] Again, this long-term goal of becoming self-employed, and the practice of

[56] See Giles A. Barrett, Trevor P. Jones and David McEvoy, 'Ethnic minority business: Theoretical discourse in Britain and North America', *Urban Studies*, 33:4–5 (1996), pp. 785–7.
[57] TWAS, MD.NC/162/1, Local Government and Racial Equality Sub-Committee of Corporate Joint Sub-Committee 18 March 1983–17 July 1985, 'Black business development project', undated report, p. 22.
[58] Ibid., p. 22.

working and saving up the sufficient financial capital to do so was not particular to Newcastle. Sheila Allen, Stuart Bentley and Joanna Bornat's Indian, Pakistani and West Indian respondents in the Bradford area followed this same pattern, with many having initially worked in factories, mills and transport.[59] Similarly, Pnina Werbner has argued that many Punjabi businessmen in Manchester often started out working in factories or in public transport.[60]

The manner in which the community got behind these businesses was witnessed in the way they were established, run and funded. Most were the result of personal entrepreneurial judgement, and businessmen rarely made use of the public advice and assistance available. Rather than approach banks, small business development agencies or the local authority, most of Newcastle's ethnic minority businessmen sought support from within their own communities and often used past successful businesses as models for future ones. The 'Black business development project' pointed out that seminars on the resources available for ethnic minority businessmen were poorly attended and predicted that leaflets with relevant information in minority languages would probably show a similar level of reponse.[61] Again, Newcastle's ethnic minority businessmen were not exceptions in this, with the refusal amongst South Asians of external business support and finance, and the preference of seeking the necessary provision from within their own families and ethnic communities being well recognised in the literature on British migrant entrepreneurship.[62]

Needless to say, there were many risks as a consequence of this system and the report highlighted a few, including the possibility of reaching a saturation point when further restaurants or corner shops become financially unsustainable, resources not being used to their maximum capacity, and the potential to create new services and employment opportunities not being realised.[63] There were numerous

[59] Sheila Allen, Stuart Bentley and Joanna Bornat, *Work, Race and Immigration* (Bradford, 1977), pp. 244, 251–2
[60] Pnina Werbner, *The Migration Process: Capital, Gifts and Offerings among British Pakistanis* (Oxford, 1990), pp. 50–78.
[61] TWAS, MD.NC/162/1, 'Black business development project', pp. 23–4.
[62] See Hilary Metcalf, Tariq Modood and Satnam Virdee, *Asian Self-Employment: The Interaction of Culture and Economics in England* (London, 1996); Anuradha Basu, 'An exploration of entrepreneurial activity among Asian small businesses in Britain', *Small Business Economics*, 10:4 (1998), pp. 313–26; and The Commission on the Future of Multi-Ethnic Britain, *The Parekh Report*, p. 202.
[63] TWAS, MD.NC/162/1, 'Black business development project', p. 23.

council documents that emerged during the mid-1980s addressing the need to make ethnic minority communities aware of the support that was available to businessmen. In fact, the economic development section of the January 1986 report entitled 'The council and racial equality: Policy statement and action plan' revolved around ethnic minority entrepreneurs, both regarding the possible need for their diversification, and ways in which to encourage business formation and equality of opportunity.[64]

Yet despite this tendency not to take advantage of available support and advice, there is no doubt that Newcastle's Muslim businessmen have not generally experienced some of the problems and obstacles that were so prevalent amongst minority groups across Britain, such as trouble securing financial assistance and being situated in areas of low profitability.[65] However, as the 'Black business development project' recognised, this was because of the support they received from within their communities rather than the result of any official system. Yet despite the apparent entrepreneurial success of the city's ethnic minority businessmen, the council appeared to subscribe to the view that a concentration of migrant communities in self-employment was the result of a lack of equal opportunity in the labour market and therefore an absence of any employment alternatives.[66]

The report concluded with a Tyne & Wear Community Relations Council proposal for a two-year project run by a Black Business Development Officer who would assist with the business development of the city's ethnic minorities. The overall aim was for ethnic minority businessmen to receive the support that they required, but also for the agencies to become better informed about local ethnic business needs.[67]

[64] See TWAS, MD.NC/162/2, Local Government and Racial Equality Sub-Committee of Corporate Joint Sub-Committee 18 September 1985–15 July 1987, 'The council and racial equality: Policy statement and action plan', January 1986, p. D.6. See also TWAS, MD.NC/162/1, City of Newcastle upon Tyne Racial Equality Sub-Committee, 'Responses to the Green Paper: Covering report', 31 May 1984, p. 22.
[65] See Rafiq, 'Ethnicity and enterprise', pp. 54–5; and Henk Flap, Adem Kumcu and Bert Bulder, 'The social capital of ethnic entrepreneurs and their business success', in Jan Rath (ed.), *Immigrant Business: The Economic, Political and Social Enviroment* (Basingstoke, 1999), pp. 142–61.
[66] TWAS, MD.NC/162/1, 'Black business development project', pp. 23–4.
[67] Ibid., pp. 24–7. See also TWAS, MD.NC/162/1, City of Newcastle upon Tyne Economic Development Committee, 'Ethnic minority groups & business development', 4 March 1985.

Although it was decided that the proposal would not go ahead at that time, it is still indicative of the importance awarded to entrepreneurialism within the city's ethnic minority communities even if its approach was one that did not appear to recognise variations in ethnic and religious backgrounds. Such variations have become increasingly identified as influential amongst what is a complex set of migrant self-employment patterns both in Britain and further afield.[68]

The council's concentration on migrant self-employment continued throughout the 1990s. Areas of focus were the problems and obstacles experienced by the city's ethnic minority businessmen. Research conducted between July 1995 and January 1996 concluded that harassment of some type was experienced by Asian traders and their families on a regular basis, including verbal abuse, assault, intimidation, theft and arson.[69] Other concerns and complaints the businessmen raised included a loss of trade due to crime, their neighbourhoods being affected by a decrease in tenants and demolition programmes, not feeling supported by certain agencies and some of the local community, and an increase in pressure and responsibilities in that they might close early due to a fear of crime or collect their own stock as a result of the area's poor reputation for deliveries. Specific experiences that the Asian traders recounted included being threatened and wounded, women and children witnessing attacks on family members, and feeling compelled to sleep above their shops for security reasons. Table 1.1 shows the problems and types of harassment experienced in Newcastle during the mid-1990s. Although the manner in which ethnic minority businesses are subjected to such incidents of crime and racial harassment have been largely neglected in the literature, there are a few studies that have emerged since the late 1980s documenting such incidents.[70]

---

[68] See Vani Kant Borooah and Mark Hart, 'Factors affecting self-employment among Indian and black Caribbean men in Britain', *Small Business Economics*, 13:2 (1999), pp. 111–29; Léo-Paul Dana (ed.), *Entrepreneurship and Religion* (Cheltenham, 2010).

[69] TWAS, MD.NC/614/2, Racial Equality Working Group 18 January 1996–6 March 1997, City of Newcastle upon Tyne Race Equality Working Group, 'Experiences of Asian traders and their families', 4 July 1996.

[70] See Paul Ekblom and Frances H. Simon with Sneh Birdi, *Crime and Racial Harassment in Asian-run Small Shops: The Scope for Prevention* (London, 1988); and David Deakins, David Smallbone, Mohammed Ishaq, Geoffrey Whittam and Janette Wyper, 'Minority ethnic enterprise in Scotland', *Journal of Ethnic and Migration Studies*, 35:2 (2009), pp. 309–30.

Table 1.1: Types of harassment suffered by Asian traders and their families in Newcastle according to a study undertaken between July 1995 and January 1996

Type of harassment	Percentage suffering
General harassment	67
Suffered at the hands of gangs and youths	55
Intimidation	50
Theft	50
Verbal racist abuse	34
Vandalism	34
Assault	28
Loss of income or debt	20
Threats	14
Burglary	14
Arson	7

Source: TWAS, MD.NC/614/2, 'Experiences of Asian traders and their families', 4 July 1996, p. 5.

Work carried out in the Scotswood area in the West End of the city showed a similar range of complaints and reported incidents. As well as problems regarding harassment, low income and theft, ethnic minority businessmen also endured problems caused by regeneration and reduced housing stock in that some people felt unsafe walking to the shops through building sites. A key point included in the report was that, despite the problems and obstacles they faced, many of them very severe and threatening, the majority of these traders had expressed a desire to remain in the area having lived and worked there for a long time.[71] This is perhaps not surprising, with the manner in which South Asian businesses in particular are deeply embedded in ethnic minority neighbourhoods and the role that location and community play being well recognised.[72] In this sense, they are surrounded by supporters of their businesses, financial or otherwise, as well as by their customers and an available labour force. Perhaps because of this, there was an

[71] See TWAS, MD.NC/614/2, City of Newcastle upon Tyne Asian Traders Working Group, 11 October 1996.
[72] See Howard Aldrich, John Cater, Trevor Jones and David McEvoy, 'Business development and self-segregation: Asian enterprise in three British cities', in Ceri Peach, Vaughan Robinson and Susan Smith (eds), *Ethnic Segregation in Cities* (London, 1981), pp. 170–90; and Ansari, *'The Infidel Within'*, pp. 196–200.

awareness that steps had to be taken in an attempt to address the situation. Some of the suggestions made included more effective support mechanisms and security, and visiting some parts of the West End in order to become better acquainted with the area.[73]

The racial harassment suffered by Newcastle's ethnic minority businessmen was again captured in interviews carried out in December 1997 and January 1998, this time in the East End of the city. Interviews were conducted with thirty Asian businessmen, seven of whom were in Byker, seven in Heaton, six in Monkchester, six in Walker and four in Sandyford. The types of businesses included nine off-licences/general stores, eight off-licences/general stores/newsagents, four takeaways, and the rest fruit shops, general stores, newsagents and post offices. The types of harassment these businessmen encountered were very similar to those affecting Asian traders in other parts of the city and are recorded in table 1.2. In total, only three out of the thirty businesses had not experienced racial harassment during the twelve months prior to the interviews taking place.[74]

The interviews also succeeded in establishing an insight into how these businessmen dealt with such incidents, and how they perceived

Table 1.2: Types of harassment suffered by Asian traders in the East End of Newcastle according to interviews carried out in December 1997 and January 1998

Type of harrassment	*Percentage suffering*	*Percentage suffering on a daily basis*
Verbal abuse	83	27
Damage to property	57	3
Graffiti	37	7
Threats	53	10
Physical attack	33	3

Source: TWAS, MD.NC/358, 'A survey of Asian traders in the East End of Newcastle. Report of a research study undertaken by the Racial Harassment Support Group (East)', March 1998, p. 5.

[73] TWAS, MD.NC/614/2, City of Newcastle upon Tyne Asian Traders Working Group, 11 October 1996; and TWAS, MD.NC/614/2, City of Newcastle upon Tyne Racial Equality Working Group, 'Site visit', 16 December 1996.
[74] TWAS, MD.NC/358, 'A survey of Asian traders in the East End of Newcastle. Report of a research study undertaken by the Racial Harassment Support Group (East)'. Research and development, Department of Community and Leisure Services, March 1998, pp. 3–4, 7.

the police and the judiciary. Of those who experienced graffiti, 55 per cent had never reported the incidents to the police. This was also the case amongst 50 per cent of those who had been threatened, 43 per cent of those who had experienced verbal abuse, 22 per cent of those who had been physically attacked and 12 per cent of those who had suffered damage to their property. Furthermore, 73 per cent did not have faith in the ability of the police to catch the perpetrators of these crimes and only 55 per cent expressed satisfaction associated with reporting racially motivated incidents. Many more of these businessmen viewed the Crown Prosecution Service in a negative light than did in a positive one, with 71 per cent finding prison sentences for racially motivated crimes too short and 68 per cent claiming that judges are ignorant of ethnic minority culture.[75]

Whilst there has been little in-depth research conducted into the extent to which racial harassment is suffered by British ethnic minority businesses, the manner in which Newcastle's ethnic minority businessmen reacted to racist incidents mirrored those of the South Asian respondents in Glasgow included in a 2010 study. It discovered that 45 per cent of respondents who had experienced racism chose to ignore it, a figure that was even higher amongst older age groups, and only 19 per cent reported such incidents to the police. In Glasgow also, there was a general lack of confidence in how the police addressed these cases.[76] Yet there was nevertheless a clear awareness on behalf of Newcastle's council that many of the incidents suffered by these ethnic minority businessmen were clearly racially motivated and thus they experienced a different set of problems to their white counterparts.[77]

As well as this focus on racial harassment, the 1990s also witnessed the council planning for the future of the city's ethnic minority businesses, especially those in the West End. This is an area close to the city centre, where a key cluster of ethnic minority businesses have traditionally been located, but it has also been a district in decline. Many of the businesses in this area were small and in the retail trade, and around 80 per cent were owned or run by members of ethnic minorities, and had difficulty accessing the usual business support. The council's vision for the area consisted of creating a shopping district for

[75] Ibid., pp. 6–9.
[76] Mohammed Ishaq, Asifa Hussain and Geoff Whittam, 'Racism: A barrier to entry? Experiences of small ethnic minority retail businesses', *International Small Business Journal*, 28:4 (2010), pp. 370–1.
[77] TWAS, MD.NC/358, City of Newcastle upon Tyne Asian Traders Working Group, 17 April 1998, p. 3.

the local population, but also establishing a specialist shopping zone that would attract people from across the city. Other proposed measures included attracting service businesses to empty properties above shops, and introducing a set of security and environmental improvements. Another suggestion was to develop a training and employment culture in the West End, with the aim of establishing an 'Asia Town', which would be seen as a key part of Newcastle alongside Chinatown and the city centre. It was hoped that this would construct a certain culture and identity that would attract people to the area in search of certain products and services. This scheme was also to include the offering of general business support for Asian-run businesses, marketing for the area and the formation of a certain image for what it was hoped would develop into a business and tourist area.[78] The potential of establishing an 'Asia Town' has also been discussed in other British cities, such as Leicester, where it has also been perceived as a diverse and exciting area that would attract tourists and professionals.[79]

Other initiatives in Newcastle included an Ethnic Minority Business Forum, which was launched in September 1995 with the aim of acting as a type of club for what was an active, yet largely isolated, ethnic minority business community. This forum was established as one way in which to address the low proportion of ethnic minority businessmen who take advantage of available business support. It was soon holding regular meetings, which attracted up to forty business representatives and enabled the discussion of relevant business issues in the city, and enjoying a continuous increase in membership, which was largely Asian from the beginning.[80] A further key initiative during the 1990s regarding ethnic minority businesses was entitled LIA-Newcastle (Local Integration (Partnership) Action-Newcastle), a project that was launched by Newcastle City Council in June 1997 with funding from

[78] See TWAS, MD.NC/614/3, Racial Equality Working Group 3 July 1997–5 March 1998, City of Newcastle upon Tyne Racial Equality Working Group, 'Asian business cluster', 5 March 1998, pp. 1–2; TWAS, MD.NC/358, City of Newcastle upon Tyne Asian Traders Working Group, 17 April 1998, pp. 1–3; and TWAS, MD.NC/358, City of Newcastle upon Tyne Asian Traders Working Group 17 April 1998, 'Asian business cluster', p. 2.
[79] See Herbert, *Negotiating Boundaries in the City*, pp. 1–2.
[80] See TWAS, MD.NC/358, City of Newcastle upon Tyne Asian Traders Working Group 17 April 1998, 'Asian business cluster', p. 1; and TWAS, MD.NC/358, City of Newcastle upon Tyne Asian Traders Working Group, 24 March 1997, p. 1.

the LIA.[81] Funding was secured under the 'ELAINE' scheme, the aim of which was to encourage the socio-economic independence of migrants and ethnic minorities through self-employment. The project included a survey of all ethnic minority businesses in Newcastle, which aimed to establish the actual number of businesses, as well as their training needs, their concerns and their interest in launching a business support network.[82]

The survey was sent out to all 465 ethnic minority businesses in the city and had a very positive response rate of 96 per cent (449 businesses). The types of businesses identified confirmed the previously mentioned pattern and included takeaways, restaurants, taxi services, post offices, newsagents, and those involved in the retail and manufacturing trade. In terms of their ethnic origin, the majority were Indian and Pakistani; other ethnicities represented included Chinese, Bangladeshi and Middle Eastern (see Table 1.3). Most of these businesses were small in that 73 per cent employed between one and ten people and 62 per cent operated as sole traders.[83]

Table 1.3: The ethnic origin of 449 ethnic minority businessmen in Newcastle, 1997

Ethnicity	*Percentage*
Indian	41
Pakistani	27
Chinese	20
Bangladeshi	7
Middle Eastern	2
Other	3

Source: TWAS, MD.NC/614/3, 'LIA-Newcastle: Minority ethnic businesses in Newcastle', Newcastle City Council, 1997, p. 21.

The results of the survey painted a picture of ethnic minority business life not dissimilar from that in other areas of Britain (and indeed Bremen). 85 per cent of businesses had not undergone any type of formal business training, the average working week was 66.5 hours

[81] LIA-Europe was a pilot initiative launched in 1996. It was developed by three networks: European Local Authority Interative Network Exchange (ELAINE), EUROCITIES and *Quartiers en Crise*.
[82] TWAS, MD.NC/614/3, *LIA-Newcastle: Minority Ethnic Businesses in Newcastle*, report of survey undertaken by Chief Executive's Department, Newcastle City Council, 1997, pp. 2, 5.
[83] Ibid., pp. iii, 9, 11, 21.

or 6.5 days, 18 per cent were dissatisfied with their location, and 22 per cent suffered crime and 17 per cent racial harassment. When asked which business skills were in need of development, the respondents identified those relating to health and safety, marketing and advertising, book-keeping, basic accounting, business planning and cash flow, and communication skills. Yet despite these businessmen admitting a lack of necessary skills and training, poor working conditions, and crime and harassment, only 35 per cent expressed an interest in partaking in a business support network.[84]

The report also comprised a list of recommendations. These included encouraging ethnic minority businesses to report racially motivated crime and harassment so that they could be addressed, improving these businesses' environment and security, promoting employment and business related training for the younger generation, encouraging the use of a Minority Ethnic Business Directory, delivering the training identified as lacking by the businesses, promoting the hiring of trainees and developing a Minority Ethnic Business Support Network.[85] At the time the report was produced, some work had already begun. The compilation of the Minority Ethnic Business Directory was under way, and it was hoped that this would increase trade for the businesses involved and enhance contact and trading relations with ethnic minority businesses more generally. Some of the businesses' training needs had also started to be addressed, including seminars on health and safety issues.[86]

Newcastle has not been alone in promoting ethnic minority entrepreneurship. In Britain more widely there has been a political interest in encouraging self-employment amongst migrant communities. This especially began to emerge following the 1981 urban disturbances after which it was believed that advancing a culture of entrepreneurship amongst ethnic minority communities would lead to increased social inclusion.[87] Yet the success of this approach has been questioned. Giles

[84] Ibid., p. iii, 14–16. See also TWAS, MD.NC/614/3, City of Newcastle upon Tyne Racial Equality Working Group, 'Survey of minority ethnic businesses (LIA-Newcastle)', 5 February 1998, p. 1.
[85] See TWAS, MD.NC/614/3, *LIA-Newcastle: Minority Ethnic Businesses in Newcastle*, pp. 23–4.
[86] Ibid., pp. 26–7.
[87] See Lord Scarman, *The Brixton Disorders, 10–12th April 1981: Report of an Inquiry by the Rt. Hon. The Lord Scarman* (London, 1982); and Barrett, Jones and McEvoy, 'Ethnic minority business: Theoretical discourse in Britain and North America', pp. 785–6.

Barrett, Trevor Jones and David McEvoy, for example, offer an assessment of the impact of available enterprise support, policies regarding urban regeneration and other political measures affecting ethnic minority businesses, and conclude that public policy has been largely unsuccessful in impacting ethnic minority entrepreneurship in the manner hoped. This was often because migrant businessmen failed to engage with the agencies, were not aware of the support available or simply because the initiatives were not relevant to their businesses.[88] Similarly, Monder Ram's study of ethnic minority business support in London, Birmingham, Manchester and Liverpool revealed the shortcomings of such provision.[89]

Yet ethnic minority businesses in Britain continue to receive political attention and recognition through such initiatives as the Ethnic Minority Business Forum, which was launched in 2000, and the 2009 Ethnic Minority Business Advocacy Network. In a pre-2010 election pledge, David Cameron went so far as to argue that he would tackle racial inequalities by promoting and supporting black businesses.[90] Even amongst academic circles there has been a recent call for the foundation of support agencies and networks, stemming from the belief that they have the potential to assist ethnic minority businessmen with business strategies and help them enter more favourable industries.[91] Yet others have questioned whether ethnic minority businesses are best served by mainstream support or by that which is rooted within their respective ethnic communities.[92] Overall there is no doubt that, as across Britain, even those schemes and programmes in Newcastle that were directly relevant to ethnic minority businesses often found themselves battling against the deeply embedded trait of refusing external assistance.

Yet ethnic minority businesses continued to play an important role on Newcastle's local government agenda and the proposal of an 'Asia Town' during the 1990s shows the extent to which they were perceived

[88] Giles A. Barrett, Trevor P. Jones and David McEvoy, 'Socio-economic and policy dimensions of the mixed embeddedness of ethnic minority business in Britain', *Journal of Ethnic and Migration Studies*, 27:2 (2001), pp. 249–54.
[89] Monder Ram, 'Enterprise support and ethnic minority firms', *Journal of Ethnic and Migration Studies*, 24:1 (1998), pp. 143–58.
[90] 'We'll Change Black Britain', *Guardian* (17 March 2010).
[91] See Basu, 'Ethnic minority entrepreneurship', p. 597.
[92] See Monder Ram and David Smallbone, 'Ethnic minority business policy in the era of the small business service', *Environment and Planning C: Government and Policy*, 20:2 (2002), p. 241.

as a permanent and influential part of the local economy. Newcastle has witnessed the emergence and development of a South Asian Muslim migrant entrepreneurial community that has been the consequence of economic aspirations, self-determination and a series of conscious business choices. This is seen through the fact that self-employment was often an ambition from the outset, with many initially pursuing other employment in order to obtain the necessary capital, thus showing their ability to successfully manipulate the local labour market to serve their long-term economic goals. The extent to which they strove for economic autonomy and independence was shown by the fact that they refused funding and support, and were determined to persevere with their businesses despite many suffering incidents of crime and racial harassment.

For too long, the literature focusing on ethnic minority businesses in Britain during the post-war era has perceived them as the unwanted consequences of unemployment, racism and discrimination in the employment sector, and promoters of ethnic enclaves which inhibit social mobility and integration into the wider economy. Whilst these theories and paradigms may be applicable in certain cases, they fail to acknowledge the more positive aspects of British Muslim immigrant businesses and the manner in which they have developed over time. This study hopes to build upon the more hopeful causes and consequences of migrant entrepreneurship, and recognises the role played by a desire for social mobility, multiculturalism, collaboration with the white British population and economic prosperity.[93]

There is no doubt that many of these positive characteristics and consequences of ethnic minority entrepreneurship are present in Newcastle. The businesses established and run by its Muslim immigrants have introduced a diverse range of new ideas and products, provided job opportunities for members of their communities, acted as a bridge between the migrant and white host populations, and offered the entrepreneurs themselves financial and social security. In essence, Newcastle's Muslim immigrants are succeeding as a result of their own self-determination, but also due to a certain understanding of and contact with their local host society. Although they have historically

---

[93] See Robin Ward, 'Economic development and ethnic business', in James Curran and Robert A. Blackburn (eds), *Paths of Enterprise: The Future of the Small Business* (London, 1991), pp. 51–67; Shaila Srinivasan, *The South Asian Petty Bourgeoisie in Britain: An Oxford Case Study* (Aldershot, 1995); and Panikos Panayi, *Spicing up Britain: The Multicultural History of British Food* (London, 2008).

portrayed a preference for self-sufficiency and economic independence, contrary to popular belief this has not necessarily been the result of a failure to integrate. Though the capital foundation of immigrant businesses has originated largely from within the ethnic communities, many have served the indigenous British population. Ethnic minority entrepreneurship should not automatically be equated with discrimination, disadvantage and a lack of integration. This pursuit of economic autonomy and independence will also be discussed as a key long-term aim amongst Muslim ethnic minorities in Bremen, and as a trait that overspills into the housing sector in both cities in the form of property ownership and neighbourhood formation.

Bremen

Throughout the twentieth century, Bremen acted as one of Germany's main economic centres, and has been a hub for shipbuilding, car and aircraft production, arms manufacturing, and machine and engineering industries. Its status as a major German port has historically ensured its position as a recipient of immigrants, whether of Eastern Europeans at the turn of the twentieth century, prisoners of war to fuel the Nazi war economy or *Gastarbeiter* during the 1960s and 1970s. Whilst Bremen's history of immigration has often been overshadowed by the role it played in the emigration of millions of European migrants making the journey to the New World, it must be recognised that, like so many others across Germany, this was a city that experienced an influx of foreign labour during the post-war period. Some of the main recruiters of guest-workers in the city included AG Weser and Bremer Vulkan, two shipbuilding companies, Bremer Woll-Kämmerei, a wool textile company, the Klöckner steel- and metal-works, and the Bremen-Vegesacker Fischerei-Gesellschaft (Bremen Vegesack fishing company). As Patrick Ireland argued, Bremen's post-war emergence as a renewed trade and industrial hub led to a vast increase in its immigrant population, which constituted fewer than 2 per cent of the total population in 1968 and almost 10 per cent in 1988.[94]

Yet Bremen's post-war economy also experienced immense change and a series of crises, causing this German city to become renowned for shipbuilders' bankruptcies and closures, and industries marred by overwhelming levels of unemployment. Between 1970 and 1980, Bremen lost an estimated 20 per cent of its manufacturing bases. By 1984, the

[94] Ireland, *Becoming Europe*, p. 86.

unemployment rate amongst foreigners in the city had reached 23.4 per cent, a figure that it has been argued was comparable to those of blacks in US cities.[95] Whilst Bremen did indeed secure economic alternatives, such as a steelworks and the Daimler-Benz aerospace plant, ethnic minority workers often failed to make the transition, and the economic activity rate amongst the Turkish community fell from 72 per cent in 1980 to 40 per cent in 1986.[96] By 1999, the unemployment rate amongst Bremen's ethnic minorities had reached 29 per cent and they constituted more than a quarter of those receiving social assistance.[97]

Nevertheless, the labour market performance of Bremen's Muslim migrant communities during the post-war period was by no means entirely dominated by unemployment and setbacks. As well as the immense initial economic contribution made by Muslim guest-workers in the city during the 1960s and 1970s,[98] their subsequent role in the local labour market must also be recognised. Government documents have repeatedly highlighted that ethnic minority communities have increasingly constituted a large and important proportion of the city's workforce, especially in shipbuilding, textiles and other types of manufacturing, the garment trade, the cleaning and personal hygiene industry, trade and commerce, and property and housing.[99] As in Newcastle, ethnic minority businesses have grown in number and progressively played a role in the city's economy. Bremen's government has perceived this entrepreneurial development in a positive light, recognising the manner in which these businesses have the potential to

[95] John D. Kasarda, Jürgen Friedrichs and Kay E. Ehlers, 'Urban industrial restructuring and minority problems in the US and Germany', in Malcolm Cross (ed.), *Ethnic Minorities and Industrial Change in Europe and North America* (Cambridge, 1992), p. 269.

[96] See Ireland, *Becoming Europe*, pp. 87–8. See also Freie Hansestadt Bremen *Statistische Monatsberichte*, 'Ausländische Arbeitnehmer in der bremischen Wirtschaft', 44. Jahrgang, August 1992, pp. 90–1.

[97] See Ireland, *Becoming Europe*, p. 96.

[98] See 'Jetzt über 2000 Gastarbeiter in Bremen-Nord. Arbeitsmarkt im März wieder stärker belebt – Kräftebedarf in fast allen Wirtschaftszweigen', *Norddeutsche Volkszeitung*, 12 April 1966; Leohold, *Die Kämmeristen*, pp. 49–55; and Çil (ed.), *Anfänge einer EPOCHE*.

[99] See Bremische Bürgerschaft Landtag 13. Wahlperiode, Drucksache 13/350, 'Kleine Anfrage der Fraktion der CDU vom 10. September 1992. Bedeutung von Ausländern für die Arbeitswelt', p. 2; and Bremische Bürgerschaft Landtag 15. Wahlperiode, Drucksache 15/368, 'Mitteilung des Senats vom 6. Juni 2000. Ausländische Mitbürgerinnen und Mitbürger in der Arbeitswelt in Bremen und Bremerhaven', 6 June 2000, p. 2.

help the local economy grow and progress, and enable integration.[100] In fact, Bremen is perceived as one of the cities in Germany that offers the most provision for ethnic minority businesses, with over fifty different advice and support measures available.[101] Indeed the performance of migrants in the labour market as a whole has been a central and vibrant part of the debate on their settlement and integration since the 1960s. Furthermore, their incorporation into the city's working and business sectors remains a fundamental area of focus of the Bremen government's efforts and measures to combat exclusion and marginalisation, and secure integration.[102]

The 1960s and 1970s: the guest-worker years

October 2011 marked the fiftieth anniversary of the 1961 recruitment agreement between West Germany and Turkey. What originally appeared to be merely another phase in Germany's history of labour recruitment, albeit one that attracted heightened attention due to the Nazi era that preceded it,[103] has gradually evolved into something far

[100] See Bremische Bürgerschaft Landtag 16. Wahlperiode, Drucksache 16/262, 'Mitteilung des Senats vom 25. Mai 2004. Das wirtschaftliche Potenzial von Unternehmern und Existenzgründern mit Migrationshintergrund', pp. 2–3; Bremische Bürgerschaft Landtag 17. Wahlperiode, Drucksache 17/503, 'Mitteilung des Senats vom 12. August 2008. Die Potenziale von Unternehmer/-innen mit Migrationshintergrund stärker nutzen', 12 August 2008, pp. 1–2; and Die Senatorin für Soziales, Kinder, Jugend und Frauen, *Konzeption zur Integration von Zuwanderern und Zuwanderinnen im Lande Bremen 2007–2011. Grundsätze, Leitbilder und Handlungsziele für die bremische Integrationspolitik* (draft dated February 2008), p. 16.

[101] See Sachverständigenrat deutscher Stiftungen für Integration und Migration, *Wirtschaftliche Selbstständigkeit als Integrationsstrategie – eine Bestandsaufnahme der Strukturen der Integrationsförderung in Deutschland* (Berlin, 2010), pp. 16–17.

[102] See Bremische Bürgerschaft Landtag 15. Wahlperiode, Drucksache 15/447, 'Antrag der Fraktion Bündnis 90/Die Grünen. Zehn-Punkte-Programm zur Integration von Zuwanderern im Lande Bremen: Konkret handeln – gemeinsame Zukunft gestalten', 8 September 2000, p. 3; and Bremische Bürgerschaft Landtag 16. Wahlperiode, Drucksache 16/176, 'Mitteilung des Senats vom 9. März 2004. Konzeption zur Integration von Zuwanderern und Zuwanderinnen im Lande Bremen 2003 bis 2007, Grundsätze, Leitlinien und Handlungsempfehlungen für die bremische Integrationspolitik', 9 March 2004, pp. 3, 6.

[103] See Schönwälder, 'West German society and foreigners in the 1960s'; and Chin, 'Guest worker migration and the unexpected return of race'.

more complex than was initially foreseen. Indeed the politics behind the originally intended guest-worker rotation system and its consequences have been well documented in both the historiography and guest-worker literature.[104] What emerges is a story involving recruitment offices, medical examinations and temporary work contracts, and one dominated by isolation, confusion, prejudice, racism and the everyday experiences of working for a German company where one is considered nothing more than a temporary supply of manpower. In many ways, Bremen was no exception to this national paradigm. As previously mentioned, the city was home to a number of companies that partook in the guest-worker recruitment scheme during the 1960s and early 1970s.

Yet because the initial employment patterns of guest-workers in Bremen were dictated by the local economy, their recruitment was distinct in several ways. Firstly, there is no doubt that Bremen's foreign worker community was smaller and more manageable than those in other cities. This was partially due to Bremen's particular economic structure. It had a smaller manufacturing sector than the German average and, because this was the industry into which guest-workers were often recruited, Bremen did not have as much need for foreign workers as did other areas. Furthermore, Bremen was often able to meet its demand for labour from its rural surroundings.[105] Secondly, whilst a large proportion of foreign workers were employed in the manufacturing sector, as was the case across Germany, Bremen had a higher percentage in the commerce and transport industry, largely as a result of the city-state's ports.

Thirdly, Bremen underwent its recruitment peak later than the German norm. This was the result of the North–South divide with regard to labour importation in that guest-workers first arrived in areas

---

[104] See Güney Dal, *Wenn Ali die Glocken läuten hört* (Berlin, 1979); Franco Biondi et al. (eds), *Im neuen Land* (Bremen, 1980); and Jürgen Fijalkowski, 'Gastarbeiter als industrielle Reservearmee? Zur Bedeutung der Arbeitsmigration für die wirtschaftliche und gesellschaftliche Entwicklung der Bundesrepublik Deutschland', *Archiv für Sozialgeschichte*, 24 (1984), pp. 399–456.

[105] See Bremische Bürgerschaft Landtag 8. Wahlperiode, Drucksache 8/600, 'Antwort des Senats zur Anfrage der Fraktion der CDU vom 26. Juni 1973 (Drs. 8/566). Ausländische Arbeitnehmer', 12 September 1973, pp. 1–2.

[106] See Freie Hansestadt Bremen *Statistische Monatsberichte*, 'Die Beschäftigung ausländischer Arbeitnehmer im Lande Bremen', 29. Jahrgang, June 1977, pp. 91–5.

in the industrial south, such as Baden-Württemberg and Hessen. This leads to the fourth point: that Bremen's foreign worker population was comprised of a much higher than average percentage of Turks. By the time guest-workers started arriving in Bremen, recruitment from countries such as Italy and Spain was slowing down. As a result, in March 1976, almost one in every two (45.6 per cent) foreign workers in Bremen was Turkish whilst the German average stood at only 27.2 per cent.[106] Between the first quarter of 1979 and March 1980, the Turkish worker community in the state of Bremen grew by 7.1 per cent to more than 9,200, constituting 47 per cent of the foreign workforce. Most worked in the city of Bremen where its 7,550 Turkish workers made up 47.4 per cent of its migrant workforce.[107]

Although Bremen's foreign worker population was much smaller than in many cities and regions across Germany, it nevertheless experienced continuous growth throughout the 1960s and early 1970s. By the end of June 1963, there was a total of 4,391 foreign workers employed in the state of Bremen.[108] This figure continued to increase throughout the 1960s, especially in northern districts of the city, such as Burglesum, Blumenthal and Vegesack, which is where the larger guest-worker recruiting companies were often located. By mid-1973, the year of the halt in recruitment, the state of Bremen had welcomed 20,388 foreign workers, 17,220 of which were employed in Bremen city.[109] After this point, the region experienced a gradual decline in foreign workers, with the size of the community sinking to just under 19,800 at the end of March 1980, and then decreasing by 22.7 per cent to 16,060 between 1980 and 1990.[110] It must be realised, however, that the number of foreign workers in Bremen was in fact much greater, but that the statistics used to compile the *Statistische Monatsberichte*

---

[107] See Freie Hansestadt Bremen *Statistische Monatsberichte*, 'Ausländische Arbeitnehmer im Lande Bremen', 33. Jahrgang, February 1981, pp. 64, 66.
[108] See Staatsarchiv Bremen, 4,124/3–694, Ausländische Arbeitskräfte in Deutschland Bd. 1 1960–1963, A letter from the Landesarbeitsamt Bremen to the Senator für Wohlfahrt und Jugend dated 11 July 1963.
[109] SB, 4,13/4–122–10–02/14, Betreuung ausländischer Arbeitnehmer 1963–1975, Reports issued by city districts during the mid-1960s; and SB, 4,124/3–645, Sozialhilfe für Ausländer und Staatenlose – Allgemeines Bd. 2b 1973, A report compiled by the Senator für Arbeit and dated 08 August 1973, p. 4.
[110] See 'Ausländische Arbeitnehmer im Lande Bremen', 33. Jahrgang, February 1981, p. 61; and 'Ausländische Arbeitnehmer in der bremischen Wirtschaft', 44. Jahrgang, August 1992, p. 91.

(Statistical Monthly Reports) included only those who were liable for National Insurance and not any workers who were either helping family members or self-employed. Therefore, the actual number of migrant workers in Bremen was substantially higher and this chapter will address those who were self-employed at a later point.

The *Statistische Monatsberichte* offer an insight into the sectors in which those liable for National Insurance were employed. As was the case throughout Germany, the manufacturing sector played a large role in the employment of guest-workers before starting to experience decline during the 1980s.[111] In March 1976, more than half (57.3 per cent) of the State of Bremen's foreign workers and 77.9 per cent of Turkish workers had jobs in the manufacturing sector. Within this sector, the most popular types of work were in shipbuilding, food and drink, and the road vehicle and aircraft industry, in which 16.7 per cent, 9.9 per cent and 6.6 per cent of the entire migrant workforce was employed respectively.[112] The important role played by manufacturing was seen in 1979–80 when, whilst this sector experienced an overall decline in its workforce, it nevertheless witnessed an increase in foreign workers, albeit a small one of 2.3 per cent. This was largely due to the textile industry, which alone saw a rise of 20 per cent amongst its migrant employees.[113] Another important sector for migrant employment was transport, storage and communications, which employed 13.4 per cent of Bremen's migrant workforce in March 1976, many of whom worked in shipping, haulage and aviation. Further noteworthy areas of work were the service sector, trade and commerce, and construction, which employed 10.8 per cent, 8.3 per cent and 5.3 per cent of foreign workers respectively. Overall, the manner in which migrants in Bremen were economically distributed reflected the local economy. As a result of the city-state's ports, higher percentages of migrant workers were employed in transport, storage and communications, and trade and commerce, and lower proportions in construction and the service sector than was the norm for Germany.[114]

In some ways, Bremen adhered to what have become the accepted

---

[111] See Alexander A. Caviedes, *Prying Open Fortress Europe: The Turn to Sectoral Labor Migration* (Lanham MD, 2010), pp. 84–5.

[112] See 'Beschäftigung ausländischer Arbeitnehmer', 29. Jahrgang, May 1977, pp. 91–2, 95.

[113] See 'Ausländische Arbeitnehmer im Lande Bremen', 33. Jahrgang, February 1981, pp. 62–3.

[114] See 'Beschäftigung ausländischer Arbeitnehmer', 29. Jahrgang, May 1977, pp. 92–5.

and well-known characteristics and intricacies of the guest-worker scheme. For example, documents held at the Staatsarchiv Bremen act as evidence that the guest-worker rotation system was indeed intended to be temporary in nature and not lead to financial costs. For example, guest-workers were issued with vocabulary booklets comprised only of words and phrases that would be needed at the workplace, some companies soon took the cheaper option of training Turkish guest-workers in Turkey rather than waiting until they had arrived in Bremen, and there was concern expressed over guest-workers who either arrived ill or became ill soon after arrival, thus putting strain on the local health infrastructure.[115] The manner in which it was perceived that guest-workers should not incur costs has been an inherent feature of the literature on the German guest-worker system, a concept that was further reinforced by the belief that these foreign workers were a temporary labour force.[116]

As tended to be the norm, Bremen's initial guest-workers were single men and there was a widely held belief in the city that provision for family members did not need to be considered. However, starting in 1962, companies in Bremen, as throughout Germany, started recruiting women.[117] By August 1965, Bremer Woll-Kämmerei had employed 250 married guest-worker couples. Not only did this result in an increase in female guest-workers, but it also freed up company accommodation for single guest-workers as married couples could be housed together.[118] Difficulties experienced by the guest-workers at the workplace included health problems and accidents, bullying and discrimination, and low wages.[119] These are all features of guest-worker life that have conventionally dominated the historiography.[120] Other problems encountered

[115] SB, 4,124/3–643, Sozialhilfe für Ausländer und Staatenlose – Allgemeines Bd. 1 1964–1972 and SB, 7,2121/1–711, Anwerbung, Vermittlung und Ausbildung ausländischer Arbeiter 1970–1973.
[116] See Chin, *The Guest Worker Question in Postwar Germany*, pp. 45–6; and Douglas B. Klusmeyer and Demetrios G. Papademetriou, *Immigration Policy in the Federal Republic of Germany: Negotiating Membership and Remaking the Nation* (New York, 2009), p. 97.
[117] See Lucassen, *The Immigrant Threat*, p. 147.
[118] SB, 4,22/2–275, Wirtschaft und Industrie in Bremen und Bremerhaven – Industrieansiedlung Bd. 3 1966–1967, A letter from the director of Bremer Woll-Kämmerei dated 25 August 1965.
[119] SB, 7,2121/1–712, Sammlung von Schriftgut zur Beschäftigung, Unterbringung und Lage der ausländischen Arbeiter auf dem Vulkan 1969–1981.
[120] See Herbert and Hunn, 'Guest workers and policy on guest workers in the Federal Republic', pp. 198–9.

by Bremen's guest-workers relating specifically to their accommodation will be explored in the following chapter on the housing sector.

Thus, in many ways, the implementation of the guest-worker system in Bremen and the experiences of its foreign workers adhered to a series of German-wide patterns and characteristics. Yet amongst the papers and documents citing incidents of discrimination and poor provision that one has come to expect from the guest-worker years was a much more positive and progressive side that detailed both an awareness regarding the intricacies of the guest-worker scheme and a keen pursuit of integration. Whilst often displaying a sense of uncertainty about the guest-workers and their future in the city, Bremen's government took part in nationwide correspondence regarding the situation of foreign workers, and implemented measures and policies across Germany. Furthermore, it recognised that future provisions for both guest-workers and their families needed to be considered, with Turks being mentioned as the group that would undoubtedly require the most attention.[121]

A striving for integration in Bremen was witnessed as early as the early 1970s, alongside a sense of pride that guest-workers in the city were being adequately provisioned for. There were widespread claims that Bremer Vulkan was not experiencing the same guest-worker problems that were so prevalent across Germany and that it was in fact a company that had long been promoting integration, a reputation that attracted the attention of the German television channel, Zweites Deutsches Fernsehen (ZDF), which enquired about the possibility of filming the first-hand experiences of the company's Turkish workers.[122] Opportunities that the company offered its foreign workers included German language classes, a cinema and a prayer room.[123]

More widely, Bremen's local authority made a clear statement that it wished to promote the integration of guest-workers. One way in which it attempted to do this was through compiling and distributing infor-

[121] SB, 4,124/3–694, Various; and SB, 4,124/3–697, Ausländische Arbeitskräfte in Deutschland Bd. 4 1971–1974, Various.
[122] SB, 7,2121/1–712, *A Bremen Special* report entitled 'Bremer Großwerft: Wir wollen Ausländer auf Dauer und nicht nur für ein Gastspiel gewinnen. Praktische Integration vor und hinter dem Fabriktor' and dated 11 September 1973, p. 2 and letter from Zweites Deutsches Fernsehen to Bremer Vulkan dated 8 August 1973; and 'Großwerft ohne Gastarbeiterprobleme. Bremer Vulkan will die Ausländer nicht nur für ein Gastspiel gewinnen – Integration wird schon längst praktiziert', *Ostbremer Rundschau* (20 September 1973).
[123] See SB, 7,2121/1–712, Various.

mation booklets that welcomed foreign workers to Bremen and provided them with information about the area. This included a map of the city, emergency telephone numbers, public transport details, information on television channels and radio stations, information about local authority offices and a welcome letter from the Senator für Arbeit.[124] This pro-integration approach taken by Bremen's government was widely publicised, with the mayor praising the situation of guest-workers in the city, something he explained not only through the comparably smaller number of foreign workers, but primarily as a result of the *Arbeitsgemeinschaft zur Betreuung ausländischer Arbeitnehmer* (Joint Venture for the Provision of Foreign Workers), which had been established in 1964.[125] These pro-integration measures were certainly a far cry from the government policy that Ulrich Herbert termed '*zukunftsblind*' or 'blind to the future', and the long-established criticisms the German government received for not considering the long-term consequences the guest-worker system might have on German society and the accompanying social aspects to what was often perceived as a purely economic migration.[126]

This two-pronged approach towards foreign workers continued throughout the 1970s. Whilst the Bremen Senate repeatedly stressed that it was keen to promote the integration of guest-workers, it simultaneously perceived them as economic assets who were there to enhance Bremen's economy in what was a changing labour market.[127] It rejected the rotation principle as a means of controlling the number of foreign labourers in Germany, recognising that it took these workers time to settle in their place of work and become acquainted with the German language. Furthermore, although restrictions were in place regarding family reunification, it acknowledged that those workers who stayed for longer periods of time could not be expected to live without their families.[128] Yet

[124] See SB, 4,124/3–644, Sozialhilfe für Ausländer und Staatenlose – Allgemeines Bd. 2a 1973.
[125] See SB, 4,63/2N-284, Gastarbeiter 1971–1973, undated interview with Mayor Hans Koschnick. See also 'Gleiche Rechte einräumen. Bürgerschaft fordert Programm zur Integration der Gastarbeiter', *Bremer Nachrichten* (5 October 1973).
[126] See Herbert, *Geschichte der Ausländerbeschäftigung in Deutschland 1880 bis 1980*; and Castles, 'Migrants and minorities in post-Keynesian capitalism', p. 42.
[127] See Bremische Bürgerschaft Landtag 8. Wahlperiode, Drucksache 8/600, 'Antwort des Senats zur Anfrage der Fraktion der CDU vom 26. Juni 1973 (Drs. 8/566)', 12 September 1973, pp. 3, 5–6.
[128] Ibid., p. 4.

Bremen's local government remained adamant that Germany was not a country of immigration and thus integration did not equate to assimilation and was not to result in naturalisation. Instead, integration was interpreted as retaining one's own citizenship and national identity, hence promoting the possibility of an eventual return to and a reintegration into the workers' countries of origin.[129]

Overall, there was an ever-increasing recognition that foreign workers could no longer be perceived solely in economic terms and that social and cultural pressures had to also be a consideration, and there was a desire to improve their living conditions during their stay in Bremen.[130] It might be that, as was the case in Newcastle, Bremen was advantaged by its smaller and more manageable migrant community, with the state being home to less than 5,000 foreign workers in 1963 and the city to just over 17,000 in 1973. The comparably smaller size of Bremen's foreign population becomes especially apparent when weighed against those of the southern *Länder*. In September 1975, for example, Bremen was home to 42,000 foreigners whilst Baden-Württemberg and Bavaria had 882,100 and 672,100 respectively.[131] Bremen might also have benefited from the fact that its recruitment of guest-workers was chronologically later and more gradual than that of other states. Therefore, it was certainly in a position to have observed the influx of foreign workers elsewhere, and thus recognise the importance of social and cultural factors.

Many of these ideas and aims came together to shape the June 1979 *Konzeption zur Integration der ausländischen Arbeitnehmer und ihrer Familienangehörigen im Lande Bremen* (Concept of the Integration of Foreign Workers and their Family Members in the State of Bremen), Bremen's most ground-breaking series of measures and concepts regarding the city-state's immigrant population in the post-war period.[132] It further reinforced the notion that the short-term stay of guest-workers and their integration were not seen as opposing goals. In other words, they may have been temporary labour

[129] Ibid., p. 6.
[130] See Bremische Bürgerschaft Landtag 8. Wahlperiode, Drucksache 8/605, 'Antrag (Entschließung) der Fraktion der SPD. Ausländische Arbeitnehmer', 26 September 1973, p. 1.
[131] See Ray C. Rist, *Guestworkers in Germany: The Prospects for Pluralism* (New York, 1978), p. 68.
[132] Der Senat der Freien Hansestadt Bremen, *Konzeption zur Integration der ausländischen Arbeitnehmer und ihrer Familienangehörigen im Lande Bremen* (June 1979).

migrants, but they could still become integrated into Bremen's society. Whilst the 1979 *Konzeption* placed a clear emphasis on the second generation and thus concentrated primarily on the education sector and, to a lesser extent, housing, it nevertheless demonstrated a clear awareness that foreign workers were to play a role in Germany's economy and society.[133]

Bremen's approach towards its guest-worker community during the 1960s and 1970s supports the thesis put forward by Karen Schönwälder and Triadafilos Triadafilopoulos who suggest that the traditional view that the settlement of guest-workers only became a political issue after the 1973 halt in recruitment is in need of revision, and that the German government made a conscious decision not to enforce the rotation principle.[134] In Bremen, integration measures and provisions for foreign workers and their families certainly intensified post-1973, but there was still a clear awareness and consciousness regarding the influx of immigrants during the 1960s. Furthermore, the rotation principle was considered and dismissed. Therefore, in Bremen at least, 1973 was not the turning point it has previously been made out to be.

The economic structural change

As Patrick Ireland asserts, by the mid-1970s, Bremen's economy had exchanged a low unemployment rate and working-class solidarity for a continuous run of economic crises. These included the closing of factories, shipbuilder bankruptcies and political controversies. The depression and unemployment that followed caused Bremen to pursue alternatives. These sprung up in the shape of a university, steelworks, defence contractors and a Daimler-Benz aerospace plant. Yet these new industries did little to help the situation of ethnic minority workers as it was the more highly qualified workers who were hired whilst migrant workers failed to make the transition, causing their unemployment rate to rise to unprecedented levels.[135] This struggle to economically readjust following the decline of industry was also

---

[133] Ibid., pp. 6–7.
[134] Triadafilopoulos and Schönwälder, 'How the Federal Republic became an immigration country'.
[135] Ireland, *Becoming Europe*, p. 87.
[136] See Hans Dietrich von Loeffelholz, 'Social and labor market integration of ethnic minorities in Germany', in Martin Kahanec and Klaus F. Zimmermann (eds), *Ethnic Diversity in European Labor Markets: Challenges and Solutions* (Cheltenham, 2011), pp. 112–13.

witnessed in other areas across Germany, such as Hessen, North Rhine-Westphalia and Baden-Württemberg.[136] It was as a result of this economic structural change that in Bremen, as in other cities, ethnic minority workers experienced a shift in their distribution and experiences within the local labour market.

Firstly, the manufacturing sector no longer attracted the large number of foreign workers it once had. Between 1980 and 1986, this sector lost 35.8 per cent of its migrant workforce, and the percentage of foreign workers employed in this sector decreased from 50.8 per cent in 1980 to 43.5 per cent in 1991.[137] Yet migrants still remained over-represented in manufacturing and it continued to be the sector that employed the most foreign workers. Secondly, there was an increase in the role the service sector played in the employment of foreign workers. By 1986, this sector had become their second largest employer, employing 20.1 per cent of them.[138] By June 1991, this figure had risen to 24.5 per cent.[139]

Overall, whilst their distribution throughout Bremen's labour market had changed, foreign workers remained largely concentrated in a few sectors, with 69.2 per cent of them working in either the manufacturing industry or the service sector in 1986 compared with 50.1 per cent of all workers.[140] Furthermore, foreign workers also experienced a clustering within sectors, with 40 per cent of those employed in the manufacturing and service sectors, for example, working in steel construction, mechanical engineering and motor manufacturing, food and drink, the accommodation and catering trade, and public health. Turks continued to be by far the largest group of foreign workers in Bremen, and they went from constituting 45.6 per cent of the foreign workforce in March 1976 to 49.5 per cent at the end of June 1986.[141] These statistics show the extent to which these ethnic minority workers were victims of a transition from a manufacturing- to a service-based economy. The historiogra-

[137] See Freie Hansestadt Bremen *Statistische Monatsberichte*, 'Ausländische Arbeitnehmer in den Stadtstaaten', 39. Jahrgang, August 1987, p. 72; and 'Ausländische Arbeitnehmer in der bremischen Wirtschaft', 44. Jahrgang, August 1992, p. 90.
[138] See 'Ausländische Arbeitnehmer in den Stadtstaaten', 39. Jahrgang, August 1987, pp. 73–4.
[139] See 'Ausländische Arbeitnehmer in der bremischen Wirtschaft', 44. Jahrgang, August 1992, p. 90.
[140] See 'Ausländische Arbeitnehmer in den Stadtstaaten', 39. Jahrgang, August 1987, p. 74.
[141] Ibid., pp. 78–9.

phy has also exposed this shift from manufacturing into the service sector in Germany more widely.[142]

Thirdly, foreign workers frequently encountered problems and obstacles during this economic structural change. Companies that had once been the powerhouses of the local economy were collapsing, most notably AG Weser in 1983 and the Vulkan shipyard which eventually closed in 1997. Whilst German workers tended to be more highly qualified and managed to make the transition from shipbuilding to road vehicle and aircraft construction, foreign workers were often unable to do so.[142] This was reflected in their unemployment rates. Throughout the mid-1970s, the unemployment figures amongst the foreign workforce increased even when the overall unemployment rate had stabilised. Unemployment for the whole of Bremen's workforce was 2.7 per cent in 1974 and 4.4 per cent in 1975, but stabilised at an average of 5.5 per cent over the following three years. That of foreign workers was consistently higher and stood at 2.7 per cent in 1974, but had reached 9.6 per cent in 1978 (see Table 1.4).[144] This growth in unemployment amongst foreign workers after the 1973 oil crisis was witnessed throughout Germany as a whole.[145]

Table 1.4: Unemployment rate amongst the State of Bremen's entire workforce and foreign workforce, 1974-78

	Percentage unemployed	
	Entire workforce	Foreign workforce
1974	2.7	2.7
1975	4.4	6.6
1976	5.4	6.3
1977	5.6	7.4
1978	5.4	9.6

Source: *Konzeption zur Integration der ausländischen Arbeitnehmer und ihrer Familienangehörigen im Lande Bremen* (June 1979), p. 22.

[142] See Wolfgang Seifert, 'Social and economic integration of foreigners in Germany', in Peter Schuck and Rainer Münz (eds), *Paths to Inclusion: The Integration of Migrants in the United States and Germany* (Oxford, 1998), p. 93 and Caviedes, *Prying Open Fortress Europe*, pp. 84–5.

[143] See 'Ausländische Arbeitnehmer in der bremischen Wirtschaft', 44. Jahrgang, August 1992, p. 91; and Ireland, *Becoming Europe*, p. 87

[144] See Der Senat der Freien Hansestadt Bremen, *Konzeption zur Integration der ausländischen Arbeitnehmer und ihrer Familienangehörigen im Lande Bremen* (June 1979), p. 22.

[145] See Stefan Bender and Wolfgang Seifert, 'On the economic and social situations of immigrant groups in Germany', in Richard Alba, Peter Schmidt and

By the early 1980s, unemployment had soared and was cited as one of the key reasons for the decline in the number of Bremen's foreign workers. In 1981, unemployment was 15.5 per cent amongst the foreign workforce and, by September 1986, it was 24.2 per cent compared to an overall unemployment rate of 15.3 per cent.[146] Migrant workers continued to be the victims of Bremen's economic difficulties throughout the 1990s. By 1999, the unemployment rate amongst ethnic minorities had reached 29 per cent and they constituted more than a quarter of those receiving social assistance.[147] Furthermore, unemployment rates amongst Bremen's foreign workers were undoubtedly much higher than these figures indicate as they only include those workers with a valid work permit who officially registered themselves as unemployed. Whilst the unemployment rate for foreigners in Germany in general has, since the mid-1970s, been higher than that experienced by German workers, that amongst Bremen's workers with a migration background has often been even greater. Whereas unemployment for Bremen's ethnic minorities stood at 29 per cent in 1999, that for Germany as a whole was 18.4 per cent.[148]

Self-employment

As in Newcastle, self-employment has also played an important role in the economic development and behaviour of Bremen's Muslim migrant community. This emergence of entrepreneurship cannot simply be perceived as a further consequence of the city's economic structural change. Indeed, is some cases, Muslim migrants in Bremen did pursue self-employment as a result of the declining manufacturing sector and difficulties encountered finding work. This has been the dominant theory in the historiography, with the *döner kebab* stands that sprung up during the 1970s often being perceived as a way to avoid both unemployment and a return to Turkey.[149] Yet, as in Newcastle, there is no doubt that many of Bremen's Muslim migrants possessed deep-

---

Martina Wasmer (eds), *Germans or Foreigners? Attitudes towards Ethnic Minorities in Post-Reunification Germany* (Basingstoke, 2003), pp. 59–60.

[146] See Freie Hansestadt Bremen *Statistische Monatsberichte*, 'Beschäftigung ausländischer Arbeitnehmer im Lande Bremen', 34. Jahrgang, September 1982, p. 279; and 'Ausländische Arbeitnehmer in den Stadtstaaten', 39. Jahrgang, August 1987, p. 69.

[147] See Ireland, *Becoming Europe*, p. 96.

[148] See Bender and Seifert, 'On the economic and social situations of immigrant groups in Germany', p. 60.

[149] See Mushaben, 'Thinking globally, integrating locally', p. 215.

rooted aims of entrepreneurialism and economic independence, and had always intended to establish businesses once this was financially possible. Ethnic minority entrepreneurialism has certainly been an increasingly widespread practice across Germany, and there is an abundant and ever-growing body of literature that reflects this.[150] Whilst as in Britain, ethnic minority entrepreneurship in Germany has traditionally been seen in a negative light, as either the result of a lack of integration or the cause of a parallel ethnic economy, this work hopes to reinforce the small, yet growing, body of literature that recognises the benefits of and developments in ethnic minority businesses that has been largely pioneered by the the *Zentrum für Türkeistudien und Integrationsforschung* (Centre for Turkish Studies and Integration Research) in Essen.

The type of entrepreneurship practised by Germany's largest group of ethnic minority businessmen, the Turkish, has largely reflected their stage of settlement. During the 1960s, for example, Turkish businesses tended to cater for the needs of labour migrants, thus taking the form of restaurants, cafes and food shops. These businesses underwent a diversification during the 1970s as a result of family reunification, and Turkish food and clothing stores began to emerge. Between the mid-1970s and mid-1980s, Germany witnessed a vast expansion in Turkish entrepreneurship. This has been explained as the direct consequence of unemployment, changes in law and policy which granted Turkish migrants greater access to self-employment, and Turks deciding to stay in Germany and invest in business the capital originally intended for their lives back in the homeland. What has since emerged is a multifaceted and complex paradigm of Turkish entrepreneurship, with businesses greatly ranging in size, specialisation and levels of interaction with the German population.[151] Self-employment has continued to be an attractive economic option for many, with the number of self-employed Turks in Germany increasing by 170 per cent from 22,000 to

[150] See Nikolinka Fertala, 'A study of immigrant entrepreneurship in Upper Bavaria', *International Journal of Entrepreneurship and Small Business*, 4:2 (2006), pp. 179–206; and Amelie Constant and Klaus F. Zimmermann, 'The making of entrepreneurs in Germany: Are native men and immigrants alike?', *Small Business Economics*, 26:3 (2006), pp. 279–300.

[151] See Zentrum für Türkeistudien, *Die Regionalen Transferstellen für ausländische Existenzgründer und Unternehmer in Nordrhein Westphalen. Ökonomische Daten der türkischen und ausländischen Selbständigen in NRW und Deutschland* (Essen, 1999); and Pécoud, '"Weltoffenheit schafft Jobs", pp. 496–7.

59,500 between 1985 and 2000.[152] As in Britain, migrant entrepreneurship is an essential aspect of any study on ethnic minority employment and economic integration in Germany.

Bremen certainly makes for a pertinent case study on migrant entrepreneurship for a number of reasons. Firstly, by 2000, Bremen was home to an estimated 1,000 self-employed Turks who constituted a higher percentage of the Turkish population than was the German average.[153] The city-state had witnessed a recent and continuous growth in the number of self-employed migrants, and numbers had increased from 904 in 1987 to 7,000 according to the micro-census of 2007.[154] This figure was far higher than what had been predicted, with government documents estimating the number of self-employed migrants at around 2,000 by 2010.[155] There has indeed been a growing realisation on behalf of Bremen's government that entrepreneurship is becoming increasingly popular amongst the Turkish community in particular. Furthermore, it has been recognised that these businessmen are no longer concentrated in the retail and catering trades, but are diversifying into other sectors, and offering innovative and modern services, as is also the case in other German cities.[156] A 2004 government document went so far as to draw comparisons with Indian and Chinese entrepreneurs in the United States.[157] Although the precise

[152] See Zentrum für Türkeistudien, *Türkische Unternehmer in Bremen und Bremerhaven. Eine Analyse ihrer Struktur, ihrer wirtschaftlichen Situation sowie ihrer Integration in das deutsche Wirtschaftsgefüge – Ergebnisse einer standardisierten telefonischen Befragung im Auftrag der Ausländerbeauftragten des Bundeslandes Bremen* (Essen, 2001), p. 10.

[153] Ibid., pp. 9–10.

[154] See Bremische Bürgerschaft Landtag 13. Wahlperiode, Drucksache 13/350, 'Kleine Anfrage der Fraktion der CDU vom 10. September 1992. Bedeutung von Ausländern für die Arbeitswelt', p. 3; and Bremische Bürgerschaft Stadtbürgerschaft 17. Wahlperiode, Drucksache 17/547S, 'Mitteilung des Senats vom 2. Februar 2010. Lebenssituation der älteren Migrantinnen und Migranten in Bremen', 2 February 2010, p. 2.

[155] See Bremische Bürgerschaft Landtag 16. Wahlperiode, Drucksache 16/262, 'Mitteilung des Senats vom 25. Mai 2004. Das wirtschaftliche Potenzial von Unternehmern und Existenzgründern mit Migrationshintergrund', p. 1.

[156] See Felicitas Hillmann, 'A look at the 'hidden side": Turkish women in Berlin's ethnic labour market', *International Journal of Urban and Regional Research*, 23:2 (1999), pp. 272–3; and Zentrum für Türkeistudien, *Die Regionalen Transferstellen für ausländische Existenzgründer und Unternehmer in Nordrhein Westphalen*.

[157] See Bremische Bürgerschaft Landtag 16. Wahlperiode, Drucksache 16/219, 'Große Anfrage der Fraktion Bündnis 90/Die Grünen. Das wirtschaftliche

number of self-employed migrants has always proved difficult to ascertain due to the fact that the ethnic and religious backgrounds of business owners and founders have never been officially recorded, a December 2006 report estimated that there were around 2,000 Muslim businesses in the state of Bremen.[158]

Secondly, government documents have highlighted a clear link between opting for self-employment and having a strong bond with Germany. Certainly, in order to pursue self-employment, a connection with the migrants' adopted country is necessary due to the risks and investments that entrepreneurship entails. This sense of attachment has unquestionably been witnessed in Bremen where the proportion of Turks who took up German citizenship was greater amongst the self-employed residents than it was amongst the wider Turkish population.[159] This same relationship between Turkish entrepreneurship and German citizenship has also been exposed in other studies.[160] This sense of commitment to Germany amongst self-employed migrants was potentially further accentuated amongst the Turkish by the fact that a return to the homeland had once been a possibility, and indeed practically a certainty, for many. In other words, founding a business was often the result of both a desire to be economically independent and a feeling of loyalty to Germany.

Yet despite self-employment playing an ever-important role in the economic activity of Bremen's ethnic minorities, it is not an area for which government-issued documents are in abundance. In fact, the city's local government does not keep separate statistics on ethnic minority businesses. Whilst this practice has been criticised elsewhere, such as in Berlin, and perceived as the result of a lack of political interest in ethnic entrepreneurship,[161] in Bremen it is not the conse-

---

Potenzial von Unternehmern und Existenzgründern mit Migrationshintergrund', 21 April 2004, p. 1.

[158] Der Senator für Arbeit, Frauen, Gesundheit, Jugend und Soziales, Referat Zuwandererangelegenheiten und Integrationspolitik, Migrations- und Integrationsbeauftragter, *Umsetzung der Konzeption zur Integration von Zuwanderinnen und Zuwanderern 2003–2007. Abschlussbericht (Stand 12/2006)*, p. 40.

[159] See Zentrum für Türkeistudien, *Türkische Unternehmer in Bremen und Bremerhaven*, pp. 20–1.

[160] See Hillmann, 'A look at the "hidden side"', p. 274.

[161] See Janet Merkel, 'Ethnic diversity and the 'creative city': The case of Berlin's creative industries', in Frank Eckardt and John Eade (eds), *Ethnically Diverse City* (Berlin, 2011), p. 570.

quence of disregard on the part of the government, but rather of a conscious effort to ensure that all entrepreneurs are treated the same regardless of ethnicity and nationality.[162] The Bremen government has stressed that there is no reason to concentrate on the economic contribution of one specific group to the local economy and that the role migrant communities play is recognised as long as they are embedded in the state's population and the relevant associations. Instead, Bremen's government approaches all entrepreneurs as one homogenous group and all are offered the same range of services. Perhaps as a consequence of this, local authority documents addressing ethnic minority entrepreneurship did not really begin to emerge until the early 2000s and thus took a somewhat retrospective approach. It should also be noted, however, that migrant businesses did emerge later in Bremen than in Newcastle, and this will have undoubtedly contributed to the comparatively narrower and chronologically delayed focus on this economic phenomenon.

The Bremen government's choice not to keep separate statistics on ethnic minority entrepreneurship has not resulted in a lack of information about the position and needs of the city's migrant businesses. On the contrary, it has regularly been kept updated by organisations such as the *Ausländerbeauftragte des Landes Bremen* (Commissioner for Foreigners of the State of Bremen) and the *BQN Beratungsstelle zur Qualifizierung ausländischer Nachwuchskräfte* (The Workers' Welfare Association's Advice Centre for the Qualification of Foreign Employees). Furthermore, there have been regular publications issued by local associations addressing ethnic minority entrepreneurs. Despite the fact that most of the relevant organisations and advisory centres do not have workers from an ethnic minority background and there is no special advisory literature issued specifically for ethnic minority businessmen, Bremen's government believes that the available support is effective and becoming increasingly recognised by the city's migrant communities.[163]

---

[162] See Bremische Bürgerschaft Landtag 17. Wahlperiode, Drucksache 17/503, 'Mitteilung des Senats vom 12. August 2008. Die Potenziale von Unternehmer/-innen mit Migrationshintergrund stärker nutzen', 12 August 2008, p. 4. See also Ireland, *Becoming Europe*, p. 88.

[163] See Bremische Bürgerschaft Landtag 16. Wahlperiode, Drucksache 16/264, 'Kleine Anfrage der Fraktion Bündnis 90/Die Grünen vom 21. April 2004. Wirtschaftsförderung für Unternehmer und Existenzgründer mit Migrationshintergrund', pp. 3–7.

The key document on ethnic minority entrepreneurship in Bremen and one that played a role in shaping subsequent government discussion and policies was issued by the *Zentrum für Türkeistudien* (Centre for Turkish Studies and Integration Research) in Essen in 2001. Based on ninety interviews with Turkish businessmen in the city of Bremen and twelve in Bremerhaven, this report went a long way in establishing a profile of the state's Turkish businesses. Amongst other factors, it investigated the background to business foundation, characteristics of the businessmen, the types of businesses run and their economic situation, and their levels of integration and incorporation within the German economy. It discovered, for example, that the majority of the Turkish self-employed were second-generation migrants and that, whilst just short of 90 per cent had been born in Turkey, two-thirds had lived in Germany for more than 20 years.[164]

Overall, the report perceived Turkish entrepreneurship in Bremen in a positive light, thus disputing the more discriminatory and restrictive explanations, characteristics and consequences of ethnic minority entrepreneurship in Germany that often dominate the historiography.[165] The reasons given by the Turkish respondents for becoming self-employed tended to revolve around personal ambition rather than negative experiences in the German labour market. A pursuit of economic independence was the most common reason given with 51 per cent of respondents citing this, and was followed by the desire for a higher income and upward social mobility. Unemployment was only cited by 15 per cent of respondents and a lack of recognition in previous employment by only 5 per cent. Other reasons provided for having opted for self-employment included wanting to better support family, ensuring the future security of children and having a promising business idea (see Table 1.5). This optimistic interpretation of migrant entrepreneurship as a conscious employment choice practised by Turks as a way in which to promote their social mobility is an argument that has largely been developed by the Centre for Turkish Studies. Since the 1990s, it has gradually been gaining credibility and support against the traditional view that sees migrant

---

[164] Zentrum für Türkeistudien, *Türkische Unternehmer in Bremen und Bremerhaven*, pp. 17–19.
[165] See Maria Kontos, 'Immigrant entrepreneurs in Germany', in Léo-Paul Dana (ed.), *Handbook of Research on Ethnic Minority Entrepreneurship: A Co-evolutionary View on Resource Management* (Cheltenham, 2007), p. 450.

Table 1.5 Reasons given for becoming self-employed by 102 Turkish businessmen in Bremen and Bremerhaven in 2001

Reason cited	Percentage
Pursuit of economic independence	51
Higher income	29
Upward social mobility	23
Offer better support to family	16
Unemployment	15
Future security of children	6
Promising business idea	6
Lack of recognition in previous employment	5

Source: Zentrum für Türkeistudien, *Türkische Unternehmer in Bremen und Bremerhaven*, p. 26.

self-employment merely as the direct result of discrimination and unemployment.[166]

This search for independence was also witnessed in the manner in which the businesses were established. As has historically been the case amongst South Asians in Newcastle, Turks in Bremen rarely sought assistance or advice. Only around one-fifth did and, of these, 75 per cent approached family and friends. In fact, only 7 per cent of the business owners took advantage of the professional advice available. Similarly, only 15.7 per cent made use of public funding, with 46 per cent having no need for it and 40 per cent not being aware of the assistance available.[167] Yet despite this overwhelming disregard of accessible advice and funds, 63.7 per cent of the respondents had experienced some type of difficulty in setting up their businesses. These included financial problems, difficulties establishing a customer base, trouble with the bureaucracy involved and with the German language, and issues that arose from a lack of business acumen.[168] Furthermore, once established, over 46 per cent of these

[166] See Zentrum für Türkeistudien (ed.), *Nur der Wandel hat Bestand. Ausländische Selbständige in Deutschland* (Essen, 1995); and Faruk Şen and Andreas Goldberg (eds), *Türken als Unternehmer. Eine Gesamtdarstellung und Ergebnisse neuerer Untersuchungen* (Opladen, 1996).
[167] Zentrum für Türkeistudien, *Türkische Unternehmer in Bremen und Bremerhaven*, pp. 28–31. See also Bremische Bürgerschaft Landtag 16. Wahlperiode, Drucksache 16/264, 'Kleine Anfrage der Fraktion Bündnis 90/Die Grünen vom 21. April 2004. Wirtschaftsförderung für Unternehmer und Existenzgründer mit Migrationshintergrund', p. 5.
[168] Zentrum für Türkeistudien, *Türkische Unternehmer in Bremen und Bremerhaven*, pp. 32–3.

Turkish businesses had no contact with German economic institutions and 62 per cent did not become members of an employers' association.[169] This tendency for Turkish businessmen to rely primarily on their families and friends for the necessary finance and support was not particular to Bremen, and the literature on Germany has stressed this as a widespread and well-established practice.[170]

Yet whilst Bremen's Turkish businesses have certainly demonstrated a sense of independence, they have also shown signs of economic integration. Firstly, they are not concentrated in the restaurant and catering trade, a sector that is often associated with ethnic minority businesses in Germany and indeed further afield. Instead, Bremen's Turkish entrepreneurs have succeeded in permeating a variety of economic sectors and, whilst many did work in the restaurant and catering trade (over 30 per cent), others owned businesses in the service sector, the retail trade, skilled crafts and trades, wholesale trading, the building trade and the manufacturing trade (see Table 1.6). This gradual diversification that has intensified with the second generation especially is undoubtedly the result of increased integration within the local economy, and adheres to what the historiography has identified as a key trend in Turkish entrepreneurship in Germany starting mainly in the 1990s.[171]

Table 1.6: The employment sectors occupied by 102 Turkish businessmen in Bremen and Bremerhaven in 2001

Employment sector	*Percentage*
Restaurant and catering trade	30.4
Service sector	21.6
Retail trade	19.6
Skilled crafts and trades	10.8
Wholesale trading	8.8
Building trade	6.9
Manufacturing trade	2

Source: Zentrum für Türkeistudien, *Türkische Unternehmer in Bremen und Bremerhaven*, p. 36.

[169] Ibid., p. 33–5.
[170] See Ali Gitmez and Czarina Wilpert, 'A micro-society or an ethnic community? Social organization and ethnicity amongst Turkish migrants in Berlin', in John Rex, Danièle Joly and Czarina Wilpert (eds), *Immigrant Associations in Europe* (Aldershot, 1987), pp. 86–125; and Kontos, 'Immigrant entrepreneurs in Germany', p. 449.
[171] Zentrum für Türkeistudien, *Türkische Unternehmer in Bremen und Bremerhaven*, pp. 36–7, 59; and Andreas Goldberg, 'Islam in Germany', in

Secondly, many of these businesses depended on interaction with their local German society. When asked about their suppliers and contractors, only 28 per cent of respondents stated that they were mostly Turkish, whilst 33 per cent said that they were mostly German and 31 per cent that they were a mixture of the two. With regard to customers, the reliance on the local German population is even more evident, with 64 per cent of businesses catering for mainly a German clientele, and only 12 per cent and 11 per cent for a mostly Turkish and mixed clientele respectively.[172] The manner in which migrant businessmen in Germany are increasingly abandoning their own ethnic communities and cultures in order to attain economic success is a pattern that has recently become more dominant in the literature.[173] This interaction with and dependence on German suppliers and customers have traditionally been recognised and looked upon favourably by Bremen's government.[174]

Thirdly, Turkish businesses in Bremen were in a fairly stable economic situation in 2001. Whilst not all were prospering economically, one-third reported a sales increase in the previous two years, 33 per cent were expecting one in the near future and almost half of the businessmen were planning to make further investments.[175] Fourthly, as previously mentioned, the pursuit of self-employment often demonstrated a clear commitment to both Bremen and Germany more broadly. In this sense, entrepreneurship must to a certain extent be recognised as an indication not just of an economic, but rather a wider integration. Indeed, Bremen's government has also increasingly perceived ethnic minority businesses in a positive light. It has argued

---

Shireen T. Hunter (ed.), *Islam, Europe's Second Religion: The New Social, Cultural, and Political Landscape* (Westport CT, 2002), p. 37.

[172] Zentrum für Türkeistudien, *Türkische Unternehmer in Bremen und Bremerhaven*, pp. 39, 41.

[173] See Pécoud, 'German-Turkish entrepreneurship and the economic dimension of multiculturalism', p. 122; Felicitas Hillmann, 'Gendered landscapes of ethnic economies: Turkish entrepreneurs in Berlin', in David H. Kaplan and Wei Li (eds), *Landscapes of the Ethnic Economy* (Lanham MD, 2006), pp. 104–5.

[174] See Bremische Bürgerschaft Landtag 15. Wahlperiode, Drucksache 15/368, 'Mitteilung des Senats vom 6. Juni 2000. Ausländische Mitbürgerinnen und Mitbürger in der Arbeitswelt in Bremen und Bremerhaven', 6 June 2000, pp. 2–3.

[175] Zentrum für Türkeistudien, *Türkische Unternehmer in Bremen und Bremerhaven*, pp. 62–3.

that, whilst their economic potential was not always fully recognised in the past, these businesses constitute an important part of the local economy, and can help it grow and progress. They have been regarded as capable of contributing to Bremen's economy, helping with the development of foreign trade and new markets, having the potential to build upon Bremen's role as an international port and foreign trade centre, and improving the economic relationship between Bremen and the businessmen's countries of origin through their knowledge of the language and economies, and their personal contacts. This is seen to be especially important following the enlargement of the European Union as Bremen's ethnic minority businesses are deemed central to extending trade and forging economic relationships with Eastern European countries.[176]

As a result of their recognised importance, a large emphasis has been placed on looking after Bremen's existing ethnic minority businesses. The local government has also acknowledged that support measures might be necessary because owners have often placed vast amounts of commitment and capital into their businesses, and therefore have an increased chance of bankruptcy. Suggested policies have included advisory services, which possess knowledge specific to entrepreneurship and the necessary intercultural skills, and maintain contact with the ethnic minority business owners and the relevant trade associations. There have also been calls to improve the manner in which the numbers and characteristics of ethnic minority businessmen are recorded, and to establish a coordinating body to work with existing organisations and representatives of migrant businesses and help increase economic development.[177] Indeed politicians and policymak-

[176] See Bremische Bürgerschaft Landtag 16. Wahlperiode, Drucksache 16/262, 'Mitteilung des Senats vom 25. Mai 2004. Das wirtschaftliche Potenzial von Unternehmern und Existenzgründern mit Migrationshintergrund', p. 3; Bremische Bürgerschaft Landtag 16. Wahlperiode, Drucksache 16/264, 'Kleine Anfrage der Fraktion Bündnis 90/Die Grünen vom 21. April 2004. Wirtschaftsförderung für Unternehmer und Existenzgründer mit Migrationshintergrund', p. 3; and Bremische Bürgerschaft Landtag 17. Wahlperiode, Drucksache 17/503, 'Mitteilung des Senats vom 12. August 2008. Die Potenziale von Unternehmer/-innen mit Migrationshintergrund stärker nutzen', 12 August 2008, p. 1.

[177] See Bremische Bürgerschaft Landtag 16. Wahlperiode, Drucksache 16/810, 'Antrag der Fraktion Bündnis 90/Die Grünen. Stärkung von Unternehmen und Unternehmensgründungen mit migrantischem Hintergrund', 29 November 2005, pp. 1–2; and Bremische Bürgerschaft Landtag 17. Wahlperiode, Drucksache 17/503, 'Mitteilung des Senats vom 12. August 2008. Die

ers across Germany are progressively recognising and focusing on ethnic minority entrepreneurship, not only because it is often perceived as a conduit of integration, but also as a result of its international dimension and the contribution it makes to a variety of sectors within the German economy.[178]

Many of the measures that have been implemented in the 2000s have been the result of the conclusions reached by the 2001 *Zentrum für Türkeistudien und Integrationsforschung* report. Bremen's government decided that certain characteristics of Turkish businessmen, such as the low percentage that took advantage of professional advice and public funding, must also be present amongst entrepreneurs of other migration backgrounds and thus decided to intensify both its offer of advice and the manner in which this is marketed. Advice centres have since discovered other problems and obstacles facing ethnic minority businessmen, such as difficulties with bookkeeping, tax and insurance laws, and acquiring the necessary capital resources.[179] Whilst Bremen's government has acknowledged the low proportion of these businessmen who seek advice and guidance, it has been encouraged by a more recent increase in the number of them making use of the services available. Around 10 per cent of entrepreneurs making credit claims with the *Bremer Aufbau-Bank GmbH*, for example, were of an ethnic minority background, as were around 30 per cent of those who approached *B.E.G.IN – Gründungsleitstelle* in 2003, an organisation that helps and advises during the process of setting up businesses. Bremen's government was reassured by these figures, and perceived them as evidence that ethnic minority businessmen were both increasingly aware of the support available and were willing to take advantage of it.[180]

As well as promoting the survival and development of ethnic minority businesses, Bremen's government also perceived them as a part of wider integration measures and thus as an indicator of integration. Minority entrepreneurship was an important aspect of both the

---

Potenziale von Unternehmer/-innen mit Migrationshintergrund stärker nutzen', 12 August 2008, pp. 1–2.

[178] See Pécoud, "Weltoffenheit schafft Jobs', pp. 498–9.

[179] See Bremische Bürgerschaft Landtag 16. Wahlperiode, Drucksache 16/264, 'Kleine Anfrage der Fraktion Bündnis 90/Die Grünen vom 21. April 2004. Wirtschaftsförderung für Unternehmer und Existenzgründer mit Migrationshintergrund', p. 5.

[180] See Bremische Bürgerschaft Landtag 16. Wahlperiode, Drucksache 16/262, 'Mitteilung des Senats vom 25. Mai 2004', p. 2.

2000 *Konzeption zur Integration von Zuwanderern und Zuwanderinnen im Lande Bremen. Grundsätze, Leitlinien und Handlungsempfehlungen für die bremische Integrationspolitik* (Integration Concept for Immigrants in the State of Bremen: Policies, Guidelines and Recommendations Regarding Bremen's Integration Policy) and the *Umsetzung der Konzeption zur Integration von Zuwanderinnen und Zuwanderern 2003–7* (Implementation of the Immigrant Integration Concept, 2003–7).[181]

Throughout the 2000s, ideas on how to realise the potential of Bremen's migrant entrepreneurship have included promoting interaction with ethnic minority businesses and organisations, providing information in mother tongues that addresses questions and concerns regarding available economic support and business foundation, and the enabling of an information exchange between ethnic minority and German businesses.[182] There is no doubt that many of these initiatives have been successful, with the *Umsetzung der Konzeption zur Integration von Zuwanderinnen und Zuwanderern 2003–7* proudly claiming that some of these businessmen had become so integrated that their ethnic minority background only became apparent upon inquiry.[183] Bremen's government has also perceived ethnic minority businesses as conduits of further integration and wants to help increase their participation in the local economy. One way in which this has been done has been through the *Beratungsstelle zur Qualifizierung ausländischer Nachwuchskräfte* (Advice Centre for the Qualification of Ethnic Minority Junior Employees), which has helped ethnic minority businesses develop into companies that take on trainees.[184] This derives from a wider initiative put forward by the *Zentrum für Türkeistudien*

---

[181] Der Senat der Freien Hansestadt Bremen, *Konzeption zur Integration von Zuwanderern und Zuwanderinnen im Lande Bremen. Grundsätze, Leitlinien und Handlungsempfehlungen für die bremische Integrationspolitik* (July 2000); and Der Senator für Arbeit, Frauen, Gesundheit, Jugend und Soziales, Referat Zuwandererangelegenheiten und Integrationspolitik, Migrations- und Integrationsbeauftragter, *Umsetzung der Konzeption zur Integration von Zuwanderinnen und Zuwanderern 2003–2007. Abschlussbericht (Stand 12/2006)*.

[182] See Bremische Bürgerschaft Landtag 16. Wahlperiode, Drucksache 16/262, 'Mitteilung des Senats vom 25. Mai 2004', p. 2.

[183] *Umsetzung der Konzeption zur Integration von Zuwanderinnen und Zuwanderern 2003–2007*, p. 40.

[184] See Bremische Bürgerschaft Landtag 15. Wahlperiode, Drucksache 15/368, 'Mitteilung des Senats vom 6. Juni 2000. Ausländische Mitbürgerinnen und Mitbürger in der Arbeitswelt in Bremen und Bremerhaven', 6 June 2000, p. 3.

as a way to promote the integration of young Turks into the labour market.[185]

Conclusion

One of this chapter's key conclusions revolves around the role played by immigration history in determining Muslim migrants' employment choices and patterns. There is no doubt that Britain and Germany's post-war immigration frameworks have influenced Newcastle and Bremen's immigrants' long-term employment behaviour. In Newcastle, as in towns and cities across the country, Britain's relatively liberal immigration policy allowed for the immediate and widespread appearance and development of ethnic minority businesses. In contrast, in Bremen and throughout Germany, the initial uncertainty and disadvantage that migrants faced as a result of the rigid guest-worker system eventually made way for the comparatively delayed emergence of economic autonomy. In other words, despite the vastly different manners in which these Muslim migrants arrived in Newcastle and Bremen, they appear to have, in many cases, adhered to a very similar long-term labour market pattern. Both cities have witnessed a strong entrepreneurial spirit amongst their Muslim migrants, a trait that was often either present from the outset or developed very quickly soon after.

Furthermore, there is no doubt that the entrepreneurship practised amongst Muslim migrants in Newcastle and Bremen has exposed the positive characteristics of ethnic minority self-employment. The businesses established and run have introduced a diverse range of new ideas and products, provided job opportunities for members of their communities, acted as a bridge between the migrant and white host populations, and offered the entrepreneurs themselves financial and social security. There is also evidence to suggest that there are strong links between entrepreneurialism and home ownership particularly amongst Newcastle's Muslim communities, and this will be discussed in the next chapter. In essence, both cities' Muslim immigrants are succeeding as a result of their own self-determination, but also due to a certain understanding of and contact with their local host society.

---

[185] See Zentrum für Türkeistudien, *Türkische Unternehmer und das duale Ausbildungssystem: Empirische Untersuchung von Möglichkeiten der beruflichen Ausbildung in türkischen Betriebsstätten in Deutschland* (Münster, 1999).

Although they have historically portrayed a preference for self-sufficiency and economic independence, contrary to popular belief, this has not necessarily been the result of a failure to integrate. In fact, Muslim migrants frequently made use of other sectors and types of work to make self-employment possible. This process has demonstrated that a certain level of economic integration is attainable. Both cities have witnessed Muslim migrants working alongside their British and German counterparts as either factory workers or public transport drivers, and there are still many instances of this taking place. Yet what has been revealed is that perhaps not economic assimilation, but rather economic independence, has often been the long-term goal of both Newcastle and Bremen's Muslim migrant communities.

This economic ambition only becomes more apparent when considering the racial discrimination and harassment endured, and difficulties encountered in founding and running businesses, and the fact that some businessmen were willing to abandon their own cultures, products and communities in favour of a more market-orientated approach. Furthermore, though the capital foundation of immigrant businesses has originated largely from within the ethnic communities, many have served the indigenous British and German populations. This notion that ethnic minority entrepreneurship should not automatically be equated with discrimination, disadvantage and a lack of integration constitutes one of this chapter's key hypotheses. The entrepreneurial success of Newcastle and Bremen's Muslim migrant businessmen has also potentially been helped by the relatively small size of both cities' migrant communities. Whilst the literature has often offered tales of failed businesses and bankruptcy, this was not an issue that featured heavily in the cities' government documents. One possible reason for this is the comparatively small and close-knit ethnic minority communities of both cities. Whilst migrant entrepreneurs in cities with larger ethnic minority populations have often suffered from business failure as a result of being unsuccessful in attracting the necessary funds, poor working conditions and enduring a concentration in a small range of overcrowded economic sectors, such as the restaurant and catering trade, this same phenomenon has not played such a prevalent role in Newcastle and Bremen. Here migrants have largely succeeded in attaining the necessary financial capital, and their products and businesses have not reached a saturation point. In Bremen especially, a city with a larger proportion of migrants than Newcastle, this has been further facilitated through the migrant businessmen's ability to diversify into other sectors.

A further key conclusion is regarding the impact that Islam has had on shaping migrant employment traits. For some time now, there has been a call for religion to be considered in the study of ethnic minority labour market patterns, which has undoubtedly been intensified by Islam's firm position at the forefront of the political and academic debate regarding immigrant communities in Europe and indeed in the West more widely. Yet despite the weight often awarded to Islam, there is no evidence here to suggest that it has played a significant part in determining the economic behaviour of Newcastle and Bremen's Muslim migrant communities. In neither city was there evidence of Muslim businessmen being disadvantaged or economically restricted as a result of their religion. On the contrary, they have shown the sufficient skills and ability necessary to shape their businesses in a manner that they believe will maximise profits. Furthermore, it seems as though Muslim migrants in both cities have adhered to traits and patterns present amongst ethnic minority groups in the West more broadly, be it Koreans in the United States, Indians in Portugal or Greeks and Italians in Australia, thus eroding the notion of both immigration frameworks and Islam as regulators or barriers to economic behaviour and integration.[186]

This chapter does not claim to represent the economic lives of all Muslim migrants in Newcastle and Bremen. Although self-employment rates are higher amongst the ethnic minority communities than the local white populations in both cities, this is an economic practice that is nevertheless pursued by only a portion of them. Furthermore, entrepreneurship was not the sole focus of Newcastle and Bremen's approach to ethnic minority employment, although it has been an area that has received much attention, especially in Newcastle. Both cities' local governments have also expressed concern over the small number of members of ethnic minorities employed in the cities' public sectors. From the mid-1980s right up to the mid-2000s, for example, Newcastle City Council focused on its position as an employer of ethnic minorities. This was largely fuelled by the 1976 Race Relations Act and the

---

[186] See Ivan Light and Edna Bonacich, *Immigrant Entrepreneurs: Koreans in Los Angeles, 1965–1982* (Berkeley CA, 1988); Jorge Malheiros, 'Indians in Lisbon: Ethnic entrepreneurship and the migration process', in Russell King and Richard Black (eds), *Southern Europe and the New Immigrations* (Brighton, 1997), pp. 93–112; and Jock Collins, 'Australia: Cosmopolitan capitalists down under', in Robert Kloosterman and Jan Rath (eds), *Immigrant Entrepreneurs: Venturing Abroad in the Age of Globalization* (Oxford, 2003), pp. 61–78.

1982 guidelines for local authorities issued by the Commission for Racial Equality on promoting the hiring of ethnic minorities,[187] and resulted in debate and measures regarding equal opportunities policies, the advertising of council posts to the city's ethnic minority communities and the improving of their recruitment, and investigations into perceptions of the council as an employer amongst the migrant population.[188]

There has also been a political concern regarding the low number of migrants employed in the public sector in Bremen. The local government has recently stressed the link between the number of ethnic minority workers employed in the civil service, their levels of integration and the overall intercultural openness of the city's administrative authority.[189] The late 1990s and early 2000s witnessed the implementation of a project centred around internships that attempted to and succeeded in increasing the number of migrants in the public sector.[190] In this sense, entrepreneurship has not been the only area Newcastle and Bremen's governments have awarded attention to, nor has it constituted the sole attempt at promoting the economic integration of their ethnic minority populations.

[187] See Iris Kalka, 'Striking a bargain: Political radicalism in a middle-class London borough', in Pnina Werbner and Muhammad Anwar (eds), *Black and Ethnic Leaderships: The Cultural Dimensions of Political Action* (London, 1991), pp. 142–3; and Romain Garbaye, *Getting into Local Power: The Politics of Ethnic Minorities in British and French Cities* (Oxford, 2005), p. 106.

[188] See TWAS, MD.NC/162/1, 'The council and racial equality: Policy statement and action plan', November 1984, pp. 3, 5; TWAS, MD.NC/162/3, City of Newcastle upon Tyne Local Government and Racial Equality Sub-Committee, 'Employment and black people', March 1988; TWAS, MD.NC/365, Black and Ethnic Minority Consultative Forum 1 September 1994–17 May 1995, 'City of Newcastle upon Tyne equal opportunities mission statement', November 1994; and TWAS, MD.NC/734, Equality Partnership Select Committee: Corporate Equality Plan Working Group 4 September 2003–27 January 2004, 'Corporate equalities plan focus groups', pp. 2–3.

[189] See Bremische Bürgerschaft Landtag 17. Wahlperiode, Drucksache 17/621, 'Kleine Anfrage der Fraktion DIE LINKE. vom 7. Oktober 2008. Beschäftigungsquote von Migrantinnen und Migranten im öffentlichen Dienst'.

[190] See Bram Frouws and Bert-Jan Buiskool, *Migrants to Work: Innovative Approaches towards Successful Integration of Third Country Migrants into the Labour Market: Final Report* (European Commission. Directorate-General for Employment, Social Affairs and Equal Opportunities) (Brussels, 2010), pp. 13, 97.

Yet next to self-employment, other labour market concentrations have largely remained secondary at best. The structure of this chapter and the strong focus on entrepreneurialism has entirely been dictated by sources, and there is no doubt that self-employment has captured the hearts and minds of both political and academic circles. In both cities, and especially in Newcastle, the local governments have awarded an overwhelming level of attention to self-employment. It is difficult to assert why this has been the case. It might be because their governments, albeit Bremen's to a larger extent, have clearly perceived ethnic minority self-employment as both the consequence of integration and as a conduit of further integration. Another reason could be the clear visibility of this employment practice, with both cities having witnessed the emergence of ethnic minority restaurants, shops and hairdressers since the 1960s. It might also be due to the manner in which self-employment has been pushed into the spotlight as a positive employment practice for ethnic groups, either by political circles in Britain or the *Zentrum für Türkeistudien und Integrationsforschung* in Germany. Furthermore, both cities' governments have repeatedly and continuously introduced measures to advise and support ethnic minority businesses despite the clear tradition of these to refrain from seeking any type of support from outside their immediate ethnic communities.

As in towns and cities across Britain and Germany, South Asian Muslim businesses in Newcastle and Turkish Muslim businesses in Bremen have undoubtedly acted as the epicentres of migrant communities. They have long been the places where adults meet to gossip and talk about politics, where children go after school, and where Muslim migrants in both cities are able to expose their religious, ethnic and cultural identities whilst engaging with their host societies. These businesses are the consequences of migrants' hard work and sacrifice, but also economic success and, most importantly, integration and commitment to their local surroundings. These businessmen have demonstrated the ability to manoeuvre their local labour markets and succeed in attaining the status of self-employment, and their businesses have gone a long way to contribute to their local economies and act as conduits of positive race relations. They have defied the discrimination and restraints that often plague Muslim migrants in Britain and Germany.

2

Neighbourhood which? The housing sector: owner-occupation and ethnic neighbourhoods

Ethnic minorities in Britain and Germany's housing sectors

The housing sector has attracted increased attention in recent years in the academic and political dialogue surrounding ethnic minorities in Britain and Germany. In Britain, the 2001 urban disturbances refuelled debate and concern regarding community cohesion, and the ethnic segregation and so-called 'parallel lives' of ethnic and religious communities.[1] Similarly in Germany, the 2000s have witnessed an increase in allegations of 'parallel societies', a growing recognition that home ownership often leads to higher levels of integration, and the inclusion of the housing sector in the ground-breaking 2007 National Integration Plan.[2] Yet this does not mean that the consideration of the housing sector is new to Britain and Germany's debate on migrant communities. On the contrary, there exists a well-established academic and political concentration on housing in both countries.

Migrants arriving independently in Britain during the 1950s and 1960s often found themselves struggling in the housing market. Studies documenting these difficulties began to emerge during the 1960s, a trait that only gathered pace during the subsequent decades. They

---

[1] See Deborah Phillips, 'Parallel lives? Challenging discourses of British Muslim self-segregation', *Environment and Planning D: Society and Space*, 24:1 (2006), pp. 25–40; and John Flint, 'Faith and housing in England: Promoting community cohesion or contributing to urban segregation?', *Journal of Ethnic and Migration Studies*, 36:2 (2010), pp. 257–74.

[2] See Karen Schönwälder and Janina Söhn, 'Immigrant settlement structures in Germany: General patterns and urban levels of concentration of major groups', *Urban Studies*, 46:7 (2009), pp. 1439–40; and Amelie F. Constant, Rowan Roberts and Klaus F. Zimmermann, 'Ethnic identity and immigrant homeownership', *Urban Studies*, 46:9 (2009), pp. 1879–80.

exposed incidents of racist discrimination, overcrowding, low access to public authority housing, segregation, residential concentration in poor quality housing in inner-city areas and barriers to achieving owner-occupation. These were difficulties that were often further exacerbated by migrants' lack of knowledge regarding the British housing market.[3] Works that drew upon the 1991 Census, the first to include a question on ethnic origin, reconfirmed many of these previously established traits and experiences, but also exposed disparities between ethnic groups. An analysis of different ethnic communities shows the extent to which their long-term housing traits and patterns have been influenced by their initial post-war migration paradigms.

The Caribbeans arrived largely as replacement workers for whites, often in public transport or the National Health Service, and many settled in London. Initially denied access to social housing, they were forced into privately rented accommodation that was often shared and overcrowded. They have since gradually gained access to council housing though have largely remained concentrated in certain districts with some dispersal having taken place. The Indian community was largely employed in white-collar work, and had a higher percentage of households with two wage earners and lower unemployment rates than other South Asian groups. This community has traditionally shown an overwhelming preference for owner-occupation, with many living in semi-detached and terraced housing in outer London, and having achieved a presence in rural areas. Many Pakistanis and Bangladeshis settled in the inner-city areas of northern textile towns, such as Oldham and Bradford, and others in areas of London, such as Tower Hamlets. Pakistanis have shown a strong preference for owner-occupation, with many becoming concentrated in nineteenth-century inner-city terraces. Yet there is also evidence to suggest that many Pakistanis with the necessary financial capital to do so have moved out of these more traditional areas of immigrant settlement into housing of higher quality in better neighbourhoods. Contrary to other migrant groups, Bangladeshi migration to Britain began later, during the early 1980s rather than the mid- to late 1970s, and did not correlate with a demand for foreign workers. In general, the Bangladeshi population was younger, consisted of large families of only one wage earner and suffered high rates of

---

[3] See Elizabeth Burney, *Housing on Trial: A Study of Immigrants and Local Government* (Oxford, 1967); Jeffrey Henderson and Valerie Karn, *Race, Class and State Housing: Inequality and the Allocation of Public Housing in Britain* (Aldershot, 1987); and Philip Sarre, Deborah Phillips and Richard Skellington, *Ethnic Minority Housing: Explanations and Policies* (Aldershot, 1989).

unemployment. Partially as a result of this, Bangledeshis have tended to live in inner-city areas, have a high dependence on council housing and low rates of owner-occupation. Chain migration has played a role in reinforcing the housing patterns and clustering of all ethnic groups.[4]

A key theme that has run throughout the literature on the housing of ethnic minorities in Britain since the 1960s has been the 'choice versus constraint' debate in which studies have deliberated over the extent to which housing market patterns and behaviour have been forced upon the migrants or been the result of their own conscious choices.[5] The foundations of the constraint argument were very much laid by John Rex and Robert Moore's 1967 ground-breaking study of the Sparkbrook area of Birmingham in which they concluded that ethnic minorities, and especially Pakistanis, suffered high levels of discrimination in the housing sector and were consequently forced into low-quality housing.[6] One of the pioneers of the choice argument was Badr Dahya who maintained that Pakistanis chose and preferred to live in shared accommodation with the aim of saving money to send home as remittances and that any discrimination suffered did not act as a catalyst for residential concentration.[7] What has since developed is a vibrant and energetic debate on migrant individual agency versus institutional racism and discrimination that has earned itself a firm place in the study of ethnic minority housing and geographical settlement.[8] In more recent years, it has gradually been extended to incorporate religion as well as ethnicity.[9] This debate is particularly relevant for this study because Newcastle's post-war Muslim immigrant communities

[4] See Ceri Peach, 'Pluralist and assimilationist models of ethnic settlement in London 1991', *Tijdschrift voor Economische en Sociale Geografie*, 88:2 (1997), pp. 120–34; Ceri Peach, 'South Asian and Caribbean ethnic minority housing choice in Britain', *Urban Studies*, 35:10 (1998), pp. 1657–80; and Deborah Phillips, 'Black minority ethnic concentration, segregation and dispersal in Britain', *Urban Studies*, 35:10 (1998), pp. 1681–1702.
[5] For a summary of the debate, see Ceri Peach, 'Does Britain have ghettos?', *Transactions of the Institute of British Geographers*, 21:1 (1996), pp. 228–9.
[6] John Rex and Robert Moore, *Race, Community and Conflict* (London, 1967).
[7] See Badr Dahya, 'The nature of Pakistani ethnicity in industrial cities in Britain', in Abner Cohen (ed.), *Urban Ethnicity* (London, 1974), pp. 77–118.
[8] See Vaughan Robinson, *Transients, Settlers and Refugees: Asians in Britain* (Oxford, 1986); and Peter Ratcliffe, 'Re-evaluating the links between "race" and residence', *Housing Studies*, 24:4 (2009), pp. 433–50.
[9] See Robinson, *Transients, Settlers and Refugees*; and Ceri Peach, 'Islam, ethnicity and South Asian religions in the London 2001 Census', *Transactions of the Institute of British Geographers*, 31:3 (2006), pp. 353–70.

have demonstrated a clear set of choices in the development of their housing patterns.

In Germany, post-war guest-workers tended to initially reside in communal accommodation provided to them by their employers. The conditions suffered in what were often sub-standard dwellings have been well documented and included overcrowding, a lack of furniture and filth.[10] Whilst a large proportion of these guest-workers had left this type of accommodation by the early to mid-1970s, they nevertheless continued to endure worse housing conditions than their German counterparts. In general, studies on the housing market experiences and behaviour of ethnic minority communities emerged comparatively later and started to be published during the 1980s.[11] Similar to that pertaining to Britain, the historiography addressing Germany has also revealed a series of difficulties encountered by the migrant population. These have included disadvantages in the social housing allocation system, discrimination suffered at the hands of private landlords and segregation into poor-quality housing stock. Furthermore, ethnic minorities have often been faced with paying higher rental prices than their German counterparts, having access to fewer amenities and have experienced limited residential mobility as a result of language difficulties.[12]

Unlike in Britain where a large proportion of certain ethnic groups have preferred owner-occupation, migrant groups in Germany have largely depended on the rental housing market. However, as in Britain, their residential patterns have at least partially been the consequence of their time of arrival to Germany, with guest-workers initially settling in predominantly industrial cities and towns, and since becoming concen-

---

[10] See Herbert, *A History of Foreign Labor in Germany*, pp. 217–20; and Panayi, *Ethnic Minorities in Nineteenth and Twentieth Century Germany*, pp. 220–1.

[11] See John O'Loughlin, 'Distribution and migration of foreigners in German cities', *Geographical Review*, 70:3 (1980), pp. 253–75; and Paul Gans, 'Intraurban migration of foreigners in Kiel since 1972. The case of the Turkish population', in Günther Glebe and John O'Loughlin (eds), *Foreign Minorities in Continental European Cities* (Wiesbaden, 1987), pp. 116–38.

[12] See Jürgen Friedrichs and Hannes Alpheis, 'Housing segregation of immigrants in West Germany', in Elizabeth D. Huttman, Wim Blauw and Juliet Saltman (eds), *Urban Housing Segregation of Minorities in Western Europe and the United States* (Duke NC, 1991), pp. 116–44; and Barbara Freyer Stowasser, 'The Turks in Germany: From sojourners to citizens', in Yvonne Yazbeck Haddad (ed.), *Muslims in the West: From Sojourners to Citizens* (Oxford, 2002), pp. 58–9.

The housing sector

trated in inner-city areas.[13] Furthermore, the settlement patterns of migrants in Germany today still very much reflect the initial labour market demands of the 1960s and 1970s. As Schönwälder and Söhn point out, there are large numbers of Turks living in former areas of heavy industry, such as Berlin and Cologne, leading one to conclude that they develop a connection to the cities or regions in which they originally settled.[14]

Yet unlike in other Western European countries, ethnic minorities in Germany do not experience high levels of residential segregation. In contrast with Britain, where London is home to almost half of the country's ethnic minority population, migrant communities in Germany are far more dispersed. For example, whilst Berlin's Turkish community may be the largest in Germany, it nevertheless only constitutes 7 per cent of the country's Turks. Furthermore, there is not one German city where one ethnic minority comprises more than 10 per cent of the population. As a result of this, Germany is not home to ethnic neighbourhoods, but rather to ethnically mixed neighbourhoods where white Germans still tend to be in the majority. Schönwälder and Söhn explain this residential dispersal in a number of ways. Firstly, it is undoubtedly largely the result of the guest-worker system. Not only did this immigration paradigm limit chain migration, especially when compared to Britain's colonial migration, but the clustering of ethnic minorities was also avoided by the fact that guest-workers tended to originate from different areas of the sending countries. In other words, there was not the same familiarity amongst ethnic minority populations that existed in Britain. A further cause of residential dispersal is the fact that rented housing plays much more of a role in Germany than owner-occupation. As a result, ethnic minorities theoretically have access to a larger proportion of available housing, which tends to be distributed throughout numerous districts of German cities.[15]

As a result of a lack of official data, there is not such a clear housing market profile for ethnic groups in Germany as there is in Britain. Yet an attempt has been made to provide a rough outline on what the experiences and traits for different ethnicities have been. Schönwälder and Söhn explain that Germany's migrant groups' housing performances have been restrained by income levels and discrimination suffered at

---

[13] See Schönwälder and Söhn, 'Immigrant settlement structures in Germany', pp. 1450, 1452.
[14] Ibid., pp. 1443–4.
[15] Ibid., pp. 1443–51.

the hands of landlords, with Turks often being more disadvantaged than other ethnic groups. They also suggest that preference plays a role, especially amongst the Turkish population, with many purposefully choosing to live in areas with other migrants, and valuing the closeness of relatives and friends.[16] Other studies have concluded that, when compared to other migrant groups, Turks suffer from more overcrowding, reside in housing of which a larger percentage requires renovations and feel more that their rent is too high. Moreover, with regard to housing conditions, the gap between Turks and other ethnic minorities actually widened during the late 1980s and 1990s.[17] Yet others have argued that Turks suffer the highest levels of segregation, often in inner-city areas.[18] In all, there is no doubt that, as with the employment sector, it is once again the Turks who have been awarded the most attention in the academic literature and are portrayed as the ethnic group that has endured the most difficult housing conditions.[19]

Muslim ethnic minorities in Britain and Germany's housing sectors

As with the employment sector, there is not an overwhelming amount of literature on the influence of religion on the housing careers of ethnic minorities in Britain and Germany. In Britain, studies on Muslim migrants' housing choices and neighbourhoods became more prevalent during the 1990s and then materialised in earnest during the 2000s following the 2001 urban disturbances. This shift in focus, both academically and politically, from ethnicity to religion was further encouraged by 9/11, the 2005 London bombings and the increasingly widespread perception of Islam as a threat. Researchers were further

---

[16] Ibid., pp. 1451–3.
[17] Anita I. Drever and William A.V. Clark, 'Gaining access to housing in Germany: The foreign-minority experience', *Urban Studies*, 39:13 (2002), pp. 2444–5.
[18] See Franz-Josef Kemper, 'Restructuring of housing and ethnic segregation: Recent developments in Berlin', *Urban Studies*, 35:10 (1998), pp. 1773, 1779–82.
[19] See Günther Glebe, 'Housing and segregation of Turks in Germany', in Sule Özüekren and Ronald van Kempen (eds), *Turks in European Cities: Housing and Urban Segregation* (Utrecht, 1997), pp. 122–57; and Sule Özüekren and Ebru Ergoz-Karahan, 'Housing experiences of Turkish (im)migrants in Berlin and Istanbul: Internal differentiation and segregation', *Journal of Ethnic and Migration Studies*, 36:2 (2010), pp. 355–72.

inspired by the 2001 Census, the first to include a question regarding religious affiliation.[20] Whilst the historiography on the housing of Muslim ethnic minorities in Britain is still very much developing, some conclusions have been reached.

Research has suggested, for example, that Muslim tenants are more likely to be victims of harassment, and experience a concentration in both poor-quality housing and areas of deprivation.[21] In his study of London, Ceri Peach concluded that Islam plays a role in residential patterns, but that it does so alongside ethnicity, region of origin and language.[22] David Varady asserted that Muslim segregation has been largely voluntary and that government policies and measures attempting to combat residential clustering are thus destined to fail.[23] Other research has further challenged the notions of 'self-segregation' and 'parallel lives' that emerged after the 2001 urban disturbances and were deemed threatening to community cohesion.[24] Whilst acknowledging that Muslims did tend to cluster together for social and cultural reasons, it also stressed that their segregation was further reinforced by the fact that certain neighbourhoods were inaccessible to them.[25] Philip Lewis's study of Bradford exposed the composition of such Muslim neighbourhoods, which hosted businesses and services that catered specifically for the social, cultural and religious needs of the local Muslim community.[26] John Flint has argued that overall there is a need for a clearer understanding of the link between faith and housing needs and aspirations in England.[27]

---

[20] See Phillips, 'Parallel lives?'; and Hussain, *Muslims on the Map*.

[21] See Open Society Institute, *Monitoring Minority Protection in the EU: The Situation of Muslims in the UK* (Budapest, 2002), p. 105; and Ansari, 'The Infidel Within', p. 179.

[22] Peach, 'Islam, ethnicity and South Asian religions in the London 2001 Census'.

[23] David Varady, 'Muslim residential clustering and political radicalism', *Housing Studies*, 23:1 (2008), pp. 45–66.

[24] Community Cohesion Review Team, *The Cantle Report – Community Cohesion: A Report of the Independent Review Team* (London, 2001).

[25] See Deborah Phillips, Ludi Simpson and Sameera Ahmed, 'Shifting geographies of minority ethnic settlement: Remaking communities in Oldham and Rochdale', in John Flint and David Robinson (eds), *Community Cohesion in Crisis? New Dimensions of Diversity and Difference* (Bristol, 2008), pp. 81–97; and Phillips, 'Minority ethnic segregation, integration and citizenship', p. 220.

[26] Lewis, *Islamic Britain*.

[27] Flint, 'Faith and housing in England'.

As with the employment sector, studies investigating the housing of Muslim migrants in Germany emerged later than those in Britain and have been fewer in number. Furthermore, the same reasons for this are applicable, including an absence of official data that clearly distinguishes between Muslim and non-Muslim ethnic minorities, and an overwhelming emphasis on the Turkish community.[28] Nevertheless, a small number of investigations into the housing experiences of Muslim migrants have been conducted. The key work is that entitled *Muslim Life in Germany*, which was published by the Federal Office for Migration and Refugees in 2009. The interviews carried out as part of this study revealed that Muslim migrants are more likely to live in predominantly ethnic minority and segregated areas than non-Muslim migrants, traits that were even more pronounced amongst Turkish Muslims. An estimated 40 per cent of Muslims lived in areas where ethnic minorities constituted the majority of the population and it was suggested that this diminished their chances of interacting with their German counterparts. Whilst more than two-thirds felt strong or very strong ties to their places of residence, Muslims felt a greater connection to their countries of origin and a lesser degree of attachment to Germany than respondents of other religions. Perhaps surprisingly, the majority of those interviewed stated that the composition of their neighbourhoods was not important, and only 3 per cent of respondents declared a preference for living in areas with other ethnic minorities. Furthermore, just over one-third expressed a desire to reside in a German environment.[29]

As with employment, the role played by the religious affiliation of Muslim ethnic minorities in Germany's housing sector is progressively being acknowledged in the historiography, albeit not yet to the same extent as in Britain. It has recently been argued, for example, that Turkish Muslims prefer to live in areas where they can fortify and sculpt their religious identities, and that they shape their neighbourhoods with religious meaning and practices.[30] Other studies have uncovered incidents of discrimination in housing offices and suggested

[28] See Lutz Holzner, 'The myth of Turkish ghettoes: A geographical case of West German response towards a foreign minority', *Journal of Ethnic Studies*, 9:4 (1982), pp. 65–85; and Heike Hanhörster, 'Whose neighbourhood is it? Ethnic diversity in urban spaces in Germany', *GeoJournal*, 51:4 (2001), pp. 329–38.

[29] Federal Office for Migration and Refugees, *Muslim Life in Germany*, pp. 280–92.

[30] See Ehrkamp, 'Beyond the mosque'; and Özüekren and Ergoz-Karahan, 'Housing experiences of Turkish (im)migrants in Berlin and Istanbul'.

that it is Muslim migrants' religious affiliation that causes them to be perceived as foreigners, which in turn leads them to form ethnic niches.[31] It is to this existing historiography on the housing of Muslim migrants in Britain and Germany that this study hopes to add.

Aims of the chapter

This chapter analyses the performance and behaviour of Muslim ethnic minority communities in both Newcastle and Bremen's housing sectors from the 1960s to the 1990s from the perspective of both local governments and the migrants themselves. As with the employment sector, there is little doubt that Britain and Germany's differing post-war immigration frameworks had a huge impact on both cities' Muslim immigrants' initial housing patterns. Whilst Newcastle's immigrants succeeded in achieving owner-occupancy from as early as the 1960s, those in Bremen were only permitted to move onto the local housing market after having first experienced the confinement of their respective employers' accommodation. As time passed, however, the housing traits of Muslim ethnic minorities in both cities gradually merged in that they have often chosen to live in predominantly ethnic areas and, when possible, in their own properties.

Thus, in this sector also, the contrasts between Britain and Germany's initial immigration paradigms were progressively replaced by grassroots housing goals and, in Germany's case, the comparatively delayed emergence of residential autonomy, an ambition that was further intensified by migrants' decisions not to return to their countries of origin, but rather remain in Bremen. This chapter seeks to go beyond the historically and historiographically insistent claims of 'poor quality housing' and 'segregation', and highlights the often neglected role that migrants themselves play in moulding their own residential patterns. It asserts that although the vast majority of both cities' Muslim migrant communities have traditionally resided in ethnic neighbourhoods, this is not evidence of a lack of integration, but rather of two minority communities that are content to coexist alongside their host populations.

This chapter draws predominantly upon existing studies and local authority correspondence, reports and minutes, which offer an insight

---

[31] See Şen, 'The historical situation of Turkish migrants in Germany', p. 110; and Amikam Nachmani, *Europe and its Muslim Minorities: Aspects of Conflict, Attempts at Accord* (Brighton, 2009), p. 62.

into local policies and measures, as well as into the views and experiences of the ethnic minority communities. An examination of the housing of Muslim migrants in Britain and Germany encounters the same problems with sources as a study of their performance in the employment sector. In other words, this chapter also seeks to investigate the patterns and experiences of Muslim immigrants before Islam was officially considered a potentially influential feature. As with the employment sector, documents are largely approached along ethnic lines and do not refer to Muslim migrants specifically. Thus, as with numerous other studies on the housing of Muslim ethnic minorities, this work relies on data that is largely based on ethnicity.[32]

There are clear parallels between some of the main conclusions reached in considering both the employment and housing sectors. Firstly, despite the growing number of studies that are being conducted along religious lines and the increasingly accepted notion that religion is an influential factor in the residential patterns of ethnic minority communities, albeit more so in Britain than in Germany, this chapter finds that Islam has played nothing more than a minor role in the housing experiences and traits of migrants in Newcastle and Bremen. In this sense, whilst the housing patterns of Muslim migrants have certainly earned themselves a firm place on both countries' political agendas in recent years, this focus on Islam has not necessarily been warranted judging from these two case studies. Furthermore, whilst their geographical clustering has indeed often been the result of their religious affiliation in that they often demonstrate a preference to live next to a mosque, an Islamic community centre or businesses that cater specifically for Muslims, such as halal butchers, their overall housing patterns and ambitions have often mirrored those of non-Muslim ethnic minority groups in Britain and Germany, and throughout the Western world.

Secondly, this study does not perceive the performance of Muslim immigrants in Newcastle and Bremen's housing sectors as having been dominated by discrimination, segregation or a lack of housing market opportunities. On the contrary, Muslim migrants have largely made conscious choices that have moulded and shaped certain neighbourhoods in both cities. In Newcastle, it was not uncommon for Muslim migrants to purchase numerous properties and rent them out, a

---

[32] See Ansari, 'The Infidel Within', pp. 179–81; and Nina Mühe, *Muslims in the EU: Cities Reports – Preliminary Research Report and Literature Survey Germany* (Budapest, 2007), pp. 39–42.

practice that further enabled their pursuit of economic autonomy and self-sufficiency. Whilst this degree of residential entrepreneurship has not been so prevalent in Bremen, there are nevertheless indications that this German city's Muslim ethnic minorities' housing practices are catching up with their British-based counterparts. This chapter does not wish to suggest that instances of discrimination and hardship have not been encountered by Muslim migrants in Newcastle and Bremen. Yet it will argue that the overall experiences in both cities have often been ones of residential satisfaction and success. It will offer a much-needed grassroots post-war assessment of Muslim migrants' experiences in the British and German housing sectors and expose their residential aspirations, arguing that choice has clearly triumphed over constraint.

Newcastle

Whilst the North East has rarely been the chosen area of studies on ethnic minority housing in Britain, this region has been awarded a substantial amount of attention in recent years. This has unquestionably been the result of the growth of its ethnic minority population. For the North East as a whole, foreign-born residents went from constituting 1.87 per cent of the population to 2.67 per cent between 1991 and 2001. Although they remain only a marginal percentage of the region's population and constitute a figure that is certainly smaller than in other areas across Britain, the relative increase during this decade was spectacular and was the second highest in the UK during this period.[33] For the city of Newcastle, the 2001 Census recorded ethnic minorities constituting 6.9 per cent of the city's total population, a substantial increase from 4.1 per cent in 1991. Whilst a proportion of this growth was the direct consequence of the arrival of asylum seekers and refugees, there was also an increase in the number of residents of South Asian descent, such as Pakistanis and Bangladeshis, who went from constituting 2.39 per cent of Newcastle's population in 1991 to 4.4 per cent in 2001. Furthermore, certain wards in the city have experienced a surge in the number of their ethnic minority residents, including Elswick (25.5 per cent), Wingrove (24.7 per cent), Moorside (16.2 per cent) and Fenham (10.1 per cent). These are traditional areas of post-war ethnic

---

[33] See Pillai, *Destination North East?*, p. 8.

minority settlement which asylum seekers and refugees have also started to move into.[34]

By the end of the 1990s, Newcastle's South Asian communities had demonstrated a certain amount of residential mobility and, in doing so, adhered to what has become the established hierarchy of ethnicities. The Indian community has been the most successful, with many having left the West End for more prestigious areas like Jesmond and Gosforth. The 1991 Census showed that only 37 per cent of Indians remained in the West End compared to 75 per cent of Bangladeshis and 74 per cent of Pakistanis.[35] Those that have remained in the West End live largely in Fenham, the most popular part, and in owner-occupied housing. The Pakistani community remains largely concentrated in the West End of the city, although it has also succeeded in securing a presence in Fenham and overwhelmingly enjoys owner-occupation. In fact, around 90 per cent of Indian and Pakistani respondents were owner-occupiers, with most having mortgages, but some owning their properties outright. As throughout Britain, the Bangladeshi community's housing patterns have remained distinct. Although some have made the transition to better areas both within and outside the West End, 52 per cent remained in council housing and many still lived on the Bentinck Estate, Newcastle's main area of initial Bangladeshi settlement.[36]

The recent movement and activity amongst ethnic minorities in Newcastle's housing sector has led to research into their housing needs, experiences and aspirations. Although these have not addressed Muslim migrants specifically, some of the conclusions reached are nevertheless pertinent to this study and are themes that will be further developed. A mid-2000s report, for example, stressed that Pakistanis and Bengalis prefer to live close to other members of their ethnic communities, and in areas where they can easily access religious establishments and ethnic shops and food. It also raised problems that

---

[34] See The Guinness Trust, *The 2003/2004 Newcastle BME Housing Research Project* (Newcastle, 2004), pp. 6–7; and David Robinson, Kesia Reeve, Rionach Casey and Rosalind Goudie, *Minority Ethnic Residential Experiences and Requirements in the Bridging NewcastleGateshead Area* (Sheffield, 2007), p. 21.

[35] See Stuart Cameron and Andrew Field, 'Community, ethnicity and neighbourhood', *Housing Studies*, 15:6 (2000), pp. 832–3.

[36] See Stuart Cameron and Andrew Field, *Housing and the Black Population of West Newcastle* (Sunderland, 1997), pp. 3, 24; and Cameron, 'Ethnic minority housing needs and diversity in an area of low housing demand', pp. 1433–4.

residents from these ethnic communities had encountered, such as high rents, overcrowding, housing being in poor condition, racial harassment, and noisy and dirty neighbourhoods.[37] A 2005 report commissioned by the North East Housing Board Unit concluded that local authorities in the region do not have a sufficient understanding of the housing needs of ethnic minority communities, and that more effort needed to be put into addressing their various cultural and religious needs.[38] A 2007 report on ethnic minority housing issues in the North East concluded that there existed a strong desire for home ownership, that social housing was often perceived as inaccessible and located in poorer low-demand neighbourhoods, people wanted more investment in ethnic minority neighbourhoods, racial harassment was suffered by a variety of ethnic groups in different locations, and that people either had limited knowledge regarding intermediate housing products, doubted their effectiveness or found them difficult to access.[39]

This is an opportune time at which to examine Newcastle's Muslim ethnic minorities' housing patterns, for numerous reasons. Firstly, the ethnic minority population is likely to continue to grow as young people have children, a practice that is far higher amongst migrant households than their white counterparts. Secondly, the younger generation leaving family homes is likely to also cause challenges in that they will initially be looking for much smaller dwellings than have traditionally been lived in by the ethnic minority communities, and some households will experience a reduction in their total income due to their departure. It has also been predicted that future years will witness a vast increase in the size of the older ethnic minority population at an even faster rate than was the case between 1991 and 2001. The result of this is likely to be a greater demand for certain types of housing, such as sheltered housing, and a need for alterations to existing housing stock.[40]

---

[37] The Guinness Trust, *The 2003/2004 Newcastle New Deal for Communities BME Housing Research Project* (Newcastle, 2004), p. 19.
[38] Andrew Petrie, *Housing Needs of Black and Minority Ethnic Communities in the North East – A Scoping Exercise* (Huddersfield, 2005), pp. 32–3.
[39] Harris Beider, Ricky Joseph and Ed Ferrari, *Report to North East Assembly BME Housing Issues* (Birmingham, 2007), pp. 4–5.
[40] See Cameron and Field, *Housing and the Black Population of West Newcastle*, p. 4; and Robinson, Reeve, Casey and Goudie, *Minority Ethnic Residential Experiences and Requirements in the Bridging NewcastleGateshead Area*, pp. 14–15.

The 1960s, 1970s and 1980s

As with the labour market, there is not a great amount of literature available on the early experiences of post-war ethnic minorities in Newcastle's housing sector. Nevertheless, there is enough information to construct a picture of their initial housing patterns and experiences. A 1967 report issued by the City of Newcastle upon Tyne singled out certain wards of the city where ethnic minorities tended to settle, such as Elswick and other areas in the west, Heaton in the east and Jesmond just north of the city centre. It pointed out that these areas were becoming increasingly popular amongst migrants because they were home to property they found suitable. This included large houses that were used by a number of different households, and the availability of both furnished and unfurnished rented accommodation.[41]

The report correctly highlighted the importance of property ownership and the manner in which it was accompanied by a sense of pride and achievement. Newcastle's South Asian population was both small and loyal, and informal measures within the community were put in place to help make home ownership possible. Migrants who were new to Newcastle tended to initially live as 'paying guests' with relatives or friends for as long as it took them to accumulate the financial capital necessary to purchase their own properties. They would then take in 'paying guests' of their own. As soon as it was financially possible, migrants would purchase a second house, live in the better of the two and rent out rooms in the other one, usually to fellow migrants. The majority of these landlords were of Indian and Pakistani origin, and preferred to have members of their own ethnic groups as tenants.[42]

The report also revealed that the majority of migrant property owners had been able to secure mortgages and that only a few had encountered difficulties in doing so. Estate agents felt that Newcastle's ethnic minorities did not suffer discrimination with regard to mortgages, although a higher deposit was often demanded from them. This was because they tended to purchase older houses and there was a general suspicion that they might not stay in the city for the long term. Also, the tendency for multiple households to share one property was often disapproved of. Yet these factors do not appear to have influenced the housing experiences of Newcastle's ethnic minorities. Overall, individual migrants seemed quite happy with their residential

---

[41] Telang, *The Coloured Immigrant in Newcastle upon Tyne*, p. 14.
[42] Ibid., p. 14.

situations and few wanted to move to a different part of the city. Furthermore, there does not seem to have been a need to rely on council housing, with the vast majority rejecting this option altogether, a pattern that will be discussed in more detail at a later stage.[43]

The report also identified a correlation between social status and area of residence, with the more educated migrants often choosing to live in Jesmond. It also raised a few other points regarding the city's ethnic minorities' housing patterns. Firstly, it recognised that they often tended to live in conditions that were deemed inferior by the local white population, but admitted that it was unclear whether this was the result of ethnic minorities consciously choosing to accept inferior housing standards or because they were simply not presented with the same range of residential opportunities. Secondly, the report warned that the concentration of ethnic minority communities would potentially have consequences for certain neighbourhoods, which it claimed were likely to experience a general deterioration in housing and garden conditions, and become increasingly less attractive to the city's white residents.[44]

Despite the pessimistic predictions regarding the long-term effects of ethnic minority settlement on Newcastle's neighbourhoods, the report portrayed their housing experiences and patterns in a largely positive light. Overall, they had established their own community support system, were managing to secure mortgages and purchase property, and were overwhelmingly content with their residential standings. Such optimistic accounts and interpretations continued to dominate what small amount of literature existed on the topic during the 1970s and into the mid-1980s. In fact, in a 1970 article, Jon Gower Davies and John Taylor used Newcastle as a case study to challenge John Rex and Robert Moore's ground-breaking 1967 work, *Race, Community and Conflict*, in which they laid the foundations of the 'constraints model', and stressed the obstacles and difficulties ethnic minorities faced when trying to secure desirable council housing and purchase their own homes. In it, they argued that Rex and Moore's thesis was not applicable to Indians and Pakistanis in Newcastle, and they offered a far more encouraging picture in which these ethnic minorities were able to access and use property in the way they chose to.[45]

[43] Ibid., p. 15
[44] Ibid., pp. 14–15.
[45] Jon Gower Davies and John Taylor, 'Race, community and no conflict', *New Society*, 9 (1970), pp. 67–9.

Davies expanded further on this research in his 1972 work on Rye Hill, an area in Newcastle's West End that, by the 1960s, was renowned for social problems and poor-quality housing. It was dominated by residents on low incomes, and houses that were of poor quality and suffered from overcrowding.[46] In this work, Davies stressed the extent to which his Indian and Pakistani respondents favoured owner-occupancy and not only shied away from council housing, but also saw themselves as being different to those people who paid rent. Whilst these ethnic minorities did often live in relatively cheap housing, it was also the type of housing that building societies were reluctant to lend money for. Yet, as Davies pointed out, many of Newcastle's Indian and Pakistani homeowners secured mortgages or bank loans and, overall, they had encountered no real problem obtaining the necessary funds in the way that they had chosen to. Others had managed to raise the financial capital through saving and borrowing from family and friends. Overall, Davies found no real evidence that Newcastle's Indians and Pakistanis were forced into borrowing money in ways they had not wished to or that racism had excluded them from certain districts of the city and the private housing market or public housing.[47] Furthermore, Davies's study also exposed the manner in which Indians and Pakistanis in Newcastle were able to manipulate and use the housing market to serve their own interests. They preferred property ownership for numerous reasons. Some felt more secure in their own homes, and others purchased multiple properties and rented them out, with some viewing them as part of their entrepreneurial portfolios alongside their shops and businesses. Overall, they seem to have had no real trouble becoming homeowners in Newcastle and some took advantage of the low property prices in certain areas, expressly buying property for the sole purpose of renting it out.[48]

Davies recognised that discrimination, although rarely actually experienced, was perceived by Indians and Pakistanis as being possible, and that this was one factor that led these migrants to property ownership. In general, there seemed to be a widespread belief that renting property from either the council or a landlord made one more vulnerable. Yet, as Davies rightly pointed out, this was only one reason why they had opted for home ownership. Others included personal

[46] Davies, *The Evangelistic Bureaucrat*, pp. 19–20.
[47] Ibid., pp. 28–33.
[48] Ibid., pp. 33–41.

ambition and a desire to make money out of property. Overall, his study clearly succeeded in challenging the Rex–Moore thesis, which still remains at the foundation of the 'constraints model'. Newcastle's Indians and Pakistanis' performance in the local housing sector was not dominated by discrimination, exclusion or constraint, but rather by their own ambitions and abilities to work the property market to their advantage. Indian and Pakistani landlords often suffered criticism as a result of the perception that they had contributed to the general decline of the Rye Hill area and the belief that they exploited white tenants. Yet, as Davies explained, these South Asian residents actually had a lot in common with their local counterparts. Rye Hill was home to a certain type of tenant in Newcastle and was an area where Indians and Pakistanis, like their white neighbours and tenants, could afford to fulfil their housing ambitions.[49]

In 1986, Davies made yet another contribution to the literature on the housing of Asians in Newcastle. He drew upon interviews in the West End of the city, and once again challenged the views and arguments of Rex and Moore. He asserted that Newcastle's Asians' housing patterns were the result of choice rather than discrimination on behalf of the local authority, poor housing conditions and disadvantage were not common, and that most lived in single-family homes as owner-occupiers.[50] This is not to say that their experiences in Newcastle's housing sector have been without racism and disadvantage. On the contrary, government documents reveal that there have certainly been incidents of both and these will be discussed at a later point. Yet Newcastle has nevertheless been home to ethnic minorities who have possessed the ability to achieve their housing aims and aspirations, and have demonstrated the importance of their own communities in doing so.

Many of these ethnic minority housing patterns and preferences that have been found to have been so prevalent in Newcastle during the 1970s and 1980s were not particular to this north-eastern city, but were also cited in other studies that emerged during this time period. These also supported the notion of self-segregation, and explained ethnic clustering as the result of migrants wanting to live close to others with similar beliefs, behaviour and attitudes. They stressed the high levels of home ownership amongst migrant groups compared to the local British population, a feature that was even more remarkable due

[49] Ibid., pp. 37–44.
[50] Jon Gower Davies, *Asian Housing in Britain* (Altrincham, 1986).

to their overwhelming concentration in either unskilled or semi-skilled employment. They also emphasised the widespread prejudice that existed against local authority housing. Furthermore, they revealed the important role played by the community when making housing market decisions, with many having been able to afford to purchase property only as a direct result of help received from family and friends. Moreover, there was also a desire to purchase housing in order to be able to sub-let to fellow migrants, a practice that was often seen as a social obligation, and a belief that home ownership brought with it a certain value and a way in which to preserve their own cultural, religious and social independence.[51]

Yet other works have highlighted the practice amongst South Asians, even those on low wages, of purchasing, refurbishing and renting out property, and have also recognised that this constitutes a type of investment and entrepreneurship.[52] Subsequent studies adhering to both the constraint and choice models have offered an insight into the continuation of many of these residential practices and patterns, and showed how they continued, and in some cases intensified, throughout the 1990s and into the 2000s amongst ethnic minorities and Muslim migrants more specifically. This has particularly been the case with regard to home ownership, which has become even more widespread amongst a greater number of ethnic minorities, and the importance of ethnic and religious communities in housing choices.[53]

---

[51] See Dahya, 'The nature of Pakistani ethnicity in industrial cities in Britain'; Vaughan Robinson, 'Choice and constraint in Asian housing in Blackburn', *Journal of Ethnic and Migration Studies*, 7:3 (1979), pp. 390–6; and Peter Ratcliffe, *Racism and Reaction: A Profile of Handsworth* (London, 1981).

[52] See Mike Bristow, 'Ugandan Asians: Racial disadvantage and housing markets in Manchester and Birmingham', *Journal of Ethnic and Migration Studies*, 7:2 (1979), pp. 203–16; and Pnina Werbner, 'South Asian entrepreneurship in Britain: A critique of the ethnic enclave economy debate', in Léo-Paul Dana (ed.), *Handbook of Research on Ethnic Minority Entrepreneurship: A Coevolutionary View on Resource Management* (Cheltenham, 2007), p. 386.

[53] See Peter Ratcliffe, '"Race", housing and the city', in Nick Jewson and Susanne MacGregor (eds), *Transforming Cities: Contested Governance and New Spatial Divisions* (London, 1997), pp. 92–3; Ludi Simpson, 'Statistics of racial segregation: Measures, evidence and policy', *Urban Studies*, 41:3 (2004), pp. 661–81; and Peach, 'Islam, ethnicity and South Asian religions in the London 2001 Census'.

The 1980s and 1990s

It has been recognised that the general view until the early to mid-1980s was that the North East's ethnic minority population did not merit special attention. A 1983 Northern Housing Associations Committee (NORHAC) report stressed that neither housing associations nor local councils in the region had implemented policies or practices targeted specifically at ethnic minority groups. On the contrary, it was believed that such initiatives were not needed, either because of the small size of the ethnic minority population or the widespread belief that they preferred owner-occupation.[54] The turning point came in the early to mid-1980s after which both Newcastle's local authority and housing organisations began to increase the amount of attention awarded to the housing of the city's ethnic minorities. The surge in levels of discussion and policies during this period was not particular to Newcastle, nor was it the result of local factors: rather it constituted a part of a much wider national development. There were several reasons why the level of attention awarded to the housing of ethnic minorities in Britain intensified at this time.

Firstly, the anti-racist movement of the 1970s played a role in that it had called for improved housing conditions amongst ethnic minorities and raised a general awareness of the subject. Secondly, as with employment, the 1976 Race Relations Act also helped place the housing of minorities on the political agenda by requiring local authorities to combat discrimination and encourage equality of opportunity. Whilst the 1976 Act has been heavily criticised for failing to achieve its aims, it nevertheless undoubtedly raised awareness regarding housing equality, and put pressure on both housing associations and local authority housing departments. An October 1984 Newcastle Housing Committee document, for example, explicitly stressed the responsibility placed on local authorities by the Race Relations Act 1976 to promote equality of opportunity between different communities.[55]

Thirdly, the 1981 urban disturbances and the Scarman Report that followed led to the realisation that some type of complementary

---

[54] Northern Housing Associations Committee, *Race and Housing in the North East: A Joint Working Party Report from the North East Housing Associations Committee and the Community Relations Council of Tyne and Wear and Cleveland County in Response to the National Federation of Housing Associations' Report 'Race and Housing'* (1983), pp. 2–3.

[55] See TWAS, MD.NC/162/1, City of Newcastle upon Tyne Housing Committee, 'Racial harassment in Newcastle', 10 October 1984, p. 1.

measures and policies were required.[56] As well as further promoting a general awareness, the disturbances also helped forge the link between disadvantage and race, a relationship that up until this point had often been neglected or dismissed, with the widespread assumption during the 1970s having been that urban problems were the result of poverty and environmental decay, not race. The culmination of these factors led to the implementation of numerous measures during the 1980s and 1990s, including schemes instigated by the Housing Corporation that sought to address the housing needs of ethnic minority communities through minority-led and financially stable housing associations.[57] Fourthly, a January 1988 report issued by Newcastle's Local Government and Racial Equality Sub-Committee highlighted the part that the 1981 Commission for Racial Equality report, *Racial Harassment on Local Authority Housing Estates*, and the 1987 report, *Living in Terror: A Report on Racial Violence and Harassment in Housing*, had in offering ground-breaking insights into racial harassment and housing, and emphasising the role that needed to be played by local authorities.[58] It was undoubtedly to some extent these overarching pressures that drove Newcastle's local government to investigate the residential situation of the city's ethnic minorities.

It is within this framework that measures implemented by Newcastle's local authority materialised and should thus be examined. Undoubtedly as a result of the context from which they emerged, the available documents concentrate on the obstacles and difficulties encountered by ethnic minorities in Newcastle's housing market. This is a direct contrast to the case regarding entrepreneurship, largely because, whilst self-employment was seen as a possible solution to the social segregation endured by minorities in the years leading up to the

[56] The Scarman Report was the result of an investigation into the 1981 riots. It found that the disorders had been sparked by long-term issues, such as a general mistrust in the police and poor social conditions amongst ethnic minorities.

[57] See Sally Tomlinson, 'Race relations and the urban context', in Peter D. Pumpfrey and Gajendra K. Verma (eds), *Race Relations and Urban Education: Contexts and Promising Practices* (Basingstoke, 1990), p. 18; Martin MacEwen, *Housing, Race and Law: The British Experience* (London, 1991), p. 2; and Harris Beider, *Race, Housing & Community: Perspectives on Policy and Practice* (Oxford, 2012), pp. 80–1, 99, 111.

[58] See TWAS, MD.NC/162/3, City of Newcastle upon Tyne Local Government and Racial Equality Sub-Committee, 'Commission for Racial Equality report on racial violence and harassment in housing: 'Living in Terror", 20 January 1988, pp. 1–2.

1981 urban disturbances, their housing experiences were suddenly perceived as one of the key catalysts. For example, the aforementioned 1983 Northern Housing Associations report expressed the belief that ethnic minorities in the North East were not offered choice within the housing market, which caused them to opt for owner-occupation and led to indirect racial discrimination. It warned that the ethnic minority population would suffer disadvantage if it did not have a grasp of the necessary procedures and available opportunities, and that policies and practices needed to be implemented to ensure that it had access to all parts of the housing system.[59] Drawing upon the 1977 National Dwelling and Household Survey, the 1981 Census and interviews, it offered an insight into housing and neighbourhood preferences, and a list of policy recommendations. A large proportion of ethnic minorities, many of whom were owner-occupiers, were housed in the private sector, and there was an overwhelming lack of awareness regarding housing associations. The recommendations centred on ways in which housing associations might make themselves more available to and better provide for ethnic minorities.[60]

Despite not awarding in-depth attention to the housing of ethnic minorities until the early to mid-1980s, Newcastle City Council was nevertheless perceived by the Tyne and Wear Community Relations Council as having adopted a proactive and positive approach compared to some local authorities and environmental health officers in the Tyne and Wear region.[61] The Community Relations Council stressed that Newcastle's local authority recognised the importance of language barriers and different cultural backgrounds, and specifically mentioned the 1984 report entitled 'The council and racial equality: Policy statement and action plan' as an example of this.[62] This was the council's first attempt at establishing its approach to racial equality, and it conveyed a clear commitment to equality of opportunity and developing Newcastle as a multi-racial city. As well as employment, housing also constituted a key part of this document, and offered a foundation of what were to be the local authority's policies and aims

---

[59] Northern Housing Associations Committee, *Race and Housing in the North East*, p. 3.
[60] Ibid., p. 14 and Appendix II.
[61] See TWAS, MD.NC/162/1, Tyne and Wear Community Relations Council, Housing and Environmental Health Panel, 'Race and environmental health', 6 June 1985, p. 1.
[62] TWAS, MD.NC/162/1, 'The council and racial equality: Policy statement and action plan', November 1984.

regarding ethnic minorities and housing over subsequent years. These included improving the monitoring of the council housing allocation system, preventing incidents of racial harassment and offering support for the victims, and awarding priority to the removal of racist graffiti.[63]

One key area of focus during the mid-1980s was the city's Bengali community, about which a series of reports were compiled in May 1984. At the time, there were approximately sixty-seven Bengali families living in Newcastle. The majority of them were living in the inner West End, seventeen of them on the Bentinck Estate, and the remainder lived in Fenham and Benwell in the west of the city, and Sandyford, Jesmond and Heaton in the east.[64] The May 1984 reports dealt overwhelmingly with those families in the inner West End and specifically with those living on the Bentinck Estate. For many members of the Bangladeshi community, the Bentinck Estate was the only area in which they would live. This resulted in the estate being full and having a waiting list, whilst the remainder of the city's council housing estates did not have significant ethnic minority populations.[65] The local government clearly viewed the Bengali community as distinct from other ethnic minorities in Newcastle. It emphasised their rural and peasant background, and their own specific individual linguistic, cultural and religious traditions. Their patterns of settlement also set them apart from other Muslim migrant groups in Newcastle, such as Pakistanis. The first phase of Bengali settlement consisted of single men who came to work in the city's restaurants and takeaways. They initially left their wives and families at home, believing that they would only be in Newcastle long enough to earn a certain amount of money and would then return home. They predominantly lived in groups in rented and overcrowded accommodation.[66] These are all traits that have been well documented regarding Bengali communities across Britain.[67]

[63] Ibid., pp. 15, 21.
[64] See TWAS, MD.NC/162/1, City of Newcastle upon Tyne Racial Equality Sub-Committee, 'The Bengali community in the inner West End of Newcastle (Bentinck Estate)', 31 May 1984, p. 1.
[65] See Cameron, 'Ethnic minority housing needs and diversity in an area of low housing demand', p. 1435; and Cameron and Field, 'Community, ethnicity and neighbourhood', p. 830.
[66] See TWAS, MD.NC/162/1, 'The Bengali community in the inner West End of Newcastle (Bentinck Estate)', 31 May 1984, pp. 1–2.
[67] See John Eade, *The Politics of Community: The Bangladeshi Community in East London* (Aldershot, 1989); and Nazli Kibria, *Muslims in Motion: Islam and National Identity in the Bangladeshi Diaspora* (London, 2011).

Newcastle's local authority appeared to perceive the Bengalis as the city's least integrated ethnic minority community. They were certainly portrayed as the most isolated, especially the women, something that was explained by their strict adherence to Islam, which the local authority claimed resulted in a limited role outside the home and thus a lack of proficiency in the English language. The Bengali community was also an exception in Newcastle in that it tended to apply for local authority housing, specifically requesting to reside in areas with other members of their own ethnic community.[68] Newcastle's Bengali community adhered to the traits and characteristics of those across Britain. It was the norm for men to arrive in Britain alone at first, a settlement pattern that has potentially led to Bengalis having a lower socio-economic status than other South Asian migrant groups because, as the women arrived later, only a small proportion of them ever entered the labour market, meaning that households have tended to rely on only one income. Furthermore, it has repeatedly been argued that they have traditionally had low levels of owner-occupation, a higher dependency on council housing and are more likely to suffer racial harassment than any other ethnic minority.[69]

It appears as though the key problems faced by Newcastle's Bengali community during the 1980s were poor housing conditions and racial harassment. Common housing problems included damp, rats and overcrowding. All of the Bengali families that were visited during these investigations complained of health problems as a result of damp. As well as problems and faults with the housing, other reasons were also given as the causes of this damp, including a poor understanding of how to work or an inability to afford the central heating system, and the fact that heating appliances were not fitted in all rooms. Overcrowding was a widespread problem, often due to the fact that Bengali families were large. Furthermore, rehousing these families in appropriate housing proved difficult because they tended to want to remain in the same area of the city within their own community, yet the council did not possess large enough housing on this estate. Offers of housing in other areas of the West End had been made, but had been turned down because the applicants had suffered racist abuse when

---

[68] See TWAS, MD.NC/162/1, 'The Bengali community in the inner West End of Newcastle (Bentinck Estate)', 31 May 1984, pp. 1–2.
[69] See Eade, *The Politics of Community*; and Sebastian M. Rasinger, *Bengali-English in East London: A Study in Urban Multilingualism* (Bern, 2007), p. 23.

going to view the properties. This meant that these families chose to live in inferior accommodation instead of moving to other areas where a higher standard of housing was available. The manner in which the anticipation of racial harassment has stopped ethnic minorities from accepting housing in certain areas has been well documented.[70] Further complications existed because a number of these families were in arrears on their rents, believing that this would force the council to re-house them quicker.[71]

As previously mentioned, Bengalis are thought to have habitually suffered the highest levels of racial harassment in Britain, and Newcastle was no exception. The reports recorded both verbal and physical abuse. There were also cases of broken windows, racist stickers and graffiti. According to an October 1984 Housing Committee report, 'the result is that children are kept in, parents rarely go out and families board themselves into their darkened homes for protection'.[72] Solutions to such incidents and experiences were difficult to find. During the 1980s, local authorities were criticised for taking the easy option by moving the victims rather than the perpetrators, with Deborah Phillips arguing that this practice increased the Bengali community's levels of segregation and concentration in low-quality housing in Tower Hamlets.[73] Yet in Newcastle, whilst it was possible to re-house families who were the victims of racial harassment, this proved difficult because these families did not wish to move to a different area of the city. Evidence showed that there was a clear fear of living outside this area of Bangladeshi settlement, especially on council housing estates that were predominantly white and had a reputation for crime and disorder.[74] Furthermore, it was also sometimes the case

[70] See David Robinson, 'Missing the target? Discrimination and exclusion in the allocation of social housing', in Peter Somerville and Andy Steele (eds), *'Race', Housing and Social Exclusion* (London, 2002), p. 100.

[71] See TWAS, MD.NC/162/1, 'Housing the Bengali community in the inner West End', 24 May 1984, pp. 1–3; TWAS, MD.NC/162/1, 'The Bengali community in the inner West of Newcastle', 31 May 1984; TWAS, MD.NC/162/1, 'The Bengali community in the inner West End of Newcastle (Bentinck Estate)', 31 May 1984, p. 3; and TWAS, MD.NC/162/1, Extract from Minutes of Housing Committee of 10th October 1984, 'Racial harassment in Newcastle', pp. 1–2.

[72] See TWAS, MD.NC/162/1, City of Newcastle upon Tyne Housing Committee, 'Racial harassment in Newcastle', 10 October 1984, p. 2.

[73] Deborah Phillips, 'What price equality? A report on the allocation of GLC housing in Tower Hamlets', *GLC Housing Research & Policy Report*, 9 (1986).

[74] See Cameron and Field, 'Community, ethnicity and neighbourhood', pp. 837–8.

that vacant and suitable properties were not available in numerous areas of the city that victims declared as their preferred choices.[75]

A further potential solution was to evict the culprits under the 1980 Housing Act though this also proved difficult because many of the victims were not comfortable coming forward as witnesses. However, some steps were taken, including the development of a clear policy for dealing with suspected cases of racial harassment; the publication of the tenancy handbook, which included information on the council's views on racial harassment, in ethnic minority languages; ensuring tenants were informed regarding the council's view on racial harassment; and the holding of public meetings between members of the Bengali community and the police as well as the Tenants Association.[76] It was decided that reports from Bengali families were to be treated with high priority, they were to have numerous contacts through which they could report incidents to the police and there was to be a higher police presence. Overall, there was a clear attempt to restore the Bengali community's confidence in the police.[77]

Furthermore, priority was given to the replacement of windows broken as a result of racist attacks as well as to the removal of racist graffiti. The Housing Committee also discussed the issuing of a statement of intent, with the aim of both threatening perpetrators with legal action and offering moral support to the ethnic minority victims in the hope of combatting feelings of isolation. It also provided training to staff in the Area Offices to ensure that they were familiar with the

[75] See TWAS, MD.NC/162/2, City of Newcastle upon Tyne, notes of case conference on racial harassment, 23 September 1985 and TWAS, MD.NC/162/2, City of Newcastle upon Tyne, notes of a case conference re racial harassment, 7 October 1985.
[76] See TWAS, MD.NC/162/1, 'Housing the Bengali community in the inner West End', 24 May 1984, p. 3; TWAS, MD.NC/162/1, 'The Bengali community in the inner West End of Newcastle (Bentinck Estate)', 31 May 1984, pp. 3–4; TWAS, MD.NC/162/1, Racial Equality Seminar, 'Report of the Housing Working Group', 12 July 1984, p. 1; TWAS, MD.NC/162/2, City of Newcastle upon Tyne Housing Committee, 'The tenancy agreement: Racial harassment', 11 September 1985, pp. 1–2; TWAS, MD.NC/162/2, Extract from minutes of tenants consultation and claims sub-committee of 29th October 1985, 'Revised draft tenancy handbook Incorporating tenancy agreement'; and TWAS, MD.NC/162/2, City of Newcastle upon Tyne Local Government and Racial Equality Sub-Committee, 'Racial harassment clause – tenancy agreement', May 1986, pp. 1–2.
[77] See TWAS, MD.NC/162/1, 'Racial harassment in Newcastle', 10 October 1984, Appendix 2.

cultural backgrounds of the ethnic minority communities in their areas. Overall, the Committee demonstrated a clear awareness that these incidents had to be perceived in terms of race rather than social problems, and there is evidence of a number of individual cases that were awarded a significant amount of attention.[78] Furthermore, Housing Sub-Committees from individual areas of Newcastle were also committed to tackling racial harassment through initiatives such as the removal of racist graffiti and attempting to engage members of ethnic minorities with the support scheme for victims.[79]

Again, the problems faced by Newcastle's Bengalis have also been discussed with regard to other areas in Britain, particularly the borough of Tower Hamlets in East London which has long been home to a large Bangladeshi community. These have included problems paying rent and heating costs, local council attempts at combatting racist violence, such as removing racist graffiti and evicting perpetrators, and lack of confidence on behalf of Bengalis in the police to adequately address the issues.[80] During the mid-1980s, Newcastle's Housing Committee itself went so far as to look into the situation amongst Bengalis in London and concluded that, whilst the problems they encountered in London were certainly on a greater scale, there were nevertheless themes and factors that were relevant to Newcastle.[81]

---

[78] See TWAS, MD.NC/162/1, 'Housing the Bengali community in the inner West End', 24 May 1984, p. 2; TWAS, MD.NC/162/1, 'Racial harassment in Newcastle', 10 October 1984, pp. 2–5; TWAS, MD.NC/162/1, Extract from minutes of Housing Committee of 10th October 1984, 'Racial harassment in Newcastle', p. 1; TWAS, MD.NC/162/2, City of Newcastle upon Tyne, notes of case conference on racial harassment, 23 September 1985; and TWAS, MD.NC/162/2, City of Newcastle upon Tyne, notes of a case conference re racial harassment, 7 October 1985.

[79] See TWAS, MD.NC/162/1, 'Extract from minutes of the Gosforth Area Housing Sub-Committee of 17th October 1984'; and TWAS, MD.NC/162/1, 'Extract from minutes of Walker Area Housing Sub-Committee of 23rd October 1984'.

[80] See Deborah Phillips, 'The rhetoric of anti-racism in public housing allocation', in Peter Jackson (ed.), *Race and Racism: Essays in Social Geography* (London, 1987), p. 194. For an insight into Bangladeshi council estate experiences, see also Anne J. Kershen, *Strangers, Aliens and Asians: Huguenots, Jews and Bangladeshis in Spitalfields 1660–2000* (London, 2005).

[81] See TWAS, MD.NC/162/1, 'Racial harassment in Newcastle', 10 October 1984, Appendix 1.

Another area to which Newcastle's local authority awarded a significant amount of attention from the mid-1980s onwards was ethnic minorities' access to council housing. From the 1970s, but especially during the 1980s and into the 1990s, local authorities across Britain came under criticism for granting ethnic minorities poor-quality housing and properties that did not meet their housing needs, and for discriminating against them with regard to waiting times and transfers.[82] In some ways, it appears as though Newcastle's council was more progressive and forward-thinking than many. In February 1984, the city's Housing Management Committee reviewed a report on race and council housing in the London borough of Hackney, which was the result of an investigation carried out by the Commission for Racial Equality that had been launched in May 1978.[83] Hackney was selected as a borough that was representative, meaning that the findings were thought to be applicable and relevant to local authorities across Britain. The study stemmed from the widespread pattern of ethnic minority communities being over-represented on poor-quality estates and having to wait a comparatively longer period of time to be rehoused. The aim of the investigation was to identify the reasons for these housing traits. It concluded that ethnic minority applicants did not perform as well within the council's housing allocation system as their white counterparts in that they received housing of poorer quality. As a result of the fact that other possible contributing factors, such as family size and housing preference, were considered and dismissed, the report deduced that the local council had indeed practised unlawful discrimination.[84]

Based on these findings, the Commission for Racial Equality made a number of recommendations, which Newcastle City Council found useful. These included the keeping and monitoring of ethnic records, visiting applicants at home, training staff in the housing requirements and patterns of ethnic minorities, and establishing a structured alloca-

[82] See John Parker and Keith Dugmore, *Colour and the Allocation of GLC Housing* (London, 1976); Deborah Phillips, *Monitoring of the Experimental Allocation Scheme for GLC Properties in Tower Hamlets* (London, 1984); and Valerie Karn and Deborah Phillips, 'Race and ethnicity in housing: A diversity of experience', in Tessa Blackstone, Bhikhu Parekh and Peter Sanders (eds), *Race Relations in Britain: A Developing Agenda* (London, 1998), p. 147.

[83] TWAS, MD.NC/162/1, City of Newcastle upon Tyne Housing Management Committee, 'Race and council housing in Hackney – report of a formal investigation by the Commission for Racial Equality', 8 February 1984.

[84] Ibid., pp. 1–2.

tion process. At the time of the report, Newcastle's local authority had already implemented these exact measures to one point or another. It was using an application form that requested information on the ethnic origins of applicants for the purpose of monitoring; it carried out home visits; some staff training had been put into effect; and it was expected that a planned computerised lettings system was going to ensure that allocations were made based on applicants' choices and the score they were awarded under a points-based system for assessing housing needs. Overall, Newcastle's Housing Management Committee, whilst recognising that further measures and developments were needed, viewed itself as having a better structured and more advanced council housing allocation system with regard to ethnic minority communities than Hackney.[85] Yet it also recognised that the points scheme could not successfully cover all possibilities and circumstances, and that the system should thus not be so inflexible that particular cases could not be addressed effectively.[86]

Newcastle's local authority also suggested measures that would combat overcrowding and do more to recognise the fact that ethnic minority households tended to be comparatively larger as a result of a greater number of children and a tendency to live within extended families. Indeed these are two of the housing traits that have long dominated the literature on both South Asians and Muslims in Britain, and are issues that continued well into the 1990s in Newcastle.[87] These measures were proposed by Newcastle's Housing Committee in February 1985 and consisted of two suggested changes to the lettings policy that it hoped would make council housing more accessible and appropriate for ethnic minority families. Firstly, it was proposed that the number of points allocated to couples with children be enhanced to more fairly reflect the number of bedrooms needed. At the time, the recognised levels of overcrowding were the same for a couple with one child as for a couple with two children under the age of ten or two

[85] Ibid., pp. 2–3.
[86] See TWAS, MD.NC/162/1, City of Newcastle upon Tyne Housing Committee, 'Officer discretion in the allocation of housing', 8 May 1985, p. 1.
[87] See Muhammad Anwar, *Between Cultures: Continuity and Change in the Lives of Young Asians* (London, 1998), pp. 103–6; Malcolm Harrison and Cathy Davis, *Housing, Social Policy and Difference: Disability, Ethnicity, Gender and Housing* (Bristol, 2001), p. 145; and The Commission on the Future of Multi-Ethnic Britain, *The Parekh Report*, p. 86. For Newcastle, see Cameron and Field, *Housing and the Black Population of West Newcastle*, pp. 2–3.

children of the same sex under the age of sixteen. It was thought that overcrowding was more severe for the couple with two children and that the points scheme should be amended to adequately reflect that. Secondly, there was to be a greater recognition on behalf of the council regarding the tendency amongst ethnic minority families, especially those of South Asian origin, for several generations to want to live together. The problem was often that the properties available in the public sector were simply not sizeable enough to accommodate such large families. The proposal was for families in this situation to be offered two properties that were situated in very close proximity to each other. Although it was uncommon for two neighbouring properties to become available at the same time, it was suggested that families could move in stages.[88]

Table 2.1: Characteristics and issues relating to council housing in Newcastle amongst whites, Chinese, South Asians and Afro-Caribbeans, 1986 (percentage reporting each issue)

	Whites	Chinese	South Asians	Afro-Caribbeans
Overcrowding	35	55	56	67
Separation	4	0	5.5	6.6
Threat of homelessness	13	15	13	42
Use of licence agreements	12	20	28	9
Transfer requests	27	10	11	13

Source: TWAS, MD.NC/162/2, 'Monitoring equal opportunity of access to council housing', April 1986, pp. 3–5.

An April 1986 report offered a further insight into the housing trends and needs of Newcastle's ethnic minority communities, and contained some relevant statistics regarding their situation in council housing (see Table 2.1).[89] Firstly, there were very few members of ethnic minorities who were on the waiting list for council housing. Only approximately 1.5 per cent of those on the waiting list were of an ethnic minority background and, of those, around 0.8 per cent were South Asian. This small percentage is most likely a reflection of the

---

[88] TWAS, MD.NC/162/1, City of Newcastle upon Tyne Housing Committee, 'Lettings policy', 14 February 1985, pp. 1–2.
[89] TWAS, MD.NC/162/2, City of Newcastle upon Tyne Race Equality Sub-Committee, 'Monitoring equal opportunity of access to council housing', April 1986.

trend for Indian and Pakistani migrants especially to prefer home ownership, a trait that emerged in Newcastle as throughout Britain.[90] Secondly, the report exposed a clear difference in the levels of overcrowding endured by white and ethnic minority tenants. Whilst 35 per cent of whites suffered from overcrowding, this figure stood at 55 per cent for Chinese, 56 per cent for South Asians and 67 per cent for Afro-Caribbeans. Thirdly, some ethnic minority groups appeared to experience higher levels of separation whilst waiting to be re-housed. 4 per cent of whites were separated from their partners and families, compared with 5.5 per cent of South Asians and 6.6 per cent of Afro-Caribbeans.[91]

Fourthly, the difference between whites and ethnic minority groups were again seen with regard to homelessness and insecurity. 13 per cent of whites had been threatened with homelessness compared to 42 per cent of Afro-Caribbeans. However, the figure amongst South Asians was also only 13 per cent. South Asians also stood out amongst all other groups regarding their use of licence agreements for accommodation. A licence agreement was often less binding than a lease. It was simpler to establish, and was often associated with more informal arrangements with family and friends. 28 per cent of them used licence agreements compared with 9 per cent of Afro-Caribbeans, 12 per cent of whites and 20 per cent of Chinese. As the report points out, this was most probably the consequence of South Asians using family and friends for temporary accommodation more than other ethnic minority communities. With regard to transfer requests, white tenants were far more likely to ask for transfers than migrant groups. Whilst the figure stood at 27 per cent amongst whites, it was only 13 per cent amongst Afro-Caribbeans, 11 per cent amongst South Asians and 10 per cent amongst Chinese. The report is correct to suggest that one possible explanation for this is that whites are more likely to be in council tenancies already. However, another reason for the comparatively lower rates of transfer requests amongst ethnic minority communities was undoubtedly their overwhelming preference to live within their own communities, a pattern that has long been present in Newcastle and across Britain amongst South Asians, and Muslims more specifically.[92] As will be further discussed, ethnic minorities in Newcastle

[90] See Karn and Phillips, 'Race and ethnicity in housing'.
[91] TWAS, MD.NC/162/2, 'Monitoring equal opportunity of access to council housing', April 1986, pp. 2–4.
[92] See Jane Lakey, 'Neighbourhoods and housing', in Tariq Modood *et al.* (eds), *Ethnic Minorities in Britain: Diversity and Disadvantage* (London, 1997) p.190; and Ansari, *'The Infidel Within'*, pp. 213–14.

have often chosen to remain in a certain property or neighbourhood despite poor housing conditions and racial harassment. Overall, despite the report drawing on only a small sample, it nevertheless offered an insight into the housing conditions and experiences of those of Newcastle's ethnic minorities who lived in local authority housing. It confirmed that ethnic minorities were more likely to experience poor housing circumstances.[93]

Newcastle's council continued to monitor the equality in opportunity of access to council housing into the mid- to late 1990s. As well as the compilation of regular statistical reports, Newcastle's Housing Department also put other measures into practice, including using equal opportunity indicators as part of policy reviews, training programmes and working with local community groups on schemes regarding housing management and investment. The first report addressed the Housing Department's ability to satisfy ethnic minority applicants' preference for both locality and property type. Overall, it concluded that the procedures in place for rehousing in the neighbourhood and dwelling of choice were not discriminating against ethnic minority households.[94]

A further area of focus was racial harassment. Whilst during the mid-1980s this was a topic that had been largely addressed with regard to the city's Bengali community, it was discussed from the point of view of ethnic minorities more widely during the 1990s. During the early 1990s, racial harassment was believed to be on the rise, and the role it played in the housing experiences and practices of ethnic minorities was increasingly emphasised.[95] In August and September 1990, an interview survey was carried out amongst 223 ethnic minority residents in five of Newcastle's wards. These wards were chosen because their populations included a percentage of ethnic minorities that was higher than the 3 per cent city average. They were Elswick (15 per cent), Wingrove (8 per cent), Moorside (7 per cent), Jesmond (4 per cent) and Heaton (4 per cent). The research conducted in these areas was complemented by a number of interviews with Afro-Caribbeans in the city. Racial harassment was a key area of the survey and the overall aim was

[93] TWAS, MD.NC/162/2, 'Monitoring equal opportunity of access to council housing', April 1986, pp. 4–6.
[94] See TWAS, MD.NC/614/3, City of Newcastle upon Tyne Tenants Consultation Sub-Committee, 'Monitoring equality of opportunity in access to council housing: Allocating council housing to different ethnic groups', February 1997.
[95] See Ratcliffe, '"Race", housing and the city', p. 91.

to establish the level, extent and nature of racial harassment experienced by the city's ethnic minority communities.[96] Whilst the cases of racism discussed were not particular to the housing sector, though many did consist of attacks against property, they nevertheless offered an insight into the problems and racial attacks experienced in the streets at a neighbourhood level. As was argued by Stuart Cameron in his study on the West End of Newcastle, South Asian residents were often more concerned with neighbourhood issues than with the quality of their individual homes. These included racial harassment as well as crime and security.[97]

The results of the interview survey showed that racial harassment was a widespread problem, with 58 per cent of respondents having been victims at some point. Out of the South Asians, 34 per cent were Bangladeshi, 29 per cent were Pakistani, 10 per cent were Indian and 27 per cent were a mixture.[98] Whilst racial harassment affected members of ethnic minorities of all ages, over half of the victims were aged between 16 and 24, and both males and females seemed to be targeted. With regard to the offenders, 95 per cent of respondents reported that they were white, a large proportion were also between the ages of 16 and 24, and most were male, although females were also involved on occasion. Most respondents had experienced racial harassment within their own wards and neighbourhoods, with 76 per cent stating that it had taken place in the street. Incidents were also reported as being common on buses and on the way to mosque.[99]

Overall, almost 50 per cent of respondents stated that either themselves, family members of friends had suffered what were referred to as serious incidents of racial harassment. The majority of cases that fell into this category consisted of verbal abuse and threats, and bodily harm, yet some had experienced broken windows, bullying, vandalism, robbery, being stoned in the street, and arson, one instance of which had resulted in a fatality.[100] These are the same types of incidents that

---

[96] See Newcastle City Library, L325, City of Newcastle upon Tyne Racial Equality Sub-Committee, 'Minority Ethnic Communities Survey 1990', 21 November 1990, pp. 1–2.
[97] Cameron, 'Ethnic minority housing needs and diversity in an area of low housing demand', p. 1434.
[98] Newcastle City Library, L325, 'Minority Ethnic Communities Survey 1990', 21 November 1990, pp. 1, 12.
[99] Ibid., pp. 4–5.
[100] Ibid., pp. 6–7.

have been recorded elsewhere in Britain.[101] Racial harassment in the form of attacks on property was the third most common type after having to walk through areas with offensive graffiti, and being subjected to personal abuse and insults. In both Elswick and Moorside, for example, almost 50 per cent of respondents had experienced some type of damage to or attack on their properties compared to a ward average of 38.5 per cent. Furthermore, a large proportion of those respondents who had suffered attacks to their properties stated that these occurred a few times a year, whilst some experienced such incidents as often as anywhere between once a month and almost daily.[102]

There were a variety of ways in which the victims reacted to the racial harassment they endured. Around 50 per cent of respondents chose to simply ignore it. A few of the South Asian female respondents stated that they would only go out when it was absolutely essential and that they would always do so in small groups. There were also a number of security measures that some of the respondents had implemented in an attempt to prevent further incidents from taking place. These included the using of security windows, door locks and letter box protection, as well as cooperating with neighbours and always walking in groups. Only 19 per cent of respondents said that they always reported incidents of racial harassment to the police, 7 per cent stated that whether they did or not depended on the severity of the incident and 20 per cent never contacted the police about such occurrences. When asked why they had not always contacted the police, the common replies given were that the incidents had not been serious enough, and that the police were inefficient, uncooperative and did not do enough to deal with reported cases of racial harassment.[103] This general unwillingness to report incidents of racial harassment against property and in neighbourhoods and the lack of faith in the police mirrored that discussed in the last chapter with regard to ethnic minority businesses. Furthermore, these are traits that have been widely documented in the literature alongside the perception that there

---

[101] See Human Rights Watch, *Racist Violence in the United Kingdom* (London, 1997); and Colin Webster, 'England and Wales', in John Winterdyk and Georgios Antonopoulos (eds), *Racist Victimization: International Reflections and Perspectives* (Aldershot, 2008), pp. 67–88.
[102] Newcastle City Library, L325, 'Minority Ethnic Communities Survey 1990', 21 November 1990, pp. 3–4.
[103] Ibid., pp. 7, 9, 11.

has been a general failure on British council estates to address racial harassment effectively.[104]

Indeed there appeared to be an overall dissatisfaction with the types of support victims of racial harassment were offered. Only 33 per cent were satisfied with the police, and 12 per cent and 15 per cent with local community organisations and Newcastle City Council respectively. Common perceptions were that the police took too long to see to reported incidents, that they needed to be awarded more power to deal with the perpetrators and that they were unsympathetic towards ethnic minority communities. There was also a fairly widespread view that Newcastle City Council did not do enough to address racial harassment. When asked what might be done to better tackle such problems, almost 60 per cent of respondents felt that more action was needed on behalf of the police, with some suggesting that there should be more regular police patrols in certain areas, and that the police should act more quickly and take harsher action against the perpetrators. Respondents also proposed that the council do more to offer support to victims of racial harassment. Other suggestions included educating young people on how to respect different communities, and the city's ethnic minority communities coming together to found projects and organisations that address such issues.[105] The general perception that not enough was being done to address racial harassment was well documented for Britain more widely.[106]

The report also offered a comparison between racial harassment in Newcastle and that in Cleveland, Sheffield and Waltham Forest in north-east London. The types of racial harassment experienced by ethnic minorities in Newcastle differed in a few ways. Firstly, Newcastle's migrant communities experienced far more attacks on their property. 45 per cent of respondents had experienced this compared to only 25 per cent, 16 per cent and 14 per cent in Sheffield, Cleveland and Waltham Forest respectively. Furthermore, neighbourhoods also seemed to play more of a role in Newcastle's racial harassment, with 76 per cent of respondents having experienced such

[104] See Commission for Racial Equality, *Living in Terror: A Report on Racial Violence and Harassment in Housing* (London, 1987); and Phillips, 'The rhetoric of anti-racism in public housing allocation', p. 194.

[105] Newcastle City Library, L325, 'Minority Ethnic Communities Survey 1990', 21 November 1990, pp. 10–11, 19.

[106] See Norman Ginsburg, 'Racism and housing: Concepts and reality', in Peter Braham, Ali Rattansi and Richard Skellington (eds), *Racism and Antiracism: Inequalities, Opportunities and Policies* (London, 1992), pp. 123–7.

incidents in the street compared with only 54 per cent and 22 per cent in Sheffield and Waltham Forest respectively, and 28 per cent nationally. Further comparisons showed that about an average share of Newcastle's ethnic minority respondents had experienced personal abuse or insults and threatening behaviour, and fewer had suffered bodily harm. Schools also appeared to be a more common place for racial harassment in Newcastle and this will be further developed in the following chapter on education.[107]

Some of the key observations and conclusions the report identified were that racial harassment was undoubtedly a widespread and common experience for ethnic minority communities living in Newcastle and that this was seen by some as an inherent part of daily life in Britain; victims lived in constant fear, often not even feeling safe in their own homes; cases of racial harassment were often so frequent that they went unreported; and there was a general lack of faith in the manner in which both the police and the council dealt with such incidents. This last point was especially seen in the fact that some members of the city's ethnic minority communities, mostly those of an Afro-Caribbean background, refused to partake in the survey because they lacked an overall confidence in the council. With regard to recommendations, the report called for more victim support and police action. The Racial Equality Sub-Committee also intended to publicise and circulate the report amongst the local community, the media and relevant local organisations. Furthermore, it proposed a consultation with the police regarding the findings the survey and report had uncovered, with the aim of addressing and rectifying the widespread discontent and frustration with the force amongst ethnic minorities. It was also hoped that the council would soon be in a position to do more to both combat racial harassment and support victims.[108]

Yet despite the identification of key problems and patterns regarding racial harassment, and potential measures to address them, very little appears to have changed in the following years. When the survey was repeated in 1995, it found that no significant developments had taken place.[109] Whilst an improvement had been witnessed in some parts of

[107] Newcastle City Library, L325, 'Minority Ethnic Communities Survey 1990', 21 November 1990, pp. 21–2.
[108] Ibid., pp. 15–16, 35.
[109] Chief Executive's Department, Newcastle City Council, *Update on Racial Harassment in Newcastle* (Newcastle, 1995). See also See TWAS, MD.NC/614/1, Racial Equality Working Group 18 January 1995-2

the city, the situation had actually deteriorated in others, with Elswick, Heaton and Wingrove being the most affected areas and Heaton having overtaken Moorside to now be in the top three areas with the most racial incidents. Overall, half of the city's black and Asian residents reported experiencing harassment, with one in twenty suffering personal insults or abuse on almost a daily basis. Furthermore, over one-third of those surveyed stated that either they themselves or a member of their families had experienced a serious incident. In Wingrove and Moorside, one in ten people reported that racial harassment was a regular occurrence, a statistic that in Elswick increased to one in five. The percentage of respondents who experienced attacks on their properties decreased in all wards between 1990 and 1995 except in Elswick, where it increased from 52 per cent to 68 per cent. Interestingly, the survey report suggested a correlation between attacks on property and type of tenure, and proposed that members of ethnic minorities were more likely to suffer attacks on their properties if they lived in rented accommodation than if they were owner-occupiers.[110] This pattern fits into wider claims that a large proportion of incidents of racial harassment took place on council estates.[111]

Again, it has not just been attacks on individual properties that have played a role in ethnic minorities' experiences in the housing sector, but also incidents of racial harassment that have taken place on local streets and in immediate neighbourhoods. In the 1995 survey, the 'local street' was the most common place for harassment to occur. 86 per cent of respondents reported that they had experienced racial harassment in or around their homes and especially in the street. Moreover, the number of victims reporting incidents of racial harassment had actually decreased. Overall, respondents felt that more action and assistance was needed from both Newcastle City Council and the police. Yet some members of the city's ethnic minority communities still felt that racism was an integral part of life in Newcastle and that there was very little that could be done to combat it.[112]

November 1995, Racial Equality Working Group, 'Racial harassment in Newcastle', 29 June 1995, Appendix A, p. 3.

[110] Chief Executive's Department, *Update on Racial Harassment in Newcastle*, pp. 2–8.

[111] See Karn and Phillips, 'Race and ethnicity in housing', p. 149; and Rafaela M. Dancygier, *Immigration and Conflict in Europe* (Cambridge, 2010), pp. 151–3.

[112] Chief Executive's Department, *Update on Racial Harassment in Newcastle*, pp. 15, 19–21.

Overall, the housing sector has developed very differently to that of employment with regard to Newcastle's Muslim ethnic minorities. Whilst Newcastle's council promoted entrepreneurship, a practice often perceived as a way to combat social exclusion, minorities' housing patterns have frequently been the source of local authority concern and anxiety. Indeed an examination of the city's Muslim migrants' post-war housing traits and experiences does not lead to the same level of promising and hopeful conclusions. This sector has also been riddled with widespread racial harassment and disadvantage yet, unlike ethnic minority entrepreneurship, it has rarely acted as a catalyst for positive race relations and multiculturalism. Nevertheless, Newcastle's Muslim ethnic minorities' housing careers have also been largely shaped by aspirations, self-determination and a series of conscious choices. This is seen in that, for many, owner-occupation was an ambition from the outset.

As has tended to be the case throughout Britain, the Indian community has been the most successful, with the vast majority having achieved owner-occupation at a very early stage. Furthermore, many eventually left the West End for more prestigious neighbourhoods like those of Jesmond and Gosforth, and those that remain live largely in Fenham, the most popular area. The Pakistani community still overwhelmingly resides in the West End of the city, but has also succeeded in securing a presence in Fenham and largely enjoys owner-occupation. In Newcastle, as throughout Britain, the Bangladeshi community has been the exception amongst South Asians with regard to housing patterns. Whilst some have made the transition to owner-occupation and to better areas both within and outside the West End, many remain concentrated in council housing on the Bentinck Estate.[113] As a result of these ethnic disparities, one might assume that these communities have pursued completely different housing paths. Indeed, Stuart Cameron has concluded that neighbourhoods like Jesmond and Gosforth are 'white' areas that lack an ethnic identity. He described a district like Fenham as having a particular ethnic identity, but also being multicultural. Lastly, he referred to areas in Newcastle like the Bentinck Estate as having an ethnic identity that is defensive and tormented because these ethnic minorities have been excluded from other parts of the city either as a result of financial constraint or fear.[114]

[113] See Cameron, 'Ethnic minority housing needs and diversity in an area of low housing demand', pp. 1433–4.
[114] Ibid., pp. 1440, 1442. See also Frederick W. Boal, 'From undivided cities to undivided cities: Assimilation to ethnic cleansing', *Housing Studies*, 14:5 (1999), pp. 585–600.

Yet whilst the differences in housing tenure and neighbourhood choice cannot be denied, these Muslim ethnic minority communities have nevertheless all shared a strong desire for residential autonomy, and success in reaching and retaining their housing aims. This is perhaps not surprising regarding the Indian community because, being the least economically disadvantaged, it has always been in the strongest position to do so. However, amongst the Muslim minorities, the Pakistanis and Bangladeshis, this has certainly been more of an accomplishment. The Pakistani community has always forcefully rejected local authority housing despite Newcastle's West End having rows of empty, yet good-quality, council houses. Whilst over half of the city's Bangladeshi community has traditionally lived in council housing, it has largely refused to live outside of the Bentinck Estate, an estate which as a consequence is full and for which there is a waiting list. Over the years, it has invested a lot into the area and the estate has gradually become the hub of the Bangladeshi community.[115] Furthermore, a 2007 report concluded that when asked about their housing aspirations, owner-occupation was a popular answer amongst Bangladeshi respondents despite this not being a financially viable option for some. It also pointed out that, over the past few years, Bangladeshis have become increasingly willing to move into areas that have not traditionally been home to ethnic minorities.[116] This shows that residential mobility is a consideration, and that Bangladeshis will increasingly demonstrate traits and aspirations that Indians and Pakistanis displayed some time ago.

Moreover, as with their employment patterns, South Asian Muslims' residential preferences and autonomy have not been overshadowed by difficulties and disadvantage, such as overcrowding and racial harassment. On the contrary, as well as increasingly succeeding in securing their preferred type of housing tenure, they have also acquired properties in their chosen areas and neighbourhoods. For both Pakistanis and Bangladeshis, housing patterns have been shaped by a desire to live amongst their own communities. They have traditionally wanted to be close to family and friends, live in areas where they feel safe, and have ethnic and religious necessities nearby such as mosques, community

---

[115] See Cameron, 'Ethnic minority housing needs and diversity in an area of low housing demand'.
[116] See Robinson, Reeve, Casey and Goudie, *Minority Ethnic Residential Experiences and Requirements in the Bridging NewcastleGateshead Area*, pp. 40, 84.

centres and specialist shops. Overall, the neighbourhood has been far more important than individual properties in making housing choices.[117] This has often meant that Newcastle's local authority's comparatively progressive approach to and understanding of the city's ethnic minorities' housing difficulties have been disregarded as Muslim migrants have 'gone it alone'. In doing so, they have demonstrated widespread levels of self-sufficiency and independence that render Davies and Taylor's conclusions still applicable.

As with the employment sector, Newcastle's Muslim immigrants are succeeding as a result of their own self-determination, but also due to a certain understanding of the local housing market and the ability to manipulate it to serve their needs. Whether it was Pakistanis securing owner-occupation during the 1960s and purchasing multiple properties as part of their entrepreneurial portfolios or Bangladeshis of the 1970s and 1980s placing their ethnic and religious identities onto the Bentinck Estate, Muslim migrants' choice has prevailed. Whilst they have historically portrayed a preference for self-sufficiency either in the form of owner-occupation or ethnic neighbourhoods, this has not necessarily been the consequence of failed integration. Whilst ethnic minorities, especially those of Bangladeshi origin, have undoubtedly suffered constraints within the local housing sector, they have nevertheless asserted their own preferences and managed to shape their own housing careers. This study hopes to build upon the more positive aspects of Muslim migrants' housing experiences and assert that residential segregation should not automatically be equated with discrimination, disadvantage and a lack of integration.

Bremen

Bremen's post-war immigrant communities suffered a shortage of housing from the outset. During the initial guest-worker years, single male workers were often housed on the same factory grounds as Second World War forced labourers and prisoners. This housing deficiency was then accentuated once family reunification began to take place, causing municipal housing authorities to take possession of cheap hotels and hostels, transform military barracks into residential units, and build tower block housing on the northern and eastern

---

[117] Cameron, 'Ethnic minority housing needs and diversity in an area of low housing demand', pp. 1434–6; and Cameron and Field, 'Community, ethnicity and neighbourhood', p. 838.

outskirts of the city. Traditionally, it has been in this type of housing, as well as in that located in more central neighbourhoods near the harbour and industrial areas, that immigrants have tended to live.[118] Bremen is not home to US-style ghettoes nor to a district that compares to Kreuzberg in Berlin, which is often referred to as a 'Turkish ghetto' or 'Little Istanbul', and in which Turks currently constitute around 35 per cent of the district's population.[119]

Yet ethnic minority clustering has nevertheless taken place. By the early 1990s, Industriehäfen, or the industrial harbour district, was over 39 per cent migrant. Older residential sub-districts, such as Lindenhof in Gröpelingen to the west of the city and Ostertor in the downtown area called Das Viertel, experienced ethnic minority concentration from the 1970s and continue to do so. Yet the 1980s witnessed the beginning of an increase in the number of ethnic minorities living in the social housing developments in areas on the outskirts of the city, such as Tenever to the east and Grohn to the north, which were around 20 per cent migrant by the early 1990s. It is these areas in Bremen that also experience high levels of social disadvantage.[120]

As well as suffering from a shortage of dwellings, Bremen's housing sector was also hit hard by the industrial crisis it experienced during the 1970s, 1980s and into the 1990s. As well as causing widespread unemployment, the deindustrialisation that took place during these decades witnessed the gradual decline of many of Bremen's traditional working-class neighbourhoods, such as Gröpelingen, which had already become the area in which a significant portion of the city's migrants had settled. This district is renowned for being the hub of the city's Turkish community. Having been home to the city's industrial harbour, the shipbuilding giant, AG Weser, and the Klöckner steel- and metalworks, Gröpelingen has experienced Turkish settlement since the beginning of the 1960s and the populations of some of its sub-districts are as high as 23 per cent Turkish. As well as being close to the

---

[118] See Ireland, *Becoming Europe*, p. 87; and Andreas Farwick, 'Behindern ethnisch geprägte Wohnquartiere die Eingliederung von Migranten?', in Olaf Schnur (ed.), *Quartiersforschung: zwischen Theorie und Praxis* (Wiesbaden, 2008), p. 211.

[119] See Ruth Mandel, 'A place of their own: Contesting spaces and defining places in Berlin's migrant community', in Barbara Daly Metcalf (ed.), *Making Muslim Space in North America and Europe* (Berkeley CA, 1996), p. 149; and Nabil Echchaibi, *Voicing Diasporas: Ethnic Radio in Paris and Berlin between Cultural Renewal and Retention* (Lanham MD, 2011), p. 144.

[120] See Ireland, *Becoming Europe*, pp. 87–8.

workplace, family and friends, Gröpelingen was also appealing to Turkish migrants because of the availability of housing caused by the increasing outflow of the local German population. This was largely the result of the growing number of job losses caused by the economic structural change, which reached its climax with the closure of AG Weser in 1983. This marked a turning point for the district in general, which came to be associated with unemployment, social grievances and urban decay.[121] Furthermore, the economic crisis also caused some housing estates, such as Osterholz-Tenever on the city's eastern periphery, to become 'problem areas' as they increasingly became home to poorer families, including many of immigrant origin.[122] Thus, in Bremen more than in Newcastle, economic downturn has had clear consequences for ethnic minority housing.

Yet the experiences of Muslim migrants in Bremen during the postwar period have not been dictated by discrimination and disadvantage despite the initial years having been characterised by the typical substandard living conditions that the guest-worker system has become renowned for. As in Newcastle, what have since developed are neighbourhoods that have been shaped by Muslim minorities with the specific aim of catering for their ethnic, cultural and religious needs.[123] Furthermore, despite suffering difficulties and prejudice, Bremen's Muslim migrants have increasingly succeeded in achieving their residential aims and ambitions. Since their settlement, Bremen's local authority has recognised the importance of the housing sector. Alongside the workplace, the neighbourhood became a key focus point in the debate on the city's ethnic minorities.

During the 1980s, this was witnessed in the form of district councils, which were involved in city administration and in which immigrants took part. The city also supported *Kulturladen* or 'culture shops' and cultural centres, which promoted and enabled cooperation between the administration and immigrant associations.[124] During the late 1980s

[121] See Farwick, 'Behindern ethnisch geprägte Wohnquartiere die Eingliederung von Migranten?', pp. 211–12; Andreas Farwick, *Segregation und Eingliederung: Zum Einfluss der räumlichen Konzentration von Zuwanderern auf den Eingliederungsprozess* (Wiesbaden, 2009), pp. 204–6; and Power, Plöger and Winkler, *Phoenix Cities*, p. 135.
[122] See Power, Plöger and Winkler, *Phoenix Cities*, p. 135.
[123] See Andreas Heinrichs, *Von Istanbul nach Gröpelingen – Alltag in der Lindenhofstraße: Fotoausstellung über die Einwanderung und das Leben in Bremen-Gröpelingen* (Kulturladen Gröpelingen, 1992).
[124] See Ireland, *Becoming Europe*, p. 92.

and into the mid-1990s, a redevelopment project took place in areas of Gröpelingen in an attempt to reverse the process of deterioration and decay.[125] The 1990s saw Bremen invest in its neighbourhoods and the funds it received to combat housing market problems were channelled specifically into Osterholz-Tenever, with the aim of reducing housing discrimination and improving the quality of life for residents in this area. The neighbourhood continued to be the focus of integration projects into the late 1990s and early 2000s.[126] Furthermore, the housing sector has always been awarded a firm position in the Bremen government's integration policies, from the ground-breaking and unprecedented 1979 *Konzeption* to its integration guidelines of the 2000s.[127] Overall, whilst often displaying a sense of uncertainty about the future of the city's ethnic minorities, Bremen's government recognised that their housing needs would need to be catered for in the long term.

The 1960s and 1970s: the guest-worker years

As has been recognised in the historiography, it was newspaper reports about guest-workers' living conditions, not their working environments, that first captured the interest of the German public. Furthermore, because employers were able to cut corners with their provision of accommodation and guest-workers were initially satisfied with low-quality and cheap housing as they still perceived their stay in Germany to be temporary, their living conditions soon became the most noticeable sign of their underprivileged status.[128] Yet this well-established account does not appear to adequately reflect the situation in Bremen. During the 1960s and 1970s, a significant amount of attention was awarded to guest-workers' housing in the city. As was

[125] See Farwick, *Segregation und Eingliederung*, p. 206.
[126] See Ireland, *Becoming Europe*, pp. 95–6; and Power, Plöger and Winkler, *Phoenix Cities*, p. 142.
[127] See Der Senat der Freien Hansestadt Bremen, *Konzeption zur Integration der ausländischen Arbeitnehmer und ihrer Familienangehörigen im Lande Bremen* (June 1979), pp. 61–5; and Bremische Bürgerschaft Landtag 16. Wahlperiode, Drucksache 16/176, 'Mitteilung des Senats vom 9. März 2004. Konzeption zur Integration von Zuwanderern und Zuwanderinnen im Lande Bremen 2003 bis 2007, Grundsätze, Leitlinien und Handlungsempfehlungen für die bremische Integrationspolitik', 9 March 2004, p. 7.
[128] See Herbert and Hunn, 'Guest workers and policy on guest workers in the Federal Republic', pp. 200–1.

The housing sector

seen with regard to their working conditions, there may have been signs portraying uncertainty over the guest-workers' future, but there was also a clear awareness and consciousness concerning their accommodation needs, as well as a vibrant debate on the topic.

Archival documents exist regarding the accommodation that was provided by numerous companies in Bremen, including AG Weser, Bremer Vulkan, Bremer Woll-Kämmerei, the Klöckner steel- and metalworks, and the Bremen-Vegesacker Fischerei-Gesellschaft.[129] Government correspondence from as early as the beginning of the 1960s detailed the nationalities of each company's workers and the number of workers being accommodated. Many accommodation blocks had a shared common room and kitchen. Documents held at the Staatsarchiv Bremen also contain blueprints, plans and descriptions of the barracks, lists of names of the people who shared rooms, and information regarding companies' financial costs and planning, rent charges and the health of guest-workers.[130] Furthermore, both the positive and negative aspects of guest-worker accommodation captured the attention of the local press during the 1960s and 1970s.[131]

As explained in the last chapter, in many ways Bremen adhered to the more negative widespread and well-documented characteristics of the guest-worker system. This was also witnessed in the initial accommodation provision through the poor conditions that workers often had to endure. One letter of complaint written by a Turkish guest-worker to Bremer Vulkan's company director detailed the way Turkish workers were treated at the hands of the on-site German interpreter. Amongst other things, he bullied and intimidated them, forced them to buy certain products from him, like bread and meat, and instigated

---

[129] See also Leohold, *Die Kämmeristen*, pp. 49–55; and Panayotidis, *Griechen in Bremen*, pp. 148–52.

[130] See SB, 7,2121/1–714, Errichtung und Ausstattung von Unterkünften für ausländische Arbeiter 1961–1981; SB, 4,130/4–250, Orts- und Wohnungshygiene – Wohnunterkünfte für ausländische Arbeiter 1962–1975; SB, 4,123/1–976, Gesundheitliche Überwachung ausländischer Arbeitskräfte 1965–1966; SB, 4,29/2–1481, Wohnungen für ausländische Arbeitnehmer 1966–1974; SB, 7,2121/1–711; SB, 4,31/6–68, Gastarbeiterwohnungen an der Rablinghauser Landstraße in Rablinghausen 1970–1975; and SB, 4,124/3–692, Unterbringung von Ausländern 1972–1979.

[131] See 'Bessere Wohnungen für ausländische Arbeiter', *Weser Kurier* (7 November 1960); and 'Gastarbeiter – ab ins Getto. Behörden wollen 200 Portugiesen in menschenleerem Hafengebiet ansiedeln', *Weser Kurier* (7 August 1973).

social unrest within the barracks.[132] Other complaints amongst Turkish guest-workers at Vulkan included overcrowding, a lack of heating and hot water, bathroom leaks and noise.[133] More widely, criticism of company accommodation across Bremen was voiced regarding poor sanitary conditions, workers having to sleep on air mattresses on the floor, barracks being too small and poorly lit, and pipes freezing in the winter resulting in no water.[134] There was also a lot of discussion about a houseboat called 'Casa Marina' that acted as guest-worker accommodation, as well as about the well-being and segregation of its residents.[135] Furthermore, whilst the religion of the city's guest-workers did not play a significant role in discussion regarding their initial housing provision, Vulkan's intention to build a mosque was questioned and the notion that their religious affiliation should be catered for challenged.[136]

Yet as with their early employment experiences, there was also a much more positive and progressive side to the Bremen guest-workers' initial accommodation. There was an awareness regarding existing and potential problems and difficulties, lively discussion and debate on the topic, and a commitment to cater for their housing needs and, as with the employment sector, there was a continuous inflow of information regarding the accommodation of foreign workers elsewhere in Germany.[137] Furthermore, company accommodation in Bremen was subject to the same guidelines as that throughout Germany, which set out clear requirements regarding the space and conditions that workers should have allocated to them.[138]

---

[132] SB, 7,2121/1–712, anonymous letter dated 6 May 1975.
[133] See SB, 7,2121/1–712, 'Besprechung mit den Türken am 30.10.76'.
[134] SB, 4,130/4–250, Various.
[135] See SB, 4,13/4–122–10–02/14; '200 Portugiesen für die bremischen Häfen. Einstellung beschlossen – Wohnschiff wird gekauft', *Bremer Nachrichten* (6 September 1973); and 'Die Portugiesen ziehen jetzt ein', *Weser Kurier* (6 November 1973).
[136] See SB, 7,2121/1–712, a letter dated 28 December 1974.
[137] See SB, 4,124/3–694; SB, 4,29/2–1479, Wohnungen für ausländische Arbeitnehmer 1960–1964; SB, 4,29/2–1480, Wohnungen für ausländische Arbeitnehmer 1965; and SB, 4,13/4–122–10–02/7, Zuzug von Familienangehörigen ausländischer Arbeitnehmer Band 2 1965–1974.
[138] See SB, 4,92/2–382, Bauvorhaben 'Wätjens Park' (Wohnungen für die Beschäftigten des Bremer Vulkan) 1970–1990, 'Richtlinien für die Unterkünfte ausländischer Arbeitnehmer in der Bundesrepublik Deutschland'. See also Dancygier, *Immigration and Conflict in Europe*, p. 226.

There was also a fear that the building of guest-worker accommodation in certain parts of the city, such as Gröpelingen, might potentially further decrease the social status of those areas.[139] Furthermore, the aim was for guest-workers to receive the same standard of accommodation as their German counterparts, and there was a desire to avoid them experiencing isolation.[140] Overall, it was acknowledged that measures needed to be in place for the successful offering of guest-worker accommodation.[141] Bremer Vulkan arranged cinema provision for its guest-workers and, for its Muslim employees, prayer rooms in some of the barracks and a dayroom that was made available especially during Ramadan.[142] The conversion of barrack rooms into prayer rooms was not an uncommon practice in Germany and these were referred to as *Hinterhof Moscheen* or 'backyard mosques'.[143]

There was also concern expressed over the length of time that guest-workers remained in company accommodation and attempts were made to help guest-workers find suitable properties on the local housing market. Because landlords were often sceptical about letting their properties to foreign workers, Bremer Vulkan would often rent them in the company's name.[144] Overall, whilst it was recognised that a concentration of foreigners in certain districts of the city could not be avoided, it was stressed that ghettoes were not forming in the city.[145] Furthermore, the residential integration of guest-workers was awarded a firm place on Bremen's political agenda, with the mayor stressing that the city was putting provisions in place with regard to their housing, and that mixed neighbourhoods of Germans and foreigners were

[139] See SB, 4,31/6–69, Gastarbeiterwohnungen am Halmerweg in Gröpelingen 1971, a letter from Bremer Treuhand to the Senator für das Bauwesen dated 13 April 1971.
[140] See SB, 4,29/2–1481, 'Protokoll über die Besichtigung des Unterkunftsgebäudes für Gastarbeiter der Aktiengesellschaft Weser in Bremen-Burg am 28. April 1971'.
[141] Ibid.; and SB, 4,29/2–1481, a letter from the Senator für Arbeit to the Senator für das Bauwesen dated 4 August 1971.
[142] See SB, 7,2121/1–712, a Bremer Vulkan report entitled 'Kinoveranstaltungen für unsere türkischen Mitarbeiter' and dated 2 July 1974; and SB, 7,2121/1–712, a Bremer Vulkan report entitled 'Bethaus für türkische Kollegen' and dated 31 January 1974.
[143] See Abadan-Unat, *Turks in Europe*, p. 125
[144] See SB, 4,29/2–1481, 'Protokoll über die Besichtigung des Unterkunftsgebäudes für Gastarbeiter der Aktiengesellschaft Weser in Bremen-Burg am 28. April 1971'; and SB, 7,2121/1–712, *Bremen Special* report.
[145] See SB, 4,124/3–644, a letter to the Senator für Arbeit dated 12 July 1973.

essential for achieving integration.[146] As with the pro-integration measures that were witnessed at this time with regard to the employment sector, those on housing also appear to have considered the long-term social consequences of the guest-worker system.

The Bremen local government's focus on ethnic minority housing continued throughout the 1970s and underwent a turning point towards the end of the decade. A September 1973 document portrayed the residential experiences of the city's foreign workers in a very positive light and stressed that reasonable housing and provisions were available for them. The document also emphasised that, unlike other German cities, Bremen was not home to 'problem areas' in which ethnic minorities were becoming increasingly concentrated and from which the local German population was increasingly moving out. In fact, there was a clear aim to avoid such segregation and ensure that migrants were distributed across the city.[147] Unlike in Berlin, Frankfurt and Munich, there were no areas in Bremen that during the 1970s were being referred to as 'Turkish ghettoes' or that had the accompanying social problems.[148]

Yet by the late 1970s, local government perception had changed. Whilst there was still a clear commitment in Bremen to provide ethnic minorities with the same housing opportunities as their German counterparts, there was also a recognition that residential clustering had started to take place. By this time, foreign workers and their families were becoming concentrated in areas of the city to which they had been attracted by cheaper rental prices, and proximity to their respective workplaces and ethnic communities, a pattern that was emerging throughout Germany.[149] In Bremen, these were areas like Hemelingen

---

[146] SB, 4,63/2N-284, undated interview with Mayor Hans Koschnick.

[147] Bremische Bürgerschaft Landtag 8. Wahlperiode, Drucksache 8/600, 'Antwort des Senats zur Anfrage der Fraktion der CDU vom 26. Juni 1973 (Drs. 8/566). Ausländische Arbeitnehmer', 12 September 1973, pp. 9–10.

[148] See Lale Yalçin-Heckmann, 'Negotiating identities: Media representations of different generations of Turkish migrants in Germany', in Deniz Kandiyoti and Ayşe Saktanber (eds), *Fragments of Culture: The Everyday of Modern Turkey* (London, 2002), p. 310; and Mandel, *Cosmopolitan Anxieties*, p. 146.

[149] See Philip L. Martin, *The Unfinished Story: Turkish Labour Migration to Western Europe, with Special Reference to the Federal Republic of Germany* (Geneva, 1991), p. 73; Leo Lucassen, 'Poles and Turks in the German Ruhr area: Similarities and differences', in Leo Lucassen, David Feldman and Jochen Oltmer (eds), *Paths of Integration: Migrants in Western Europe (1880–2004)* (Amsterdam, 2006), p. 32; and Schönwälder and Söhn, 'Immigrant settlement structures in Germany', p. 1450.

and Tenever in the east near Daimler-Benz and the Bremer Silberwarenfabrik (Bremen Silverware Factory); Gröpelingen, Lindenhof and Ohlenhof in the west near AG Weser; and Blumenthal and Aumund-Hammersbeck in the north near Bremer Vulkan and Bremer Woll-Kämmerei. Other parts of the city that gradually appealed to migrants as a result of the availability of affordable housing have included Blockdiek and Tenever in the east, Kattenturm in the South and Lüssum-Bockhorn in the north, all of which have become areas associated with both ethnic minorities and those at the bottom of Bremen's social hierarchy.[150] It was believed that this concentration would make integration more difficult, especially because these areas of the city that tended to attract migrants often suffered from social and cultural disadvantage.[151]

These settlement patterns constitute a key disparity between Bremen and Newcastle. Although South Asian Muslims in Newcastle have also historically become clustered into certain districts of the city, sometimes in dwellings that suffered from overcrowding and structural problems, the attraction to these areas has been the result of a pursuit of affordable housing and a desire to live amongst people of similar ethnic and religious backgrounds. Yet Bremen's Turkish Muslims tended to initially settle in districts in which their employers were based when first venturing onto the city's housing market and only later did other factors start to have a widespread influence on their housing choices. Whilst many of the key areas of ethnic minority settlement, such as Ostertor and Lindenhof, kept hold of large numbers of migrants, the 1980s witnessed many Turks and other ethnic groups being drawn towards the large social housing developments on the outskirts of the city, such as Tenever and Grohn.[152] On the whole, Turks in Bremen have experienced a more delayed and rigid development, with their residential patterns showing signs of constraint and dependency well into the 1990s. In contrast, in Newcastle, Indian, Pakistani and Bangladeshi streets and neighbourhoods emerged more organically from the outset, with many immigrants having succeeded in

---

[150] See Freie Hansestadt Bremen *Statistische Monatsberichte*, 'Die Segregation der ausländischen Bevölkerung in Bremen', 35. Jahrgang, October 1983, p. 248; and Freie Hansestadt Bremen *Statistische Monatsberichte*, 'Ausländer nach Ortsteilen der Stadt Bremen', 37. Jahrgang, October 1985, pp. 146–8.

[151] See Bremische Bürgerschaft Landtag 9. Wahlperiode, Drucksache 9/1061, 'Kleine Anfrage der Fraktion der FDP vom 2. April 1979. Ausländer im Lande Bremen', pp. 4–5.

[152] See Ireland, *Becoming Europe*, pp. 87–8.

Table 2.2: Districts in Bremen in which the ethnic minority population constituted a minimum of 6 per cent, April 1977

District	Percentage
Mitte	11.6%
Gröpelingen	11.4%
Östliche Vorstadt	9.2%
Neustadt	8.7%
Blumenthal	8.5%
Vegesack	8.3%
Hemelingen	8.1%
Woltmershausen	7%
Walle	6.7%

Source: 'Die ausländische Wohnbevölkerung der Stadt Bremen', 31. Jahrgang, 1979, p. 127.

breaking out into the more prestigious areas of Gosforth and Jesmond during the 1980s and 1990s.

The link between area of employment and housing was seen in Bremen throughout the 1970s. Between June 1973 and April 1977, for example, the districts of Osterholz and Gröpelingen experienced an 89.3 per cent and 45.9 per cent increase in the size of their migrant populations respectively. Overall, by April 1977, there were three city districts that were over 9 per cent ethnic minority. These were Mitte (11.6 per cent), Gröpelingen (11.4 per cent) and Östliche Vorstadt (9.2 per cent). There were a further six for which this figure stood between 6 per cent and 9 per cent: Walle, Woltmershausen, Hemelingen, Vegesack, Blumenthal and Neustadt (see Table 2.2). The Häfen district was over 50 per cent migrant, but this figure is misleading because of its small total number of residents. By April 1977, over 70 per cent of the city's ethnic minorities were concentrated in eight districts and one-third lived in Gröpelingen (12.2 per cent), Neustadt (11.8 per cent) and Hemelingen (9.6 per cent). Turks constituted more than 40 per cent of the ethnic minority populations of ten districts. The areas with the most Turkish residents were Gröpelingen with around 2,950, Neustadt with approximately 2,450, and Hemelingen, Vegesack and Blumenthal with around 1,650 each.[153]

What gradually emerged in Bremen during the 1970s was an approach to migrant housing that paralleled that to ethnic minority

[153] See Freie Hansestadt Bremen *Statistische Monatsberichte*, 'Die ausländische Wohnbevölkerung der Stadt Bremen', 31. Jahrgang, 1979, pp. 126–8.

businesses. Firstly, there was a lack of extensive migrant-specific housing provision and there were no housing construction programmes devised especially for them. Instead the aim was for them to have the same opportunities as their German counterparts. Secondly, Bremen's government again reiterated its two-pronged approach in that whilst integration was to be pursued, this was not to equate to assimilation so that migrants could retain their own identity and a return to the homeland would remain a possibility.[154] As was the case regarding local measures on ethnic minority employment during the 1970s, those addressing housing also came together to form the 1979 *Konzeption zur Integration der ausländischen Arbeitnehmer und ihrer Familienangehörigen im Lande Bremen* (Concept of the Integration of Foreign Workers and their Family Members in the State of Bremen), Bremen's most ground-breaking set of policies and concepts on ethnic minorities to emerge during the post-war period. It highlighted a few difficulties and concerns regarding ethnic minority housing. Firstly, it reiterated that migrants were becoming increasingly residentially concentrated, albeit in a larger number of districts. Secondly, it stressed that they often found it difficult to qualify for social housing and that there was thus a tendency to live in privately rented accommodation. Furthermore, around 60 per cent of the public housing awarded to ethnic minorities was located in inner-city areas.[155]

The 1979 *Konzeption* also specified a list of measures, which were either planned or had already been implemented, and which aimed to offer migrants and their families adequate and reasonably priced housing, shield them from discrimination in the housing market, and present them with the same opportunities as their German counterparts. On the whole, these strategies were based around the notion that traditional guest-worker accommodation was becoming increasingly redundant and that, as migrants' stays in Bremen were becoming lengthier and the process of family reunification was taking place, the demand was increasingly for family homes. The city-state's government believed that newly built housing was often too expensive for migrants. Instead, the emphasis was placed on the renovation of older housing stock. It argued that the fixing up of old, strained and disadvantaged

[154] See Bremische Bürgerschaft Landtag 9. Wahlperiode, Drucksache 9/1061, 'Kleine Anfrage der Fraktion der FDP vom 2. April 1979. Ausländer im Lande Bremen', pp. 4–5.
[155] Der Senat der Freien Hansestadt Bremen, *Konzeption zur Integration der ausländischen Arbeitnehmer und ihrer Familienangehörigen im Lande Bremen* (June 1979), pp. 61–4.

districts would advantage ethnic minorities because it was in these types of areas that they overwhelmingly chose to live. The areas in Bremen that had been singled out as the targets of renovation plans, such as Lindenhof, Vegesack and Grohn, were home to over 35 per cent of the city's migrant population. Other measures included offering ethnic minorities the available older and more affordable council housing, as well as housing-based translation services.[156]

As with the employment sector, the housing needs of migrants did not become a political issue in Bremen only after the recruitment halt in 1973. Furthermore, there does not appear to have been a dismissal of the notion that adequate housing for guest-workers and their families was going to be needed in the city. Whether in reference to the guest-worker barracks of the 1960s or properties on the city's housing market during the 1970s, concern was continuously expressed over the levels of integration, segregation and discrimination migrants were experiencing, and there was a real commitment to attempt to meet their housing, and even their religious, needs. Again, whilst measures and provisions certainly intensified as the 1970s unfolded, these were implemented on a firm foundation of awareness and deliberation. This was a trait that both continued and escalated during the 1980s.

The 1980s and 1990s

The tendency for migrant groups from the recruitment countries to become concentrated in poor-quality housing in certain neighbourhoods continued into the 1980s and 1990s. As these migrant populations grew and their levels of residential concentration intensified, so did the number of government reports and correspondence on the topic. Overall, there was a stress on integration, a recognition of problems that ethnic minorities tended to face in Germany's housing sector and deliberation regarding possible solutions.[157] Indeed there were certain disadvantages that ethnic minorities suffered when compared to the local German population. According to a 1981 local government report, for example, 83 per cent of migrant households with five or more people lived in homes that were under 80m^2

---

[156] Ibid., pp. 64–5.
[157] See Bremische Bürgerschaft Landtag 10. Wahlperiode, Drucksache 10/895, 'Mitteilung des Senats. Fortschreibung der Konzeption zur Integration der ausländischen Arbeitnehmer und ihrer Familienangehörigen im Lande Bremen', 6 September 1982, pp. 2, 28–30.

compared with only 19 per cent of the local German population. Amongst Turkish families the situation was much bleaker, with 79 per cent and 51.6 per cent living in dwellings of under 60m^2 and 40m^2 respectively. This same report highlighted the fact that only 28 per cent of those immigrants with a permit actually received social housing.[158] The higher levels of overcrowding and the difficulties encountered by ethnic minorities when trying to access social housing have been repeatedly stressed in the historiography.[159]

Government documents also emphasised the fact that migrants often did not have much knowledge of the German housing market, potentially causing them to acquire dwellings of poorer quality. They also often tended to gravitate towards older and cheaper housing in deteriorating areas from which the German population was moving out. In general, the worries expressed were concerning both the quality of dwellings and residential distribution, aspects of ethnic minority housing experiences that have traditionally been discussed and remain key features of the academic debate.[160] Bremen's local authority believed that these traits and patterns were leading to a residential environment that was not in the long-term interest of migrants and were decreasing their overall chances of integration.[161]

As was the case regarding the Bremen local government's wider approach to its migrant population during the 1980s and 1990s, its focus on housing also revolved around the Turkish community due to its comparatively greater size. By the mid-1990s, like Newcastle, Bremen was home to some smaller Muslim ethnic minority communities, many of which had arrived as refugees and asylum seekers, were completing their studies in the city or worked in the local import and export business. These included migrants from Iran, Lebanon, Tunisia, Morocco and

---

158   See Der Senator für das Bauwesen, *Wohnen in Bremen*. Heft 2 der Reihe 'Der Senator für das Bauwesen informiert' (June 1981), pp. 3–4.
159   See William Clark and Anita Drever, 'Residential mobility in a constrained housing market: Implications for ethnic populations in Germany', *Environment and Planning A*, 32:5 (2000), pp. 835–6; and Stowasser, 'The Turks in Germany', p. 58.
160   See Lucassen, *The Immigrant Threat*, p. 159; and Jocelyne Cesari, 'Islamophobia in the West: A comparison between Europe and the United States', in John L. Esposito and Ibrahim Kalin (eds), *Islamophobia: The Challenge of Pluralism in the 21st Century* (Oxford, 2011), p. 26.
161   See Freie Hansestadt Bremen *Statistische Monatsberichte*, 'Räumlich – strukturelle Analyse der Ausländerkonzentration in der Stadt Bremen', 34. Jahrgang, October 1982, p. 310.

Table 2.3: The seven districts in Bremen with the highest ethnic minority population constitutions, February 1980

District	Percentage
Gröpelingen	12
Mitte	10.6
Neustadt	8.5
Blumenthal	8.3
Vegesack	7.9
Östliche Vorstadt	7.8
Hemelingen	7.7

Source: 'Die ausländische Wohnbevölkerung in der Stadt Bremen', 33. Jahrgang, 1981, p. 92.

Afghanistan. Whilst these ethnic groups have also become clustered into certain areas and neighbourhoods, they have been almost entirely overshadowed by the Turkish population. This is understandable as the largest Muslim community, after the Turks, during the early 1990s were the Iranians with just over 2,000 people. Not only was the Turkish community comparatively vast with over 24,000 members, but it had been settled in the city much longer and, as throughout Germany, had captured the attention of both the government and the public.[162] Furthermore, during the 1980s and 1990s, the residential patterns and experiences of those ethnic minorities who originated from the recruitment countries and either initially arrived as guest-workers themselves or as dependents thereof, and migrants from other countries, was still being assessed.[163]

During the 1980s and 1990s, the residential concentration of migrant groups continued in the aforementioned areas that were both geographically close to their places of work, such as Hemelingen, Gröpelingen and Blumenthal, and in those that offered affordable housing, such as Tenever, Kattenturm and Lüssum-Bockhorn.[164] All of

---

[162] See Freie Hansestadt Bremen *Statistische Monatsberichte*, 'Demographische Situation von Ausländerinnen und Ausländern im Lande Bremen', 45. Jahrgang, February 1994, pp. 127–8; and Freie Hansestadt Bremen *Statistische Monatsberichte*, 'Ausländer in der Stadt Bremen', 45. Jahrgang, March 1994, pp. 191–5.

[163] See Freie Hansestadt Bremen *Statistische Monatsberichte*, 'Residentielles Verteilungsmuster ausländischer Bevölkerungsgruppen in der Stadt Bremen', 37. Jahrgang, December 1985, pp. 168–70.

[164] See 'Ausländer nach Ortsteilen der Stadt Bremen', 37. Jahrgang, October 1985, pp. 146–8.

the city districts that were home to the largest concentrations of ethnic minorities during the mid- to late 1970s continued to be so whilst experiencing a slight decline in their overall migrant constitution. The only exception was Gröpelingen, which in February 1980 was 12 per cent ethnic minority (see Table 2.3).

Furthermore, despite these areas of concentration, Bremen's ethnic minorities were also succeeding in dispersing into other districts across the cities. By February 1980, nineteen districts, almost one-quarter of the city, were between 5 per cent and 7.5 per cent ethnic minority. This figure stood between 7.5 per cent and 10 per cent for thirteen districts, over 10 per cent for seven districts and over 15 per cent for three districts. Yet individual groups tended to continue to be found in certain areas, with around 60 per cent of Turks living in Gröpelingen, Neustadt, Blumenthal, Vegesack and Hemelingen. Within these five districts, they made up anywhere between 4.2 per cent (Hemelingen) and 8.5 per cent (Gröpelingen) of the total population.[165]

There were also a number of reports that sought to assess the extent to which Bremen had neighbourhoods or areas that could be perceived as ghettoes and the likelihood of these developing. Overall, the results were quite positive. In an analysis of forty-two sub-neighbourhood ethnic minority areas of concentration, it was concluded that only one had more migrants than German residents, and that there were only two others that were over 30 per cent ethnic minority. Whilst residential clustering was undoubtedly greater amongst the Turkish community, with the migrant population of five of these areas being over 90 per cent Turkish, it was nevertheless established that Bremen was not home to any one area that fulfilled the definition of a ghetto. Overall, only 52.4 per cent of Bremen's ethnic minority population lived in these forty-two areas and, as a result of the manner in which migrants were spread across the city, it was deemed that they were experiencing few problems adjusting to the local housing market.[166] This was confirmed in a 1982 report that pointed out that, even in areas of the city with high ethnic minority concentrations, there were more Germans than migrants in 97.7 per cent of cases.[167] Therefore, as has historically been the case in Newcastle, although Bremen's Muslim

---

[165] Ibid., p. 93.
[166] Freie Hansestadt Bremen *Statistische Monatsberichte*, 'Keine Ausländergettos in der Stadt Bremen', 33. Jahrgang, May 1981, pp. 169–73.
[167] 'Räumlich – strukturelle Analyse der Ausländerkonzentration in der Stadt Bremen', 34. Jahrgang, October 1982, p. 327.

ethnic minorities have often preferred to live amongst people from their own ethnic and religious backgrounds, this residential clustering has taken place in what have traditionally been working-class neighbourhoods, such as Gröpelingen, in which they have lived alongside the local white population.[168]

Other hypotheses regarding residential concentration also emerged from Bremen local authority documentation. Firstly, it was recognised that levels of clustering were greater the larger the ethnic minority group, yet it was also expected that residential concentration would decrease the longer migrants remained in the city.[169] In Bremen, as throughout Germany, it has been the Turkish population during the post-war period that has played the largest role in shaping the culture, streets and identities of certain neighbourhoods.[170] Furthermore, Bremen's government recognised that as migrants' stays in Germany evolved, their housing demands and willingness to pay rent became increasingly similar to those of the German population.[171] It was also found that Turks who lived outside the areas of migrant concentration displayed more similarities with the German population than those within them.[172]

The 1980s also witnessed a series of measures and policies that Bremen's local authority devised in an attempt to both improve migrants' quality of housing and decrease their levels of residential concentration. It was recognised that certain districts of the city were continuing to experience an influx of ethnic minorities and that, as a result, levels of segregation were increasing in some areas. Tenever, for example, housed 1.9 per cent of the city's foreigners and 2.1 per cent of the city's Germans in 1980 and, by the beginning of 1983, was home to 4.1 per cent of foreigners and 1.9 per cent of Germans.[173] Furthermore,

[168] See Farwick, 'The effect of ethnic segregation on the process of assimilation', p. 241.
[169] See 'Räumlich – strukturelle Analyse der Ausländerkonzentration in der Stadt Bremen', 34. Jahrgang, October 1982, p. 313.
[170] See Patricia Ehrkamp, 'Placing identities: Transnational practices and local attachments of Turkish immigrants in Germany', *Journal of Ethnic and Migration Studies*, 31:2 (2005), pp. 345–64.
[171] See Bremische Bürgerschaft Landtag 10. Wahlperiode, Drucksache 10/895, 'Mitteilung des Senats. Fortschreibung der Konzeption zur Integration der ausländischen Arbeitnehmer und ihrer Familienangehörigen im Lande Bremen', 6 September 1982, p. 29.
[172] See Freie Hansestadt Bremen *Statistische Monatsberichte*, 'Integration von Ausländern in der Stadt Bremen', 34. Jahrgang, November 1982, p. 361.
[173] 'Die Segregation der ausländischen Bevölkerung in Bremen', 35. Jahrgang, October 1983, p. 252.

it was believed that Bremen's ethnic minority residents were barely benefiting from efforts made in an attempt to improve the quality of the city's housing, something Bremen's government hoped would soon change. A number of properties in Lindenhof and Ohlenhof in Gröpelingen were awarded funding from a national project that aimed to modernise and renovate housing. This project was to be further assisted by state funds as well. For a minimum of nine years, 50 per cent of this housing was to be reserved for ethnic minorities.[174] There was also an increasing awareness regarding the religious and cultural needs of ethnic minorities, with discussions on neighbourhoods like Gröpelingen now addressing such topics as the building of a mosque, Turkish sport clubs, a German-Turkish festival, a Qur'an school, and sacrificial and slaughtering feasts.[175]

Yet despite local authority efforts, ethnic minority residential clustering continued into the 1990s and increased in some city districts. In January 1993, apart from Häfen which was 49.5 per cent migrant as a result of its exceptionally small total population (738), Gröpelingen remained the district with the largest ethnic minority constitution (16.3 per cent). Other city districts with high migrant compositions were Osterholz, Mitte, Neustadt, Hemelingen, Blumenthal and Vahr all of which had minority populations of well over 10 per cent (see Table 2.4). Residential concentration was even greater in certain sub-districts. By the end of 1992, Tenever was 29 per cent ethnic minority and other sub-districts with large migrant populations included Lesum, Hemelingen, Blockdiek, Grohn, Ohlenhof and Huckelriede (see Table 2.5).[176]

Yet again, government documents stressed that Bremen was not home to any areas that could be described as ghettoes and argued that the levels of concentration were not that high when compared to those

---

[174] See Bremische Bürgerschaft Landtag 10. Wahlperiode, Drucksache 10/895, 'Mitteilung des Senats. Fortschreibung der Konzeption zur Integration der ausländischen Arbeitnehmer und ihrer Familienangehörigen im Lande Bremen', 6 September 1982, pp. 28–9. See also Bremische Bürgerschaft (Stadt), 'Modernisierungsmaßnahmen im Ortsteil Lindenhof mit dem Ziel, für deutsche und ausländische Mieter besseren Wohnraum zu schaffen', 11. Wahlperiode, 11. Sitzung am 7 December 1984.
[175] See Bremische Bürgerschaft Stadtbürgerschaft 10. Wahlperiode, Drucksache 10/457S, 'Kleine Anfrage der Fraktion der FDP vom 10. März 1982. Ausländerbeiräte bei den Ortsämtern', p. 2.
[176] The sub-district of Häfen has been excluded because of its remarkably small total population.

Table 2.4: The seven districts in Bremen with the highest ethnic minority constitutions, January 1993

District	Percentage
Gröpelingen	16.3
Osterholz	16.1
Mitte	14.6
Neustadt	13.1
Hemelingen	12.1
Blumenthal	11.7
Vahr	11.7

Source: 'Einwohner und Ausländeranteile nach Stadtteilen der Stadt Bremen im Januar 1993', 46. Jahrgang, June 1994, p. 10.

Table 2.5: The seven sub-districts in Bremen with the highest ethnic minority constitutions, December 1992

District	Percentage
Tenever	29
Lesum	25
Hemelingen	23
Blockdiek	23
Grohn	23
Ohlenhof	22
Huckelriede	22

Source: 'Demographische Situation von Ausländerinnen und Ausländern im Lande Bremen', 45. Jahrgang, February 1994, p. 125.

found in some neighbourhoods in other German cities, such as Berlin-Kreuzberg and Munich-Ludwigsvorstadt. Residential concentration continued to be an issue alongside overcrowding, which was caused by larger families and the issue of affordability. Yet the standards of ethnic minority housing had improved and, by the 1990s, their housing was no longer lagging behind the German standard with regard to amenities, such as toilet facilities and central heating.[177]

An aspect of housing that has not played such a role in Bremen's local government documentation as in Newcastle's is home ownership. The city's measures and policies appear to have traditionally been towards improving the housing conditions of ethnic minorities in the rental sector and owner-occupation has certainly not been as wide-

[177] Ibid., pp. 127, 133.

spread as in Newcastle. On a broader scale, home ownership amongst Muslim migrants in Germany has not been the prevalent practice it has been in Britain. As the literature has correctly pointed out, one reason for this is the low overall rate of home ownership in Germany which, at around 42 per cent, is one of the lowest in Europe.[178] Yet levels of home ownership amongst foreign residents in Germany have been rising progressively since the 1970s, with those in West Germany increasing from 3.5 per cent in 1972 to 8.1 per cent in 1987 to 12.4 per cent in 1998.[179] Furthermore, it has been predicted that this figure will continue to rise due to the fact that one-third of Turks in Germany have saving agreements in building societies.[180]

Indeed, home ownership amongst Muslim ethnic minorities emerged as a practice much later than amongst those in Newcastle. Whilst owner-occupation and residential independence were immediate goals amongst Newcastle's South Asian Muslims from the time of their settlement, home ownership began to emerge at a much later date in Bremen. The situation in Bremen supports the conclusions reached of late by Amelie Constant, Rowan Roberts and Klaus Zimmermann in that home ownership appears to be the consequence of a commitment to the host society.[181] Even more recently, Sule Özüekren and Ebru Ergoz-Karahan stressed the increase in the number of Turkish homeowners in Germany from the late 1980s onwards once permanent settlement had become definite, and argued that this shift towards home ownership has developed simultaneously to that of entrepreneurship.[182] In this sense, purchasing a home, like establishing a business, acted as an investment in the local community. Yet this delay in residential autonomy has not stopped ethnic streets and neighbourhoods from developing in Bremen. On the contrary, as in Newcastle, certain districts of the city have become pebble-dashed with mosques, ethnic food stores, and cultural and religious youth centres. As in other German cities, certain areas that once held a magnetism over the city's Muslim migrants due to their proximity to

[178] See Constant, Roberts and Zimmermann, 'Ethnic identity and immigrant homeownership', p. 1880.
[179] See Bill Edgar, Joe Doherty and Henk Meert, *Immigration and Homelessness in Europe* (Bristol, 2004), p. 65.
[180] See Kemper, 'Restructuring of housing and ethnic segregation', p. 1772.
[181] Constant, Roberts and Zimmermann, 'Ethnic identity and immigrant homeownership', pp. 1879–98.
[182] Özüekren and Ergoz-Karahan, 'Housing experiences of Turkish (im)migrants in Berlin and Istanbul', p. 366.

the workplace and affordable housing have maintained their attraction through family and friends, and the development of a particular ethnic and religious identity, suggesting a degree of migrant agency.[183] Yet as with the employment sector, the key difference remains that these housing patterns began to develop at a later stage in Bremen due to the initial restraints of the guest-worker system.

The performance and experiences of ethnic minorities within the local housing sector continued to be a local government consideration throughout the 2000s, with a large emphasis being placed on improving both the quality of housing and neighbourhoods.[184] The *Konzeption zur Integration von Zuwanderern und Zuwanderinnen im Lande Bremen 2003 bis 2007* (Immigrant Integration Concept in the State of Bremen, 2003–2007) included a section on migrants' housing situations, and a list of measures and aims for the future. These included the increased participation of migrants in developments, improving the standards of living in areas with high ethnic minority concentrations through established projects and programmes, and doing more to engage the district and sub-district advisory boards.[185] The 2000s has also seen Bremen's government aiming to encourage integration at a neighbourhood level by promoting more involvement amongst migrants with individual districts in the city.[186]

---

[183] See Levent Tezcan, 'Kulturelle Identität und Konflikt: Zur Rolle politischer und religiöser Gruppen der türkischen Minderheitsbevölkerung', in Wilhelm Heitmeyer and Reimund Anhut (eds), *Bedrohte Stadtgesellschaft: Soziale Desintegrationsprozesse und ethnisch-kulturelle Konfliktkonstellationen* (Weinheim, 2000), pp. 401–48; and Ehrkamp, 'Beyond the mosque'. For Bremen, see 'Räumlich – strukturelle Analyse der Ausländerkonzentration in der Stadt Bremen', 33. Jahrgang, May 1981, p. 313; and knauf and Schröder (eds), *Fremde in Bremen*, p. 173.

[184] See Der Senat der Freien Hansestadt Bremen, *Umsetzung der Konzeption zur Integration von Zuwanderern und Zuwanderinnen im Lande Bremen – Abschlußbericht – (Planungsbögen zum Stand 12/2002)*, pp. 28–30.

[185] Bremische Bürgerschaft Landtag 16. Wahlperiode, Drucksache 16/176, 'Mitteilung des Senats vom 9. März 2004. Konzeption zur Integration von Zuwanderern und Zuwanderinnen im Lande Bremen 2003 bis 2007, Grundsätze, Leitlinien und Handlungsempfehlungen für die bremische Integrationspolitik', 9 March 2004, p. 7.

[186] See Die Senatorin für Soziales, Kinder, Jugend und Frauen, *Konzeption zur Integration von Zuwanderern und Zuwanderinnen im Lande Bremen 2007–2011, Grundsätze, Leitbilder und Handlungsziele für die bremische Integrationspolitik*, pp. 16–17.

Conclusion

As with the last chapter on employment, one of this chapter's key conclusions also revolves around the impact initial immigration paradigms have had on the long-term housing patterns and experiences of Muslim ethnic minorities. In both Newcastle and Bremen, residential behaviour has been shaped by their respective country's post-war immigration framework. As was the case throughout Britain, Muslim ethnic minorities in Newcastle found themselves on the open local housing market as soon as they arrived. As was seen with regard to the development of entrepreneurialism, their independence and self-sufficiency was also immediately apparent in the housing sector. In contrast, in Bremen, as throughout Germany, these attributes were delayed, firstly, as a result of their accommodation for the first phase of their stay having been largely provided by their employers and, secondly, because residential progression and autonomy emerged gradually alongside their long-term commitment to the city. Therefore, as in the employment sector, the patterns displayed by Muslim ethnic minorities in both Newcastle and Bremen's housing markets are progressively converging despite the different circumstances under which they initially settled. In both cities, they have placed their ethnic and religious identities in neighbourhoods, succeeded in breaking away from ethnic minority residential hubs when choosing to do so, and aspired to owner-occupation, albeit at a slower pace in Bremen than in Newcastle.

In general, the residential autonomy and housing experiences amongst ethnic minority communities in Britain and Germany have rarely been portrayed in a positive light, with ethnic neighbourhoods often perceived as the homes of poor-quality housing and 'parallel societies'. Yet in neither Newcastle nor Bremen do Muslim migrants' housing choices and careers appear to be dictated by disadvantage and constraint. Contrary to what a large proportion of the academic literature suggests, an exclusion from council housing and a forced concentration into inadequate housing have never featured widely amongst Newcastle's South Asian Muslims. Similarly, Bremen's Turkish Muslims have not extensively reported the discrimination at the hands of private landlords and the limited residential mobility documented in the historiography. Whilst there is no doubt that Muslim migrants in both cities have encountered disadvantage and been the subjects of discrimination, this has certainly not been on the scale of that in other British and German cities. This might again be the consequence of Newcastle and Bremen's comparatively smaller and more close-knit ethnic minority communities. These are characteristics that have potentially helped them secure the necessary financial capital and their preferred properties without putting too much strain on the available housing stock.

Furthermore, Muslim migrants in both cities have again largely succeeded as a result of their own self-determination and an understanding of their respective host society and, therefore, their residential clustering and housing choices have not been the result of a failure to integrate. On the contrary, Muslim ethnic minorities in both cities have overwhelmingly succeeded in making their own conscious and well-considered housing decisions. In Newcastle, they have tended to either become owner-occupiers, with many purchasing multiple properties and renting them out as part of their entrepreneurial portfolios, or secure local authority housing in areas of their choosing. In Bremen, there has been an absence of ghettoisation and residential dispersal has occurred. In both cities, but particularly in Newcastle, Muslim migrants' past and current residential choices and patterns demonstrate an understanding of the local housing market and an ability to command it to suit their long-term needs and ambitions.

As is the case with the employment sector, their residential determination and aspirations are only accentuated when considering the discrimination and racial harassment that has often been suffered. Muslim ethnic minorities have been willing to endure racial harassment, overcrowding and housing of a poorer quality if it has meant being able to live in their preferred properties and neighbourhoods. Furthermore, it must be recognised that whilst residential segregation has taken place in both cities, this has often been in neighbourhoods, such as Fenham and Gröpelingen, in which Muslim migrants live alongside the local white working classes.

Another main conclusion is regarding the extent to which Islam has influenced both cities' ethnic minorities' housing patterns and experiences. Although not as developed as that concerning the labour market, there has been a call for religion to be considered in the study of migrants' housing sector behaviour and performances. Yet as was the case with the employment sector, Islam does not appear to have played more than a small role in influencing the long-term housing careers amongst Newcastle and Bremen's Muslim migrants. Initially, Muslim ethnic minorities in both cities were attracted to certain areas and neighbourhoods as a result of either affordable housing or proximity to the workplace. As time progressed, however, Islam certainly did become more of an influential factor in that properties were undoubtedly partially chosen either because they were near or at a distance from the core of each city's migrant community and its accompanying amenities, including mosques, Islamic community centres and ethnic minority businesses.

This conscious choice to residentially align oneself alongside either the migrant or the local British or German population mirrors the manner in which Muslim businessmen either embraced or abandoned their ethnic and religious affiliation depending on whether they chose to cater for either a migrant or British or German clientele. However, there is no evidence of Muslim owner-occupiers or tenants having been disadvantaged or discriminated against as a consequence of their religion. Furthermore, as was the case with their labour market behaviour, housing experiences and traits amongst Muslim migrants in Newcastle and Bremen have paralleled those amongst ethnic minority groups in the West more broadly, be it amongst Puerto Ricans in New York, the Vietnamese in Sydney or the Surinamese in Amsterdam.[187] This challenges the notion that immigration frameworks and Islam have a significant long-term impact on ethnic minorities' residential patterns and integration.

The structure of this chapter has also been dictated by the available sources. The local authorities in both Newcastle and Bremen have historically expressed high levels of concern regarding the housing provision and experiences of the cities' ethnic minority communities. This was seen in the government reports and correspondence on racial harassment, overcrowding and residential segregation. Yet Muslim migrants in both cities have often fulfilled their housing aims despite local government initiatives. Many purchased property years ago and others undoubtedly still have ambitions to do so. Some formed part of an ethnic concentration and lived in multicultural neighbourhoods alongside both migrants and members of either the British or German population. Others succeeded in 'breaking out' into 'white' areas in which their housing experiences and ambitions increasingly resembled those of their British or German neighbours. Both groups have

[187] See Peter Jackson, 'Paradoxes of Puerto Rican segregation in New York', in Ceri Peach, Vaughan Robinson and Susan Smith (eds), *Ethnic Segregation in Cities* (London, 1981), pp. 109–26; Kevin Dunn, 'Rethinking ethnic concentration: The case of Cabramatta, Sydney', *Urban Studies*, 35:3 (1998), pp. 503–27; and Hans van Amersfoort and Cees Cortie, 'Housing and population: Spatial mobility in twentieth-century Amsterdam', in Liza Nell and Jan Rath (eds), *Ethnic Amsterdam: Immigrants and Urban Change in the Twentieth Century* (Amsterdam, 2009), pp. 75–102.

achieved residential integration. Overall, Muslim ethnic minorities have demonstrated the ability to manoeuvre within their local housing markets as well as a commitment to their neighbourhoods and surroundings. Whilst these traits emerged later in Bremen than in Newcastle as a result of the initial restrictions caused by the guest-worker system, choice has often triumphed over constraint amongst Muslim migrants in both cities.

3

The education sector: the three Rs – race, relations and arithmetic

Ethnic minorities in Britain and Germany's education sectors

Education has potentially been the most complex and most discussed topic regarding the settlement of immigrants and their descendants in Britain and Germany in the post-war period. Not only has it traditionally secured a place at the centre of political and academic debate in both countries, but it has also often been perceived as having the power to determine young ethnic minorities' long-term integration. In Britain, many Afro-Caribbean and East African refugee children arrived during the 1960s, and those of Indian, Pakistani and Bangladeshi origin followed during the family reunification process that began in the 1970s.[1] It has been argued that educational disadvantage was present amongst many of these immigrants from the beginning, with many being less educationally qualified than their white counterparts, a trait that continues for some groups still today.[2] Much of the academic literature has stressed that Britain's education system was unprepared for the arrival of post-war immigrant youths and thus did not effectively cater for them. Panikos Panayi, for example, has argued that local education authorities during the 1960s and 1970s had no real concept of how to address the growing number of ethnic minority schoolchildren.[3] Sally Tomlinson has claimed that Britain lacked a clear notion of how to integrate migrant youths, and that post-war education policies have too often been influenced by society's xenophobic and racist senti-

---

[1] See Tariq Modood and Stephen May, 'Multiculturalism and education in Britain: An internally contested debate', *International Journal of Educational Research*, 35:3 (2001), pp. 305–6.
[2] See Ansari, *'The Infidel Within'*, pp. 184–8.
[3] Panayi, *An Immigration History of Britain*, p. 209.

ments.[4] Similarly, Gajendra Verma and Douglas Darby have asserted that individual schools and teachers have often struggled to integrate ethnic minority children and meet their education needs, and received very little help or support.[5]

In Germany, guest-worker children, especially those of Turkish origin, started arriving in large numbers during the 1970s despite an overall decline in foreign workers: despite the 1973 recruitment halt, many foreign workers already in Germany wished to unify their families. The 1975 change to children's allowances (*Kindergeld*) was a further factor. Prior to this, no distinction was made between children living inside or outside Germany, but from 1975 higher payments were to be made for children living in Germany.[6] As in Britain, educational disadvantage was arguably present amongst Germany's guest-workers from the beginning. Having been recruited to largely carry out manual work, many were less educationally qualified than their German counterparts, and it has often been mistakenly assumed that their children are not interested in education.[7] Regarding Germany, the academic literature has been even more forceful than that addressing Britain in its blaming of the government and local authorities for issues and problems that have arisen regarding the education of ethnic minority schoolchildren. It has often been argued that, as a result of the nature of the guest-worker rotation system, they were very slow to acknowledge that a substantial proportion of the guest-worker population and their families were settling in Germany.[8] There have also been two other key factors that have undoubtedly contributed to educational hardship amongst migrant children. Firstly, education in Germany is state-controlled, meaning that there has historically been a lack of any type of national overarching policy or accountability. Secondly, it has

---

[4] Sally Tomlinson, *Race and Education: Policy and Politics in Britain* (Maidenhead, 2008), p. 177.

[5] Gajendra K. Verma and Douglas Darby, 'Immigrant policies and the education of immigrants in Britain', in Dr Pirkko Pitkänen, Devorah Kalekin-Fishman and Gajendra K. Verma (eds), *Education and Immigration: Settlement Policies and Current Challenges* (London, 2002), pp. 11–47.

[6] See Czarina Wilpert, 'Children of foreign workers in the Federal Republic of Germany', *International Migration Review*, 11:4 (1977), p. 475; and Abadan-Unat, *Turks in Europe*, pp. 117–18.

[7] See Ira N. Gang and Klaus F. Zimmermann, 'Is child like parent? Educational attainment and ethnic origin', *The Journal of Human Resources*, 35:3 (2000), pp. 552–3.

[8] See Klopp, *German Multiculturalism*, pp. 103–4.

been argued that the inherent structure of the education system, in which there is a strong link between socio-economic status and education performance and pupils are streamed at an early age, disadvantages ethnic minority children.[9]

In order to undertake an assessment of ethnic minority education in Britain and Germany at a grassroots level, it is necessary to have a grasp of overarching national policies. During the 1960s and early 1970s, the British government adopted an assimilationist approach to the education of migrant children, which was best witnessed in the government education literature published in 1965 and 1971, both of which were entitled *The Education of Immigrants*. This approach was based on the belief that immigrant children should be absorbed into British society, and that therefore the acquisition of the English language should be the key priority whilst the preservation of minority languages and cultures was viewed as less significant.[10] Part of this assimilationist policy was the notion that local education authorities should not allow ethnic minority children to constitute more than one-third of any school or classroom's total number of pupils. Therefore, in an attempt to promote a quicker integration and preserve individual school's British characters and principles, a dispersal policy was introduced through which surplus migrant children were to be bussed to schools in other neighbourhoods.[11]

This assimilationist approach was challenged by contemporaries and has been criticised consistently since. It was believed that it would reinforce the idea that immigrant children were the cause of education problems and that it was about nothing more than reassuring white British parents that their children's education would not be harmed by 'excessive numbers' of ethnic minority children.[12] It has also been

---

[9] See Worbs, 'The second generation in Germany', p. 1025
[10] See Linda Thompson, Michael Fleming and Michael Byram, 'Languages and language policy in Britain', in Michael Herriman and Barbara Burnaby (eds), *Language Policies in English-Dominant Countries: Six Case Studies* (Clevedon, 1996), pp. 108–9; and Andrew Dorn and Paul Hibbert, 'A comedy of errors: Section 11 funding and education', in Barry Troyna (ed.), *Racial Inequality in Education* (Abingdon, 2012), pp. 60–2.
[11] See David L. Kirp, 'The vagaries of discrimination: Busing, policy, and law in Britain', *The School Review*, 87:3 (1979), pp. 269–94; and Ronald Manzer, *Educational Regimes and Anglo-American Democracy* (Toronto, 2003), pp. 220–2.
[12] See Gajendra Verma, Paul Zec and George Skinner, *The Ethnic Crucible: Harmony and Hostility in Multi-Ethnic Schools* (Abingdon, 1994), p. 13; and Kevin Myers and Ian Grosvenor, 'Policy, equality and inequality: From the

argued, for example, that it portrayed the migrant communities rather than individual schools or the education system as the problem, and that it demonstrated a limited understanding on behalf of the government of the issues regarding cultural diversity that the British education system had been handling during the 1950s and 1960s.[13] Furthermore, the dispersal policy arguably resulted in neglect of the positive steps being taken by both schools and local authorities in areas with large numbers of migrant schoolchildren.[14]

As the 1970s progressed, it was increasingly recognised that changes needed to be made within the education system to prepare children for a multicultural society and that ethnic minority children could no longer be perceived simply in terms of 'disadvantage'.[15] A 1977 Green Paper entitled *Education in Schools: A Consultative Document* stressed that Britain was a multi-racial society and should have an education system that reflected this.[16] The 1981 Rampton Report offered measures through which education could tackle racism, and was concerned with combatting underachievement amongst ethnic minority youth and advocating 'cultural tolerance'. Overall, it recognised that Britain was a culturally diverse country and that education should draw upon and teach about an array of different cultures, thus offering children a multicultural education.[17] This multicultural approach to education was best documented in the 1985 Swann Report, which stressed that the learning needs of youths of all ethnicities should be met, and that schoolchildren should be taught about ethnic and cultural differences and how to respect them.[18] The education policies

---

past to the future', in Dave Hill and Mike Cole (eds), *Schooling and Equality: Fact, Concept and Policy* (London, 2001), p. 259.

[13] See Richard Race, *Multiculturalism and Education* (London, 2011), pp. 17–18.

[14] See Tomlinson, *Race and Education*, p. 30.

[15] Ibid., pp. 68, 82.

[16] See Gajendra K. Verma, 'Cultural diversity in primary schools: Its nature, extent and cross-curricular implications', in Gajendra K. Verma and Peter D. Pumpfrey (eds), *Cross Curricular Contexts, Themes and Dimensions in Primary Schools* (London, 1994), pp. 6–7.

[17] See Josna Pankhania, *Liberating the National History Curriculum* (London, 1994), p. 50; and Harry Tomlinson, 'International perspectives on education: The response of the mother country', in Carl A. Grant and Joy L. Lei (eds), *Global Constructions of Multicultural Education: Theories and Realities* (Mahwah NJ, 2001), p. 322.

[18] See Gajendra K. Verma, 'Diversity and multicultural education: Cross-cutting issues and concepts', in Gajendra K. Verma, Christopher R. Bagley and Madan

of the 1990s have been criticised for permitting the gradual abandonment of a multicultural anti-racist education. Largely as a result of funding cutbacks and the political climate, this decade witnessed English language support again taking priority, multicultural advisers being made redundant, the decline of effective systems for monitoring ethnic minority pupils, a persistence in ethnic differences in educational attainment, teachers no longer being given adequate preparation to teach in a multicultural society, and complaints that schools were not adequately providing for Muslim worship.[19]

It proves more difficult to offer a framework of national education policy in Germany. This is because, as previously mentioned, education in Germany is state-controlled. Yet there were a series of policy recommendations issued through the Standing Conference of the Ministers of Education and Cultural Affairs of the Länder in the Federal Republic of Germany (*Ständige Konferenz der Kultusminister der Länder in der Bundesrepublik Deutschland*, or KMK), a political body that advised on policies, but did not actually implement them. The first was that of May 1964, which extended compulsory education to include all foreign schoolchildren and youths, and outlined a two-pronged approach in which provision would be made for both a stay in Germany and a return to the homeland. In other words, immigrant youths were to be taught both German and their respective mother-tongue language. The second was that of December 1971, which advocated that ethnic minority schoolchildren should be prepared solely for a future in Germany, and should become integrated within the German school system so that they would be able to partake in German society. German language instruction was to be conducted in preparatory classes (*Vorbereitungsklassen*) in which immigrant youths would spend a certain amount of time before joining the mainstream classroom. The third was that of April 1976, which at first glance appears to have reverted back to the two-pronged policy of 1964, but an examination of the suggested measures reveals a clear withdrawal of any previous commitment to integration. It advocated that it was the responsibility of schools to maintain pupils' ethnic identities, and recommended special and bilingual classes, initiatives that all derived from the belief that these schoolchildren would eventually return 'home'. This was

---

Mohan Jha (eds), *International Perspectives on Educational Diversity and Inclusion: Studies from America, Europe and India* (Abingdon, 2007), p. 21.

[19] Tomlinson, *Race and Education*, pp. 114–23.

further reinforced in 1979 when it was decided that migrant pupils in secondary education could choose their mother-tongue language as a school subject in place of a foreign language.[20]

These policies have come under a considerable amount of criticism in the academic literature, with some of the key arguments being that the 1976 policy withdrew any previous commitment to integration and awarded too much flexibility to individual states, and that the dual approach should be perceived as a failure due to the fact that the educational achievement of immigrant schoolchildren barely improved in the years that followed.[21] Indeed what emerged from these central KMK recommendations was a series of *Länder*-specific policies, many of which, it has been forcefully argued, have failed to meet the educational needs of migrant schoolchildren. The historiography has often focused on the measures adopted by Bavaria and Berlin, the two German states that have traditionally been seen as adopting contrasting approaches. Bavaria's policies involved separate classes for guestworker children, assuming that they were to be in Germany only for the short term and thus did not need to become fully integrated into German society. Berlin's was based on the notion that these children's futures were likely to be in Germany and thus it implemented an education policy that strove for full integration, which involved a strong focus on the German language alongside optional mother-tongue language instruction.[22]

Another approach was the combined model, such as that implemented in the city of Krefeld. This middle position involved German and migrant children studying some subjects together and others separately, with the aim of them eventually merging in all subjects. The

[20] See Rist, *Guestworkers in Germany*, pp. 188–96; Hartmut Esser and Hermann Korte, 'Federal Republic of Germany', in Tomas Hammar (ed.), *European Immigration Policy: A Comparative Study* (Cambridge, 1985), p. 194; Peter Broeder and Guus Extra, *Language, Ethnicity and Education: Case Studies of Immigrant Minority Groups and Immigrant Minority Languages* (Clevedon, 1999), p. 82; and Klopp, *German Multiculturalism*, pp. 104–5.

[21] See Klopp, *German Multiculturalism*, pp. 104–5; and Ulrike Behrens, Sabine Tost and Reinhold S. Jäger, 'German policy on foreigners and the education of immigrants in the Federal Republic of Germany', in Dr Pirkko Pitkänen, Devorah Kalekin-Fishman and Gajendra K. Verma (eds), *Education and Immigration: Settlement Policies and Current Challenges* (London, 2002), pp. 113–14.

[22] See Ray C. Rist, 'On the education of guest-worker children in Germany: A comparative study of policies and programs in Bavaria and Berlin', *The School Review*, 87:3 (1979), pp. 242–68; and Ireland, *Becoming Europe*, pp. 101–2.

crucial aspect of this model was that foreign children learnt both German and their respective mother-tongue languages, and thus pursued integration through the recognition of both German and minority languages and cultures.[23] Although one might assume that there are benefits to implementing local measures for local immigrant communities, each of these approaches has been heavily criticised, and the benefits and shortcomings of these different models have been the topic of fierce debates both in the academic literature and amongst German educators.

In fact, the education of ethnic minorities in both Britain and Germany continues to be perceived as crucial to overall integration. For many migrant children and youths, a school classroom is the first opportunity to spend a sustained period of time with their British and German counterparts. Furthermore, educational attainment naturally also has clear links with future employment and life opportunities. Yet it is perhaps this sector more than others that is most clearly afflicted by shortcomings, conflict and underachievement. At the beginning of the 2000s, the extent to which Britain's education system had accepted its role as a challenger to discrimination, racism and inequality was still being assessed.[24] In Germany, the condemnation of the manner in which the education system has provided for the learning needs of ethnic minorities has been even more extensive. This was further publicised by the PISA (Programme for International Student Assessment) studies of the 2000s, which found that there was a wide gap between the educational performance and attainment of pupils with a migrant background and those without, and high rates of social inequality within the system.[25] These results caused both a 'PISA shock' and vigorous debate amongst German political and educational circles. It is within the contexts of both these political histories and recent developments that this study will be situated.

---

[23] See Karl-Heinz Dickopp, *Erziehung ausländischer Kinder als pädagogische Herausforderung: das Krefelder Modell* (Dusseldorf, 1982); and Barry McLaughlin and Peter Graf, 'Bilingual education in West Germany: Recent developments', *Comparative Education*, 21:3 (1985), p. 247.

[24] See Tomlinson, *Race and Education*, p. 180.

[25] See Manfred Prenzel, Jürgen Baumert, Werner Blum, Rainer Lehmann, Detlev Leutner, Michael Neubrand, Reinhard Pekrun, Jürgen Rost and Ulrich Schiefele (eds), *PISA 2003: Der zweite Vergleich der Länder in Deutschland – Was wissen und können Jugendliche?* (Münster, 2005).

Muslim ethnic minorities in Britain and Germany's education sectors

As with the employment and housing sectors, it has only been fairly recently that the academic literature on Britain and Germany's ethnic minority education experiences and performances has started to perceive Islam as an influential factor. In Britain, it was not until the 1990s that research of this type began to emerge in earnest and it has since undergone an intensification. Many studies have focused on pupils' academic performances, arguing that Muslims educated in the British state system are hindered academically and culturally, and that too many are failing to attain high-level grades and qualifications. This has particularly been stressed for those of Pakistani, Bangladeshi, Turkish and Somali backgrounds.[26] Others have exposed the existence of bullying and racism as a result of religious differences, and the extent to which Muslim youths suffer discrimination at the hands of both the education system and teachers.[27] Recent research has also revealed that the manner in which Islam has been the victim of negative stereotyping has impacted Muslim youths' educational engagement, motivation and success.[28] The education of Muslim schoolchildren in Britain has also often been a source of tension, with some Muslim parents not approving of a Christian-orientated education system, and questions being asked about whether this system can meet Muslim pupils' learning needs.[29]

As with the employment and housing sectors, the consideration of Islam in the literature on the educational performances and experiences

---

[26] See Zubaida Haque, 'The ethnic minority 'underachieving' group? Investigating the claims of 'underachievement' amongst Bangladeshi pupils in British secondary schools', *Race, Ethnicity and Education*, 3:2 (2000), pp. 145–68; Louise Archer, *Race, Masculinity and Schooling: Muslim Boys and Education* (Maidenhead, 2003); and Hussain, *Muslims on the Map*, pp. 53–5.

[27] See Mike Eslea and Kafeela Mukhtar, 'Bullying and racism among Asian schoolchildren in Britain', *Educational Research*, 42:2 (2000), pp. 207–17; and David Gilbert, 'Racial and religious discrimination: The inexorable relationship between schools and the individual', *Intercultural Education*, 15:3 (2004), pp. 253–66.

[28] See Saeeda Shah, 'Leading multi-ethnic schools: Adjustments in concepts and practices for engaging with diversity', *British Journal of Sociology of Education*, 29:5 (2008), pp. 526–7.

[29] See Marie Parker-Jenkins, 'Muslim matters: An examination of the educational needs of Muslim children in Britain', *American Journal of Islamic Social Sciences*, 9:3 (1992), pp. 351–69.

of ethnic minorities in Germany emerged slightly later than that addressing Britain, and studies have been fewer in number. Again, a large focus has traditionally been awarded to the Turkish community, about which it has repeatedly been argued that they possess the lowest levels of school-leaving qualifications compared to both their German counterparts and migrant youths from other former recruitment countries.[30] Whilst the education sector also suffers from an absence of official data that distinguishes between Muslim and non-Muslim ethnic minorities, the number of works considering Islam is increasing. Again, the most definite conclusions were reached by the 2009 Federal Office for Migration and Refugees study, which found that Muslims possess a significantly lower educational level than people of other religious affiliations in Germany, and that Turks perform the least well out of all Muslim groups.[31] Other investigations have established that, in addition to poor educational attainment, Muslims in Germany also suffer from a lack of proficiency in the German language and poor vocational training.[32] It has also been argued that Muslim parents are often confused by the complexity of the German education system, and that communication between them and schools should be increased.[33] The overall importance of education in the integration process has been repeatedly stressed. Not only did education constitute a key part of the 2007 National Integration Plan, but it has even been suggested that multicultural education could help reduce Islamophobia.[34]

The consideration of Islam within Britain and Germany's education

---

[30] See Kalter, 'Ethnische Kapitalien und der Arbeitsmarkterfolg Jugendlicher türkischer Herkunft', p. 404; and Manuel Siegert, 'Schulische Bildung von Migranten in Deutschland', *Working Paper of the Bundesamt für Migration und Flüchtlinge*, 13 (Nuremberg, 2008).

[31] Federal Office for Migration and Refugees, *Muslim Life in Germany*, pp. 200–13.

[32] See Robert J. Pauly, Jr., *Islam in Europe: Integration or Marginalization?* (Aldershot, 2004), p. 71.

[33] See Andreas Hieronymus, 'Muslim identity formations and learning environments', in Abdulkader Tayob, Inga Niehaus and Wolfram Weisse (eds), *Muslim Schools and Education in Europe and South Africa* (Münster, 2011), pp. 151–2.

[34] See Rod Gardner, Yasemin Karakaşoğlus and Sigrid Luchtenberg, 'Islamophobia in the media: A response from multicultural education', *Intercultural Education*, 19:2 (2008), pp. 119–36; and Patrick Stevenson and Livia Schanze, 'Language, migration and citizenship in Germany: Discourses on integration and belonging', in Guus Extra, Massimiliano Spotti and Piet van Avermaet (eds), *Language Testing, Migration and Citizenship* (London, 2009), pp. 94–5.

sectors is undoubtedly a far more complex and discussed topic than its role within the employment and housing markets. This is because Muslims in both countries' school systems have been affected as a result of their religion in a number of ways. Britain has been home to a headscarf controversy and a fiery debate on Muslim faith schools.[35] Germany has also witnessed a headscarf debate of its own as well as heated political discussion on Islamic religious education.[36] It is topics such as these that act as evidence that the education sector is an area in which Muslim migrants in both countries have traditionally had to negotiate their identities. Contrary to the labour and housing markets in which not all national and local policies and measures affected Muslim ethnic minorities, education is an area in which they have been forced to interact with the system and engage with a white British or German society. Despite this, there is a lack of research on the post-war educational patterns and performances of local Muslim migrant communities in both countries. This chapter aims to make a small contribution to this historiographical void.

Aims of the chapter

This chapter examines and analyses the education of Muslim ethnic minorities in Newcastle and Bremen from the 1960s to the 1990s from the perspective of both cities' local governments and the migrants themselves.[37] As with the employment and housing sectors, Britain and Germany's post-war immigration frameworks played an overwhelming role in shaping Newcastle and Bremen's initial education policies and both cities' Muslim migrants' educational experiences. It is undoubtedly an assessment of this sector that best exposes the sense of uncertainty and ambiguity that accompanied the settlement of guest-workers and their families in Bremen, characteristics that become further accentuated when

[35] See Ansari, *'The Infidel Within'*, pp. 337–9; and Christian Joppke, *Veil: Mirror of Identity* (Cambridge, 2009), pp. 81–106.

[36] See Albrecht Fuess, 'Islamic religious education in Western Europe: Models of integration and the German approach', *Journal of Muslim Minority Affairs*, 27:2 (2007), pp. 215–39; and Hilal Elver, *The Headscarf Controversy: Secularism and Freedom of Religion* (Oxford, 2012), pp. 129–52.

[37] For a more succinct insight into both cities' policies, see Sarah E. Hackett, 'A learning curve: The education of immigrants in Newcastle upon Tyne and Bremen from the 1960s to the 1980s', in Zvi Bekerman and Thomas Geisen (eds), *International Handbook of Migration, Minorities and Education – Understanding Cultural and Social Differences in Processes of Learning* (Dordrecht, 2011), pp. 349–64.

compared with the situation in Newcastle. It has also been this area that has been influenced the most by Britain's centralised and Germany's federal administration. Whilst Newcastle's approach to the education of ethnic minorities has largely reflected national mandate, Bremen's has often differed from that adopted in other German states.

Yet as was seen regarding the employment and housing markets, similarities were also witnessed in both cities' education policies the longer Muslim ethnic minorities remained in Newcastle and Bremen. Both local governments introduced measures aimed at enhancing educational performance, promoting English and German language acquisition, and improving migrant youths' chances of integration from an early age. The conclusions reached from an analysis of both cities deviate from the historically and historiographically adamant claims of policy failures and educational underachievement. On the contrary, both Newcastle and Bremen's local authorities and Muslim ethnic minority communities have fared much better than what has often been argued regarding other British and German cities. Newcastle once again benefited from its small close-knit Muslim migrant population whilst Bremen profited from an immediate commitment to guest-worker children's educational needs and a series of pro-integration measures. It is the Bremen government's dedication to the learning needs of migrant children that becomes especially apparent, a feature that is repeatedly witnessed in the vast quantity of policies implemented and the manner in which education has traditionally been awarded a central position on the city's integration agenda.

This chapter draws largely upon local government correspondence, minutes and reports, which together enable an understanding of local policies and approaches, and offer an insight into the experiences of the cities' migrant communities. An assessment of the education of Muslim ethnic minorities in Britain and Germany from the 1960s to the 1990s faces the same difficulties regarding source material as the previous chapters on employment and housing. As a result of the fact that the religious affiliation of migrants was rarely considered a significant factor during this time period, the relevant documents are again largely compiled according to ethnicity and thus do not often refer to Muslims specifically. As a result, works have often tended to be conducted along ethnic lines and have traditionally had to draw upon data that is organised according to ethnicity.[38]

[38] See Ansari, 'The Infidel Within'; and Siegert, 'Schulische Bildung von Migranten in Deutschland'.

Whilst there were clear parallels between the conclusions reached in the employment and housing chapters, an assessment of the education sector is different. The self-determination and pursuit of independence that has traditionally played such a role amongst Muslim migrants in both Newcastle and Bremen's labour and housing markets has not featured to the same extent in their education sector's behaviour and performances. Instead, Muslim children have been subjected to local government policies under which there was little room for educational autonomy. Yet it is the education sector that better exposes some of the other key arguments and themes that run throughout this book. As previously mentioned, an assessment of education policies offers a comprehensive insight into the manner in which Newcastle's government prepared for the permanent settlement of its ethnic minority communities, as well as the Bremen local authority's sense of uncertainty and ambiguity regarding the future of its guest-worker population.

Regarding Newcastle, the size of the Muslim migrant population again plays a role, leading to a more successful educational performance and fewer difficulties and problems compared to what has often been the case in British cities with larger ethnic minority communities. Lastly, Islam influences Muslim migrants' educational experiences to a greater extent than was seen in both employment and housing. Irrespective of the quantity and quality of Newcastle and Bremen's policies and provisions, both cities' local authorities have only traditionally catered for a segment of Muslim children's educational needs. As a result, learning has not been confined to the classroom, but rather been dispersed across Muslim ethnic minority communities in the form of mosques and Islamic community centres. Yet despite this, the provision in both cities for Muslim migrant education was the result of an understanding of the local ethnic minority communities. Bremen's policies in particular were commendable when one considers both the context of the guest-worker system and the approaches adopted by other German *Länder*.

Newcastle

Both positive and negative practices have been revealed regarding the education of ethnic minorities in Newcastle. The 1980s especially was a period of debate and activity, undoubtedly as a result of the national push towards a multicultural education system and curriculum. Teachers and educational advisers from the area published reports of problems and difficulties they had encountered first-hand, including high levels of racism amongst schoolchildren, the Newcastle Local Education Authority's equal opportunities policy not being effectively distributed amongst school staff, the isolation of South Asian parents from their children's schools, and the ineffectiveness and misdirection of policies regarding Section 11 funding and posts.[39] Yet more positive experiences and events were also documented, such as the establishment of an Asian mothers' group, the maintaining of mother-tongue languages, raising awareness about different religions and food, and the role that the Muslim community centre in the West End played in the community's religious education and in promoting a multicultural society.[40]

The 1980s also witnessed other local initiatives, including the foundation of North Tyneside's LEA Multicultural Centre, a Newcastle branch of the National Association for Multiracial Education (NAME), and the teacher-dominated Gateshead Federation to Combat Racism.[41] One study on anti-racism went so far as to assert that, in

---

[39] See Wim Mould, 'No rainbow coalition on Tyneside', *Multicultural Teaching*, 4:3 (1986), pp. 9–12; Carrie Supple, 'Anti-racist teaching in the North East: A personal view', *Multicultural Teaching*, 4:3 (1986), p. 16; Elizabeth French, 'Parental involvement – an evolving process', *Multicultural Teaching*, 4:3 (1986), pp. 18–19; and Naseem Shah, 'A black perspective on current policy initiatives in the North East', *Multicultural Teaching*, 4:3 (1986), pp. 28–9.

Under the Section 11 scheme, local authorities in areas of high ethnic minority concentration could apply for funding from the Home Office to employ extra teachers on projects that would help migrant children overcome disadvantage. Whilst there is no doubt that this available funding was a sign that it was gradually being recognised that the educational needs specific to ethnic minority children needed to be met, it has also traditionally been perceived as a way in which local authorities were compensated for the 'burden' that migrant pupils had placed upon them. In general, Section 11 teaching has been heavily criticised for being inconsistent and not directly helping migrant children, having only marginal benefits, not attracting the support of mainstream teachers and being nothing more than a way in which to attempt to achieve the quicker assimilation of ethnic minority children. See Julios, *Contemporary British Identity*, p. 102; Dorn and Hibbert, 'A comedy of errors'; and The Commission on the Future of Multi-Ethnic Britain, *The Parekh Report*, p. 150.

[40] See Surinder K. Samra, 'Section 11 teaching: A new ball game', *Multicultural Teaching*, 4:3 (1986), pp. 20–3; and Qureshi, 'The Newcastle mosque and Muslim mommunity centre'.

[41] See Alastair Bonnett, 'Anti-racism as a radical educational ideology in London and Tyneside', *Oxford Review of Education*, 16:2 (1990), p. 262.

comparison to London, Tyneside LEAs, and especially that of Newcastle, had helped secure the issue of racism a place on the local education agenda and promoted the beginning of a debate on the topic.[42] Examples of good practice have also been implemented more recently. A few examples are Newcastle's New Deal for Communities, one of the few to award any significant attention to ethnic minority communities in its education work, local authority initiatives such as the Ethnic Minority, Traveller and Refugee Pupil Achievement Service (EMTRAS), and numerous community organisations that aim to improve the education levels of migrant groups.[43]

Furthermore, as with entrepreneurship, there is no doubt that ethnic minorities' education and qualifications are increasingly being perceived as an asset to the North East. A 2006 Institute for Public Policy Research report, for example, stressed the fact that a significant portion of the region's migrants are better educated than both those born in Britain and living in the North East, and their migrant counterparts in the UK. There are also fewer migrants in the region with no qualifications than is the case for the rest of the country. Furthermore, even when comparing the North East to individual regions, it still has one of the greatest levels of highly skilled migrants in the UK. The report also highlighted the manner in which these highly qualified migrants have played a central role in the region's economy, but that there remain many whose skills are not being taken advantage of. It even went so far as to argue that migrants could go a long way to helping the North East's workforce's qualification levels catch up with those of the UK, an aim that has been branded a key priority in regional planning documents.[44] Therefore, as with employment and housing, this is an opportune time at which to examine Newcastle's Muslim ethnic minorities' experiences in the education sector.

The 1960s and 1970s

As with the employment and housing sectors, there are a handful of archival documents and studies that together provide an insight into

---

[42] See Alastair Bonnett, *Radicalism, Anti-Racism and Representation* (London, 1993), pp. 140–2.

[43] Marie Lall and David Gillborn, *Beyond a Colour Blind Approach: Addressing Black and Minority Ethnic Inclusion in the Education Strand of New Deal for Communities*, New Deal for Communities, The National Evaluation, 49 (Sheffield Hallam University, 2004).

[44] Pillai, *Destination North East?*, pp. 28–9, 34, 38.

the early experiences of Newcastle's post-war ethnic minorities in the local education system. Again, the 1967 report compiled by the City of Newcastle upon Tyne offered some of the earliest information derived from interviews, questionnaires, observations and group activities. It estimated that there were around 220 immigrant children in the city's primary schools in 1966–67, most of whom were concentrated in schools in the West End. There were also over ninety ethnic minority pupils at Slatyford Comprehensive School in the west of the city. The report also demonstrated an awareness regarding the problems that could potentially arise amongst immigrant schoolchildren. Firstly, it recognised that those who arrived in Newcastle having already started school in their home countries might encounter certain difficulties, especially with the English language. Secondly, it predicted that there might be issues in the future as a result of certain schools experiencing a concentration of ethnic minority pupils. However, it seemed to suggest that major or widespread problems had not yet arisen, and that the education of immigrant schoolchildren was being handled effectively. At Slatyford school, for example, new ethnic minority pupils were grouped into a reception class where they were taught by an immigrant teacher, thus ensuring that their presence did not delay the progress made in mainstream classrooms.[45] As previously mentioned, this was a very common aspect of the 1960s assimilationist approach, which tended to perceive ethnic minority children as the 'problem' and as a potential threat to white British pupils' education.[46]

The 1967 report also addressed education more widely. It stressed that Newcastle was home to immigrant students of all levels, including some undertaking practical training with companies like Reyrolles in Hebburn, which hired ethnic minority draughtsmen, clerks and technicians. Some attended part-time or evening classes that were linked to their employment, and there were language and conversation classes held on a weekly basis. The report recognised that South Asian women often experienced difficulties learning English either because of domestic responsibilities or a lack of an educational background. It also acknowledged that efforts to improve the educational and English language standards of the South Asian population were coming from within the immigrant community, and in particular through the

[45] Telang, *The Coloured Immigrant in Newcastle upon Tyne*, pp. 15–16.
[46] See Peter Figueroa, 'Intercultural education in Britain', in Kenneth Cushner (ed.), *International Perspectives on Intercultural Education* (Mahwah NJ, 1998), p. 128.

Pakistan Association. Lastly, some of the report's recommendations revolved around education. These included the offering of classes on the English language and life in Britain, the promoting of public libraries and inter-racial playgroups, and encouraging Newcastle's ethnic minority university students to play an educationally supportive role amongst the city's immigrant communities.[47] Overall, there seemed to be an awareness of the educational difficulties and needs of the city's ethnic minority children and adults, as well as an identification of potentially valuable proposals as early as the mid- to late 1960s.

A December 1967 Education Committee report further expressed concern regarding language acquisition and a concentration of immigrant pupils in certain schools. It explained that records of Newcastle's ethnic minority schoolchildren had been kept since January 1964 and that, since then, numbers had increased quite dramatically. Indeed, between January 1964 and November 1967, the number of immigrant pupils in the city's primary and secondary schools rose from 259 to 350 and 89 to 235 respectively. This was a total increase from 348 to 585. Furthermore, these ethnic minority schoolchildren were not evenly distributed amongst Newcastle's schools, but rather some schools received more than others. The report highlighted how there were ten primary schools in the city that had ten or more immigrant children in their student body and together had over 72 per cent of all ethnic minority primary school pupils. There were two schools in the West End in particular, Westgate Hill Junior and Westgate Hill Infant, which by November 1967 were 19.8 per cent and 20 per cent ethnic minority respectively. Some primary schools, such as Elswick Road Junior, Westgate Hill Junior and St Paul's CE Primary School, also faced language problems in that they had a significant number of immigrant pupils who either had no knowledge of English or had some knowledge of the English language, but required assistance with both speaking and writing.[48]

When looking at individual class years at both Westgate Hill Infant and Westgate Hill Junior, there were a few where the ethnic minority constitution was significantly higher than those for the schools as a whole. The highest percentage of immigrant pupils in a class at

---

[47] Telang, *The Coloured Immigrant in Newcastle upon Tyne*, pp. 16–17, 30, 33–4.
[48] TWAS, MD.NC/149, Commonwealth Immigrants Working Group of Planning Committee 19 September 1966–6 May 1968, Education Committee, 'Immigrant pupils in schools', 5 December 1967, p. 1.

Westgate Hill Infant was around 26 per cent whilst at Westgate Hill Junior it was 34 per cent. Whilst the Education Committee recognised the Department of Education and Science's recommendation regarding the dispersal of ethnic minority schoolchildren, and Newcastle had a few individual classes where the immigrant composition was either close to or surpassed the suggested one-third limit, schools preferred to address any difficulties that might arise themselves. Head teachers agreed that instead of sending their ethnic minority pupils to a separate reception centre, additional teaching assistance was to be introduced in some schools to help with additional pressures. However, they were concerned that continuing to admit an unrestricted number of immigrant schoolchildren would lead to problems for their schools.[49]

By the late 1960s, ethnic minority secondary school pupils were also becoming concentrated in a handful of Newcastle's schools, a characteristic that was also witnessed in Bremen. Almost 90 per cent were clustered into only five schools and one school alone, the aforementioned Slatyford Comprehensive School, had over 52 per cent of them. Slatyford was also the only secondary school to have a language problem in that there were a significant number of immigrant children arriving at the school with little or no English and with few years left in education. They often showed little interest in becoming integrated into the school and tended to form a group of their own. In November 1967, the school had eighteen ethnic minority pupils who had no knowledge of the English language, twenty-one who had some knowledge of English but needed help with both speaking and writing, and thirty-four who spoke English to an acceptable standard but needed special help with writing. As was the case regarding the city's primary schools, the intention was for any problems to be addressed within the school.[50] This was a view that was headed by the Commonwealth Immigrants Working Group, which was against any notion of separating migrant pupils from their white British counterparts, preferring instead for extra English language tuition to be offered within the normal curriculum.[51] Many of those schoolchildren at Slatyford with language problems were learning English within a special teaching unit at the school and extra staff had been appointed specifically for this purpose.

[49] Ibid., p. 2.
[50] Ibid., p. 3.
[51] See TWAS, MD.NC/149, Commonwealth Immigrants Working Group, 8 November 1967, p. 4.

Lastly, the report also stressed the importance of special training courses for teachers of ethnic minority pupils.[52] On the whole, it was argued that despite difficulties with the English language and self-segregation amongst Newcastle's migrant schoolchildren, the majority seemed happy and cases of discrimination between them and white British pupils were rare.[53] Yet there was concern regarding the English language acquisition of ethnic minority pupils well into the 1970s, with a 1975 survey showing that out of a total of 680 children from a non-English-speaking background, thirty-four had no English, eighty-six had a limited amount and 400 had only enough to cope in the classroom.[54] Overall, the difficulties encountered during the 1960s and 1970s, such as language problems, the concentration of ethnic minority pupils in certain schools, and also low levels of inter-ethnic friendship, were not particular to Newcastle, but have been widely documented as having been commonplace across Britain.[55]

Yet despite the problems encountered and the anxieties expressed, Taylor's study of all Indian and Pakistani boys who reached leaving age in Newcastle's schools between 1962 and 1967 revealed that his respondents performed better educationally than their white English counterparts. His conclusions derived from preliminary research conducted in 1968 and a follow-up investigation carried out during the early 1970s. Overall, out of the four measures of educational attainment that Taylor applied, the South Asians performed better in three and matched the English control sample in one. Firstly, the Indian and Pakistani youths stayed on longer at school, with 53 per cent of them having pursued full-time studies beyond the minimum leaving age of fifteen compared to only 23 per cent of English youths. Secondly, a larger proportion of the Asian respondents stayed on longer in full-time education and, at the time of the interviews, 34 per cent of them were still studying compared to only 7 per cent of their English counterparts.[56]

[52] TWAS, MD.NC/149, 'Immigrant pupils in schools', 5 December 1967, p. 4.
[53] See TWAS, MD.NC/149, Commonwealth Immigrants Working Group, 6 May 1968, p. 3.
[54] See TWAS, MD.NC/162/1, Racial Harmony Working Group, 'Mother tongue teaching', 23 January 1983.
[55] See Milena M. Jelinek and Elaine M. Brittan, 'Multiracial education 1. Inter-ethnic friendship patterns', *Educational Research*, 18:1 (1975), pp. 44–53; Ansari, *'The Infidel Within'*, pp. 299–300; and Christina Julios, *Contemporary British Identity: English Language, Migrants, and Public Discourse* (Aldershot, 2008), p. 103.
[56] Taylor, *The Half-way Generation*, pp. 147, 149.

Thirdly, the Indian and Pakistani youths had much higher aspirations and long-term educational success rates. 17 per cent had secured a place in higher education compared to only 4 per cent of the English sample. Moreover, Taylor's Asian respondents showed determination and persistence in pursuing higher education. Some, for example, had retaken their A-Level examinations if necessary and surpassed their teachers' expectations of them. The last indicator of educational attainment measured the certificates they attained upon leaving school. It was in this category that the English and South Asian respondents performed equally as well. The educational success of Taylor's Indian and Pakistani youths is further accentuated by the fact that 58 per cent did not arrive in England until after the age of 10 and 42 per cent until after the age of 12.[57]

Not only did Taylor's South Asian respondents perform better than local English youths, but their educational success also constituted a clear deviation away from the widespread underachievement that was argued to be present amongst ethnic minority schoolchildren in Britain at the time.[58] Taylor offered explanations for why be believed South Asian youths in Newcastle performed better. He suggested that educational achievement was encouraged by the two castes, Jat and Khatri, to which the majority of the parents belonged, by the importance that Indo-Pakistani culture awards to education, and by the supportive and close-knit families from which his respondents came. He also argued that they had inherited the ability to adapt to the British school system and the determination to do well from their parents. Whilst these characteristics could be applied to Indian and Pakistani pupils across the country, Taylor also provided a reason for educational achievement that was particular to Newcastle. He argued that his respondents were helped by the fact that a high proportion of them had either been born in England or had arrived in the country before the age of eleven. He compared this with studies conducted in Birmingham and Ealing where a high percentage of ethnic minority pupils had attended school in England for much less time before reaching leaving age. Overall, Taylor believed that Indian and Pakistani parents' cultures and values succeeded in influencing their children's educational careers because they had largely been in England from a young age.[59]

[57] Ibid., pp. 148–53.
[58] See David Beetham, *Immigrant School Leavers and the Youth Employment Service in Birmingham* (London, 1967); and Alan Little, Christine Mabey and Graham Whitaker, 'The education of immigrant pupils in Inner London primary schools', *Race & Class*, 9:4 (1968), pp. 439–52.
[59] Taylor, *The Half-way Generation*, pp. 166–9.

There were other explanations for the educational success of Newcastle's South Asians that Taylor considered, but appears to have dismissed. Yet it is the belief of this study that two of these were also influential. Firstly, he referred to a significant proportion of his respondents' families as 'a small-scale entrepreneurial middle class' as a result of their high levels of self-employment and home ownership, and the fact that over one-third owned more than one property.[60] In contrast, the majority of the English youths' fathers were employees and tenants, and belonged to the local working class. Although Taylor concludes that class cannot be used to explain why the Indian and Pakistani pupils performed better than their white counterparts, it seems likely that there was still a correlation between the South Asian fathers' employment and residential status and their sons' educational achievements. In other words, it appears entirely possible that the same self-determination that played such a role in the employment and housing sectors was also present in education. Indeed, as Taylor admits, a commitment to education and a desire to do well at school was reinforced by parents much more amongst the Indian and Pakistani youths than was the case regarding the English sample.[61]

The second explanation for the educational achievements of Newcastle's South Asian youth is to do with the size of the city's ethnic minority population. As with their success in the employment sector, Taylor briefly considered the notion that his South Asian respondents might have performed to a higher level in school than was the norm for ethnic minorities in Britain because they did not constitute more than a small percentage of the total number of school pupils in the city. This meant that they tended to comprise only a small proportion of individual schools and classrooms, and were therefore in a position to learn English quicker and become absorbed into the education system.[62] Yet regardless of the reason, there is no doubt that Newcastle's Indian and Pakistani youths' early educational performances set them far apart from ethnic minority communities across Britain. Contrary to the employment and housing sectors in which the city's South Asians portrayed similar patterns and characteristics to those in other cities and towns, albeit often on a more widespread scale and for different reasons, their initial achievements in the local education system appear to be overwhelmingly unique.

[60] Ibid., p. 159.
[61] Ibid., pp. 159–63.
[62] Ibid., p. 168.

The 1980s and 1990s

As with both the employment and housing sectors, the amount of attention granted to the education of ethnic minorities by Newcastle's local authority increased greatly during the 1980s. Again, this was largely not the result of local factors, but rather formed part of a national development, and there were several reasons why this took place. Firstly, as with employment and housing, the 1976 Race Relations Act required local authorities to eliminate discrimination, and promote positive race relations and equality of opportunity in education. Although heavily criticised for not successfully combating racial discrimination, there is no doubt that, as in the housing sector, the 1976 Act both raised awareness and acted as a foundation for future legislation. Secondly, it was from the findings of the 1981 Rampton Report that the debate on the educational challenges encountered by ethnic minority children that evolved during the 1980s developed. The report compared the educational performances of white, Asian and West Indian children, and found that West Indian pupils coped the least well within the education system and that the majority of those of an Asian origin did less well than their white British counterparts. The Rampton Report also discussed a number of possible explanations for this migrant underachievement, including racism in both society and schools, negligence on behalf of local authorities, and socio-economic factors. It made a total of eighty-one recommendations and stressed that not sufficient progress had been made in the area of multicultural education.[63]

Yet it was the publication in 1985 of *Education for All*, or the Swann Report, which continued and extended the work of the Rampton Report, and has come to be perceived as the true breakthrough in multicultural education in Britain. Having immediately sparked extensive debate, this report of over 800 pages recognised the manner in which the assimilationist and integrationist approaches to education had failed ethnic minority children, and stressed the importance of a multicultural education, which would educate all children irrespective of their ethnic backgrounds. Amongst other things, it assessed the educational achievement and underachievement of ethnic minority

---

[63] See Interim Report of the Committee of Inquiry into the Education of Children from Ethnic Minority Groups, *West Indian Children in Our Schools, The Rampton Report* (London, 1981); Brian D. Jacobs, *Black Politics and Urban Crisis in Britain* (Cambridge, 1986), pp. 125–7; Verma, Zec and Skinner, *The Ethnic Crucible*, p. 10; and Tomlinson, *Race and Education*, p. 55.

youth, and provided a list of particular areas that required attention, such as the learning of English and mother-tongue languages, the hiring of ethnic minority teachers and religious education.[64]

Whilst the Swann Report has traditionally been perceived as the crucial piece of legislation concerning ethnic minority education during the 1980s, it is important to realise that it formed part of a wider context. This decade also witnessed other initiatives that either addressed or impacted aspects of ethnic minority schooling, including the developing of LEA multicultural education policies, the dilemmas caused by the 1980 and 1988 Education Acts, and efforts by the Commission for Racial Equality to eliminate racial discrimination in schools. The 1980s also saw grassroots incidents that contested the notion of a multicultural education. These included the 1984 Honeyford Affair in which a Bradford head teacher was suspended for criticising multicultural education, the 1986 murder of a Bangladeshi boy at a school in Manchester, and numerous instances of white British parents removing their children from multi-racial schools.[65]

Whilst the 1980s was a decade of activity, race in education during the 1990s became what has been referred to as an 'absent presence'.[66] Indeed John Major's Conservative government has been heavily criticised for overlooking racial tensions and problems encountered by ethnic minorities in Britain's schools. There was a cut in the funding available to help with the education of migrant children, some ministers were opposed to changes being made in the National Curriculum that would allow it to better reflect Britain's multi-ethnic society and the education system was seen as neglecting its legal responsibilities following the murder of Stephen Lawrence in

[64] For an insight into the Swann Report, its context and some of the criticism it received, see Barry Troyna, '"Swann's song": The origins, ideology and implications of Education for All', *Journal of Education Policy*, 1:2 (1986), pp. 171–81; Gajendra K. Verma (ed.), *Education for All: A Landmark in Pluralism* (Lewes, 1989); and Peter Figueroa, *Education and the Social Construction of 'Race'* (London, 1991), pp. 76–88.

[65] See Olivia Foster-Carter, 'The Honeyford Affair: Political and policy implications', in Barry Troyna (ed.), *Racial Inequality in Education* (London, 1987), pp. 44–58; Ian MacDonald, Reena Bhavnani, Lily Khan and Gus John, *Murder in the Playground: The Report of the MacDonald Inquiry into Racism and Racial Violence in Manchester Schools* (London, 1989); Ranjit Arora, *Race and Ethnicity in Education* (Aldershot, 2005), pp. 38–9; and Tomlinson, *Race and Education*, pp. 72–5, 90.

[66] See Tomlinson, *Race and Education*, pp. 100–25.

1993.[67] Overall, the multicultural and anti-racist approach to education that played such a role during the 1980s gradually receded during the 1990s and, due to the arrival of refugees and asylum seekers, the education system faced new challenges and the needs of long-settled ethnic minority children were once again grouped together.[68]

Yet the 1990s also witnessed some progress and development. In 1992, for example, the National Union of Teachers published antiracist curriculum guidelines and the publication of the fourth Policy Studies Institute survey in 1997 revealed the vast disparities that existed between the educational performances and qualifications of different ethnic groups. Overall, however, education policies until 1997 were afflicted by funding cuts and an unwillingness to implement changes that would allow the education system to better provide for ethnic minority children, two characteristics that resulted in local authorities' policies and procedures not enjoying further development and improvement. In fact, it was not until the late 1990s and early 2000s that race was once again awarded a place on the government's education agenda under New Labour.[69]

It is within this context that measures implemented by Newcastle's local authority emerged and should therefore be assessed. Furthermore, local measures in the city during both the 1980s and 1990s adhered to this national framework. Although Newcastle was not home to the large numbers of ethnic minority schoolchildren that were present in cities like Birmingham and Bradford, great consideration and attention was nevertheless awarded to the development of a multicultural education system. This becomes evident through a series of mid-1980s documents and is best outlined in the 1984 report entitled 'The council and racial equality: Policy statement and action plan'. This was the council's first step towards setting out a clear policy regarding racial equality, and its measures and recommendations acted as the founda-

---

[67] See Horace Lashley and Peter Pumfrey, 'Countering racism in British education', in Gajendra K. Verma and Peter D. Pumfrey (eds), *Cross-Curricular Contexts: Themes and Dimensions in Secondary Schools* (London, 1993), pp. 115–16; David Gillborn, *Racism and Education: Coincidence or Conspiracy?* (London, 2008), p. 118; and Tomlinson, *Race and Education*, p. 101.

[68] See Sally Tomlinson, 'The education of migrants and minorities in Britain', in Sigrid Luchtenberg (ed.), *Migration, Education and Change* (Abingdon, 2004), pp. 86–102; and Tomlinson, *Race and Education*, p. 123.

[69] See Tomlinson, *Race and Education*, pp. 103–4, 124, 148.

tion of local policies during both the 1980s and 1990s. It conveyed a strong commitment to combatting racism, discrimination and disadvantage and, alongside employment and housing, education constituted a key sector through which this was to be attempted.[70] The importance awarded to the education system in promoting racial equality and equality of opportunity was further proclaimed by local schools and organisations in a preparatory document.[71]

The 1984 *Policy Statement and Action Plan* stressed that multicultural education was to be advocated in all schools, and would consist of spreading anti-racist sentiment as well as promoting an understanding of all cultures amongst schoolchildren. The report made clear that the council's racial equality policy was intended to be applied in all schools and even in those which either had very few or no ethnic minority pupils at all. Some institutions were asked to review their approaches towards multicultural and anti-racist education, and the library service was given the responsibility of removing books and learning material that were perceived to encourage racism. One key strand to education policy was language and skills development. For example, the teaching of mother-tongue languages in schools was discussed, and additional English language provision was under consideration for both secondary school pupils and adults. Furthermore, there was an intention to offer courses in numeracy and literacy for ethnic minority children who arrived in Newcastle in their teens and required extra help, and it was believed that the Youth Training Scheme could widen pupils' opportunities and career choices.[72]

Other initiatives outlined in the report included encouraging ethnic minority parents to become more involved in their children's schools and appointing members of ethnic minorities to school governing bodies. The school meals service already catered for the dietary needs of ethnic minority pupils and Careers Service staff were made aware of the particular problems and difficulties often encountered by ethnic minority youths. Lastly, a monitoring system was to be put in place to both oversee all multicultural education initiatives and guarantee the

---

[70] TWAS, MD.NC/162/1, 'The council and racial equality: Policy statement and action plan', November 1984.

[71] See TWAS, MD.NC/162/1, City of Newcastle upon Tyne Racial Equality Sub-Committee, 'Responses to the Green Paper: Covering report', 31 May 1984, pp. 10–12.

[72] TWAS, MD.NC/162/1, 'The council and racial equality: Policy statement and action plan', November 1984, pp. 7–8.

official reporting of all racist incidents in the city's schools.[73] Many of the measures outlined in this 1984 report were very typical of the 1980s shift towards a multicultural education. For example, although their effectiveness has been questioned, the recognition within education of ethnic minority identities and experiences, the fostering of mother-tongue languages, the focus on anti-racism, the provision of halal food in schools, attempts to include migrant parents, and the careful monitoring of practices and learning material are all initiatives that have been widely recognised in the literature as having emerged at this time.[74] Furthermore, the concentration on these areas in Newcastle both continued and intensified as the 1980s progressed.[75]

The publication of the Swann Report was officially acknowledged by Newcastle's local authority in an Education Committee and Racial Equality Sub-Committee meeting in the autumn of 1985. The report that emerged recognised that the Swann Report advocated a pluralist view of society in which different races, cultures and faiths were accepted and respected, and stressed that the educational policies of the Newcastle authority mirrored and supported this view. Overall, the report demonstrated a clear engagement with and understanding of the Swann Report. It provided a summary of each of its chapters, and showed how the recommendations and proposals were being met in Newcastle whilst also challenging some of its requests and seeking further clarification.[76]

[73] Ibid., pp. 8–9. See also TWAS, MD.NC/162/1, Commission for Racial Equality Annual Report 1984, 'The Commission's work in the North of England'; and TWAS, MD.NC/162/1, Racial Equality Seminar, 'Report of the Education Working Groups', 12 July 1984.

[74] See James Lynch, *Multicultural Education: Principles and Practice* (London, 1986); Colin Baker, *Key Issues in Bilingualism and Bilingual Education* (Clevedon, 1988), p. 63; David Gillborn, 'Anti-racism: From policy to praxis', in Bob Moon, Sally Brown and Miriam Ben-Peretz (eds), *Routledge International Companion to Education* (London, 2000), pp. 477–9; Arora, *Race and Ethnicity in Education*, p. 26; and Ansari, 'The Infidel Within', pp. 313, 319–20.

[75] See TWAS, MD.NC/162/2, 'The council and racial equality policy statement and action plan', January 1986, pp. 1–2, D.2; and TWAS, MD.NC/162/3, Newcastle City Council Local Government and Racial Equality Sub-Committee 16 December 1987 and Education (Schools) Sub-Committee 13 October 1987, 'Monitoring of racial incidents in schools'.

[76] TWAS, MD.NC/162/2, City of Newcastle upon Tyne Education Committee Schools Sub-Committee 8 October 1985 and Racial Equality Sub-Committee 18 September 1985, 'The Swann Report'.

For example, it argued that racism within the education system was being combated through measures that included schools reviewing their curricular, administrative and organisational policies, and learning materials, for any racist components. It clearly stated that Newcastle's authority was pursuing a multicultural education policy in an attempt to meet the needs of ethnic minority schoolchildren and prepare all pupils for a future in a multi-racial society. It also firmly advocated the notion that a multicultural education should have a place in all schools regardless of the number of ethnic minority pupils enrolled. It also called for stronger leadership from the Department of Education and Science in this area, which it believed would result in a greater consistency in multicultural education measures that were being implemented in LEAs across the country. There were a number of other ways in which multicultural education was being pursued in Newcastle, which included the appointment of an adviser and officer who had the responsibility of enforcing these policies, and by monitoring the application of schools' multicultural policy statements.[77]

The Newcastle local authority's report agreed that religious education should adopt a multicultural approach to faith, but that there needed to be a more effective review of how to go about this. It also approved of the importance awarded to teacher education, such as initial teacher training, in-service courses and Racism Awareness Training, and stated that a Racism Awareness Training course was being prepared for teachers in Newcastle. Support was also shown for the proposal to hire more teachers from an ethnic minority background.[78] Both anti-racist and multicultural training, and efforts to increase the number of ethnic minority teachers in the city, were initiatives that remained on the agenda throughout the late 1980s.[79]

Another key element of the Swann Report was language education and it was this aspect that Newcastle's local authority appears to have given the most immediate attention to. It agreed that the languages of ethnic minority communities should be recognised and respected. However, it disagreed with the notion that language centres are racist,

---

[77] Ibid., pp. 1–3.
[78] Ibid., p. 4.
[79] See TWAS, MD.NC/162/2, 'Racial equality action plan monitor', July 1986, pp. 7–9; and TWAS, MD.NC/162/2, City of Newcastle upon Tyne Local Government and Racial Equality Sub-Committee, 'Strategies for combatting racism – head teachers' courses report of Head of Education Department', 18 March 1987.

and argued that they provided ethnic minority pupils with an arena that supported their cultures and identities at a time when they were having to adjust to a new environment. Whilst it was recognised that such centres could lead to instances of disadvantage, it was argued that these would be avoided in Newcastle through consistent monitoring.[80] Indeed whilst language centres in Britain were heavily criticised both at the time and subsequently for permanently isolating pupils and encouraging racial discrimination, such problems do not appear to have arisen in Newcastle.[81]

Newcastle's debate on mother-tongue teaching was further developed in a September 1985 report issued by the Schools Sub-Committee and the Racial Equality Sub-Committee. In this report, Newcastle's local authority questioned the Swann Report's assertion that the teaching of mother-tongue languages was best carried out within the ethnic minority communities themselves rather than in mainstream schools. This declaration was based on the belief that mother-tongue teaching in schools offered students a 'separate provision', which might cause or confirm divisions between ethnic minority pupils and their white counterparts. However, Newcastle's local authority disagreed with this view, arguing that ethnic minority pupils' cognitive development might be restricted if they were not receiving mother-tongue language support. It stressed that migrant children should be given the chance to develop both their mother tongue and the English language, and that there was no reason why this had to result in separating them from mainstream classrooms and experiencing a different or limited curriculum.[82] Indeed the mother-tongue teaching that had taken place in Newcastle up until this point had been largely community-based and had taken place at mosques or at schools in the evenings and at weekends. These classes were often

---

[80] TWAS, MD.NC/162/2, 'The Swann Report', p. 3.

[81] See Barrie Wade and Pam Souter, *Continuing to Think: The British Asian Girl: An Exploratory Study of the Influence of Culture upon a Group of British Asian Girls with Specific Reference to the Teaching of English* (Clevedon, 1992), p. 29; and Jill Bourne, 'Centralization, devolution and diversity: Changing educational policy and practice in English schools', in Guofang Wan (ed.), *The Education of Diverse Student Populations: A Global Perspective* (Dordrecht, 2008), p. 32.

[82] TWAS, MD.NC/162/2, City of Newcastle upon Tyne Schools Sub-Committee and Racial Equality Sub-Committee, 'Mother-tongue teaching report on the schools language survey conducted in Newcastle upon Tyne schools, Autumn 1984', 18 September 1985, p. 2.

spontaneous and depended on teachers being available.[83] The local authority believed that mother-tongue teaching should not be left to ethnic minority communities because not all children would have the same opportunities, the classes offered might be restricted or serve specific purposes, and because removing mother-tongue teaching from schools would highlight differences between pupils and result in these languages not being perceived as important. As a result, it was decided that mother-tongue teaching was to take place in Newcastle's primary and secondary schools in a way that would ensure that ethnic minority pupils remained in the mainstream classroom and had access to the full curriculum. In primary schools, this was to be achieved through a team of peripatetic mother-tongue teachers who would assist with the mother-tongue development of migrant children under the direct supervision of the classroom teacher. In secondary schools, this same method was to be applied in Years 1–3, whilst in Years 4 and 5 major mother tongues were to be available as an option in certain schools.[84]

The report also documented the results of a language survey that had been conducted in the autumn of 1984 and included all pupils in all of the city's schools. The survey found that over 2,000 children or 4.9 per cent of the schools' pupil body spoke a mother tongue that was not English. The five most widely spoken languages were Punjabi, Urdu, Bengali, Cantonese and Hindi, which together were spoken by over 75 per cent of the city's ethnic minority pupils. Of these, Punjabi was the most common with 893 speakers, followed by Urdu with 389 and Bengali with 198. Furthermore, it was stressed that there were still large numbers of younger children coming through the education system who spoke these three languages. The areas requiring the most assistance were Westgate Hill, Wingrove Road and Canning Street in the West End and Sandyford in the east of the city.[85]

Based on these findings, the report detailed specific recommendations regarding the teaching of mother-tongue languages in Newcastle's schools. It was decided that pupils speaking the five dominant mother tongues would receive language support at all stages of their education. This was to be carried out by twenty peripatetic teachers of which fifteen were assigned to Punjabi and Urdu, two to Bengali, two to

[83] See TWAS, MD.NC/162/1, Racial Harmony Working Party, 'Mother tongue teaching', 23 January 1983.
[84] TWAS, MD.NC/162/2, 'Mother-tongue teaching report on the schools language survey conducted in Newcastle upon Tyne schools, Autumn 1984', p. 2.
[85] Ibid., p. 3, Appendix A, Appendix C.

Cantonese and one to Hindi. As previously mentioned, these teachers were to work alongside main classroom teachers and pupils were not to be separated from their white counterparts. Other recommendations were also listed. These included increased training opportunities for teachers for the purpose of raising awareness and knowledge in the area of ethnic minority languages, aiming to hire more teachers from an ethic minority background, the awarding of qualifications in ethnic minority languages in secondary schools, promoting positive attitudes towards these languages and the training of all teaching staff in the area of language teaching methodology.[86] Newcastle's local authority was not alone in questioning the Swann Report's approach to mother-tongue languages. In fact, the notion that mother-tongue language teaching should not take place in mainstream schools attracted many critics who claimed that the report was proposing linguistic assimilation rather than pluralism, and that it failed to appreciate the connection between a child's first and second language development, and that between language and culture.[87] Furthermore, there were LEAs and schools across Britain who incorporated mother-tongue languages into their curriculums and appointed specialist teaching teams.[88]

The 1980s also saw Newcastle's local authority concentrating heavily on ethnic minority pupils' English language acquisition. It primarily did this by applying for Section 11 grants under the 1966 Local Government Act. Despite the fact that Section 11 grants received a great deal of criticism, Newcastle made much use of them and continued to do so throughout the 1980s. Like local authorities across Britain, Newcastle's primarily sought this funding for the teaching of English amongst its ethnic minority children, with some being awarded to adult education.[89] In December 1983, the Home Office approved an

---

[86] Ibid., pp. 3–4.
[87] See Sandra Lee McKay, *Agendas for Second Language Literacy* (Cambridge, 1993), pp. 43–4.
[88] See Dennis Ager, *Language Policy in Britain and France: The Processes of Policy* (London, 1996), p. 92; and Naz Rassool, 'Language policies for a multicultural Britain', in Ruth Wodak and David Corson (eds), *Encyclopedia of Language and Education. Volume 1: Language Policy and Political Issues in Education* (Dordrecht, 1997), p. 120.
[89] See Khurshid Ahmed, 'Birmingham: Local initiatives to associate immigrants in the integration process', in OECD, *Immigrants, Integration and Cities: Exploring the Links* (Paris, 1998), p. 182; and Julios, *Contemporary British Identity*, p. 102.

application for seven teaching posts and the appointed staff quickly became engaged with language work, liaising with ethnic minority families in seven of the city's primary schools.[90] A mid-1984 report issued by the Racial Equality Sub-Committee and the Education Committee outlined the need for additional posts in the city, which would especially allow Newcastle's local authority to further pursue its goals of offering specialist language help for ethnic minority children and establishing a multicultural education system. The posts applied for included a teacher/adviser of multicultural education, four additional members of teaching staff, a multicultural resources officer and a technical/clerical support officer.[91]

The four teaching posts were identified for schools that had been singled out as having particularly widespread language problems. The first was Hotspur Primary School in Heaton which, at the time of the report, was about to open. It was estimated that the school's student body would be between 10 per cent and 16 per cent ethnic minority, and that an additional teacher would be required for both mother-tongue and English language teaching. The second was St Paul's CE Primary School in the West End which in the autumn of 1984 was expected to admit more students as a result of the closure of a neighbouring school. The school was already 14 per cent ethnic minority, a figure that was much higher in the nursery school, and had cases of severe language problems. The third was West Jesmond Junior School where 12 per cent of the pupils originated from New Commonwealth countries, over half of them displaying language problems. The fourth was Chillingham Road Primary School in Heaton, which required additional assistance with the language development of South Asian children. It was expected that all four teaching posts would also promote the development of multicultural education in the city.[92] It was predicted that a further school, Rutherford School in Fenham, might require additional teaching staff in the near future as it was 25 per cent ethnic minority and it had not yet been confirmed if the

---

[90] See TWAS, MD.NC/162/1, Local Government and Racial Equality Sub-Committee, 'Report of Director of Education: Section 11 appointments', undated report.

[91] TWAS, MD.NC/162/1, City of Newcastle upon Tyne Racial Equality Sub-Committee 31 May 1984 and Education Committee 5 June 1984, 'Local Government Act 1966 Section 11 Education Service – proposed submission', attached report entitled 'Proposals for the establishment of posts in the Education Service under Section 11', pp. 1–3.

[92] Ibid., pp. 1–2.

The education sector

existing teaching staff could meet their language and learning needs.[93]

Furthermore, the teacher/adviser position would have the role of offering leadership to the area of multicultural education in the city and the multicultural resources officer would have the responsibility of ensuring that the necessary resources were available. These included language materials, books that portrayed Britain as a multicultural society, and resources that ethnic minority pupils could identify with. Lastly, the technical/clerical post would provide support to all Section 11 initiatives. Newcastle's local authority also submitted applications for two posts concerning adult education. These were for a Senior Community Language Co-ordinator and a post to cover crèche provision. The former was needed to coordinate language provision for ethnic minority adults, to develop English language classes, and arrange the recruitment and training of teaching volunteers. The latter stemmed from the recognition that many South Asian women were unable to partake in language classes because of childcare responsibilities. It was thought that a crèche would solve this problem. Newcastle's local government also wanted to create a post for a youth and community worker to develop youth clubs around the needs of ethnic minorities, to work closely with the Community Relations Council and community leaders, and liaise with other agencies like schools and social services. The last group of proposed positions were in the College of Arts and Technology and revolved largely around the teaching of English. Overall, there was a clear awareness regarding the language needs of the city's ethnic minority communities and a commitment to meet them and engage with ethnic minority parents in an attempt to promote integration.[94]

Investigation into the language needs of Newcastle's ethnic minority pupils continued and a further major report was compiled by the city's Education Committee in December 1984. It stressed the difference between the Teaching of English as a Second Language (ESL), aimed

---

[93] See TWAS, MD.NC/162/1, City of Newcastle upon Tyne Racial Equality Sub-Committee 31 May 1984 and Education Committee 5 June 1984, 'Local Government Act 1966 Section 11 Education Service – proposed submission', p. 1.

[94] See TWAS, MD.NC/162/1, 'Proposals for the establishment of posts in the Education Service under Section 11', pp. 1–5. See also TWAS, MD.NC/162/1, City of Newcastle upon Tyne Continuing Education Sub-Committee 20 March 1985, 'Teaching English to ethnic minorities'; and TWAS, MD.NC/162/3, Education Committee, 'Section 11 posts in the Education Service', 6 November 1987, p. 2.

primarily at ethnic minority pupils who had lived in Britain for some time, and the Teaching of English as a Foreign Language (EFL), which was for those who had little or no familiarity with the English language or environment. In doing so, Newcastle's local authority was challenging the view endorsed by the Swann Report that downplayed the different language needs of ESL students, preferring instead to mainstream them. At the time of the report, Newcastle was home to two specialist language units that had been established in secondary schools. These units were set up with the aim of helping ethnic minority pupils who had grown up in Britain and required ESL support. However, it quickly became apparent that there were a significant number of children who had recently arrived in Britain, spoke their mother tongue at home and had very little knowledge of English. As a result of this, the language units had to try to also meet their learning needs. An additional problem was that not all ethnic minority pupils who needed language help attended one of the two schools with language units. Furthermore, because there was not an official city policy for establishing which children required support and what this should consist of, the report conceded that many ethnic minority pupils were not receiving suitable language provision.[95]

It also documented the results of a survey of the language units at Heaton Manor and Redewood schools, and of a review of the available provision for ethnic minority pupils with language difficulties at Rutherford School. These three schools were undoubtedly chosen because they had the greatest numbers of ethnic minority pupils. Rutherford had 348 pupils of Commonwealth origin whilst Heaton Manor had ninety-six and Redewood fifty-nine. Furthermore, it was these three schools that had the highest numbers of migrant children requiring additional language support. Rutherford had 110 pupils who fell into this category whilst Redewood had fifty-eight and Heaton Manor thirty-five. The report found that although staff in the Redewood and Heaton Manor centres would have benefited from further qualifications and resources, they appeared to be effectively meeting the language needs of their pupils. The situation at Rutherford School was certainly more pressing. It did not have the resources to cope with all of its migrant children with language difficulties and thus around eighty were receiving no specialist help whatsoever. The two

[95] TWAS, MD.NC/162/1, City of Newcastle upon Tyne Education Committee, 'Report on provision for the teaching of English as a second language and as a foreign language in Newcastle secondary schools', 11 December 1984, p. 1.

specialist language teachers working at the school suffered from a lack of resources and storage space, and their role and purpose was not recognised or supported by the rest of the school staff. Overall, it was impossible for a small team of two to address the needs of all the ethnic minority pupils at the school who required additional language assistance.[96]

The report also offered a city-wide assessment of primary and secondary school pupils who needed help with the English language, but were not attending specialist language units. However, these pupils' needs were being met in other ways. For example, teachers attached to the Learning Support Service helped children within primary schools, some schools were granted additional members of staff by the LEA and there was an outreach agenda concerning ethnic minority parents. Overall, there were only a total of six pupils in five of the city's schools who were deemed as requiring specialist language help, but not receiving it. Finally, the report made a series of recommendations, including that additional language teachers be appointed to Redewood, Heaton Manor and Rutherford Schools, and that the schools be granted the necessary outreach staff, learning resources and in-service training. Lastly, it suggested that appropriate criteria be developed so that ethnic minority pupils requiring support could be identified and their needs evaluated.[97]

Adhering to the national paradigm, whilst the 1980s saw Newcastle's local authority implement a series of new measures in an attempt to secure a multicultural and anti-racist education system, the 1990s was a period of cuts and continuation rather than innovation. With race having largely slipped from Britain's national education agenda, the initiatives carried out in Newcastle were either scaled back due to a lack of funding or, when possible, were extensions of those that had been implemented during the 1980s. In 1993, for example, concern was expressed over the Bilingual Support Service having to be discontinued as a result of funding cuts. This service offered additional teaching support for children whose first language was not English, provided help and advice for teachers through in-class support and training, and carried out home visits and maintained links with ethnic minority parents. This meant that any support subsequently offered to bilingual children would have to be financed through the Aggregated Schools Budget, a fund from which LEAs received a smaller share

---

[96] Ibid., pp. 2–4, Appendix 1.
[97] Ibid., pp. 5–6, Appendix 1.

following the 1988 Education Reform Act.[98]

Newcastle's local authority conceded that, from 1993 onwards, there would be a reduction in the support available to bilingual children and that schools with a small number of ethnic minority pupils that had traditionally been granted small amounts of money would potentially miss out altogether. Furthermore, the expertise and support that had been provided by the Bilingual Support Service's central team would no longer be available.[99] Despite the reductions, Newcastle was still the recipient of some Home Office funds that supported schools with large numbers of ethnic minority pupils and language problems.[100]

Other bids for projects aimed at helping bilingual children in the city's schools had to be scaled down due to Section 11 funding cuts. As a result, it was decided that the best approach in Newcastle would be to concentrate on children between the ages of three and five. The idea behind such a proposed project was to identify at an early age those bilingual children at risk of not performing well in the education system and provide support for these pupils by involving their parents. It was also to comprise training for members of staff and parental workshops. The focus was to be overwhelmingly on those schools that had the largest numbers of pupils for whom English was not their first language. Newcastle's local authority declared that such a bid from the Education Committee would have priority over all other submissions.[101] Concern was also expressed over the availability of mother-tongue language classes. Due to a lack of resources, those lessons that had been offered at the Bangladeshi Muslim Association were no longer running and, because of the manner in which the Home Office prioritised the English language, doubts were expressed over funding being allocated to mother tongues.[102]

There also continued to be a focus on racial harassment in Newcastle's schools. Both in Newcastle and across Britain the late

---

[98] See Stephen Gorard, Chris Taylor and John Fitz, *Schools, Markets and Choice Policies* (London, 2003), p. 9.

[99] See TWAS, MD.NC/613, Racial Equality Officer Working Group 2 December 1992–17 May 1995, Racial Equality Officers Working Group, 'Racial equality – budget appraisal', 17 February 1993, pp. 2–3.

[100] See TWAS, MD.NC/365, Education Committee, 'Section 11 bid', 16 December 1994.

[101] Ibid., p. 3.

[102] See TWAS, MD.NC/365, City of Newcastle upon Tyne Black and Minority Ethnic Consultative Forum 14 December 1994, p. 3.

1980s and 1990s witnessed an increasing awareness regarding racial incidents in schools.[103] As a result, a Racial Harassment Support Working Group was established in the city with the intention of offering advice and support to pupils who had been racially harassed, and their families. There was concern that the LEA's guidelines on racial harassment were not being effectively implemented and this group was to help head teachers apply them and improve practices.[104] Furthermore, the Education Committee applied measures it hoped would raise awareness amongst schools of its anti-racist policy and the procedures for dealing with racial harassment. All schools were informed of the general guidelines, and were provided with a checklist of what to do in cases of racial harassment and an outline of the behaviour that was expected from members of staff.[105] Overall, despite financial cutbacks, Newcastle's local authority was committed to the education of the city's ethnic minorities.[106]

An assessment of the education of Muslim ethnic minorities in Newcastle during the post-war period follows a different trajectory to those of the employment and housing sectors. Through their behaviour and performances in the local labour and housing markets, Newcastle's Muslim migrants demonstrated widespread self-determination, independence and an understanding of their host societies. These are traits and characteristics that the city's Muslim ethnic minorities have not had the same opportunity to enact in education although a pursuit of

[103] For Newcastle see Newcastle City Library, L325, 'Minority Ethnic Communities Survey 1990', 21 November 1990, p. 5; TWAS, MD.NC/613, Newcastle City Council Racial Equality Sub-Committee, 'Reported racial incidents in schools, summer 1993', 6 January 1993; and Chief Executive's Department, *Update on Racial Harassment in Newcastle*, p. 15. For Britain see Commission for Racial Equality, *Learning in Terror: A Survey of Racial Harassment in Schools and Colleges in England, Scotland and Wales, 1985–1987* (London, 1988); and Barry Troyna and Richard Hatcher, 'Racist incidents in schools: A framework for analysis', in Dawn Gill, Barbara Mayor and Maud Blair (eds), *Racism and Education: Structures and Strategies* (London, 1992), pp. 187–207.
[104] See TWAS, MD.NC/614/1, Racial Equality Working Group, 'Work of the Racial Harassment Support Group', 2 March 1995, p. 4.
[105] See TWAS, MD.NC/614/2, Newcastle City Council Education Committee, 'Anti-racist policy and procedures for dealing with racial harassment', 5 November 1996, pp. 1, 5–9.
[106] See TWAS, MD.NC/614/2, City of Newcastle upon Tyne Racial Equality Working Group, 'The Single Regeneration Budget Challenge Fund – round III', 7 March 1996, p. 3.

self-determination potentially played a role in influencing educational achievements and aspirations. Yet it is an assessment of this sector that particularly exposes two of the other key themes running throughout this study. Firstly, more so than in both employment and housing, the Newcastle local authority's policies and measures from the 1960s to the 1990s regarding the education of ethnic minorities demonstrated a clear adherence to a national mandate that catered for their long-term settlement. Whether it was the assimilationist approach of the 1960s or the multicultural stance of the 1980s, legislation assumed a future in Britain. The role that this supposition played becomes further accentuated when compared with the Bremen context.

Secondly, there is no doubt that the size of Newcastle's ethnic minority community once again had an impact. As a result of this, the education of the city's Muslim migrant pupils has been more manageable and not resulted in some of the widespread difficulties that have arisen in other areas. The number of ethnic minority pupils in Newcastle has always been smaller than in the larger hubs of migrant concentration. For example, whilst Newcastle had 585 immigrant pupils towards the end of 1967, there were fifty LEAs that had over 1,000 by January 1970 and those of Birmingham, Bradford, Manchester and Inner London had over 1,000 Pakistani pupils alone. Similarly, whilst in the autumn of 1984 Newcastle was home to around 2,000 schoolchildren whose mother tongue was not English, Bradford in 1983 already had almost 14,000 pupils whose home languages were Punjabi, Urdu, Bengali or Pushto.[107] It is true that the number of ethnic minority pupils did not necessarily influence local authorities' policies. For example, like Newcastle, both Inner London and Birmingham rejected the dispersal policy of the 1960s and many, including those of Leicester and Manchester, disregarded the Swann Report recommendations and offered provision for mother-tongue teaching in schools.[108]

Yet Newcastle's Muslim migrant pupils have nevertheless often had a different educational experience than those in cities with far larger ethnic minority populations. The highest ethnic minority constitution of a Newcastle school in the mid-1980s was 25 per cent, a far cry from figures of over 70 per cent in nineteen schools in Bradford.[109] As a

---

[107] See Jørgen S. Nielsen, *Towards a European Islam: Migration, Minorities and Citizenship* (Basingstoke, 1999), pp. 48–9.

[108] See David H. McKay and Andrew W. Cox, *The Politics of Urban Change* (London, 1979), p. 235; and Baker, *Key Issues in Bilingualism and Bilingual Education*, p. 66.

result, schools in the city have rarely struggled to respond effectively to their migrant pupils' needs and have overwhelmingly managed to address any existing problems themselves. Furthermore, ethnic minority schoolchildren have not tended to suffer from persistent language problems and isolation. Furthermore, the manageable size of Newcastle's ethnic minority population has meant that the city's local authority, whilst largely abiding by national directives, was able to mould practices and measures around the requirements of migrant pupils, and demonstrate an awareness and understanding of their learning needs.

Yet as across Britain, Newcastle's schools were only managing to respond to the learning demands of a certain proportion of the city's Muslim pupils. As was the case with the employment and housing sectors (and as will also be discussed regarding Bremen) the Muslim ethnic minority communities have also played a significant role in the educational process.[110] Mosques, youth and community centres, and even Muslim migrant businesses and neighbourhoods have traditionally acted as conduits of cultural and religious education. It has been in these spaces that Newcastle's Muslim youths have become acquainted with Islam, mother-tongue languages, and their ethnic and religious cultures, and had the opportunity to engage with Islamic learning materials and study groups. In other words, the education of Muslim youths in Newcastle, as in towns and cities across Britain, has traditionally taken place in two separate, yet complementary, spheres.

Furthermore, in contrast to what has often been argued is the case for British Muslims, it does not appear as though Newcastle's local authority can be accused of educationally failing the city's Muslim youth or of not doing enough to meet their specific needs.[111] Overall, whilst Muslim pupils in Newcastle have undoubtedly experienced incidents of disadvantage, hardship and racism, these have not been widespread, nor have they dominated their educational experiences. This study has exposed the advantages of a small and close-knit Muslim migrant population, and demonstrated that education policies

---

[109] See Jean Conteh, *Succeeding in Diversity: Culture, Language and Learning in Primary Classrooms* (Stoke on Trent, 2003), p. 29.

[110] See Lewis, *Islamic Britain*, pp. 76–112; and Ansari, 'The Infidel Within', p. 311.

[111] See Anwar, 'Muslims in Britain: Issues, policy and practice', pp. 32–4; and Joel S. Fetzer and J. Christopher Soper, *Muslims and the State in Britain, France, and Germany* (Cambridge, 2005), p. 42.

have not always revelled in racism and xenophobia, or resulted in underachievement and non-integration.

Bremen

Bremen's government has traditionally awarded more attention to the education of its ethnic minorities than to any other aspect of their lives. From the time of their initial settlement in the city, policies have been implemented in an attempt to accommodate migrant pupils within the local education system and meet their learning needs. The aim of Bremen's local authority from the beginning was to mainstream immigrant pupils as quickly as possible. At nursery and kindergarten level, there was a dispersal policy in place, meaning that ethnic minority children were not permitted to become concentrated past a certain level. At primary and secondary schools, migrant pupils received help with their homework, and bilingual and mother-tongue instruction. They also benefited from supplementary German language classes that were taught by native teachers alongside ethnic minority instructors, and there was a strong emphasis on vocational training. Efforts on behalf of Bremen's local authority increased and intensified even at times of economic hardship. During the 1990s, initiatives persevered with the hiring of ethnic minority teachers, and mother-tongue teaching taking place in both supplementary and mainstream classes. Furthermore, efforts appeared to be working. Fewer ethnic minority youths were leaving secondary school without a diploma, and there were increasing numbers attending both kindergartens and *Gymnasium*, the highest tier of the German secondary school education system. By the early 2000s, Bremen had also witnessed a vast surge in the number of migrants enrolling on vocational training programmes.[112]

The role played by ethnic and religious communities in education has been even more visible in Bremen than in Newcastle. The city has long been home to migrant cultural organisations, such as the Umbrella Federation of Immigrant Cultural Associations in Bremen or the DAB (Dachverband der Ausländer-Kulturvereine in Bremen). The DAB's monthly magazine, *Stimme* (Voice), offered an insight into city policies and immigrant experiences, and education was a regular focal point.

---

[112] See Ireland, *Becoming Europe*, pp. 89, 95–7.
[113] See Daniel Faas, *Negotiating Political Identities: Multiethnic Schools and Youth in Europe* (Farnham, 2010), p. 49.

Mosques, Turkish associations, youth clubs and community and cultural centres have traditionally played a significant role in provisioning for Islamic religious education, cultural festivals and traditions and mother-tongue teaching. The education of Bremen's ethnic minorities has also been a much-discussed subject at the city's *Integrationswoche* (Integration Week) in recent years. Furthermore, Islam has specifically been a topic of heated debate in Bremen's education system, with Bremen being one of the German states to have enforced a ban on the wearing of visible religious clothing and symbols amongst teachers in public schools.[113]

Even more contentious and divisive a topic in Bremen, and indeed throughout Germany, is that of religious education. In Germany, religious education is part of the curriculum at public schools, and is an official subject in most *Länder*; provision is the responsibility of both the state and the religious communities. It is taught in accordance with the principles of the respective religious communities and is overwhelmingly confessional. Religious education has traditionally followed Christian lines, however, with Islam being largely neglected due to the fact that no Islamic organisation has been officially recognised at a state level. However, more recently, and since 9/11 especially, most German states have introduced some type of Islamic religious education in their schools.[114] Bremen, however, has always been an exception because its 1947 state constitution specifies that state schools must teach biblical history in a Christian context. This is referred to as the 'Bremen clause' or the *Bremer Klausel*. This has meant that although some projects have been introduced to offer Islamic religious education to Muslim pupils in the state, these have not been authorised by an Islamic religious body, nor are they directed by practising Muslims. For decades, the content of Bremen's religious education and how best to develop it has been the topic of heated debate amongst politicians, Islamic associations and members of the city's Muslim communities.[115]

[114] See Fuess, 'Islamic religious education in Western Europe', pp. 225–32; and Dan-Paul Jozsa, 'Islam and education in Europe. With special reference to Austria, England, France, Germany and the Netherlands', in Robert Jackson, Siebren Miedema, Wolfram Weisse and Jean-Paul Willaime (eds), *Religion and Education in Europe: Developments, Contexts and Debates* (Münster, 2007), pp. 75–9.

[115] See Jørgen S. Nielsen, *Muslims in Western Europe* (Edinburgh, 2004), p. 37; Yasemin Karakaşoğlu and Sigrid Luchtenberg, 'Islamophobia in German educational settings: Actions and reactions', in Barry van Driel (ed.),

Alongside the status of Islam within Bremen's education system, the educational achievement of migrant schoolchildren is a subject that has recently attracted heightened levels of attention in the city-state. Despite local authority initiatives and progress being made, the PISA studies revealed that there was a significant gap between the educational attainment levels of migrant pupils and their German counterparts. Between the 2000 and the 2003 studies, this was shown to be the case for mathematics and reading skills. Furthermore, Bremen was the worst performing of the German states overall.[116] Therefore, this is a topic with both current relevance and historical poignancy. It has been at the centre of government debate and policies since the 1960s, and continues to be perceived as a key feature and indicator of integration. Overall, as with the employment and housing sectors, whilst often displaying a sense of uncertainly about the future of the city's immigrant communities, there was a clear realisation from the beginning that their educational needs required catering for in the long term.

The 1960s and 1970s

As was the case across Germany, the initial belief in Bremen was that guest-workers constituted a temporary supply of manpower. During the early 1960s, as a result of the small number of workers whose families had joined them in Bremen, it was still believed that any type of provision for children was unnecessary.[117] Yet from this point onwards, both Bremen's government and the local press began realising

---

Confronting Islamophobia in Educational Practice (Stoke on Trent, 2004), p. 42; Fetzer and Soper, *Muslims and the State in Britain, France, and Germany*, p. 113; and Fuess, 'Islamic religious education in Western Europe', pp. 231–2.

[116] See Gesa Ramm, Oliver Walter, Heike Heidemeier and Manfred Prenzel, 'Soziokulturelle Herkunft und Migration im Ländervergleich', in Manfred Prenzel, Jürgen Baumert, Werner Blum, Rainer Lehmann, Detlev Leutner, Michael Neubrand, Reinhard Pekrun, Jürgen Rost and Ulrich Schiefele (eds), *PISA 2003: Der zweite Vergleich der Länder in Deutschland – Was wissen und können Jugendliche?* (Münster, 2005), pp. 282–5; and Ursula Rotte, 'Education reform in Germany: Efforts and experiences in Bavaria after PISA 2000', in Ralph Rotte (ed.), *International Perspectives on Education Policy* (New York, 2006), p. 109.

[117] See Staatsarchiv Bremen, 4,13/4–122–10–02/0 Grundsätzliche Vereinbarungen für die Behandlung ausländischer Arbeitnehmer und deren Angehörigen. Allgemeines. 1951–1972, A letter from the Stadt- and Polizeiamt Bremen to the Senator für das Bauwesen dated 18 November 1960; and 'Für die Bambinos ist kein Platz. Nur vereinzelte ausländische Arbeiter können Kind und Kegel nach Bremen nachholen', *Weser Kurier* (17 June 1961).

that increasing numbers of foreign workers in the city were sending for their families.[118] Bremen's local authority focused heavily on the education and learning needs of ethnic minority youths, and the initiatives it implemented were soon recognised as examples of good practice across Germany.[119] Due to the fact that Bremen experienced the recruitment of guest-workers later than most areas of Germany, it still had only a small number of foreign pupils in its schools during the 1960s. In June 1965, there were fifty-four foreign workers' children who attended schools in Bremen and the three main nationalities represented were Spanish, Turkish and Greek with eighteen, fifteen and twelve pupils respectively. Of these children, fifty-two attended either primary school or *Hauptschule*, the lowest tier of Germany's secondary education system. The remaining two pupils went to a *Gymnasium*, the most academic level of secondary education that prepares pupils for entry into university.[120] By March 1966, there were fifty-seven guest-workers' children in Bremen's daycare centres and, by October of that year, the number of Turkish pupils had increased to ninety-two.[121] This was a far cry from a city like West Berlin, for example, that was already home to 2,840 foreign students in 1968.[122]

Yet despite its low numbers, Bremen's local authority placed a strong emphasis on these migrant children having the same educational opportunities as their German counterparts and on establishing what provision they required. Government documents repeatedly stressed that, according to the state's May 1957 law on the education system, all foreign children living in Bremen that were of school age had equal access to public schools and the same obligation to attend school as their German

[118] See 'Wenn Gastarbeiter keine Gäste mehr sind. Viele Ausländer lassen sich mit ihren Familien in Deutschland nieder', *Weser Kurier* (29 October 1965).
[119] See 'Bremen will Gastarbeiterkindern besseren Unterricht anbieten', *Frankfurter Rundschau* (11 April 1978); and 'Die soziale Zeitbombe tickt nicht überall. Bremens Schule an der Schmidtstraße als Modell für die Integration', *Stuttgarter Zeitung* (21 September 1979).
[120] SB, 4,111/5–2272, Beschulung der Kinder ausländischer Arbeitnehmer – KMK – Rundschreiben (Mitteilungen, Beschlüsse) Bd. 5 1974–1979, 'Zur 108. Sitzung der Ständigen Konferenz der Kultusminister, Plenum, am 7./8. Juli 1965 in Kiel', 30 June 1965.
[121] See SB, 4,124/3–695, Ausländische Arbeitskräfte in Deutschland Bd. 2 1964–1968, A letter from Jugendamt Bremen to the Senator für Wohlfahrt und Jugend dated 7 March 1966; and SB, 4,111/5–2279, Beschulung der Kinder ausländischer Arbeitnehmer – Regelung in Bremen: Kinder türkischer Gastarbeiter 1966–1970.
[122] See Rist, *Guestworkers in Germany*, p. 225.

counterparts.[123] There was also a recognition that these pupils posed difficulties for the city's schools as a result of their lack of proficiency in the German language and there was a clear commitment to ensuring that schools in the city could cater for them appropriately.[124] For example, amongst the aforementioned fifty-four foreign workers' children who attended schools in Bremen in June 1965, only 35 per cent possessed the German language skills required to partake in lessons.[125] The language difficulties experienced by guest-worker pupils and their educational consequences have been repeatedly stressed in the literature for Germany as a whole.[126] Each German state approached these children differently and the Bremen government's aim during the 1960s was to integrate guest-worker children as quickly as possible. This was to be achieved by mainstreaming them rather than separating them from their German peers, and by promoting a swift acquisition of the German language. This approach was like that taken in Berlin and was practically the opposite of that pursued in conservative southern states like Bavaria and Baden-Württemberg where migrant pupils were segregated from German children into classes in which there was a heavy focus on mother-tongue languages.[127]

Furthermore, foreign workers' children in Bremen were to be dispersed amongst as many schools in the city as possible as it was believed that this would allow them to learn German faster and not become segregated. There were not to be more than twenty-five migrant pupils in any one school. For younger children, it was believed that additional German language classes were often not successful and

[123] See SB, 4,111/5–2276, Beschulung der Kinder ausländischer Arbeitnehmer – Regelung in Bremen: Allgemeines 1965–1976, A letter from the Senator für das Bildungswesen to schools in Bremen dated 1 February 1965; and SB, 4,111/5–2277, Beschulung der Kinder ausländischer Arbeitnehmer – Regelung in Bremen: Durchführung (Grundsatzfragen, Einzelfälle) 1962–1971, A letter dated 14 June 1966.
[124] See SB, 4,13/4-122-10-02/7, Zuzug von Familienangehörigen ausländischer Arbeitnehmer Band 1 1965–1974, A letter from the Senator für das Bildungswesen to the Senator für Inneres dated 14 October 1965.
[125] See SB, 4,111/5–2272, 'Zur 108. Sitzung der Ständigen Konferenz der Kultusminister'.
[126] See Eva Kolinsky, 'Non-German minorities in contemporary German society', in David Horrocks and Eva Kolinsky (eds), *Turkish Culture in German Society Today* (Oxford, 1996), p. 102; and Kalter, 'The second generation in the German labor market'.
[127] See Rist, *Guestworkers in Germany*, p. 226; and Lucassen, *The Immigrant Threat*, p. 165.

that German was often best learnt alongside German youngsters in the mainstream classrooms of kindergartens and primary schools. Older children were only to receive additional German tuition if necessary and, if there were not sufficient numbers to form a class, they were to be given extra help within the mainstream classroom. German language groups were to consist of around five pupils and were not supposed to be held for more than six hours a week. Furthermore, they were to be taught by teachers who were not acquainted with the children's mother tongues and the classes were to comprise pupils of different nationalities. Overall, the learning of German was seen as both essential for integration and as part of a wider initiative to help these children and their families settle into life in Germany.[128]

During the 1960s, Bremen's local authority repeatedly stressed that all schoolchildren were to have the same educational opportunities and that, as a result, schools with Turkish as the language of instruction were not to be established in Bremen. Yet the Turkish consul general requested that Turkish children in the city attend mother-tongue language classes so as not to lose ties with their homeland. Whilst Bremen's government was adamant that these classes were not to replace mainstream lessons within schools, it agreed to offer the use of classrooms in the afternoon; these sessions took place in schools across the city and were run by native speakers. However, they were the responsibility of the Turkish Ministry of Education and Cultural Affairs and, because Bremen's local authority provided all children with equal education opportunities, they were to be paid for by the sending country.[129] Indeed mother-tongue language classes

---

[128] See SB, 4,111/5–2276, A letter from the Senator für das Bildungswesen to schools in Bremen dated 1 February 1965; SB, 4,111/5–2272, 'Zur 108. Sitzung der Ständigen Konferenz der Kultusminister, Plenum, am 7./8. Juli 1965 in Kiel'; SB, 4,111/5–2277, A report entitled 'Deutschunterricht für Kinder von Ausländern' dated 16 February 1967; SB, 4,111/5–2277, 'Konferenz über Fragen des Deutschunterrichts für Gastarbeiterkinder am 6. März 1969 für Schulen in Bremen-Nord'; and SB, 4,111/5–2281, Durchführung des Unterrichts für Kinder ausländischer Arbeitnehmer – Allgemeines 1967–1984, Report entitled 'Gastarbeiter' dated 27 November 1969.

[129] See SB, 4,111/5–2290, Beschulung der Kinder ausländischer Arbeitnehmer – Allgemeines (1955) Bd. 1 1964–1971, A letter dated 14 June 1966; SB, 4,111/5–2277, A letter from the Senator für das Bildungswesen to schools in Bremen dated 17 October 1966; SB, 4,111/5–2277, A letter from the Chef der Senatskanzlei to the consul general dated 6 January 1967; SB, 4,111/5–2277, A letter dated 19 February 1969; and SB, 4,111/5–2281, Report entitled 'Gastarbeiter' dated 27 November 1969.

became increasingly widespread in Germany throughout the 1970s as family reunification took place, and the manner in which they were run and where the responsibility for them lay depended on individual states.[130]

During the 1970s, the number of guest-worker children in Bremen's schools increased dramatically, as did the amount of attention awarded to their education by Bremen's local authority. Government reports and correspondence from this decade repeatedly reinforced a commitment to providing for ethnic minority pupils' needs, and further stressed that they were to have the same educational opportunities as their German counterparts. The main aim was still for them to become integrated into the city's schools as quickly as possible, something that was to be largely achieved through intensive German language tuition.[131] The level of dedication of the Bremen government to the education of guest-worker youths during the 1970s is reflected in the vast amount of discussion that took place, and the policy suggestions and recommendations put forward.[132]

In September 1970, the city was home to 893 migrant pupils, of which the largest group, the Turkish, constituted 308.[133] By the beginning of the 1972–73 school year, there were 1,288 foreign

[130] See Nermin Abadan-Unat, 'Turkish migration to Europe, 1960–1975: A balance sheet of achievements and failures', in Nermin Abadan-Unat et al., *Turkish Workers in Europe, 1960–1975: A Socio-economic Reappraisal* (Leiden, 1976), pp. 38–9.

[131] See SB, 4,124/3–645, Der Senator für Arbeit, 'Kleine Anfrage der Fraktion der CDU vom 26. Juni 1973. Ausländische Arbeitnehmer', 8 August 1973, pp. 21–2, 26–9; and Bremische Bürgerschaft Landtag 8. Wahlperiode, Drucksache 8/600, 'Antwort des Senats zur Anfrage der Fraktion der CDU vom 26. Juni 1973 (Drs. 8/566). Ausländische Arbeitnehmer', 12 September 1973, pp. 14, 16.

[132] See SB, 4,111/5–241, Beschulung der Kinder ausländischer Arbeitnehmer – Vorlagen für die Referentensitzungen 1972–1973, 'Modellvorstellungen zur Frage sprachintegrierter Schulen', 22 May 1972; and SB, 4,124/3–644, A letter from the Gesellschaft für Wohnungs- und Siedlungswesen e.V. to the Senator für Wohlfahrt und Jugend der Freien Hansestadt Bremen dated 27 January 1973.

[133] See SB, 4,111/5–2278, Beschulung der Kinder ausländischer Arbeitnehmer – Regelung in Bremen: Durchführung (Grundsatzfragen, Einzelfälle) 1962–1971, 'Zur schulischen Situation der Kinder von Ausländern in der Stadtgemeinde Bremen', 02 November 1970, p. 1.

[134] See SB, 4,111/5–2281, Vorlage für die Referentensitzung am 08 November 1972, 'Zur Situation der Kinder ausländischer Arbeitnehmer an bremischen Schulen mit Beginn des Schuljahres 1972/73', p. 1.

workers' children in Bremen's schools, of which 808 were Turkish.[134] As a consequence of the family reunification process, by the 1978–79 school year, the total number of migrant children in the city's schools had increased to 4,573, of which 3,855 were from the recruitment countries of Greece, Italy, Yugoslavia, Portugal, Spain and Turkey. The Turks were still the largest group with 2,902 pupils.[135] Although the number of ethnic minority pupils in Bremen had grown substantially throughout the 1970s, it remained small compared to those found in areas and cities of migrant worker concentration. During the 1976–77 school year, for example, there were 33,200 guest-worker children in Bavarian public schools, whilst West Berlin was home to 19,241 foreign students.[136]

Although on a smaller scale, Bremen experienced the same problems and obstacles regarding the education of guest-worker children as have been documented for Germany more widely. Furthermore, by the early 1970s, the city's local authority already appears to have had an in-depth appreciation of what these were. It demonstrated an understanding of the background of migrant schoolchildren and the difficulties they faced in the city's schools, as well as a firm idea of how to improve their educational experiences and achievements. A 1970 report, for example, highlighted what some of the problems were and raised issues that acted as the backbone of the political debate in the city throughout the decade. Firstly, there were cases of children not being sent to school. This was largely put down to parents coming from a culture that did not place much value on education and a tendency amongst them of not perceiving schooling in Bremen as necessary because their stay was only to be temporary. There were also some who chose to keep their children at home for fear they would face discrimination in a German school.[137]

Throughout the 1970s, measures were implemented in Bremen in an attempt to get all guest-worker children of school age to attend school. These included letters and packs with information on education laws

[135] See Der Senat der Freien Hansestadt Bremen, *Konzeption zur Integration der ausländischen Arbeitnehmer und ihrer Familienangehörigen im Lande Bremen* (June 1979), pp. 33–4.
[136] See Rist, *Guestworkers in Germany*, pp. 212, 225.
[137] SB, 4,111/5–2278, 'Zur schulischen Situation der Kinder von Ausländern in der Stadtgemeinde Bremen', 02 November 1970, pp. 2–3. See also SB, 4,111/5–242, Beschulung der Kinder ausländischer Arbeitnehmer – Anfragen aus Bremen, A letter from the Arbeiterkammer Bremen to the Senator für Bildung, Kunst und Wissenschaft dated 9 February 1972.

and local schools being sent to parents.[138] The fact that there was a link between the paying out of *Kindergeld* and enrollment was expected to help.[139] It was also anticipated that the regulation that came into effect in October 1978 would help further as it stated that foreign workers who had been living legally in Germany for a period of five years, and their immediate families, could be granted an indefinite residence permit on the condition that any children of school age were in fact attending school.[140] Indeed the fact that a significant number of guest-worker children, and especially Turkish girls, were not sent to school in Germany has been widely documented, with German authorities having been criticised for not doing enough to ensure attendance.[141] However, in Bremen, this was a government concern from the outset.

The second issue raised was the difficulty encountered by guest-worker pupils in trying to learn and maintain both German and their mother tongues. It was the older children especially who struggled the most. Because they arrived to Germany at a later age, they often suffered from language difficulties throughout the remainder of their school careers. As a result, the most prestigious school-leaving certificate they achieved tended to be that from *Hauptschule*, with those successfully completing *Realschule* (the middle tier of the secondary system) or *Gymnasium* being exceptions.[142] A concentration of ethnic minority pupils into *Hauptschule* was a pattern witnessed in Bremen throughout the 1970s, although improvements were made throughout the decade.[143] Of those secondary school youths in Bremen during the 1978–79 school year from Greece, Italy, Yugoslavia, Portugal Spain and Turkey, 492 went to *Hauptschule*, 259 to *Realschule* and 117 to

[138] See SB, 4,111/5–242, Draft letters to parents; and SB, 4,111/5–246, Beschulung der Kinder ausländischer Arbeitnehmer – Sonstige soziale Betreuung ausländischer Arbeitnehmer und ihrer Kinder: Private Träger, Bürgerinitiativen, etc. Bd. 1 1972–1975, Information about schools for Turkish parents.
[139] See SB, 4,111/5–2272, 'Kleine FDP-Anfrage in der Bürgerschaft am 27.04.1977 – Kinder ausländischer Arbeitnehmer. Vorlage vom 12.04.1977 für die Sitzung des Senats am 25.04.1977', 12 April 1977, pp. 2–3.
[140] See Der Senat der Freien Hansestadt Bremen, *Konzeption zur Integration der ausländischen Arbeitnehmer und ihrer Familienangehörigen im Lande Bremen* (June 1979), p. 46.
[141] See Abadan-Unat, *Turks in Europe*, p. 19.
[142] SB, 4,111/5–2278, 'Zur schulischen Situation der Kinder von Ausländern in der Stadtgemeinde Bremen', 02 November 1970, pp. 3–4.
[143] See Freie Hansestadt Bremen *Statistische Monatsberichte*, 'Schulbesuch und Schulerfolg ausländischer Schüler', 30. Jahrgang, 1978, p. 101.

Gymnasium. Amongst the Turkish secondary school pupils, 388 went to *Hauptschule*, 175 to *Realschule* and 58 to *Gymnasium*.[144]

This concentration of migrant youths, and especially Turks, into secondary education's lowest tier has long been, and remains, at the centre of both the political and academic debate on ethnic minority education in Germany. Various explanations have been provided for this pattern, including the late arrival of migrant children in Germany, their socio-economic background and their parents' lack of proficiency in the German language.[145] Yet despite the overwhelming clustering of ethnic minority youths into *Hauptschule*, there was an increase during the 1970s of those succeeding in attaining a school-leaving diploma. Whilst in 1973 only 33.7 per cent of migrant *Hauptschule* graduates secured a diploma, this figure had risen to 51.1 per cent in 1977.[146]

The third issue raised in the 1970 report was that the city's additional German language classes were not running smoothly. Ethnic minority children were grouped together in these classes irrespective of nationality, age and ability, and progress was often disrupted by new arrivals. Furthermore, these lessons lacked any official theoretical or methodological foundation, and their content and structure depended entirely on individual teachers. They also suffered from a lack of teachers, learning materials and enough available teaching hours for them to take place. As a result, of the 259 migrant pupils who urgently required additional German tuition at the time, only 191 were receiving it.[147] Fourthly, the report argued that some ethnic minority children were being overloaded with afternoon mother-tongue language classes and that this was having an effect on their academic

[144] See Der Senat der Freien Hansestadt Bremen, *Konzeption zur Integration der ausländischen Arbeitnehmer und ihrer Familienangehörigen im Lande Bremen* (June 1979), p. 34.
[145] See Richard D. Alba, Johann Handl and Walter Müller, 'Ethnic inequalities in the German school system', in Peter Schuck and Rainer Münz (eds), *Paths to Inclusion: The Integration of Migrants in the United States and Germany* (Oxford, 1998), pp. 127–34; and Lucassen, 'Poles and Turks in the German Ruhr area', p. 36.
[146] See 'Schulbesuch und Schulerfolg ausländischer Schüler', 30. Jahrgang, 1978, p. 102.
[147] SB, 4,111/5–2278, 'Zur schulischen Situation der Kinder von Ausländern in der Stadtgemeinde Bremen', 2 November 1970, p. 4. See also SB, 4,111/5–2287, Beschulung der Kinder ausländischer Arbeitnehmer – Ressortübergreifende Arbeitsgruppe 'Integration ausländischer Arbeitnehmer': Grundsätzliches, Protokolle, Konzepte, etc. 1974–1978, A report compiled by the Senator für Bildung, Wissenschaft und Kunst dated 6 November 1974, p. 2.

performance. This was further accentuated by the fact that some parents perceived the learning of mother tongues as more important than the curriculum within German schools.[148] The last issue the report highlighted was that some migrant pupils were having trouble adapting. They often struggled to understand the rules and structure of German schools, and it was especially tough for teachers in classes with high numbers of ethnic minority children.[149] Certainly, the difficulties encountered by guest-worker children in adjusting to a new education system and the consequences of 'living in two worlds' should not be underestimated.[150]

The 1970 report also detailed a series of recommendations it hoped would help improve the educational experiences and performances of Bremen's guest-worker pupils. These included using translators to help teachers and pupils, and establish contact with ethnic minority parents; providing German language teachers with more preparation opportunities; rescheduling mother-tongue classes to the morning; sending migrant pupils to initiation classes until they had acquired the necessary German language level to join mainstream classes; and hiring additional members of staff. Overall, the report stressed that promoting the integration of ethnic minority children was a way of helping their entire families settle into Bremen.[151] Thus, the early 1970s was largely a period of continuation regarding the education of guest-worker children in Bremen. As during the 1960s, the aim was to integrate them as quickly as possible into mainstream classrooms and offer them the same standard of education as that received by their German counterparts. Furthermore, there was a sense of pride in Bremen regarding the manner in which the integration of migrant pupils was being pursued. In an early 1970s interview, for example, the mayor stressed that the local authority's education policies, alongside those concerning employment and housing, set Bremen's provision for guest-workers and their families apart from that of other German states.[152]

[148] SB, 4,111/5–2278, 'Zur schulischen Situation der Kinder von Ausländern in der Stadtgemeinde Bremen', 2 November 1970, p. 4.
[149] Ibid., p. 5.
[150] See Elçin Kürsat-Ahlers, 'The Turkish minority in German society', in David Horrocks and Eva Kolinsky (eds), *Turkish Culture in German Society Today* (Oxford, 1996), p. 130; and Abadan-Unat, *Turks in Europe*, pp. 115, 117.
[151] SB, 4,111/5–2278, 'Zur schulischen Situation der Kinder von Ausländern in der Stadtgemeinde Bremen', 2 November 1970, pp. 5–8.
[152] See SB, 4,63/2N-284, undated interview with Mayor Hans Koschnick.

The education sector

Yet by the beginning of the 1970s, Bremen's government had become aware that the continuous increase in the city's number of migrant schoolchildren meant that a more intensive type of tuition would soon be required if integration was to be attained.[153] This came in the form of *Vorbereitungsklassen* or preparation classes that ran in Bremen for the first time during the 1972–73 school year. In accordance with the KMK's 1971 policy recommendation, their aim was to prepare migrant schoolchildren solely for a future in Germany and promote a swift integration into the German school system. In February 1973, there were ten preparation classes running for Turkish pupils, one for Greek children and two that were comprised of youths of various nationalities. Each class consisted of between twelve and fifteen pupils, and met for ten to fifteen hours a week. Furthermore, there were also 379 migrant children receiving up to six hours a week of additional German language tuition in groups of around eight pupils called *Kursgruppen*. Whilst those youths in preparation classes tended to have almost no knowledge of German, those in the smaller groups had a basic foundation in the language. *Kursgruppen* were also organised in areas of the city where there were fewer ethnic minority pupils and where therefore preparation classes were not organised. There were twelve Turkish and one Yugoslav teacher to help with both types of lessons. More preparation classes were added the following year and involved German and/or Turkish teaching staff.[154]

Yet these classes were not without problems, with the academic literature arguing that they were poorly organised, that they isolated migrant children and kept them at a lower level of education, and that many children were either never transferred to the German mainstream classroom or could not cope once they got there.[155] In Bremen,

[153] See SB, 4,111/5–2278, a letter from a local education officer to the Senator für Arbeit entitled 'Eingliederung ausländischer Arbeitnehmer' dated 20 October 1970.

[154] See SB, 4,111/5–2281, 'Deutschunterricht für Kinder von Ausländern', 16 February 1967; and SB, 4,111/5–2270, Beschulung der Kinder ausländischer Arbeitnehmer – KMK – Rundschreiben (Mitteilungen, Beschlüsse) Bd. 3 1972–1973, 'Erläuterungen zur schulischen Betreuung von Kindern ausländischer Arbeitnehmer', 27 February 1973. See also SB, 4,111/5–2283, Durchführung des Unterrichts für Kinder ausländischer Arbeitnehmer – Fördermaßnahmen: Vorbereitungskurse 1972–1981.

[155] See M. Sitki Bilmen, 'Educational problems encountered by the children of Turkish migrant workers', in Nermin Abadan-Unat *et al.*, *Turkish Workers in Europe, 1960–1975: A Socio-economic Reappraisal* (Leiden, 1976), p. 247; Schole Raoufi, 'The children of guest-workers in the Federal Republic of

preparation classes were often disadvantaged by the different ages of the pupils, the Turkish teachers speaking Turkish better than German themselves, not having appropriate rooms and children not becoming prepared quickly enough to join the mainstream classroom. The smaller groups experienced difficulty securing enough members of staff. However, there was a clear commitment in the city to making improvements, some of which involved dedicating more hours to additional German language teaching, granting better rooms to these classes and introducing a system that did not allow new pupils to disrupt the progress being made. When not in these German language classes, migrant children joined regular classes with their German peers. This tended to be for subjects like music and physical education.[156]

Furthermore, as was the case in Newcastle, ethnic minority pupils were not spread evenly around the city, but were becoming concentrated in certain schools. During the 1970s, there was a greater proportion of younger migrant children in the city and thus it was primary schools that were experiencing the highest levels of ethnic minority concentration. The schools with the highest proportion of migrant pupils were the Schmidtstraße primary school and *Hauptschule* in the Östliche Vorstadt, which in the 1977–78 school year had 175 and 59 ethnic minority pupils and were 36.1 per cent and 38.1 per cent ethnic minority respectively. Other primary schools in the city with high concentrations of migrant children were Kirchenallee and Halmerweg in Gröpelingen which were 29.7 per cent and 23.7 per cent ethnic minority respectively, and Buntentorsteinweg in Neustadt for which the figure stood at 22.4 per cent. Other *Hauptschule* in Bremen with large numbers of migrant pupils included Kornstraße in Neustadt (33.7 per cent) and Hemelinger Straße in Östliche Vorstadt

---

Germany: Maladjustment and its effects on academic performance', in Joti Bhatnagar (ed.), *Educating Immigrants* (London, 1981), p. 123; and Hartmut Haberland and Tove Skutnabb-Kangas, 'Political determinants of pragmatic and sociolinguistic choices', in Herman Parret, Marina Sbisà and Jef Verschueren (eds), *Possibilities and Limitations of Pragmatics* (Amsterdam, 1981), pp. 301–3.

[156] See SB, 4,111/5–2281, 'Die schulische Betreuung von Kindern ausländischer Arbeitnehmer im Raum Bremen-Nord', 16 June 1972, p. 3; and SB, 4,111/5–2281, Vorlage für die Referentensitzung am 8 November 1972, 'Zur Situation der Kinder ausländischer Arbeitnehmer an bremischen Schulen mit Beginn des Schuljahres 1972/73', pp. 4–5.

(19.2 per cent).[157] As is to be expected, the districts in which these schools were located were some of the ones that experienced the highest levels of residential concentration during the 1970s.

As in Newcastle, there was one school in particular, the aforementioned Schule an der Schmidtstraße, that attracted the local government's attention. Throughout the late 1960s and 1970s, the school kept Bremen's authority informed regarding its ethnic minority pupils, often suggesting measures and approaches it believed would lead to a quicker and more successful integration. The school experienced a sudden increase in its number of migrant children for which it was unprepared, meaning that the appropriate measures were not in place. This was further heightened by the fact that the secondary school was attended by pupils from four of the city's primary schools and, because ethnic minority pupils rarely got into *Realschule* or *Gymnasium*, the majority ended up at the Schmidtstraße *Hauptschule*.[158]

In September 1969, the school had forty migrant children of which nine spoke no German, twelve had a basic grasp of the language but were largely unable to follow classes, nine could understand lessons but had trouble with spelling and arithmetic, and ten achieved the same level as some of the German pupils. A further problem was that many of these children were concentrated in years 5 to 7 and lessons were suffering as a result of classes being over 20 per cent ethnic minority. Whilst it was agreed that these migrant pupils should remain in mainstream classrooms so as to experience a German-speaking environment, it was suggested that they receive two hours of special language tuition a day in order to encourage a faster integration. It was argued that this should take place during regular school hours so as not to overburden them. Furthermore, it was suggested that ethnic minority pupils be able to use more suitable books and learning materials.[159]

By September 1970, the school was questioning migrant children's ability to cope in mainstream German classrooms. It argued that these pupils slowed down the progress made in lessons and that teachers

---

[157] See 'Schulbesuch und Schulerfolg ausländischer Schüler', 30. Jahrgang, 1978, p. 103.

[158] See SB, 4,111/5–253, Durchführung des Unterrichts für Kinder ausländischer Arbeitnehmer – Berichte, Meldungen und Anfragen der Schule Schmidtstraße 1969–1976, A letter from the school's headmaster to the Senator für Bildung, Wissenschaft und Kunst dated 16 April 1974.

[159] See SB, 4,111/5–253, A letter from the school's headmaster to the Senator für das Bildungswesen dated 5 September 1969.

found it difficult to deal with them. Furthermore, it stressed that even ethnic minority children who had been in Germany for a long period of time behaved differently to their German counterparts. At the time, there were a few classes at the school that were over 20 per cent migrant.[160] Throughout the early 1970s, the Schmidtstraße school repeatedly expressed concern regarding the increase in its number of guest-worker pupils and its status as having a high proportion of migrant children was widely recognised in the city.[161] In April 1974, the headmaster declared the school to be in a state of emergency and asked Bremen's local authority to award it a special status to enable it to more effectively pursue the integration of its migrant children. It requested the allocation of additional teaching hours, and more German and mother-tongue teachers.[162]

There are two key reports that offer an insight into the levels of migrant pupils' integration at the school. The first addresses pupils in years 1–6 and the second focuses on youths in years 7–9. The first argued that, out of the twenty-two guest-worker children in years 1–6, only one had been accepted by its German peers. Furthermore, it stressed that, out of these twenty-two pupils, twelve often arrived at school late and without having completed their homework, and eleven still did not have the level of German necessary to follow lessons. The migrant children tended to socialise only amongst themselves, and even those that had only ever been in the German education system were not integrated and were the worst-performing pupils of their years. The report argues that these guest-worker children were not accepted by their German counterparts because of general negative attitudes towards Turks, and because their behaviour in lessons and attitude towards learning caused them to not be taken seriously in the classroom.[163]

[160] See SB, 4,111/5–253, A letter from the school's headmaster to the Senator für das Bildungswesen dated 17 September 1970.
[161] See SB, 4,111/5–242, A letter from the Arbeiterkammer Bremen to the Senator für Bildung, Kunst und Wissenschaft dated 9 February 1972, p. 4; SB, 4,111/5–253, A letter from the school to the Senator für Bildung, Wissenschaft und Kunst dated 12 October 1972; and SB, 4,111/5–253, A letter from the school to the Senator für Bildung, Wissenschaft und Kunst dated 29 November 1972.
[162] See SB, 4,111/5–253, A letter from the school to the Senator für Bildung, Wissenschaft und Kunst dated 16 April 1974.
[163] See SB, 4,111/5–253, 'Die soziale Integration der Gastarbeiterkinder in den Klassen 1–6', undated report.

The second report addressing migrant pupils in *Hauptschule* years 7–9 was equally negative. It argued that only 21 per cent of the guest-worker youths had become integrated into the school and that 54 per cent spoke barely enough German to make themselves understood. Many had become concentrated at the bottom of their classes and, out of the twenty-eight guest-worker pupils, twenty had either already left school or were expected to leave without a diploma. Overall, the report stressed that guest-worker children were not integrated and were often not likely to achieve integration as a result of their lack of German, and that even amongst those that did speak German integration was unlikely.[164]

Cases of isolation and underachievement were common amongst Turkish guest-worker children in Germany, especially during the 1960s and 1970s when problems adjusting remained widespread and many guest-worker families did not value German education because of their intention to return 'home'.[165] Furthermore, Turkish pupils were also at a disadvantage in the German education system where the daily number of contact hours was low and there was a great importance placed on homework with which it was assumed parents would be able to help.[166] Indeed helping ethnic minority children with their homework was an initiative that was discussed and implemented in Bremen.[167]

Despite the problems at the Schmidtstraße school, some improvements were being made due to a series of measures. In initiation classes, guest-worker children were undergoing intensive German language tuition until they were ready to join the mainstream classroom, but still studied a few subjects alongside German pupils. Instruction took place in both German and Turkish, with the overall aim being integration. In the primary school, Turkish pupils were mainstreamed for some

---

[164] See SB, 4,111/5–253, 'Die soziale Integration der Gastarbeiterkinder in den Klassen 7–9', undated report.

[165] See Kürsat-Ahlers, 'The Turkish minority in German society', p. 130; and Lucassen, 'Poles and Turks in the German Ruhr area', p. 35.

[166] See Stowasser, 'The Turks in Germany', p. 63; and Maurice Crul, 'How do educational systems integrate? Integration of second-generation Turks in Germany, France, the Netherlands, and Austria', in Richard Alba and Mary C. Waters (eds), *The Next Generation: Immigrant Youth in a Comparative Perspective* (New York, 2011), p. 275.

[167] See SB, 4,111/5–2272, 'Kleine FDP-Anfrage in der Bürgerschaft am 27.04.1977 – Kinder ausländischer Arbeitnehmer. Vorlage vom 12.04.1977 für die Sitzung des Senats am 25.04.1977', 12 April 1977, p. 4.

subjects, including physical education and arts and crafts. In the *Hauptschule*, they participated in physical education with their German counterparts and were able to choose other electives such as cooking and arts and crafts.[168] Other initiatives included giving learning materials to migrant children in their mother tongues in an attempt to get them to connect with classes. Suggestions were also made on how to foster contact between German and migrant pupils.[169] Other ideas on how to promote integration and interaction during the 1970s involved the showing of films about Turkey to encourage understanding, and organising activities that would bring pupils together.[170]

The 1970s also witnessed other initiatives on behalf of Bremen's local authority that demonstrated a proactive and attentive approach to the education of its guest-worker children. For example, Bremen was one of the first states to offer teachers training in the education of migrant pupils.[171] Ethnic minority youth was also offered preparation for entrance into higher education.[172] Bremen's government also placed a large emphasis on raising the level of kindergarten attendance, which stood at only 25.1 per cent amongst ethnic minority children between the ages of three and six in January 1978.[173] Kindergarten attendance is a factor that it has increasingly been argued influences migrant

---

[168] See SB, 4,111/5–2269, Beschulung der Kinder ausländischer Arbeitnehmer – KMK – Rundschreiben (Mitteilungen, Beschlüsse) Bd. 2 1970–1971, A Schule an der Schmidtstraße report entitled 'Einführungsklasse für türkische Kinder (E-Kl)' dated 26 May 1971.

[169] See SB, 4,111/5–253, 'Die soziale Integration der Gastarbeiterkinder in den Klassen 7–9', undated report.

[170] See SB, 4,111/5–2278, 'Hilfen für Kinder ausländischer Arbeitnehmer', 31 March 1970.

[171] See SB, 4,111/5–2302, Beschulung der Kinder ausländischer Arbeitnehmer – Bericht über den Modellversuch 'Kompaktkurs zur Fortbildung von Lehrern für den Unterricht ausländischer Kinder' 1978. See also Arlette C. Hill, 'Democratic education in West Germany: The effects of the new minorities', *Comparative Education Review*, 31:2 (1987), p. 285.

[172] See SB, 4,124/3–649, Sozialhilfe für Ausländer und Staatenlose – Allgemeines Bd. 6 1979–1980, 'Modellversuch Vorbereitungsstudium für Kinder türkischer Arbeitnehmer am Studienkolleg Bremen zur Vorbereitung auf die 'Prüfung zur Feststellung der Hochschulreife", undated report; and SB, 4,111/7–254, Studienkolleg Bremen – Sonderkurs für Gastarbeiterkinder 1979–1983.

[173] See Der Senat der Freien Hansestadt Bremen, *Konzeption zur Integration der ausländischen Arbeitnehmer und ihrer Familienangehörigen im Lande Bremen* (June 1979), p. 26.

pupils' later educational placement and attainment.[174] It has been claimed that Muslim ethnic minority parents in Germany often refused to send their children to kindergartens because many were run by the Roman Catholic Church and they did not want them to be religiously influenced.[175] Others have pointed out that parents had little awareness about the German education system and the opportunities that were available for their children.[176] As well as its positive and conscientious approach throughout the 1960s and 1970s, Bremen's local authority also possessed a detailed understanding of what measures and policies were being implemented in other federal states, and partook in a vibrant national debate in the manner it did regarding employment and housing.[177]

The last major initiative of the 1970s was the ground-breaking 1979 *Konzeption zur Integration der ausländischen Arbeitnehmer und ihrer Familienangehörigen im Lande Bremen* (Concept of the Integration of Foreign Workers and their Family Members in the State of Bremen). As was the case regarding both the employment and housing sectors, the *Konzeption* brought together and expanded on the existing policies and measures, and reinforced the commitment of Bremen's local authority to ethnic minority education. Some of the key points concerned kindergarten and day-care centres, training for both German and ethnic minority teachers, German language and mother-tongue teaching, after-school homework support and social activities, and vocational schools.[178]

---

[174] See C. Katharina Spiess, Felix Büchel and Gert G. Wagner, 'Children's school placement in Germany: Does *Kindergarten* attendance matter?', *Early Childhood Research Quarterly*, 18:2 (2003), pp. 255–70.

[175] See Hill, 'Democratic education in West Germany', p. 278; and Faruk Şen, 'The economic, social and political impact of Turkish migration', in Sarah Spencer (ed.), *Immigration as an Economic Asset: The German Experience* (Stoke on Trent, 1994), p. 100.

[176] See Mandel, *Cosmopolitan Anxieties*, p. 269.

[177] See SB, 4,111/5–2268, Beschulung der Kinder ausländischer Arbeitnehmer – KMK – Rundschreiben (Mitteilungen, Beschlüsse) Bd. 1 1964–1971; and SB, 4,111/5–2286, Beschulung der Kinder ausländischer Arbeitnehmer – Regelung in anderen Bundesländern: Umfrageergebnisse über Ausländerkinder allgemein, Fördermaßnahmen und Religionsunterricht für Kinder und Jugendliche islamischen Glaubens an öffentlichen Schulen 1974–1979.

[178] Der Senat der Freien Hansestadt Bremen, *Konzeption zur Integration der ausländischen Arbeitnehmer und ihrer Familienangehörigen im Lande Bremen* (June 1979), pp. 26–32, 40–5, 47–51.

Additional German language tuition was to continue at the centre of ethnic minority education, and measures were in place to develop this amongst both adults and children. Mother-tongue languages were to remain the responsibility of the sending countries although pupils at some types of school were to be given the option of choosing their mother tongue instead of a foreign language. It was also hoped that school attendance could be increased. The report also placed a special emphasis on Turkish youth and stressed the important role played by children and youths in the integration process. With more attention being awarded to education than to any other sector or area, the 1979 *Konzeption* portrayed the significance Bremen's local authority attached to ethnic minority educational success.[179]

As was the case within both the employment and housing sectors, the educational needs of guest-workers and their children in Bremen became a political concern prior to the 1973 recruitment halt and before the process of family reunification began in earnest. By the mid-1960s, not only had Bremen's government realised that educational provisions needed to be put in place, but it also showed an admirable commitment to securing ethnic minority children and youths' integration. Whether it was its pledge to provide guest-worker children with the same educational opportunities as their German counterparts or the plethora of measures it implemented, Bremen's local authority demonstrated a clear awareness and understanding of the problems and obstacles migrant, and especially Turkish, youths encountered in the German school system. Furthermore, its perception of education as the key to integration continued into the 1980s and 1990s.

The 1980s and 1990s

The number of migrant pupils in Bremen's schools continued to increase during the 1980s and 1990s. During the 1980–81 school year, the city was home to 6,478 ethnic minority pupils of which over 88 per cent originated from former recruitment countries, and 4,570 or 70.5 per cent were Turks. The distribution pattern of migrant children amongst Bremen's schools mirrored that of the 1960s and 1970s, and they constituted 13.9 per cent of all pupils in primary schools, 13.9 per cent of those enrolled at *Hauptschule*, 6.6 per cent of those at *Sonderschule*, 4.2 per cent at *Realschule* and only 1.6 per cent at *Gymnasium*. Besides Turks, there were other Muslim pupils in the city from countries such as Morocco (forty-six), Indonesia (twenty-six),

[179] Ibid., pp. 23, 25–6, 40–1, 45–6, 56–9.

Tunisia (fourteen) and Pakistan (five) although their numbers were very small.[180] By the 1999–2000 school year, there were 11,400 ethnic minority pupils in the state of Bremen which constituted 15.2 per cent of the total, a percentage that was the second highest amongst the German states after that of Hamburg.[181]

Not only did Bremen experience a continuous increase in its number of migrant pupils, but also an intensification in their levels of concentration. By the 1980–81 school year, the districts in which the largest groups of ethnic minority children attended school were Gröpelingen, Neustadt, Vegesack, Blumenthal, Osterholz, Hemelingen and Östliche Vorstadt (see Table 3.1). The districts of Osterholz and Vegesack especially had experienced a vast growth in their numbers of migrant schoolchildren over the previous four years of 123 per cent and 70.9 per cent respectively. These were areas to which ethnic minorities had traditionally been attracted either as a result of work or the availability of affordable housing.[182] This concentration continued throughout the 1990s. In January 1993, for example, 18 per cent of primary school-aged children (between the ages of 6 and 10) were ethnic minority. In certain districts, however, this figure was much higher. These included Osterholz, Mitte, Neustadt, Vahr, Gröpelingen, Blumenthal and Hemelingen (see Table 3.2).[183] During the mid- to late 1990s, schools in areas like Osterholz and Gröpelingen remained the targets of local government measures due to their high numbers of migrant pupils.[184]

With regard to policies, both the 1980s and 1990s largely acted as a direct continuation of the 1970s in that the 1979 *Konzeption* was the foundation of the decades' major measures and areas of focus. In this sense, the education sector in Bremen is different from those of employment and housing. Whilst the late 1970s and early 1980s represented something of a turning point as former guest-workers and their families

---

[180] See Freie Hansestadt Bremen *Statistische Monatsberichte*, 'Schulbesuch und Schulerfolg ausländischer Schüler an den allgemeinbildenden Schulen', 33. Jahrgang, June 1981, pp. 187–90.
[181] See Marcel Daniel, 'Streiflichter bundesdeutscher Zuwanderung – Reise auf abwechslungsreichen Wegen', in Karin Meendermann (ed.), *Migration und politische Bildung – Integration durch Information* (Münster, 2003), p. 77.
[182] See 'Schulbesuch und Schulerfolg ausländischer Schüler an den allgemeinbildenden Schulen', 33. Jahrgang, June 1981, p. 191.
[183] Häfen has again been excluded.
[184] See Bremische Bürgerschaft Landtag 14. Wahlperiode, Drucksache 14/857, 'Kleine Anfrage der Fraktion der CDU vom 23. Oktober 1997. Förderung von Kindern mit geringen Deutschkenntnissen', p. 2.

Table 3.1: The seven districts in Bremen with the highest numbers of ethnic minority pupils, 1980-81

District	Number
Gröpelingen	799
Neustadt	651
Vegesack	552
Blumenthal	552
Osterholz	513
Hemelingen	471
Östliche Vorstadt	451

Source: 'Schulbesuch und Schulerfolg ausländischer Schüler an den allgemeinbildenden Schulen', 33. Jahrgang, June 1981, p. 191.

Table 3.2: The seven districts in Bremen with the highest constitutions of ethnic minority primary school-aged children, January 1993

District	Percentage
Osterholz	24.7%
Mitte	24.7%
Neustadt	22.5%
Vahr	22.1%
Gröpelingen	21.9%
Blumenthal	20.7%
Hemelingen	19.9%

Source: 'Kinder im Grundschulalter und Ausländeranteile in der Stadt Bremen im Januar 1993 nach Stadtteilen', 46. Jahrgang, July 1994, p. 77.

ventured onto the local labour and housing markets as independent agents, the underpinning of education policies remained the same. However, they did acknowledge both the increasing numbers of ethnic minority schoolchildren and assumed that the vast majority of them were going to remain in Germany and that therefore this was the future they needed to be prepared for. Furthermore, Bremen's government did not act in isolation, but was again aware of procedures and measures being implemented across Germany.[185] At the beginning of the 1980s, Bremen's local authority renewed its commitment to migrant pupils' education provision, and both the acquisition of the German language and the swift mainstreaming of ethnic minority children remained key

[185] See SB, 4,111/5–2345, Berufsbildung für Ausländer – Bremen und bundesweit (Konzepte, Statistiken, v.a. Ausländeranteil, Prognosen) Bd. 5 1981–1982; and SB, 4,124/3–5, Planung in Bremen – Konzeption Bd. 2 1986.

priorities. However, the intention was not for these youths' native identities to be neglected, but rather that they became acquainted with multiple languages, religions and sets of customs.[186]

The individual policies and areas of concentration were largely an extension of those devised in the 1970s. For example, the aim of not allowing the ethnic minority constitution of individual classes to surpass 20 per cent remained. Whilst this had not previously been enforced for pragmatic reasons, there was now an intention to impose this limit. Yet there was also a recognition that because of the recent influx of migrant families into the city and the manner in which they were becoming concentrated into certain districts, it was inevitable that the 20 per cent limit was exceeded in some cases. Indeed during the second half of the 1979–80 school year, there were 344 classes that were over 20 per cent ethnic minority, with some having greatly surpassed this threshold. One pre-school class at Kirchenallee school in Gröpelingen, for example, was 83 per cent migrant, and two of its primary school classes were 53 per cent and 54 per cent ethnic minority respectively. Schmidtstraße school in Östliche Vorstadt had one primary school class and two *Hauptschule* classes that were 46 per cent, 53 per cent and 55 per cent migrant respectively. Other classes with high concentrations of ethnic minority pupils included a *Hauptschule* class at Kornstraße school in Neustadt (48 per cent) and a primary school class at Halmerweg school in Gröpelingen (31 per cent). Schools and classes with high numbers of migrant children were to be awarded additional teaching hours. Overall, the aim was to provide educationally for ethnic minority pupils whilst ensuring that schools remained satisfactory for German children and their parents.[187]

Vorbereitungsklassen or preparation classes were to remain at the centre of German language learning for migrant children. They were to consist of between twelve and twenty pupils, and ethnic minority pupils were not to remain in one of these classes for longer than two years, a limit that was also imposed in other German states.[188] They

---

[186] See Bremische Bürgerschaft Landtag 10. Wahlperiode, Drucksache 10/300, 'Mitteilung des Senats. Bericht über die Lage der schulpflichtigen Kinder von Ausländern', 1 September 1980, p. 11.

[187] Ibid., pp. 7–8, 19–21. See also 'Ausländerflut drängt in die Schulen. In Anfängerklassen der Schule Kirchenallee Deutsche klar in der Minderheit / Ausschuß geplant', *Weser Kurier* (8 July 1980).

[188] See Ingelore Oomen-Welke and Guido Schmitt, 'Teaching the mother tongue in Germany', in Witold Tulasiewicz and Anthony Adams (eds), *Teaching the Mother Tongue in a Multilingual Europe* (London, 1998), p. 144; and Broeder and Extra, *Language, Ethnicity and Education*, p. 82.

were also to be structured in a way so that work and progress was not disrupted by the arrival of new pupils. For those schools at which there were not sufficient ethnic minority children, those needing additional German language tuition were to continue to receive help in smaller groups. Other initiatives included allowing pupils to study their mother tongue in place of a foreign language, training programmes for both German and migrant teachers, and further integrating ethnic minority youths into the vocational school system.[189] Bremen was not alone in this and such provision also emerged in other German states and cities during the 1980s.[190] Other schemes documented in a September 1982 report included those aimed at very young Turkish children and their parents.[191]

There is no doubt that progress was made in Bremen during the late 1970s and early 1980s. There was a higher number of Turkish youths enrolled at vocational schools, additional teaching staff had been appointed, and migrant children were benefiting from help they received with their homework and supplementary learning materials.[192] Furthermore, kindergarten attendance amongst ethnic minority children had increased from 25.1 per cent in 1977–78 to 56.1 per cent in 1982, and the percentage of migrant youths attaining school-leaving diplomas was greater in the state of Bremen than for Germany as a whole. At the end of the 1980–81 school year, the figure in Bremen stood at 62.5 per cent whilst the German average was only

[189] See Bremische Bürgerschaft Landtag 10. Wahlperiode, Drucksache 10/300, 'Mitteilung des Senats. Bericht über die Lage der schulpflichtigen Kinder von Ausländern', 1 September 1980, pp. 19–29. See also SB, 4,111/5–2274, Beschulung der Kinder ausländischer Arbeitnehmer – Besondere Bestimmungen, Sammlung von Rechtsvorschriften/Land Bremen 1982–1984.
[190] See Sabine Bühler-Otten and Sara Fürstenau, 'Multilingualism in Hamburg', in Guus Extra and Kutlay Yağmur (eds), *Urban Multilingualism in Europe: Immigrant Minority Languages at Home and School* (Clevedon, 2004), pp. 163–91; and H. Julia Eksner, *Ghetto Ideologies, Youth Identities and Stylized Turkish German: Turkish Youths in Berlin-Kreuzberg* (Berlin, 2006), p. 29.
[191] Bremische Bürgerschaft Landtag 10. Wahlperiode, Drucksache 10/895, 'Mitteilung des Senats. Fortschreibung der Konzeption zur Integration der ausländischen Arbeitnehmer und ihrer Familienangehörigen im Lande Bremen', 6 September 1982, p. 11.
[192] See Bremische Bürgerschaft Landtag 10. Wahlperiode, Drucksache 10/300, 'Mitteilung des Senats. Bericht über die Lage der schulpflichtigen Kinder von Ausländern', 1 September 1980, pp. 9, 12–13, 17.

around 40 per cent.[193] By the 1985–86 school year, there was also a much more even distribution of migrant pupils amongst types of secondary school, with 33 per cent at *Hauptschule*, 32.2 per cent at *Realschule*, 24.8 per cent at *Gymnasium* and 10 per cent at *Gesamtschule* (comprehensive school).[194]

As well as these achievements, by the early 1980s a much larger emphasis was being placed on vocational training, with Bremen's local authority perceiving a recognised vocational education or a vocational qualification as ways of improving migrant youths' chances of integration.[195] A further area that Bremen's local authority continued to award a significant amount of attention to during the 1980s and 1990s was migrant children's kindergarten attendance. Indeed, as previously mentioned, kindergarten attendance has increasingly been perceived as imperative for ethnic minority children's long-term integration into Germany. Despite attendance not being mandatory for either German or migrant children, Bremen's government recognised kindergarten as an opportunity to promote interaction between ethnic minority children and their German counterparts at an early age, and as an important conduit of integration. There was a concern because, whilst ethnic minority kindergarten attendance had increased steadily throughout the late 1970s, it began to drop again during the early to mid-1980s. Numerous reasons were given for this, including uncertainty amongst Turkish parents regarding their families' future in Germany, the tendency to keep children at home and the cost involved.[196]

Thus, in an attempt to raise the profile of kindergartens amongst Bremen's ethnic minority communities, information packets and letters

[193] See Bremische Bürgerschaft Landtag 10. Wahlperiode, Drucksache 10/895, 'Mitteilung des Senats. Fortschreibung der Konzeption zur Integration der ausländischen Arbeitnehmer und ihrer Familienangehörigen im Lande Bremen', 6 September 1982, pp. 14, 18–19.
[194] See Bremische Bürgerschaft Landtag 11. Wahlperiode, Drucksache 11/764, 'Antrag der Fraktion der SPD. Muttersprachlicher Unterricht für die Kinder ausländischer Mitbürger', 5 November 1986.
[195] See Bremische Bürgerschaft Landtag 10. Wahlperiode, Drucksache 10/300, 'Mitteilung des Senats. Bericht über die Lage der schulpflichtigen Kinder von Ausländern', 1 September 1980, pp. 23–9.
[196] See SB, 4,124/3–4, Planung in Bremen – Konzeption Bd. 1 1985, A letter from the Senator für Jugend und Soziales to the Jugendamt Bremen dated 3 December 1984; and SB, 4,124/3–5, A report compiled by the Senator für Jugend und Soziales entitled 'Ausländische Kinder in städtischen Kindergärten' and dated 18 February 1986.

continued to be sent out in both German and other languages, and some children were able to attend free of charge or at reduced rates. The importance awarded to kindergartens in the integration process cannot be exaggerated, with this topic having received a vast amount of local authority attention in Bremen during the 1980s especially.[197] This continued throughout the 1990s and they were at the centre of local government plans to promote the learning of German alongside the migrant's mother tongue.[198]

As well as kindergartens, there was also a large emphasis placed on youth and social work involving ethnic minority youth and their families. This included the organisation and running of activities and initiatives that often sought to enable educational and employment success, as well as promote a positive relationship between migrant youths and their German counterparts, and an overall integration.[199] Furthermore, particular attention was awarded to Turkish girls in Bremen as it was recognised that they often struggled upon finding themselves caught between two cultures, an aspect of Turkish settlement in Germany that has been widely recognised in the academic literature.[200]

There were a variety of social activities organised by the city's youth welfare office that were aimed specifically at them in the hope that they would not become isolated. There were also cases of Turkish girls who wished to remain in Bremen against the wishes of their parents. Some were expected to return to Turkey alone or with the family, whilst others had marriages arranged for them. This was a topic during the 1980s that captured the attention of Bremen's government and press, but also the hearts and minds of the city's German and Turkish popu-

[197] See SB, 4,124/3–1, Aufnahmeordnung – Kindergarten – Hortgesetz Bd. 2 1980–1981; SB, 4,124/3–2, Aufnahmeordnung – Kindergarten – Hortgesetz Bd. 3 1981–1984; SB, 4,124/3–4; SB, 4,124/3–5; and SB, 4,124/3–7, Planung in Bremen – Allgemeines Bd. 6 1985–1986.

[198] See Bremische Bürgerschaft Stadtbürgerschaft 14. Wahlperiode, Drucksache 14/804S, 'Antrag der Fraktionen der SPD und der CDU. Verbesserte Förderung der deutschen Sprache in Kindergärten', 23 February 1999.

[199] See SB, 4,124/3–9, Außerschulische Jugendarbeit Bd. 1 1979–1981; SB, 4,124/3–22, Neustrukturierung der Sozialarbeit für ausländische Familien Bd. 3 1981; SB, 4,124/3–10, Außerschulische Jugendarbeit Bd. 2 1982; and SB, 4,124/3–8, Außerschulische Jugendarbeit Bd. 3 1983–1986.

[200] See Martin, *The Unfinished Story*, pp. 31–2; and Viola-Donata Rauch, 'More than an urban stage for conflict – the city's impact of self-representation of children of immigrants in Berlin', in Frank Eckardt and John Eade (eds), *Ethnically Diverse City* (Berlin, 2011), pp. 473–94.

lations. Bremen's local authority opened a residence for Turkish girls who had fled their parents' houses, a scheme that was criticised by some sections of the local Turkish community. Furthermore, this conflict amongst Turkish families in the city arguably led to a greater exposure of their religious practices and beliefs.[201]

During the 1980s, Islam also began to feature in the discussion on Bremen's ethnic minority youths in other ways. For example, it gradually began to appear in documentation pertaining to work and initiatives regarding the city's Turkish community.[202] Furthermore, plans and models were drawn up and discussed regarding Islamic religious instruction for the city's Muslim schoolchildren. As with mother-tongue language classes, this was to take place after school and was to be run by Islamic religious associations. Bremen's local authority stressed that because of the so-called *Bremer Klausel*, Islamic instruction could not be part of the official curriculum. There was, however, some concern that the content of such teachings could not be controlled.[203] Indeed this is a worry that has been raised regarding Islamic teaching in Germany as a whole. Furthermore, it has also been asserted that in keeping Islamic instruction separate, Muslim migrants in Germany remain a separate entity and that, if it were allowed to become embedded within the German state, it could act as a conduit of integration.[204] This was also the line of reasoning put forward at the 2008 German Islam Conference (*Islamkonferenz*).

---

[201] See SB, 4,124/3–15, Wohngemeinschaft für türkische Mädchen und Frauen Bd. 2 1980–1985; SB, 4,124/3–11, Türkische Mädchen und Frauen Bd. 1 1983–1984; SB, 4,124/3–14, Wohngemeinschaft für türkische Mädchen und Frauen Bd. 1 1985; SB, 4,124/3–13, Türkische Mädchen und Frauen Bd. 3 1986–1988; and SB, 4,124/3–16, Wohngemeinschaft für türkische Mädchen und Frauen Bd. 3 1986–1988. See also 'Zuflucht vor elterlicher Gewalt. Neue Wohngemeinschaft für junge Türkinnen wird im Juli eröffnet', *Weser Kurier* (15 June 1985); and 'Junge Türkinnen oft im Konflikt mit den Eltern. Wohngemeinschaft der AW bietet Schutz und Hilfe', *Weser Kurier* (9 May 1987).

[202] See SB, 4,124/3–22, Jugendamt Bremen, 'Konzeptionsentwurf für die Sozialarbeit mit türkischen Familien Teil I und II', March 1981.

[203] See SB, 4,111/5–2216, Teilnahme ausländischer Kinder nichtchristl. Bekenntnisses am Unterricht in Biblischer Geschichte, Überlegungen zum alternativen Koran-Unterricht 1980–1982; and SB 4,111/5–2292, Durchführung des Unterrichts für Kinder ausländischer Arbeitnehmer – Korankurse, Islamischer Religionsunterricht: Regelung in Bremen 1982–1983.

[204] See James Helicke, 'Turks in Germany: Muslim identity 'between' states', in Yvonne Yazbeck Haddad and Jane I. Smith (eds), *Muslim Minorities in the West: Visible and Invisible* (Oxford, 2002), p. 183; and Faas, *Negotiating Political Identities*, p. 53.

Whilst Bremen's state law stands in the way of Islamic religious education securing a place on the official curriculum, some steps have been taken. There have been trials of Islam being taught in one of the city's schools. This was said to have had a positive influence on the school's atmosphere and on the parents' behaviour towards the school in general. These classes were taught in German and all learning materials are in the German language.[205] These classes have been expanded into other schools during the 2000s and have become a part of Bremen's integration policies.[206] Furthermore, plans have been put in place so that Muslim girls in certain schools in the city can be exempt from coeducational physical education classes.[207] Indeed, this is also a debate that in recent years has gained momentum both throughout Germany and further afield.[208] Overall, Bremen increasingly recognised Islam in its debate on ethnic minority education as guest-workers became Muslim immigrants. Yet the founding principles of the city's migrant communities' education have stayed the same since they were first established in the mid-1960s. There remains a heavy emphasis placed on kindergarten attendance and the acquisition of the German language, and recent and on-going measures and initiatives still perceive the integration of children as the key to the successful integration of entire families and communities.[209]

---

[205] See Bremische Bürgerschaft Landtag 17. Wahlperiode, Drucksache 17/348, 'Antrag der Fraktion der CDU. Islamkunde als Ersatzfach im Lande Bremen', 8 April 2008. See also Karakaşoğlu and Luchtenberg, 'Islamophobia in German educational settings', p. 42.

[206] See Bremische Bürgerschaft Landtag 16. Wahlperiode, Drucksache 16/176, 'Mitteilung des Senats vom 9. März 2004. Konzeption zur Integration von Zuwanderern und Zuwanderinnen im Lande Bremen 2003 bis 2007, Grundsätze, Leitlinien und Handlungsempfehlungen für die bremische Integrationspolitik', 9 March 2004, p. 5.

[207] See *Umsetzung der Konzeption zur Integration von Zuwanderern und Zuwanderinnen im Lande Bremen – Abschlußbericht – (Planungsbögen zum Stand 12/2002)*, p. 14.

[208] See Cesari, 'Islamophobia in the West', p. 37.

[209] See Bremische Bürgerschaft Landtag 15. Wahlperiode, Drucksache 15/447, 'Antrag der Fraktion Bündnis 90/Die Grünen. Zehn-Punkte-Programm zur Integration von Zuwanderern im Lande Bremen: Konkret handeln – gemeinsame Zukunft gestalten', 8 September 2000; Bremische Bürgerschaft Landtag 16. Wahlperiode, Drucksache 16/735, 'Mitteilung des Senats vom 30. August 2005. Stand der Integrationsarbeit in Bremen und Bremerhaven', 30 August 2005; and Bremische Bürgerschaft Landtag 16. Wahlperiode, Drucksache 16/1370, 'Mitteilung des Senats vom 10. April 2007. Konzeption zur

Overall, Islam has been awarded more recognition in the official debate on the education of ethnic minorities in Bremen than in Newcastle. Yet as in Newcastle and cities across Germany, schools in Bremen only managed to provide for a certain proportion of Muslim schoolchildren's learning needs. As was also the case in both the employment and housing sectors, educational experiences were also deeply rooted in and inherently linked to the city's Muslim ethnic minority communities. Mosques and Muslim community centres and organisations have also played an educational role in Muslim youths' lives. It has traditionally been where they read the Qur'an, studied their mother tongues and become acquainted with their ethnic and religious cultures. Despite the attention awarded to the debate on Islamic religious education in Bremen and the efforts the city's local authority has made to recognise Islam in schools, as in Newcastle, the education of Muslim ethnic minorities in Bremen has been and remains two-pronged.

Conclusion

As with the chapters on employment and housing, one of this chapter's key conclusions concerns the manner in which initial immigration paradigms influenced Newcastle and Bremen's education policies and their Muslim migrant communities' experiences. Indeed the policies devised and implemented by both cities' local authorities were intrinsically linked to their respective country's post-war immigration framework. As was the case throughout Britain, the measures employed in Newcastle, be it the assimilationist approach of the 1960s or the multicultural outlook of the 1980s, reflected a national mandate that assumed permanent settlement. In contrast, in Bremen, as throughout Germany, policies were developed amidst a sense of uncertainty regarding the future of the city's guest-workers and their families.

Yet this did not result in Newcastle's approach being more successful or comprehensive than Bremen's. In fact, the educational experiences and performances of Muslim ethnic minorities in both cities appear to have exceeded what has been the norm for Britain and Germany more widely. In Newcastle, South Asian Muslim schoolchildren often achieved higher qualifications than their English counterparts, and did not suffer from the racial harassment and

---

Integration von Zuwanderern und Zuwanderinnen im Lande Bremen 2003 bis 2007; Abschlussbericht', 10 April 2007.

language difficulties to the same extent as in other British cities. They also did not experience the same levels of concentration and social isolation. In Bremen, Turkish Muslim pupils have enjoyed increasingly higher success rates regarding the securing of places at *Realschule* and *Gymnasium*, and the attaining of a school-leaving diploma. They also benefited from initiatives aimed at helping with homework and liaising with parents. Overall, whilst there were certainly cases of discrimination, underachievement and language deficiency, there is no doubt that both cities often surpassed the British and German standard. Although in the 2000s Bremen has been heavily criticised for its poor PISA results, it must be recognised that it was both German and migrant children who performed less well than their counterparts in other German states. In fact, when looking at the individual elements that were assessed and the scores awarded, there was often less variation between those of German and migrant children in Bremen than in other states, such as Bayern and Berlin.[210]

In all, Muslim ethnic minority children and youths in both Newcastle and Bremen have experienced certain benefits. In Newcastle, it appears as though the relatively small size of the city's Muslim migrant population again acted as an advantage. This resulted in any problems and difficulties that arose being addressed and managed within individual schools. Furthermore, because levels of concentration and isolation were lower, it arguably resulted in a quicker integration of Muslim South Asian pupils. Moreover, Newcastle's local authority was largely able to shape measures and practices around the needs and requirements of the city's migrant pupils. They were able to learn in multicultural schools and classrooms in which they did not become segregated and excluded, but rather were able to achieve integration.

Bremen, however, did not have the advantage of a small migrant population. Yet neither its growing number of migrant schoolchildren nor the ambiguous context in which it was operating appears to have fazed Bremen's local authority. From the outset, it was committed to meeting Turkish pupils' learning needs and integrating them into the city's education system as quickly as possible. Furthermore, the situation in Bremen has potentially benefited from a consistency in approach. From the initial guest-worker years, throughout the family reunification phase and into the period in which Islam secured a firm

---

[210] See Ramm, Walter, Heidemeier and Prenzel, 'Soziokulturelle Herkunft und Migration im Ländervergleich', pp. 282, 284–5.

position in the debate, the foundations of Bremen's policies remained unchanging. Bremen's local authority can certainly not be criticised for educationally failing its ethnic minorities as has so often been argued is the case in Germany. In fact, as early as the 1960s and 1970s, Bremen's government debated and tackled many of the issues and factors that have since come to dominate both the political and academic debate on migrant educational achievement in Germany, including the securing of places in *Gymnasium* and the recognition that ethnic minority pupils often suffered in an education system where so much emphasis was placed on homework.

In essence, the differences in overarching immigration frameworks had little effect on the Newcastle and Bremen local authorities' implemented policies and approaches. This was not because the inherent dissimilarities between permanent and temporary migrants were not present, but rather because Bremen's government eroded these differences with what can only be described as a proactive approach to the city's ethnic minority schoolchildren. In fact, in Bremen, it was the Turkish Muslim migrant population rather than Bremen's local authority whose behaviour was most shaped by the intended temporary nature of the guest-worker system. This was seen in the conduct of some parents especially during the 1960s, 1970s and early 1980s. As a result of the fact that a return to the homeland was still a reality for many, it was frequently the case that little importance was awarded to children attending kindergarten or to the German curriculum. This was a direct contrast to the situation in Newcastle during this period where the self-determination that played such a role amongst Muslim migrants in the employment and housing sectors potentially spread into children's educational performance. Furthermore, as their settlement was intended to be permanent from the outset, there were also undoubtedly links made between educational attainment and future labour and housing market success and independence.

Another key conclusion is regarding the extent to which Islam has influenced both cities' ethnic minority educational performances and experiences. Again, the education sector differs from both employment and housing. Whilst Islam played a limited role in shaping Newcastle and Bremen's work and housing patterns, it has not done so in education, at least not within mainstream schools. Indeed there has been a call in both Britain and Germany for Islam to be further recognised in both countries' education systems, whether in the form of state-funded Muslim schools or the incorporation of Islamic religious education into school curriculums.[211] Yet it cannot be argued that

Newcastle and Bremen's local governments have failed Muslim ethnic minority children. On the contrary, they have benefited from mainstream school education as well as that provided by their migrant communities. It is also important to contextualise this community education within both cities' Muslim migrant populations' employment and housing patterns. For Muslims in both cities, the source of Islamic religious and cultural education has not been confined to mosques and official organisations, but rather such education has also undoubtedly taken place in Muslim migrant-run businesses and neighbourhoods. In this sense, there is a clear link between education and the employment and housing sectors. There is no doubt, however, that Islam will increasingly feature in both cities' future political deliberations on the education of ethnic minority youth. Indeed, in Bremen, it has already begun to do so.

As with those addressing employment and housing, the structure of this chapter has also been dictated by the available source material. As has been seen, Newcastle and Bremen's local authorities awarded a vast amount of attention to the educational provision of their respective migrant schoolchildren. Whilst the consideration in Newcastle matched the amount granted to the employment and housing sectors, that in Bremen far surpassed any other area of ethnic minorities' lives. Indeed Bremen's government has traditionally seen education as the key not just to the integration of ethnic minority children, but to that of entire migrant communities. In both cities, Muslims have increasingly become integrated into their respective education system. They have resisted the underachievement and limitations that have often afflicted Muslim migrants in Britain and Germany, and have achieved integration whilst simultaneously preserving their own Muslim identities.

---

[211] See Jürgen Henze, 'Muslim minorities and education in Germany – The case of Berlin', in Holger Daun and Geoffrey Walford (eds), *Educational Strategies among Muslims in the Context of Globalization: Some National Case Studies* (Leiden, 2004), pp. 233–6; and Gilliat-Ray, *Muslims in Britain*, pp. 151–5.

4

Conclusion: comparing communities, challenging conceptions

By the turn of the millennium, Newcastle and Bremen bore clear signs of being home to well-established Muslim ethnic minority communities. As many of Newcastle's South Asian immigrants and Bremen's Turkish guest-workers of the 1960s and 1970s abandoned 'the myth of return', and catered for their religious, cultural and social needs and customs, both cities gradually became comprised of Muslim residential streets and neighbourhoods, mosques, halal food stores, and Muslim institutions and businesses. Whilst it might be easy to mistakenly assume that they formed self-sufficient groups within their wider communities, Muslims in both Newcastle and Bremen progressively immersed themselves in their local surroundings in which their everyday lives unfolded. These features and characteristics were obviously not particular to the often-forgotten Muslim ethnic minorities of these two cities, but rather could be observed across Britain and Germany, and most notably in the larger and often-studied communities of Bradford, London, Berlin and Frankfurt.

Yet it is not the belief of this study that Newcastle and Bremen act as British and German microcosms. On the contrary, it is evident that South Asian Muslims in Newcastle and Turkish Muslims in Bremen during the post-war period have performed better in the employment, housing and education sectors than their migrant counterparts in many other British and German towns and cities. Many have succeeded in attaining a long sought-after economic independence in the form of businesses, which acted as both evidence and conduits of integration. Residential autonomy and self-determination took the form of owner-occupation and neighbourhood formation. Educational success and attainment were often the result of small and close-knit ethnic minority communities, and well-directed local government initiatives. Achievements amongst Muslim ethnic minorities in both cities were frequently further accentuated by instances of racial discrimination and hardship, the ability to manipulate local labour and housing markets to suit their long-term aims and ambitions, and a clear commitment to their British and German surroundings.

An analysis of Muslim migrant performance in both Newcastle and Bremen's employment, housing and education sectors allows conclusions to be reached concerning the six prime arguments and themes that have run throughout this study. The first relates to Britain and Germany's differing post-war immigration frameworks. There is no doubt that whilst these did have an initial impact on Muslim migrant behaviour and success in all three spheres, self-determination and autonomy soon took charge. Therefore, regarding long-term integration, the legacies of Britain and Germany's post-war immigration histories should not be seen as contrasting. On the contrary, South Asian Muslims in Newcastle and Turkish Muslims in Bremen displayed increasing similarities in their performances and attitudes in all three areas between the 1960s and 1990s. In what is the first work to offer a comparative assessment of Muslim ethnic minorities at a local level in Britain and Germany, these findings offer an additional tier to the existing historiography on the integration of ethnic minorities in Europe.[1]

Yet parallels in Newcastle and Bremen were not only visible amongst the Muslim migrant communities, but also in local government legislation in both cities. There were countless similarities between integration policies, for example, from attempts to encourage ethnic minority entrepreneurship to the concern expressed over the concentration of migrant schoolchildren in certain schools. This convergence goes some way to challenging the traditional, and still popular, view that Britain and Germany's post-war immigration histories and political structures should be seen as contrasting. Whilst disparities certainly existed at a national level, including those regarding their histories of immigration frameworks, and notions of nationhood and citizenship, it is clear that, in Newcastle and Bremen, local needs and demands prevailed.

In Newcastle, where the long-term settlement of South Asian Muslims was assumed from the outset, there were immediate strategies put into

---

[1] See Adrian Favell, *Philosophies of Integration: Immigration and the Idea of Citizenship in France and Britain* (Basingstoke, 1998); Schuck and Münz, *Paths to Inclusion*; Ireland, *Becoming Europe*; Lucassen, *The Immigrant Threat*; and Lucassen, Feldman and Oltmer, *Paths of Integration*.

place to cater for their integration. Perhaps more surprisingly, this was also the case regarding Turkish Muslims in Bremen where integration was sought prior to the guest-worker rotation system being phased out, and long before official political dialogue abandoned the claim that Germany is 'not a country of immigration' and German citizenship was made more attainable. Although this integration was initially only intended to be temporary in many cases, many of the proposed and implemented measures and procedures did in fact go on to form the basis of subsequent long-term policies. Whilst the definition of the term 'integration' and what this process entails has certainly undergone numerous modifications over the decades, and has been the subject of countless local, national and Europe-wide debates, it has long remained a constant in both Newcastle and Bremen's local authority policies.

These similarities regarding both local measures and Muslim ethnic minority attitude and performance support the body of existing literature that recognises a convergence both in Britain and Germany's post-1945 immigration histories, and European nations' immigration and integration policies more widely. Panikos Panayi and Simon Green have exposed growing similarities between Britain and Germany's immigration and integration goals and developments of multiculturalism, and attributed these to the influx of asylum seekers, terrorism, demographic and skills shortages, and their statuses as modern liberal democracies.[2] The emergence of parallels between the two countries have additionally been accredited to the European Union and the accompanying 'Europeanisation' of immigration, as a result of which Christian Joppke argued at the end of the 1990s that 'Germany and Great Britain no longer live in two separate immigration worlds'.[3] Yet it has not only been Britain and Germany that have experienced a convergence in their immigration and integration policies, and the extent to which this has also been the case amongst other European countries has been recognised.[4] Overall, the literature seems to

---

[2] Panayi, 'The evolution of multiculturalism in Britain and Germany'; and Green, 'Divergent traditions, converging responses'.

[3] Joppke, *Immigration and the Nation-State*, p. 276. For an insight into the 'Europeanisation' of immigration policy, see Rey Koslowski, 'European Union migration regimes, established and emergent', in Christian Joppke (ed.), *Challenge to the Nation-State: Immigration in Western Europe and the United States* (Oxford, 1998), pp. 153–88; and Geddes, *The Politics of Migration and Immigration in Europe*.

[4] See Hollifield, *Immigrants, Markets, and States*; Geddes, *The Politics of Migration and Immigration in Europe*; Heckmann and Schnapper, *The*

overwhelmingly suggest that similarities between Britain and Germany emerged progressively during the latter part of the twentieth and into the twenty-first century, have been the result of overarching and communal pressures and factors, and have formed part of a wider European process. Yet what is being proposed here is that, in Newcastle and Bremen at least, this merging of ideas and policies began much earlier, and developed for the most part as a result of local conditions and concerns.

A review of the measures implemented by Newcastle and Bremen's local authorities also exposes the extent to which they adhered to wider post-1945 British and German policies and practices. It is clear that Newcastle largely followed national mandate, whether it was regarding the impact of race relations legislation, the pursuit of assimilation and multiculturalism, or the types of measures implemented pertaining to employment, housing and education. Overall, Newcastle portrayed a distinct compliance to national immigration and race politics throughout the period.[5] The actions of Bremen's local government, on the contrary, challenge the traditional understanding and assessment of Germany's guest-worker system and, in doing so, support the theories put forward by Triadafilos Triadafilopoulos and Karen Schönwälder.[6] The long-accepted argument that German policymakers perceived migration as nothing more than a labour market issue and neglected its accompanying political and social ramifications, as pioneered by Ulrich Herbert and Stephen Castles amongst others, is in need of revision.[7] Moreover, there has been a widespread tendency to assume that the long-term settlement of guest-workers and their families only became a political issue after the 1973 halt in recruitment, and a habit of neglecting any concerns that already existed during the 1950s and 1960s. The conclusions reached here show that, in Bremen at least, 1973 was not the turning point that it is often assumed to have been, certainly not concerning political

---

Integration of Immigrants in European Societies; and Wayne A. Cornelius, Philip L. Martin and James F. Hollifield (eds), *Controlling Immigration: A Global Perspective* (Stanford CA, 2004).

[5] See Spencer, *British Immigration Policy since 1939*; and Hansen, *Citizenship and Immigration in Post-war Britain*.

[6] Triadafilopoulos and Schönwälder, 'How the Federal Republic became an immigration country'.

[7] See Herbert, *A History of Foreign Labor in Germany*; and Castles, 'Migrants and minorities in post-Keynesian capitalism'.

and social provision or an awareness regarding widespread immigration and the possibility of long-term settlement.[8]

Instead, as Triadafilopoulos and Schönwälder argue was the case in Germany at a national level,[9] Bremen's local government had doubts over the enforcing of the rotation principle. Whilst they suggest that rotation could not be implemented in a post-war Germany that was trying to break away from its recent troubled past,[10] in Bremen, there appeared to exist a clear concern for the welfare of guest-workers. It was recognised, for example, that it took them time to settle into their places of work and become acquainted with the German language, and that they could not be expected to live without their families for the long term. Furthermore, not only was rotation often not imposed, but there was a clear digression from the principle that guest-workers should not be socially provided for or incorporated into society. In essence, whilst the social provision of guest-workers in Bremen certainly intensified after 1973, it was nevertheless already a consideration during the pre-1973 period.

The second key argument is regarding the extent to which Islam influenced migrant behaviour and experiences. Overall, religious affiliation did not play an overwhelming role in shaping Newcastle's South Asian Muslims and Bremen's Turkish Muslims' employment, housing and education careers. Although the historiography is increasingly calling for Islam to be recognised as an influencing factor in all three sectors and revelling in claims that Europe is failing to integrate its Muslim migrant communities, there is no evidence to suggest that Islam acted as a barrier to integration in Newcastle or Bremen.[11] Whilst it undoubtedly sometimes played a role in determining the types of products their shops sold, the neighbourhoods in which they lived and the community-led education they experienced, religious affiliation does not appear to have disadvantaged or hindered either city's Muslim ethnic minority population. Moreover, the notion that Islam acts as a defining factor in the migratory experience is further undermined by the fact that Muslim migrants in both Newcastle and Bremen adhered

---

[8] See Joppke, *Immigration and the Nation-State*; Herbert and Hunn, 'Guest workers and policy on guest workers in the Federal Republic', pp. 211–12; and Stephen Castles, 'The factors that make and unmake migration policies', *International Migration Review*, 38:3 (2004), p. 853.

[9] Triadafilopoulos and Schönwälder, 'How the Federal Republic became an immigration country'.

[10] See also Schönwälder, 'West German society and foreigners in the 1960s'.

[11] See Shore, *Breeding Bin Ladens*; and Bawer, *While Europe Slept*.

to patterns and traits that have been exhibited by Muslim and non-Muslim ethnic minority communities in Britain, Germany, Europe and across the Western world, be it amongst Mexican and Pakistani entrepreneurs in the United States or Surinamese neighbourhoods in Amsterdam.[12] Indeed, as has been correctly pointed out by some, one must be careful not to exaggerate the part that Islam has played in Muslims' lives.[13]

This conclusion makes a valuable contribution to the debate on the integration of Europe's ethnic minorities and that of Muslim migrants more specifically. As has been argued by Leo Lucassen, the integration of migrant communities is a relatively new concern, one that is 'now constantly measured, discussed, and put under the magnifying glass'.[14] As the topic of immigration has gathered pace both within the political and public domains, Europeans have increasingly become preoccupied with how non-Western migrant groups fit into their societies. Fears about the possibility of underclass formation, polarised communities and cultures that are deemed as being incompatible with their own have become more widespread. This has particularly been the case regarding Muslims whose values, it is often perceived, are at odds with those of the West, constituting what Samuel P. Huntington notoriously termed the 'clash of civilizations'.[15] This is a time at which Islam continues to be linked with violence, the multiculturalism challenge remains largely associated with Muslim migrants, and many question their integration and indeed their chances of achieving it. Some have identified events such as the murder of Theo van Gogh and the Madrid and London bombings as evidence that Islam poses a serious threat to European society.[16]

[12] See Caroline B. Brettell and Kristoffer E. Alstatt, 'The agency of immigrant entrepreneurs: Biographies of the self-employed in ethnic and occupational niches of the urban labor market', *Journal of Anthropological Research*, 63:3 (2007), pp. 383–97; and van Amersfoort and Cortie, 'Housing and population: Spatial mobility in twentieth-century Amsterdam'.

[13] See Ansari, '*The Infidel Within*', p. 166; and Aziz Al-Azmeh and Effie Fokas (eds), *Islam in Europe: Diversity, Identity and Influence* (Cambridge, 2007).

[14] Lucassen, *The Immigrant Threat*, p. 204.

[15] Samuel P. Huntington, *The Clash of Civilizations and the Remaking of World Order* (New York, 1996).

[16] See Shore, *Breeding Bin Ladens*; and Bawer, *While Europe Slept*. For an insight into the debate on Islam and Europe and the West more widely, see Lewis, *Islam and the West*; John L. Esposito, *The Islamic Threat: Myth or Reality?* (Oxford, 1999); and Jonathan Laurence, *The Emancipation of Europe's Muslims: The State's Role in Minority Integration* (Princeton NJ, 2012).

Yet there have also been those who have argued against the belief that there exists a confrontation between Western states and their Muslim populations and it is this thesis that this study supports. Bhikhu Parekh, for example, asserts that European anxiety regarding Muslim communities is greatly exaggerated, whilst Jonathan Laurence challenges the notion that Europe's Muslims pose a threat to liberal democracy and offers optimistic predictions regarding the future of Islam in Europe.[17] Similarly, Jytte Klausen recognises the difficulties Europe can face when trying to accommodate large Muslim populations yet refutes the 'clash of civilizations' theory.[18] By drawing upon historical comparisons, Leo Lucassen contests the common perception that ethnic minorities in today's Europe are not achieving integration at as fast a pace as those in the past and the notion that Islam acts as a definite barrier to integration.[19]

Indeed, this study on Newcastle and Bremen makes an in-depth local British-German contribution to the previously mentioned ever-growing number of works on the integration of Europe's ethnic minorities, but also to those on Muslim migrant communities more specifically.[20] Its assessment of the 'everyday' experiences of Muslims challenges the current trend of migrant populations being identified and assessed primarily according to their religious affiliation, and the notion that the manner in which they interact with their local surroundings and the extent to which they achieve integration is determined by it. Whilst the conclusions reached for Newcastle and Bremen cannot claim to be applicable to Britain and Germany more widely, they nevertheless expose the danger that the current academic

---

[17] Bhikhu Parekh, 'European Liberalism and "The Muslim Question"', *International Institute for the Study of Islam in the Modern World*, 9 (2008); and Laurence, *The Emancipation of Europe's Muslims*.

[18] Jytte Klausen, *The Islamic Challenge: Politics and Religion in Western Europe* (Oxford, 2005).

[19] Lucassen, *The Immigrant Threat*.

[20] See Steven Vertovec and Ceri Peach (eds), *Islam in Europe: The Politics of Religion and Community* (Basingstoke, 1997); Tariq Modood, Anna Triandafyllidou and Ricard Zapata-Barrero (eds), *Multiculturalism, Muslims and Citizenship: A European Approach* (Abingdon, 2006); Federal Office for Migration and Refugees, *Muslim Life in Germany*; Gilliat-Ray, *Muslims in Britain*; Anna Triandafyllidou (ed.), *Muslims in 21st Century Europe: Structural and Cultural Perspectives* (London, 2010); and Hakan Yilmaz and Çağla E. Aykaç (eds), *Perceptions of Islam in Europe: Culture, Identity and the Muslim 'Other'* (London, 2012).

and political fixation with Islam is distorting the debate on the countries' ethnic minority communities.

The third key argument concerns the role played by self-determination amongst Muslim migrants in both Newcastle and Bremen. This study concludes that the development of self-employment and Muslim ethnic minority neighbourhoods was not overwhelmingly the result of discrimination, enforced segregation or a lack of alternative opportunities. Contrary to the dominant historiographical argument, this work argues for the triumph of migrant agency over institutional and non-institutional constraints. In the employment and housing sectors of both cities, the performances and conduct of Muslim South Asians and Turks were often the direct result of consciously made choices and decisions, many of which reflected long-term ambitions. Whilst the same levels of self-determination were unachievable in the cities' education systems, these migrants nevertheless showed evidence of integration and attainment.

It is certainly not this study's intention to unreservedly challenge and dispute the vast array of literature on ethnic minorities in Britain and Germany that has stressed disadvantage and inequality. Indeed in relation to all three of the sectors discussed, discrimination and constraint have long constituted the dominant narrative, and Newcastle and Bremen's Muslim migrants have certainly been victims of both on occasion. Furthermore, this work does not claim that Newcastle's South Asian Muslims and Bremen's Turkish Muslims have comprised two homogenous groups in which all members have displayed identical employment, housing and education patterns and performances. Whilst it has exposed the fact that many Muslim migrants in both cities have experienced incidents of success and self-determination, it also recognises that there have undoubtedly been those who have not. Nevertheless, the positive account that has run throughout supports the relatively small body of literature that both acknowledges the role ethnic minorities have played in shaping their own paths and destinies, and accentuates the more hopeful interpretations of migrant behaviour in all three sectors. In Newcastle and Bremen, as elsewhere, this has been witnessed, for example, in their pursuit of economic independence and higher wages, the importance awarded to home ownership and neighbourhood formation, and indicators of increasing educational success, all of which constitute markers of integration in both cities.

Whilst Newcastle's South Asian Muslims and Bremen's Turkish Muslims often displayed self-determination and autonomy, their achievements were also further facilitated by several other factors. These constitute the remaining three arguments that have run throughout this study which, although they do not contribute to the wider debates on migration to the same extent as those already discussed, have nevertheless played important roles in Newcastle and Bremen. Indeed this work's fourth key point, despite being controversial and possibly provocative, is that Muslims in Newcastle clearly benefited from belonging to relatively small and close-knit communities. Not only did this mean that they were often successful in securing the necessary financial capital and resources from within their own populations, but also that businesses rarely reached a saturation point, affordable housing stock was seldom exhausted, and schools were able to contain and manage any difficulties that arose. The historiography has often recognised the manner in which ethnic minorities in Britain have drawn upon their own families and communities in order to fulfil their employment and housing goals,[21] yet a debate regarding the possibility that smaller migrant populations might achieve higher levels of success and integration has been absent from the literature. Whilst this study does not advocate limiting the size of migrant communities, there is certainly a real need for further research on numerically smaller and often neglected ethnic minority populations, which would offer a new sphere to the study of integration in Britain.

The fifth theme concerns the association between local policies and the cities' Muslim communities. There is no doubt that whilst Muslims in Newcastle were advantaged by the size and formation of their communities, Turkish Muslims in Bremen benefited from the local authority's proactive and persistent commitment to their integration. Indeed Bremen's government demonstrated an understanding of and dedication towards its guest-worker population from an early stage, characteristics that were especially witnessed with regard to education and which clearly set Bremen apart from what has commonly been argued was the case in other German cities and across the country as a whole.[22] Yet this does not mean that all policies and measures

[21] See Shaw, *Kinship and Continuity*, pp. 89–93; Monder Ram, Tahir Abbas, Balihar Sanghera, Gerald Barlow and Trevor Jones, 'Making the link: Households and small business activity in a multi-ethnic context', *Community, Work and Family*, 4:3 (2001), pp. 327–48; and Ansari, '*The Infidel Within*', pp. 196–7.

[22] See Rist, *Guestworkers in Germany*; Herbert, *A History of Foreign Labor in Germany*; and Klaus J. Bade, 'Immigration and integration in Germany since 1945', *European Review*, 1:1 (1993), pp. 75–9.

implemented were effective and led to positive results, though the underlying continuous encouraging and fostering of integration was certainly ever-present in Bremen. Indeed in both cities there was often a breach between local government policies and their Muslim migrant communities. This was especially the case in Newcastle where daily life appears to have often continued almost in willing ignorance of local authority policies and plans. This is not the consequence of impractical or misdirected policies, but rather evidence of the extent to which self-determination and a desire for independence enabled migrant communities' success despite them.

The sixth and final theme concerns regional identity and the extent to which it acted as either an advocate or barrier to Muslim ethnic minority integration. Whilst the possibility of a regional patriotism that influences migrant experiences in both cities existing is certainly intriguing, and was one of the reasons Newcastle and Bremen were chosen as case studies, such identities prove difficult to measure. Yet regardless of their presence, there is no doubt that these cities' Muslim migrants were often provided with opportunities that were not available for minority groups across Britain and Germany more widely. Both local policies and migrants' behaviour and performances promoted integration and often set Newcastle and Bremen apart from cities with larger ethnic minority populations like Birmingham and Berlin. Many Muslims have come to play a part in their local surroundings and can truly be referred to as 'Geordie Muslims' or 'Bremer Muslims'. Thus, whilst neither city's regional identity presented itself in a tangible or visible form, and whilst I have previously argued against Newcastle's 'welcoming host' hypothesis, it cannot be denied that, in some aspects at least, Muslims in both cities lived in remarkable and truly multicultural locations.[23]

The themes and arguments that have run throughout this work have been further exposed and enriched as a result of three characteristics in its approach. Firstly, through its investigation into the employment, housing and education sectors, it has offered an assessment of three areas that have traditionally been overwhelmingly studied on an individual basis. The conclusions reached, therefore, make a contribution to the historiographies of each of these fields as well as to the academic debate on the long-term integration, performances and experiences of ethnic minorities in Britain and Germany more widely. Secondly, despite its historical foundation, this work has engaged with studies on

---

[23] See Hackett, 'The Asian of the north'.

migration that have emerged from a variety of disciplines, including geography, demography, sociology, political science and anthropology. In doing so, it recognises the importance of not seeing these bodies of literature as disparate and hopes to complement the small, yet growing, number of works in the field of migration studies that are truly interdisciplinary.[24] Thirdly, there is no doubt that this book's comparative approach has permitted a more in-depth analysis of its arguments and ideas. Consequently, it endorses the practice of going beyond the study of one ethnic minority group in a singular local or national context, and fully recognises the benefits of drawing upon numerous case studies and comparative migration history.[25] On the whole, all three of these traits have allowed for a more comprehensive and wide-ranging study of Newcastle and Bremen's Muslim ethnic minority communities than would otherwise have been the case.

Overall, despite the debate on the integration of Muslim migrant communities in the West being marred by claims of struggle and conflict, it is clear that Muslim ethnic minorities in both Newcastle and Bremen are becoming integrated at a faster pace than is often assumed to be the case for Britain and Germany more widely. Indeed whilst the perceived incompatibility of Europe and its Muslims is being discussed on one level, Muslim migrants' everyday lives are being carried out on another. Overall, there appears to be a breach between what is often a historiographical and political search for conflict, and the daily experiences of Europe's ethnic minority communities. This is not to say that incidents of racism, discrimination and Islamophobia do not take place. Indeed the difficulties faced by migrant populations in Britain, Germany and further afield have been well documented and some

[24] See Caroline Brettell and James F. Hollifield (eds), *Migration Theory: Talking across Disciplines* (New York, 2000); Virginie Guiraudon and Christian Joppke (eds), *Controlling a New Migration World* (New York, 2001); Lucassen, *The Immigrant Threat*; and Craig A. Parsons and Timothy M. Smeeding (eds), *Immigration and the Transformation of Europe* (Cambridge, 2006).

[25] For examples of other comparative works, see Joppke, *Immigration and the Nation-State*; Joel Fetzer, *Public Attitudes toward Immigration in the United States, France, and Germany* (Cambridge, 2000); Schönwälder, *Einwanderung und ethnische Pluralität*; Riva Kastoryano, *Negotiating Identities: States and Immigrants in France and Germany*, trans. Barbara Harshav (Princeton NJ, 2002); Erik Bleich, *Race Politics in Britain and France: Ideas and Policymaking since the 1960's* (Cambridge, 2003); and Schain, *The Politics of Immigration in France, Britain, and the United States*.

examples have been provided in this study. Nevertheless, there is often a clear discrepancy between the media and academic frenzy, and the grassroots reality. As has been seen regarding both Newcastle and Bremen, positive relations between the cities' Muslim ethnic minorities and their British and German counterparts have been frequent and examples of integration common.

This work does not claim to represent all aspects and features of Muslim migrants' experiences in Newcastle and Bremen's employment, housing and education sectors, nor does it assert that the behaviour patterns and attitudes portrayed are necessarily those of both cities' Muslim majorities. Furthermore, there are numerous other indicators of integration that have not been applied here, including political participation and intermarriage rates. Yet it offers a glimpse of hope regarding their integration. Whilst this study agrees with Leo Lucassen's assertion that it is colonial immigrants who succeed in identifying with the cultures of their receiving societies the fastest, it also exposes the extent to which former guest-workers are catching up.[26] Furthermore, despite the fact that the long-term settlement of post-war immigrant communities in both Britain and Germany was largely unwanted, an attitude that was often reflected in policy and legislation, long-term integration is taking place.[27]

This book's historical underpinning champions the notion that ethnic minorities in today's Europe cannot be understood without an awareness of the past. Whilst it might be tempting for some to succumb to the alarmist, and often sensationalised, claims that Muslim ethnic minorities and Europe are incompatible, this study has shown that not only is integration possible, but that in Newcastle and Bremen it has been under way for some time. Both cities embraced and overcame the challenges that the arrival of post-war immigrants presented them with and there is no reason to believe that it will be any different regarding either the younger generations or the smaller migrant groups that continue to settle at the beginning of the twenty-first century. As did those before them, they are likely to become embedded in their local surroundings and create spaces for themselves within the multicultural landscapes that comprise both cities.

[26] Lucassen, *The Immigrant Threat*, p. 207.
[27] See Spencer, *British Immigration Policy since 1939*; Hansen, *Citizenship and Immigration*; Simon Green, *The Politics of Exclusion: Institutions and Immigration Policy in Contemporary Germany* (Manchester, 2004); and Klusmeyer and Papademetriou, *Immigration Policy in the Federal Republic of Germany*.

Bibliography

Primary sources

Newcastle City Library

L325, City of Newcastle upon Tyne Racial Equality Sub-Committee, 'Minority Ethnic Communities Survey 1990', 21 November 1990

Tyne & Wear Archives Service, Newcastle

MD.NC/149, Commonwealth Immigrants Working Group of Planning Committee 19 September 1966–6 May 1968

MD.NC/162/1, Local Government and Racial Equality Sub-Committee of Corporate Joint Sub-Committee 18 March 1983–17 July 1985

MD.NC/162/2, Local Government and Racial Equality Sub-Committee of Corporate Joint Sub-Committee 18 September 1985–15 July 1987

MD.NC/162/3, Local Government and Racial Equality Sub-Committee of Corporate Joint Sub-Committee 6 August 1987–16 March 1988

MD.NC/358, Asian Traders Working Group 4 July 1996–17 April 1998

MD.NC/365, Black and Ethnic Minority Consultative Forum 1 September 1994–17 May 1995

MD.NC/554, Multi Agency Panel on Racial Incidents Interdepartmental Forum 7 June 1995–29 January 1996

MD.NC/613, Racial Equality Officer Working Group 2 December 1992–17 May 1995

MD.NC/614/1, Racial Equality Working Group 18 January 1995–2 November 1995

MD.NC/614/2, Racial Equality Working Group 18 January 1996–6 March 1997

MD.NC/614/3, Racial Equality Working Group 3 July 1997–5 March 1998

MD.NC/734, Equality Partnership Select Committee: Corporate Equality Plan Working Group 4 September 2003–27 January 2004

MD.NC/765, Equality Partnership Select Committee 15 January 2003–5 May 2004

Bremen Parliament reports and documentation

Bremische Bürgerschaft Landtag 8. Wahlperiode, Drucksache 8/600, 'Antwort des Senats zur Anfrage der Fraktion der CDU vom 26. Juni 1973 (Drs. 8/566). Ausländische Arbeitnehmer', 12 September 1973

Bremische Bürgerschaft Landtag 8. Wahlperiode, Drucksache 8/605, 'Antrag (Entschließung) der Fraktion der SPD. Ausländische Arbeitnehmer', 26 September 1973

Bremische Bürgerschaft Landtag 9. Wahlperiode, Drucksache 9/1061, 'Kleine Anfrage der Fraktion der FDP vom 2. April 1979. Ausländer im Lande Bremen'

Bremische Bürgerschaft Landtag 10. Wahlperiode, Drucksache 10/300, 'Mitteilung des Senats. Bericht über die Lage der schulpflichtigen Kinder von Ausländern', 1 September 1980

Bremische Bürgerschaft Landtag 10. Wahlperiode, Drucksache 10/895, 'Mitteilung des Senats. Fortschreibung der Konzeption zur Integration der ausländischen Arbeitnehmer und ihrer Familienangehörigen im Lande Bremen', 6 September 1982

Bremische Bürgerschaft Landtag 11. Wahlperiode, Drucksache 11/764, 'Antrag der Fraktion der SPD. Muttersprachlicher Unterricht für die Kinder ausländischer Mitbürger', 5 November 1986

Bremische Bürgerschaft Landtag 13. Wahlperiode, Drucksache 13/350, 'Kleine Anfrage der Fraktion der CDU vom 10. September 1992. Bedeutung von Ausländern für die Arbeitswelt'

Bremische Bürgerschaft Landtag 14. Wahlperiode, Drucksache 14/857, 'Kleine Anfrage der Fraktion der CDU vom 23. Oktober 1997. Förderung von Kindern mit geringen Deutschkenntnissen'

Bremische Bürgerschaft Landtag 15. Wahlperiode, Drucksache 15/368, 'Mitteilung des Senats vom 6. Juni 2000. Ausländische Mitbürgerinnen und Mitbürger in der Arbeitswelt in Bremen und Bremerhaven', 6 June 2000

Bremische Bürgerschaft Landtag 15. Wahlperiode, Drucksache 15/447, 'Antrag der Fraktion Bündnis 90/Die Grünen. Zehn-Punkte-Programm zur Integration von Zuwanderern im Lande Bremen:

Konkret handeln – gemeinsame Zukunft gestalten', 8 September 2000

Bremische Bürgerschaft Landtag 15. Wahlperiode, Drucksache 15/1417, 'Mitteilung des Senats vom 18. März 2003. Konzeption zur Integration von Zuwanderern und Zuwanderinnen im Lande Bremen – Abschlussbericht', 18 March 2003

Bremische Bürgerschaft Landtag 16. Wahlperiode, Drucksache 16/176, 'Mitteilung des Senats vom 9. März 2004. Konzeption zur Integration von Zuwanderern und Zuwanderinnen im Lande Bremen 2003 bis 2007, Grundsätze, Leitlinien und Handlungsempfehlungen für die bremische Integrationspolitik', 9 March 2004

Bremische Bürgerschaft Landtag 16. Wahlperiode, Drucksache 16/219, 'Große Anfrage der Fraktion Bündnis 90/Die Grünen. Das wirtschaftliche Potenzial von Unternehmern und Existenzgründern mit Migrationshintergrund', 21 April 2004

Bremische Bürgerschaft Landtag 16. Wahlperiode, Drucksache 16/262, 'Mitteilung des Senats vom 25. Mai 2004. Das wirtschaftliche Potenzial von Unternehmern und Existenzgründern mit Migrationshintergrund', 26 May 2004

Bremische Bürgerschaft Landtag 16. Wahlperiode, Drucksache 16/264, 'Kleine Anfrage der Fraktion Bündnis 90/Die Grünen vom 21. April 2004. Wirtschaftsförderung für Unternehmer und Existenzgründer mit Migrationshintergrund', 26 May 2004

Bremische Bürgerschaft Landtag 16. Wahlperiode, Drucksache 16/735, 'Mitteilung des Senats vom 30. August 2005. Stand der Integrationsarbeit in Bremen und Bremerhaven', 30 August 2005

Bremische Bürgerschaft Landtag 16. Wahlperiode, Drucksache 16/810, 'Antrag der Fraktion Bündnis 90/Die Grünen. Stärkung von Unternehmen und Unternehmensgründungen mit migrantischem Hintergrund', 29 November 2005

Bremische Bürgerschaft Landtag 16. Wahlperiode, Drucksache 16/1370, 'Mitteilung des Senats vom 10. April 2007. Konzeption zur Integration von Zuwanderern und Zuwanderinnen im Lande Bremen 2003 bis 2007; Abschlussbericht', 10 April 2007

Bremische Bürgerschaft Landtag 17. Wahlperiode, Drucksache 17/348, 'Antrag der Fraktion der CDU. Islamkunde als Ersatzfach im Lande Bremen', 8 April 2008

Bremische Bürgerschaft Landtag 17. Wahlperiode, Drucksache 17/503, 'Mitteilung des Senats vom 12. August 2008. Die Potenziale von Unternehmer/-innen mit Migrationshintergrund stärker nutzen', 12 August 2008

Bremische Bürgerschaft Landtag 17. Wahlperiode, Drucksache 17/621, 'Kleine Anfrage der Fraktion DIE LINKE. vom 7. Oktober 2008. Beschäftigungsquote von Migrantinnen und Migranten im öffentlichen Dienst'

Bremische Bürgerschaft (Stadt), 'Modernisierungsmaßnahmen im Ortsteil Lindenhof mit dem Ziel, für deutsche und ausländische Mieter besseren Wohnraum zu schaffen', 11. Wahlperiode, 11. Sitzung am 7 December 1984

Bremische Bürgerschaft Stadtbürgerschaft 10. Wahlperiode, Drucksache 10/457S, 'Kleine Anfrage der Fraktion der FDP vom 10. März 1982. Ausländerbeiräte bei den Ortsämtern'

Bremische Bürgerschaft Stadtbürgerschaft 14. Wahlperiode, Drucksache 14/804S, 'Antrag der Fraktionen der SPD und der CDU. Verbesserte Förderung der deutschen Sprache in Kindergärten', 23 February 1999

Bremische Bürgerschaft Stadtbürgerschaft 17. Wahlperiode, Drucksache 17/547S, 'Mitteilung des Senats vom 2. Februar 2010. Lebenssituation der älteren Migrantinnen und Migranten in Bremen', 2 February 2010

Freie Hansestadt Bremen Statistische Monatsberichte (Reports issued by Bremen's Statistical Land Office)

'Die Beschäftigung ausländischer Arbeitnehmer im Lande Bremen', 29. Jahrgang, June 1977, pp. 90–6

'Schulbesuch und Schulerfolg ausländischer Schüler', 30. Jahrgang, May 1978, pp. 99–104

'Die ausländische Wohnbevölkerung der Stadt Bremen', 31. Jahrgang, July 1979, pp. 124–9

'Ausländische Arbeitnehmer im Lande Bremen', 33. Jahrgang, February 1981, pp. 60–6

'Die ausländische Wohnbevölkerung in der Stadt Bremen', 33. Jahrgang, May 1981, pp. 89–101

'Keine Ausländergettos in der Stadt Bremen', 33. Jahrgang, May 1981, pp. 169–73

'Schulbesuch und Schulerfolg ausländischer Schüler an den allgemeinbildenden Schulen', 33. Jahrgang, June 1981, pp. 186–91

'Beschäftigung ausländischer Arbeitnehmer im Lande Bremen', 34. Jahrgang, September 1982, pp. 275–9

'Räumlich – strukturelle Analyse der Ausländerkonzentration in der Stadt Bremen', 34. Jahrgang, October 1982, pp. 309–27

'Integration von Ausländern in der Stadt Bremen', 34. Jahrgang, November 1982, pp. 354–70
'Die Segregation der ausländischen Bevölkerung in Bremen', 35. Jahrgang, October 1983, pp. 245–52
'Ausländer nach Ortsteilen der Stadt Bremen', 37. Jahrgang, October 1985, pp. 146–8
'Residentielles Verteilungsmuster ausländischer Bevölkerungsgruppen in der Stadt Bremen', 37. Jahrgang, December 1985, pp. 168–70
'Ausländische Arbeitnehmer in den Stadtstaaten', 39. Jahrgang, August 1987, pp. 69–79
'Ausländische Arbeitnehmer in der bremischen Wirtschaft', 44. Jahrgang, August 1992, pp. 87–93
'Demographische Situation von Ausländerinnen und Ausländern im Lande Bremen', 45. Jahrgang, February 1994, pp. 122–34
'Ausländer in der Stadt Bremen', 45. Jahrgang, March 1994, pp. 191–5
'Einwohner und Ausländeranteile nach Stadtteilen der Stadt Bremen im Januar 1993', 46. Jahrgang, June 1994, pp. 10–11
'Kinder im Grundschulalter und Ausländeranteile in der Stadt Bremen im Januar 1993 nach Stadtteilen', 46. Jahrgang, July 1994, pp. 77–8

Government reports

Der Senat der Freien Hansestadt Bremen, *Konzeption zur Integration der ausländischen Arbeitnehmer und ihrer Familienangehörigen im Lande Bremen* (June 1979)
Der Senat der Freien Hansestadt Bremen, *Konzeption zur Integration von Zuwanderern und Zuwanderinnen im Lande Bremen. Grundsätze, Leitlinien und Handlungsempfehlungen für die bremische Integrationspolitik* (July 2000)
Der Senat der Freien Hansestadt Bremen, *Umsetzung der Konzeption zur Integration von Zuwanderern und Zuwanderinnen im Lande Bremen – Abschlußbericht – (Planungsbögen zum Stand 12/2002)*
Der Senator für Arbeit, Frauen, Gesundheit, Jugend und Soziales, Referat Zuwandererangelegenheiten und Integrationspolitik, Migrations- und Integrationsbeauftragter, *Umsetzung der Konzeption zur Integration von Zuwanderinnen und Zuwanderern 2003–2007. Abschlussbericht (Stand 12/2006)*
Der Senator für das Bauwesen, *Wohnen in Bremen*. Heft 2 der Reihe 'Der Senator für das Bauwesen informiert' (June 1981)
Die Senatorin für Soziales, Kinder, Jugend und Frauen, *Konzeption zur Integration von Zuwanderern und Zuwanderinnen im Lande*

Bremen 2007–2011. Grundsätze, Leitbilder und Handlungsziele für die bremische Integrationspolitik (draft dated February 2008)

Staatsarchiv Bremen

4,13/4–122–10–02/0, Grundsätzliche Vereinbarungen für die Behandlung ausländischer Arbeitnehmer und deren Angehörigen. Allgemeines. 1951–1972

4,13/4–122–10–02/7, Zuzug von Familienangehörigen ausländischer Arbeitnehmer Band 1 1965–1974

4,13/4–122–10–02/7, Zuzug von Familienangehörigen ausländischer Arbeitnehmer Band 2 1965–1974

4,13/4–122–10–02/9, Arbeitskreis für Fragen der Beschäftigung ausländischer Arbeitnehmer 1965–1973

4,13/4–122–10–02/12, Schnellinformationen über die Anwerbung und Vermittlung ausländischer Arbeitnehmer 1969–1972

4,13/4–122–10–02/14, Betreuung ausländischer Arbeitnehmer 1963–1975

4,13/4–122–10–05/1, Ausländerpolitik des Bundes 1977–1979

4,13/4–122–10–05/2, Ausländerpolitik der Bundesländer 1971–1977

4,22/2–275, Wirtschaft und Industrie in Bremen und Bremerhaven – Industrieansiedlung Bd. 3 1966–1967

4,29/2–1479, Wohnungen für ausländische Arbeitnehmer 1960–1964

4,29/2–1480, Wohnungen für ausländische Arbeitnehmer 1965

4,29/2–1481, Wohnungen für ausländische Arbeitnehmer 1966–1974

4,31/6–68, Gastarbeiterwohnungen an der Rablinghauser Landstraße in Rablinghausen 1970–1975

4,31/6–69, Gastarbeiterwohnungen am Halmerweg in Gröpelingen 1971

4,63/2N-284, Gastarbeiter 1971–1973

4,92/2–378, Bremer Vulkan, Bremen-Vegesack: Allgemeines Bd. 4 1989–1994

4,92/2–382, Bauvorhaben 'Wätjens Park' (Wohnungen für die Beschäftigten des Bremer Vulkan) 1970–1990

4,111/5–240, Beschulung der Kinder ausländischer Arbeitnehmer – Lehraufträge für Deutschunterricht 1965–1971

4,111/5–241, Beschulung der Kinder ausländischer Arbeitnehmer – Vorlagen für die Referentensitzungen 1972–1973

4,111/5–242, Beschulung der Kinder ausländischer Arbeitnehmer – Anfragen aus Bremen

4,111/5–246, Beschulung der Kinder ausländischer Arbeitnehmer –

Sonstige soziale Betreuung ausländischer Arbeitnehmer und ihrer Kinder: Private Träger, Bürgerinitiativen, etc. Bd. 1 1972–1975

4,111/5–247, Beschulung der Kinder ausländischer Arbeitnehmer – Sonstige soziale Betreuung ausländischer Arbeitnehmer und ihrer Kinder: Private Träger, Bürgerinitiativen, etc. Bd. 2 1976–1977

4,111/5–248, Beschulung der Kinder ausländischer Arbeitnehmer – Arbeitsgemeinschaft ausländischer Arbeiter Bd. 1 1972

4,111/5–249, Beschulung der Kinder ausländischer Arbeitnehmer – Arbeitsgemeinschaft ausländischer Arbeiter Bd. 2 1974

4,111/5–253, Durchführung des Unterrichts für Kinder ausländischer Arbeitnehmer – Berichte, Meldungen und Anfragen der Schule Schmidtstraße 1969–1976

4,111/5–1723, Lehrerfortbildung – Fortbildung für den Unterricht ausländischer Schüler, Kompaktkurs (Modellversuch) 1977–1980

4,111/5–1971, Grundsätzliche Angelegenheiten der Abendhauptschule – Regelung in Bremen 1964–1980

4,111/5–2216, Teilnahme ausländischer Kinder nichtchristl. Bekenntnisses am Unterricht in Biblischer Geschichte, Überlegungen zum alternativen Koran-Unterricht 1980–1982

4,111/5–2234, Konzeption zur Integration ausländischer Schüler/Jugendlicher, Berichte über die Lage der schulpflichtigen Kinder von Ausländern 1979–1980

4,111/5–2342, Berufsbildung für Ausländer – Bremen und bundesweit (Konzepte, Statistiken, v.a. Ausländeranteil, Prognosen) Bd. 2 1979

4,111/5–2343, Berufsbildung für Ausländer – Bremen und bundesweit (Konzepte, Statistiken, v.a. Ausländeranteil, Prognosen) Bd. 3 1980

4,111/5–2344, Berufsbildung für Ausländer – Bremen und bundesweit (Konzepte, Statistiken, v.a. Ausländeranteil, Prognosen) Bd. 4 1980–1981

4,111/5–2345, Berufsbildung für Ausländer – Bremen und bundesweit (Konzepte, Statistiken, v.a. Ausländeranteil, Prognosen) Bd. 5 1981–1982

4,111/5–2268, Beschulung der Kinder ausländischer Arbeitnehmer – KMK – Rundschreiben (Mitteilungen, Beschlüsse) Bd. 1 1964–1971

4,111/5–2269, Beschulung der Kinder ausländischer Arbeitnehmer – KMK – Rundschreiben (Mitteilungen, Beschlüsse) Bd. 2 1970–1971

4,111/5–2270, Beschulung der Kinder ausländischer Arbeitnehmer – KMK – Rundschreiben (Mitteilungen, Beschlüsse) Bd. 3 1972–1973

4,111/5–2271, Beschulung der Kinder ausländischer Arbeitnehmer – KMK – Rundschreiben (Mitteilungen, Beschlüsse) Bd. 4 1972–1975

4,111/5–2272, Beschulung der Kinder ausländischer Arbeitnehmer –

KMK – Rundschreiben (Mitteilungen, Beschlüsse) Bd. 5 1974–1979
4,111/5–2273, Beschulung der Kinder ausländischer Arbeitnehmer – KMK-Datenkommission (Statistiken, Länderergebnisse) 1977–1979
4,111/5–2274, Beschulung der Kinder ausländischer Arbeitnehmer – Besondere Bestimmungen, Sammlung von Rechtsvorschriften/Land Bremen 1982–1984
4,111/5–2275, Beschulung der Kinder ausländischer Arbeitnehmer – Bundesgesetze, rechtliche Bestimmungen und bremische Verordnungen 1965, 1977–1985
4,111/5–2276, Beschulung der Kinder ausländischer Arbeitnehmer – Regelung in Bremen: Allgemeines 1965–1976
4,111/5–2277, Beschulung der Kinder ausländischer Arbeitnehmer – Regelung in Bremen: Durchführung (Grundsatzfragen, Einzelfälle) 1962–1971
4,111/5–2278, Beschulung der Kinder ausländischer Arbeitnehmer – Regelung in Bremen: Durchführung (Grundsatzfragen, Einzelfälle) 1962–1971
4,111/5–2279, Beschulung der Kinder ausländischer Arbeitnehmer – Regelung in Bremen: Kinder türkischer Gastarbeiter 1966–1970
4,111/5–2281, Durchführung des Unterrichts für Kinder ausländischer Arbeitnehmer – Allgemeines 1967–1984
4,111/5–2283, Durchführung des Unterrichts für Kinder ausländischer Arbeitnehmer – Fördermaßnahmen: Vorbereitungskurse 1972–1981
4,111/5–2286, Beschulung der Kinder ausländischer Arbeitnehmer – Regelung in anderen Bundesländern: Umfrageergebnisse über Ausländerkinder allgemein, Fördermaßnahmen und Religionsunterricht für Kinder und Jugendliche islamischen Glaubens an öffentlichen Schulen 1974–1979
4,111/5–2287, Beschulung der Kinder ausländischer Arbeitnehmer – Ressortübergreifende Arbeitsgruppe 'Integration ausländischer Arbeitnehmer': Grundsätzliches, Protokolle, Konzepte, etc. 1974–1978
4,111/5–2290, Beschulung der Kinder ausländischer Arbeitnehmer – Allgemeines (1955) Bd. 1 1964–1971
4,111/5–2291, Beschulung der Kinder ausländischer Arbeitnehmer – Allgemeines (1955) Bd. 2 1971–1975
4,111/5–2292, Durchführung des Unterrichts für Kinder ausländischer Arbeitnehmer – Korankurse, Islamischer Religionsunterricht: Regelung in Bremen 1982–1983
4,111/5–2301, Beschulung der Kinder ausländischer Arbeitnehmer – Bericht über die Lage der schulpflichtigen Kinder von Ausländern

(Senatsvorlage, Mitteilung des Senats an die Bremische Bürgerschaft) 1980

4,111/5-2302, Beschulung der Kinder ausländischer Arbeitnehmer – Bericht über den Modellversuch 'Kompaktkurs zur Fortbildung von Lehrern für den Unterricht ausländischer Kinder' 1978

4,111/5-2303, Beschulung der Kinder ausländischer Arbeitnehmer – Bericht über die schulische Förderung der Ausländer- und Umsiedlerkinder (1976–) 1980–1981

4,111/5-2304, Beschulung der Kinder ausländischer Arbeitnehmer – Ausländerprogramm 1982 zur Senatsvorlage 'Fortschreibung der Konzeption zur Integration der ausländischen Arbeitnehmer und ihrer Familienangehörigen im Lande Bremen' 1982

4,111/5-2341, Berufsbildung für Ausländer – Bremen und bundesweit (Konzepte, Statistiken, v.a. Ausländeranteil, Prognosen) Bd. 1 1979

4,111/7-254, Studienkolleg Bremen – Sonderkurs für Gastarbeiterkinder 1979–1983

4,123/1-976, Gesundheitliche Überwachung ausländischer Arbeitskräfte 1965–1966

4,124/3-1, Aufnahmeordnung – Kindergarten – Hortgesetz Bd. 2 1980–1981

4,124/3-2, Aufnahmeordnung – Kindergarten – Hortgesetz Bd. 3 1981–1984

4,124/3-3, Planung in Bremen – Allgemeines Bd. 5 1982–1984

4,124/3-4, Planung in Bremen – Konzeption Bd. 1 1985

4,124/3-5, Planung in Bremen – Konzeption Bd. 2 1986

4,124/3-6, Planung in Bremen – Konzeption Bd. 3 1986

4,124/3-7, Planung in Bremen – Allgemeines Bd. 6 1985–1986

4,124/3-8, Außerschulische Jugendarbeit Bd. 3 1983–1986

4,124/3-9, Außerschulische Jugendarbeit Bd. 1 1979–1981

4,124/3-10, Außerschulische Jugendarbeit Bd. 2 1982

4,124/3-11, Türkische Mädchen und Frauen Bd. 1 1983–1984

4,124/3-12, Türkische Mädchen und Frauen Bd. 2 1985–1986

4,124/3-13, Türkische Mädchen und Frauen Bd. 3 1986–1988

4,124/3-14, Wohngemeinschaft für türkische Mädchen und Frauen Bd. 1 1985

4,124/3-15, Wohngemeinschaft für türkische Mädchen und Frauen Bd. 2 1980–1985

4,124/3-16, Wohngemeinschaft für türkische Mädchen und Frauen Bd. 3 1986–1988

4,124/3-19, Ausbildungsförderung für Ausländer der 2. und 3. Generation 1985–1986

4,124/3–20, Neustrukturierung der Sozialarbeit für ausländische Familien Bd. 1 1979–1980
4,124/3–21, Neustrukturierung der Sozialarbeit für ausländische Familien Bd. 2 1980–1981
4,124/3–22, Neustrukturierung der Sozialarbeit für ausländische Familien Bd. 3 1981
4,124/3–23, Behördenwegweiser für türkische Familien 1983–1985
4,124/3–25, Angebote für ausländische Familien 1984–1985
4,124/3–643, Sozialhilfe für Ausländer und Staatenlose – Allgemeines Bd. 1 1964–1972
4,124/3–644, Sozialhilfe für Ausländer und Staatenlose – Allgemeines Bd. 2a 1973
4,124/3–645, Sozialhilfe für Ausländer und Staatenlose – Allgemeines Bd. 2b 1973
4,124/3–646, Sozialhilfe für Ausländer und Staatenlose – Allgemeines Bd. 3 1974–1975
4,124/3–647, Sozialhilfe für Ausländer und Staatenlose – Allgemeines Bd. 4 1976–1977
4,124/3–648, Sozialhilfe für Ausländer und Staatenlose – Allgemeines Bd. 5 1977–1979
4,124/3–649, Sozialhilfe für Ausländer und Staatenlose – Allgemeines Bd. 6 1979–1980
4,124/3–650, Arbeitsgemeinschaft ausländischer Arbeiter (AGaA) 1974
4,124/3–651, Sozialhilfe für Ausländer und Staatenlose – Allgemeines Bd. 2c 1973
4,124/3–691, Ausländer – Allgemeines und Verschiedenes aus älterer Zeit 1952–1960
4,124/3–692, Unterbringung von Ausländern 1972–1979
4,124/3–693, Betreuung heimatloser Ausländer 1951–1969
4,124/3–694, Ausländische Arbeitskräfte in Deutschland Bd. 1 1960–1963
4,124/3–695, Ausländische Arbeitskräfte in Deutschland Bd. 2 1964–1968
4,124/3–696, Ausländische Arbeitskräfte in Deutschland Bd. 3 1969–1970
4,124/3–697, Ausländische Arbeitskräfte in Deutschland Bd. 4 1971–1974
4,124/3–698, Ausländische Arbeitskräfte in Deutschland Bd. 5 1975–1977
4,124/3–699, Ausländische Arbeitskräfte in Deutschland Bd. 6 1977–1978

4,130/4–250, Orts- und Wohnungshygiene – Wohnunterkünfte für ausländische Arbeiter 1962–1975

4,130/4–251, Orts- und Wohnungshygiene – Wohnunterkünfte für ausländische Arbeiter 1973–1990

7,2121/1–652, Betriebausschußsitzungen 1961–1984

7,2121/1–711, Anwerbung, Vermittlung und Ausbildung ausländischer Arbeiter 1970–1973

7,2121/1–712, Sammlung von Schriftgut zur Beschäftigung, Unterbringung und Lage der ausländischen Arbeiter auf dem Vulkan 1969–1981

7,2121/1–713, Sammlung von Schriftgut zu Personalmarketing, Beschäftigung und Unterbringung von ausländischen Arbeitern, zur Stahlbauerschule und zu Auszubildenden und Lehrlingen 1944–1975

7,2121/1–714, Errichtung und Ausstattung von Unterkünften für ausländische Arbeiter 1961–1981

Newspaper articles

'City Busmen Protest Over New Coloured Crews', *Evening Chronicle* (24 February 1958)

'Coloured Busmen Get No Special Treatment', *Evening Chronicle* (25 February 1958)

'Give the Coloured Bus Crews a Chance: Let's Show TRUE Geordie 4 Spirit' (Letter to the editor), *Evening Chronicle* (27 February 1958)

'Bus Crews Say: "No More Coloured Men"', *Evening Chronicle* (17 November 1958)

'100 Millionen für Ausländer-Wohnungen', *Bremer Nachrichten* (5 November 1960)

'Bessere Wohnungen für ausländische Arbeiter', *Weser Kurier* (7 November 1960)

'Our City Busmen … A Passenger Praises Coloured Workers', *Evening Chronicle* (1 February 1961)

'Für die Bambinos ist kein Platz. Nur vereinzelte ausländische Arbeiter können Kind und Kegel nach Bremen nachholen', *Weser Kurier* (17 June 1961)

'Gastarbeiter-Kinder lernen Sprache schnell. Notfalls hilft die ganze Klasse mit', *Bremer Nachrichten* (1 May 1965)

'Ali sucht den Zaunkönig unter „S". Gastarbeiterkinder werden mit Sonderkursen in die deutsche Sprache eingeführt', *Weser Kurier* (12 July 1965)

'Wenn Gastarbeiter keine Gäste mehr sind. Viele Ausländer lassen sich mit ihren Familien in Deutschland nieder', *Weser Kurier* (29 October 1965)

'Jetzt über 2000 Gastarbeiter in Bremen-Nord. Arbeitsmarkt im März wieder stärker belebt – Kräftebedarf in fast allen Wirtschaftszweigen', *Norddeutsche Volkszeitung* (12 April 1966)

'Beirat lehnte Einrichtung von Baracken für Ausländer ab. AG „Weser" wollte 200 Arbeiter in Burg unterbringen', *Bremer Nachrichten* (28 January 1971)

'Schon acht türkische Lehrer unterrichten. Vorbereitungsklassen für Gastarbeiterkinder geplant', *Bremer Nachrichten* (23 June 1972)

'Gastarbeiter – ab ins Getto. Behörden wollen 200 Portugiesen in menschenleerem Hafengebiet ansiedeln', *Weser Kurier* (7 August 1973)

'200 Portugiesen für die bremischen Häfen. Einstellung beschlossen – Wohnschiff wird gekauft', *Bremer Nachrichten* (6 September 1973)

'Großwerft ohne Gastarbeiterprobleme. Bremer Vulkan will die Ausländer nicht nur für ein Gastspiel gewinnen – Integration wird schon längst praktiziert', *Ostbremer Rundschau* (20 September 1973)

'Gleiche Rechte einräumen. Bürgerschaft fordert Programm zur Integration der Gastarbeiter', *Bremer Nachrichten* (5 October 1973)

'DGB kritisiert den Kauf des Gastarbeiter-Wohnschiffs', *Bremer Nachrichten* (9 October 1973)

'Die Portugiesen ziehen jetzt ein', *Weser Kurier* (6 November 1973)

'Bremen will Gastarbeiterkindern besseren Unterricht anbieten', *Frankfurter Rundschau* (11 April 1978)

'Deutschlehrer büffeln Türkisch. Bremen will 80 weitere Pädagogen für Klassen von Gastarbeiterkindern ausbilden', *Weser Kurier* (11 April 1978)

'Zusätzlich 20 Lehrer für Gastarbeiterkinder. Die gleiche Anzahl ab 1. August auch an Schwerpunktschulen der Ausländerförderung', *Bremer Nachrichten* (12 January 1979)

'Jugendliche helfen Türkenkindern. Freizeitbetreuung und Sprachunterricht im Ostertor', *Bremer Nachrichten* (18 April 1979)

'Hilfe nicht nur bei Schulaufgaben. Studenten möchten Ausländerkinder betreuen / Domizil schon gefunden', *Weser Kurier* (6 July 1979)

'Die soziale Zeitbombe tickt nicht überall. Bremens Schule an der Schmidtstraße als Modell für die Integration', *Stuttgarter Zeitung* (21 September 1979)

'Ausländerflut drängt in die Schulen. In Anfängerklassen der Schule Kirchenallee Deutsche klar in der Minderheit / Ausschuß geplant', *Weser Kurier* (8 July 1980)

Hilfe für junge Türkinnen in Not. Bei familiären Konflikten jetzt Aufnahme in Wohngemeinschaft', *Bremer Nachrichten* (15 June 1985)

'Zuflucht vor elterlicher Gewalt. Neue Wohngemeinschaft für junge Türkinnen wird im Juli eröffnet', *Weser Kurier* (15 June 1985)

'Bremen als Vorreiter? Initiative fordert kommunales Wahlrecht für Ausländer', *Frankfurter Rundschau* (9 May 1986)

'Junge Türkinnen oft im Konflikt mit den Eltern. Wohngemeinschaft der AW bietet Schutz und Hilfe', *Weser Kurier* (9 May 1987)

'We'll Change Black Britain', *Guardian* (17 March 2010)

Secondary sources and official reports

Abadan-Unat, Nermin, 'Turkish migration to Europe, 1960–1975: A balance sheet of achievements and failures', in Nermin Abadan-Unat et al., *Turkish Workers in Europe, 1960–1975: A Socio-economic Reappraisal* (Leiden, 1976), pp. 1–44

Abadan-Unat, Nermin, *Turks in Europe: From Guest Worker to Transnational Citizen* (Oxford, 2011)

Abadan-Unat, Nermin et al., *Turkish Workers in Europe, 1960–1975: A Socio-economic Reappraisal* (Leiden, 1976)

Abbas, Tahir, 'Teacher perceptions of South Asians in Birmingham schools and colleges', *Oxford Review of Education*, 28:4 (2002), pp. 447–71

Abbas, Tahir, *The Education of British South Asians: Ethnicity, Capital and Class Structure* (Houndmills, 2004)

Abbas, Tahir (ed.), *Muslim Britain: Communities under Pressure* (London, 2005)

Ager, Dennis, *Language Policy in Britain and France: The Processes of Policy* (London, 1996)

Ahmed, Khurshid, 'Birmingham: Local initiatives to associate immigrants in the integration process', in OECD, *Immigrants, Integration and Cities: Exploring the Links* (Paris, 1998), pp. 173–91

Al-Azmeh, Aziz and Fokas, Effie (eds), *Islam in Europe: Diversity, Identity and Influence* (Cambridge, 2007)

Alba, Richard D., Handl, Johann and Müller, Walter, 'Ethnic inequalities in the German school system', in Peter Schuck and Rainer Münz (eds), *Paths to Inclusion: The Integration of Migrants in the United*

States and Germany (Oxford, 1998), pp. 115–54

Aldrich, Howard, Cater, John, Jones, Trevor and McEvoy, David, 'Business development and self-segregation: Asian enterprise in three British cities', in Ceri Peach, Vaughan Robinson and Susan Smith (eds), *Ethnic Segregation in Cities* (London, 1981), pp. 170–90

Alexander, Claire, 'Imagining the politics of BrAsian youth', in N. Ali, V.S. Kalra and S. Sayyid (eds), *A Postcolonial People: South Asians in Britain* (Cambridge, 2008), pp. 258–71

Algan, Yann, Dustmann, Christian, Glitz, Albrecht and Manning, Alan, 'The economic situation of first and second-generation immigrants in France, Germany and the United Kingdom', *The Economic Journal*, 120:542 (2010), pp. F4–F30

Al-Hamarneh, Ala and Thielmann, Jörn (eds), *Islam and Muslims in Germany* (Leiden, 2008)

Alladina, Safder, 'South Asian languages in Britain', in Guus Extra and Ludo Verhoeven (eds), *Immigrant Languages in Europe* (Clevedon, 1993), pp. 55–66

Allen, Joan and Allen, Richard C., 'Competing identities: Irish and Welsh migration and the North East of England, 1851–1980', in Adrian Green and A.J. Pollard (eds), *Regional Identities in North-East England, 1300–2000* (Woodbridge, 2007), pp. 133–59

Allen, Sheila, Bentley, Stuart and Bornat, Joanna, *Work, Race and Immigration* (Bradford, 1977)

AlSayyad, Nezar and Castells, Manuel (eds), *Muslim Europe or Euro-Islam: Politics, Culture, and Citizenship in the Age of Globalization* (Lanham MD, 2002)

Ammermueller, Andreas, 'Poor background or low returns? Why immigrant students in Germany perform so poorly in the Programme for International Student Assessment', *Education Economics*, 15:2 (2007), pp. 215–30

Ansari, Humayun, *'The Infidel Within': Muslims in Britain since 1800* (London, 2004)

Anwar, Muhammad, *Between Cultures: Continuity and Change in the Lives of Young Asians* (London, 1998)

Anwar, Muhammad, 'Muslims in Britain: Issues, policy and practice', in Tahir Abbas (ed.), *Muslim Britain: Communities under Pressure* (London, 2005), pp. 31–46

Apple, Michael, 'The absent presence of race in educational reform', *Race, Ethnicity and Education*, 2:1 (1999), pp. 9–16

Archer, Louise, *Race, Masculinity and Schooling: Muslim Boys and Education* (Maidenhead, 2003)

Armgort, Arno, *Bremen, Bremerhaven, New York: Geschichte der europäischen Auswanderung über die bremischen Häfen* (Steintor, 1991)
Arora, Ranjit, *Race and Ethnicity in Education* (Aldershot, 2005)
Bade, Klaus J. (ed.), *Population, Labour and Migration in 19th- and 20th-Century Germany* (Leamington Spa, 1987)
Bade, Klaus J., 'Immigration and integration in Germany since 1945', *European Review*, 1:1 (1993), pp. 75–9
Bade, Klaus J., *Europa in Bewegung: Migration vom späten 18. Jahrhundert bis zur Gegenwart* (Munich, 2000)
Bagley, Christopher, 'The educational performance of immigrant children', *Race & Class*, 10:1 (1968), pp. 91–4
Baker, Colin, *Key Issues in Bilingualism and Bilingual Education* (Clevedon, 1988)
Ballard, Roger and Ballard, Catherine, 'The Sikhs: The development of South Asian settlements in Britain', in James L. Watson (ed.), *Between Two Cultures: Migrants and Minorities in Britain* (Oxford, 1977), pp. 21–56
Barfuss, Karl Marten, 'Foreign workers in and around Bremen, 1884–1918', in Dirk Hoerder and Jörg Nagler (eds), *People in Transit: German Migrations in Comparative Perspective, 1820–1930* (Cambridge, 1995), pp. 201–24
Barrett, Giles A., Jones, Trevor P. and McEvoy, David, 'Ethnic minority business: Theoretical discourse in Britain and North America', *Urban Studies*, 33:4–5 (1996), pp. 783–809
Barrett, Giles A., Jones, Trevor P. and McEvoy, David, 'Socio-economic and policy dimensions of the mixed embeddedness of ethnic minority business in Britain', *Journal of Ethnic and Migration Studies*, 27:2 (2001), pp. 241–58
Barrett, Giles A., Jones, Trevor P. and McEvoy, David, 'United Kingdom: Severely constrained entrepreneurialism', in Robert Kloosterman and Jan Rath (eds), *Immigrant Entrepreneurs: Venturing Abroad in the Age of Globalization* (Oxford, 2003), pp. 101–22
Basu, Anuradha, 'An exploration of entrepreneurial activity among Asian small businesses in Britain', *Small Business Economics*, 10:4 (1998), pp. 313–26
Basu, Anuradha, 'Ethnic minority entrepreneurship', in Mark Casson, Bernard Yeung, Anuradha Basu and Nigel Wadeson (eds), *The Oxford Handbook of Entrepreneurship* (Oxford, 2006), pp. 580–600

Baumert, Jürgen, Klieme, Eckhard, Neubrand, Michael, Prenzel, Manfred, Schiefele, Ulrich, Schneider, Wolfgang, Stanat, Petra, Tillmann, Klaus-Jürgen and Weiß, Manfred (eds), *PISA 2000: Basiskompetenzen von Schülerinnen und Schülern im internationalen Vergleich* (Opladen, 2001)

Bawer, Bruce, *While Europe Slept: How Radical Islam is Destroying the West from Within* (London, 2006)

Beetham, David, *Immigrant School Leavers and the Youth Employment Service in Birmingham* (London, 1967)

Behrens, Ulrike, Tost, Sabine and Jäger, Reinhold S., 'German policy on foreigners and the education of immigrants in the Federal Republic of Germany', in Dr Pirkko Pitkänen, Devorah Kalekin-Fishman and Gajendra K. Verma (eds), *Education and Immigration: Settlement Policies and Current Challenges* (London, 2002), pp. 96–123

Beider, Harris, *Race, Housing & Community: Perspectives on Policy and Practice* (Oxford, 2012)

Beider, Harris, Joseph, Ricky and Ferrari, Ed, *Report to North East Assembly BME Housing Issues* (Birmingham, 2007)

Bender, Stefan and Seifert, Wolfgang, 'Zuwanderer auf dem Arbeitsmarkt: Nationalitäten- und geschlechtsspezifische Unterschiede', *Zeitschrift für Soziologie*, 25:6 (1996), pp. 473–95

Bender, Stefan and Seifert, Wolfgang, 'On the economic and social situations of immigrant groups in Germany', in Richard Alba, Peter Schmidt and Martina Wasmer (eds), *Germans or Foreigners? Attitudes towards Ethnic Minorities in Post-Reunification Germany* (Basingstoke, 2003), pp. 45–68

Bilmen, M. Sitki, 'Educational problems encountered by the children of Turkish migrant workers', in Nermin Abadan-Unat *et al.*, *Turkish Workers in Europe, 1960–1975: A Socio-economic Reappraisal* (Leiden, 1976), pp. 235–52

Biondi, Franco *et al.* (eds), *Im neuen Land* (Bremen, 1980)

Bird, Karen, Saalfeld, Thomas and Wüst, Andreas M. (eds), *The Political Representation of Immigrants and Minorities: Voters, Parties and Parliaments in Liberal Democracies* (London, 2011)

Blaschke, Jochen, and Ersöz, Ahmet, *Herkunft und Geschäft-saufnahme türkischer Kleingewerbetreibender in Berlin* (Berlin, 1987)

Bleich, Erik, *Race Politics in Britain and France: Ideas and Policymaking since the 1960's* (Cambridge, 2003)

Boal, Frederick W., 'From undivided cities to undivided cities: Assimilation to ethnic cleansing', *Housing Studies*, 14:5 (1999), pp. 585–600

Bonnett, Alastair, 'Anti-racism as a radical educational ideology in London and Tyneside', *Oxford Review of Education*, 16:2 (1990), pp. 255–67

Bonnett, Alastair, *Radicalism, Anti-Racism and Representation* (London, 1993)

Borooah, Vani Kant and Hart, Mark, 'Factors affecting self-employment among Indian and black Caribbean men in Britain', *Small Business Economics*, 13:2 (1999), pp. 111–29

Bourne, Jill, 'Centralization, devolution and diversity: Changing educational policy and practice in English schools', in Guofang Wan (ed.), *The Education of Diverse Student Populations: A Global Perspective* (Dordrecht, 2008), pp. 29–43

Boyes, Roger and Huneke, Dorte, *Is it Easier to be a Turk in Berlin or a Pakistani in Bradford?* (London, 2004)

Braham, Peter, Rattansi, Ali and Skellington, Richard (eds), *Racism and Antiracism: Inequalities, Opportunities and Policies* (London, 1992)

Bremer, Peter, *Ausgrenzungsprozesse und die Spaltung der Städte: Zur Lebenssituation von Migranten* (Opladen, 2000)

Brettell, Caroline B. and Alstatt, Kristoffer E., 'The agency of immigrant entrepreneurs: Biographies of the self-employed in ethnic and occupational niches of the urban labor market', *Journal of Anthropological Research*, 63:3 (2007), pp. 383–97

Brettell, Caroline and Hollifield, James F. (eds), *Migration Theory: Talking across Disciplines* (New York, 2000)

Bristow, Mike, 'Ugandan Asians: racial disadvantage and housing markets in Manchester and Birmingham', *Journal of Ethnic and Migration Studies*, 7:2 (1979), pp. 203–16

Broeder, Peter and Extra, Guus, *Language, Ethnicity and Education: Case Studies of Immigrant Minority Groups and Immigrant Minority Languages* (Clevedon, 1999)

Brown, Colin, *Black and White Britain: The Third PSI Survey* (London, 1984)

Brown, Colin and Gay, Pat, *Racial Discrimination: Seventeen Years after the Act* (London, 1985)

Brown, Mark S., 'Religion and economic activity in the South Asian population', *Ethnic and Racial Studies*, 23:6 (2000), pp. 1035–61

Brubaker, Rogers, *Citizenship and Nationhood in France and Germany* (Cambridge MA, 1992)

Brüß, Joachim, 'Experiences of discrimination reported by Turkish, Moroccan and Bangladeshi Muslims in three European cities',

Journal of Ethnic and Migration Studies, 34:6 (2008), pp. 875–94

Bühler-Otten, Sabine and Fürstenau, Sara, 'Multilingualism in Hamburg', in Guus Extra and Kutlay Yağmur (eds), *Urban Multilingualism in Europe: Immigrant Minority Languages at Home and School* (Clevedon, 2004), pp. 163–91

Bukta, Susanne, 'Der lange Weg – Islamischer Religionsunterricht in Deutschland', *Stimme*, 14:5 (2000), pp. 6–9

Burkert, Carola and Seibert, Holger, 'Labour market outcomes after vocational training in Germany – equal opportunities for migrants and natives?', *IAB Discussion Paper* 31 (2007)

Burleigh, Michael and Wippermann, Wolfgang, *The Racial State: Germany 1933–1945* (Cambridge, 1991)

Burney, Elizabeth, *Housing on Trial: A Study of Immigrants and Local Government* (Oxford, 1967)

Buse, Dieter K., 'Urban and national identity: Bremen, 1860–1920', *Journal of Social History*, 26:3 (1993), pp. 521–37

Buse, Dieter K., 'Federalism and identity: Bremen, 1945–1960s', *Debatte: Journal of Contemporary Central and Eastern Europe*, 10:1 (2002), pp. 33–50

Byrne, David, 'Immigrants and the formation of the North Eastern industrial working class', *North East Labour History Society Bulletin* 30 (1996), pp. 29–36

Cabinet Office, *Ethnic Minorities and the Labour Market: Final Report* (London, 2003)

Çağlar, Ayse S., 'Constraining metaphors and the transnationalisation of spaces in Berlin', *Journal of Ethnic and Migration Studies*, 27:4 (2001), pp. 601–13

Cameron, Stuart, 'Ethnic minority housing needs and diversity in an area of low housing demand', *Environment and Planning A*, 32:8 (2000), pp. 1427–44

Cameron, Stuart and Field, Andrew, *Housing and the Black Population of West Newcastle* (Sunderland, 1997)

Cameron, Stuart and Field, Andrew, 'Community, ethnicity and neighbourhood', *Housing Studies*, 15:6 (2000), pp. 827–43

Carey, Séan and Shukur, Abdus, 'A profile of the Bangladeshi community in East London', *Journal of Ethnic and Migration Studies*, 12:3 (1985), pp. 405–17

Carr, Barry, 'Black Geordies', in Robert Colls and Bill Lancaster (eds), *Geordies: Roots of Regionalism* (Newcastle upon Tyne, 2005), pp. 133–48

Cashmore, Ellis and Troyna, Barry, *Introduction to Race Relations*

(London, 1990)

Castles, Stephen, 'Migrants and minorities in post-Keynesian capitalism: The German case', in Malcolm Cross (ed.), *Ethnic Minorities and Industrial Change in Europe and North America* (Cambridge, 1992), pp. 36–54

Castles, Stephen, 'The factors that make and unmake migration policies', *International Migration Review*, 38:3 (2004), pp. 852–84

Caviedes, Alexander A., *Prying Open Fortress Europe: The Turn to Sectoral Labor Migration* (Lanham MD, 2010)

Cesari, Jocelyne, 'Islamophobia in the West: A comparison between Europe and the United States', in John L. Esposito and Ibrahim Kalin (eds), *Islamophobia: The Challenge of Pluralism in the 21st Century* (Oxford, 2011), pp. 21–43

Chief Executive's Department, Newcastle City Council, *Update on Racial Harassment in Newcastle* (Newcastle, 1995)

Chin, Rita, *The Guest Worker Question in Postwar Germany* (Cambridge, 2007)

Chin, Rita, 'Guest worker migration and the unexpected return of race', in Rita Chin, Heide Fehrenbach, Geoff Eley and Atina Grossmann (eds), *After the Nazi Racial State: Difference and Democracy in Germany and Europe* (Ann Arbor, 2009), pp. 80–101

Chivers, Terry S. (ed.), *Race and Culture in Education: Issues Arising from the Swann Committee Report* (Windsor, 1987)

Çil, Hasan (ed.), *Anfänge einer EPOCHE. Ehemalige türkische Gastarbeiter erzählen* (Berlin, 2003)

Clark, Kenneth and Drinkwater, Stephen, 'Ethnicity and self-employment in Britain', *Oxford Bulletin of Economics and Statistics*, 60:3 (1998), pp. 383–407

Clark, Kenneth and Drinkwater, Stephen, 'Pushed in or pulled out? Self-employment among ethnic minorities in England and Wales', *Labour Economics*, 7:5 (2000), pp. 603–28

Clark, Kenneth and Drinkwater, Stephen, 'Dynamic and diversity: Ethnic employment differences in England and Wales, 1991–2001', *IZA Discussion Paper* 1698 (Bonn, 2005)

Clark, William and Drever, Anita, 'Residential mobility in a constrained housing market: Implications for ethnic populations in Germany', *Environment and Planning A*, 32:5 (2000), pp. 833–46

Clyne, Michael, *The German Language in a Changing Europe* (Cambridge, 1995)

Collins, Jock, 'Australia: Cosmopolitan capitalists down under', in Robert Kloosterman and Jan Rath (eds), *Immigrant Entrepreneurs:*

Venturing Abroad in the Age of Globalization (Oxford, 2003), pp. 61–78

Collins, Sydney, *Coloured Minorities in Britain: Studies in British Race Relations Based on African, West Indian and Asiatic Immigrants* (London, 1957)

Colls, Robert, *The Pitmen of the Northern Coalfield: Work, Culture, and Protest, 1790–1850* (Manchester, 1987)

Commission for Racial Equality, *Living in Terror: A Report on Racial Violence and Harassment in Housing* (London, 1987)

Commission for Racial Equality, *Learning in Terror: A Survey of Racial Harassment in Schools and Colleges in England, Scotland and Wales, 1985–1987* (London, 1988)

Commission for Racial Equality, *Racial Discrimination in Liverpool City Council: Report of a Formal Investigation into the Housing Department* (London, 1989)

Commission for Racial Equality, *Housing Allocations in Oldham: Report of a Formal Investigation* (London, 1993)

Community Cohesion Review Team, *The Cantle Report – Community Cohesion: A Report of the Independent Review Team* (London, 2001)

Constant, Amelie and Zimmermann, Klaus F., 'The making of entrepreneurs in Germany: Are native men and immigrants alike?', *Small Business Economics*, 26:3 (2006), pp. 279–300

Constant, Amelie, Roberts, Rowan and Zimmermann, Klaus F., 'Ethnic identity and immigrant homeownership', *Urban Studies*, 46:9 (2009), pp. 1879–98

Conteh, Jean, *Succeeding in Diversity: Culture, Language and Learning in Primary Classrooms* (Stoke on Trent, 2003)

Conway, Cheryl, Coombes, Mike, and Humphrey, Lynne, *Mapping Ethnicity in the North East Labour Market (Draft Report)* (Newcastle upon Tyne, 2006)

Cooter, Roger, *When Paddy Met Geordie: The Irish in County Durham and Newcastle, 1840–1880* (Sunderland, 2005)

Cornelius, Wayne A., Martin, Philip L. and Hollifield, James F. (eds), *Controlling Immigration: A Global Perspective* (Stanford CA, 2004)

Crul, Maurice, 'How do educational systems integrate? Integration of second-generation Turks in Germany, France, the Netherlands, and Austria', in Richard Alba and Mary C. Waters (eds), *The Next Generation: Immigrant Youth in a Comparative Perspective* (New York, 2011), pp. 269–82

Dahya, Badr, 'The nature of Pakistani ethnicity in industrial cities in

Britain', in Abner Cohen (ed.), *Urban Ethnicity* (London, 1974), pp. 77–118

Dal, Güney, *Wenn Ali die Glocken läuten hört* (Berlin, 1979)

Dana, Léo-Paul (ed.), *Entrepreneurship and Religion* (Cheltenham, 2010)

Dancygier, Rafaela M., *Immigration and Conflict in Europe* (Cambridge, 2010)

Dangschat, Jens, 'Concentration of poverty in the landscapes of "boomtown" Hamburg: The creation of a new urban underclass?', *Urban Studies*, 31:7 (1994), pp. 1133–47

Daniel, Marcel, 'Streiflichter bundesdeutscher Zuwanderung – Reise auf abwechslungsreichen Wegen', in Karin Meendermann (ed.), *Migration und politische Bildung – Integration durch Information* (Münster, 2003), pp. 53–82

Daniel, William W., *Racial Discrimination in England: Based on the PEP Report* (London, 1968)

Davies, Jon Gower, *The Evangelistic Bureaucrat. A Study of a Planning Exercise in Newcastle upon Tyne* (London, 1972)

Davies, Jon Gower, *Asian Housing in Britain* (Altrincham, 1986)

Davies, Jon Gower and Taylor, John, 'Race, community and no conflict', *New Society*, 9 (1970), pp. 67–9

Deakins, David, Ram, Monder, Smallbone, David and Fletcher, Margaret, 'Ethnic minority entrepreneurs and the commercial banks in the UK: Access to formal sources of finance and decision-making by their bankers', in Curt H. Stiles and Craig S. Galbraith (eds), *Ethnic Entrepreneurship: Structure and Process* (London, 2004), pp. 293–314

Deakins, David, Smallbone, David, Ishaq, Mohammed, Whittam, Geoffrey and Wyper, Janette, 'Minority ethnic enterprise in Scotland', *Journal of Ethnic and Migration Studies*, 35:2 (2009), pp. 309–30

Dickopp, Karl-Heinz, *Erziehung ausländischer Kinder als pädagogische Herausforderung: das Krefelder Modell* (Dusseldorf, 1982)

Dorn, Andrew and Hibbert, Paul, 'A comedy of errors: Section 11 funding and education', in Barry Troyna (ed.), *Racial Inequality in Education* (Abingdon, 2012), pp. 59–76

Drever, Anita I. and Clark, William A.V., 'Gaining access to housing in Germany: The foreign-minority experience', *Urban Studies*, 39:13 (2002), pp. 2439–53

Drinkwater, Stephen, 'Self-employment amongst ethnic and migrant groups in the United Kingdom', in OECD, *Open for Business:*

Migrant Entrepreneurship in OECD Countries (Paris, 2010), pp. 189–98

Dunn, Kevin, 'Rethinking ethnic concentration: The case of Cabramatta, Sydney', *Urban Studies*, 35:3 (1998), pp. 503–27

Dünzelmann , Anne E., *Aneignung und Selbstbehauptung: Zum Prozess der Integration und Akkulturation von >GastarbeiterInnen< in Bremen* (Göttingen, 2005)

Eade, John, *The Politics of Community: The Bangladeshi Community in East London* (Aldershot, 1989)

Eade, John, 'Identity, nation and religion: Educated young Bangladeshi Muslims in London's "East End"', *International Sociology*, 9:3 (1994), pp. 377–94

Echchaibi, Nabil, *Voicing Diasporas: Ethnic Radio in Paris and Berlin between Cultural Renewal and Retention* (Lanham MD, 2011)

Edgar, Bill, Doherty, Joe and Meert, Henk, *Immigration and Homelessness in Europe* (Bristol, 2004)

Edwards, Viv and Redfern, Angela, *The World in a Classroom: Language in Education in Britain and Canada* (Clevedon, 1992)

Ehrkamp, Patricia, 'Placing identities: Transnational practices and local attachments of Turkish immigrants in Germany', *Journal of Ethnic and Migration Studies*, 31:2 (2005), pp. 345–64

Ehrkamp, Patricia, 'Beyond the mosque: Turkish immigrants and the practice and politics of Islam in Duisburg-Marxloh, Germany', in Cara Aitchison, Peter Hopkins and Mei-Po Kwan (eds), *Geographies of Muslim Identities: Diaspora, Gender and Belonging* (Aldershot, 2007), pp. 11–28

Ekblom, Paul and Simon, Frances H. with Birdi, Sneh, *Crime and Racial Harassment in Asian-run Small Shops: The Scope for Prevention* (London, 1988)

Eksner, H. Julia, *Ghetto Ideologies, Youth Identities and Stylized Turkish German: Turkish Youths in Berlin-Kreuzberg* (Münster, 2006)

Elkeles, Thomas and Seifert, Wolfgang, 'Immigrants and health: Unemployment and health-risk of labour migrants in the Federal Republic of Germany', *Social Science and Medicine*, 43:7 (1996), pp. 1035–47

Elver, Hilal, *The Headscarf Controversy: Secularism and Freedom of Religion* (Oxford, 2012)

Eslea, Mike and Mukhtar, Kafeela, 'Bullying and racism among Asian schoolchildren in Britain', *Educational Research*, 42:2 (2000), pp. 207–17

Esposito, John L., *The Islamic Threat: Myth or Reality?* (Oxford, 1999)
Esser, Hartmut and Korte, Hermann, 'Federal Republic of Germany', in Tomas Hammar (ed.), *European Immigration Policy: A Comparative Study* (Cambridge, 1985), pp. 165–205
Faas, Daniel, *Negotiating Political Identities: Multiethnic Schools and Youth in Europe* (Farnham, 2010)
Faist, Thomas, 'From school to work: Public policy and underclass formation among young Turks in Germany during the 1980s', *International Migration Review*, 27:2 (1993), pp. 306–31
Farwick, Andreas, 'Behindern ethnisch geprägte Wohnquartiere die Eingliederung von Migranten?', in Olaf Schnur (ed.), *Quartiersforschung: zwischen Theorie und Praxis* (Wiesbaden, 2008), pp. 209–32
Farwick, Andreas, *Segregation und Eingliederung: Zum Einfluss der räumlichen Konzentration von Zuwanderern auf den Eingliederungsprozess* (Wiesbaden, 2009)
Farwick, Andreas, 'The effect of ethnic segregation on the process of assimilation', in Matthias Wingens, Michael Windzio, Helga de Valk and Can Aybek (eds), *A Life-Course Perspective on Migration and Integration* (Dordrecht, 2011), pp. 239–58
Favell, Adrian, *Philosophies of Integration: Immigration and the Idea of Citizenship in France and Britain* (Basingstoke, 1998)
Federal Office for Migration and Refugees, *Muslim Life in Germany. A Study Conducted on Behalf of the German Conference on Islam* (Nuremberg, 2009)
Fertala, Nikolinka, 'A study of immigrant entrepreneurship in Upper Bavaria', *International Journal of Entrepreneurship and Small Business*, 4:2 (2006), pp. 179–206
Fetzer, Joel, *Public Attitudes toward Immigration in the United States, France, and Germany* (Cambridge, 2000)
Fetzer, Joel S. and Soper, Christopher J., *Muslims and the State in Britain, France, and Germany* (Cambridge, 2005)
Figueroa, Peter, *Education and the Social Construction of 'Race'* (London, 1991)
Figueroa, Peter, 'Intercultural education in Britain', in Kenneth Cushner (ed.), *International Perspectives on Intercultural Education* (Mahwah NJ, 1998), pp. 122–44
Fijalkowski, Jürgen, 'Gastarbeiter als industrielle Reservearmee? Zur Bedeutung der Arbeitsmigration für die wirtschaftliche und gesellschaftliche Entwicklung der Bundesrepublik Deutschland',

Archiv für Sozialgeschichte, 24 (1984), pp. 399–456
Flap, Henk, Kumcu, Adem and Bulder, Bert, 'The social capital of ethnic entrepreneurs and their business success', in Jan Rath (ed.), *Immigrant Business: The Economic, Political and Social Environment* (Basingstoke, 1999), pp. 142–61
Flett, Hazel, *Council Housing and Location of Ethnic Minorities* (Bristol, 1977)
Flint, John, 'Faith and housing in England: Promoting community cohesion or contributing to urban segregation?', *Journal of Ethnic and Migration Studies*, 36:2 (2010), pp. 257–74
Foster-Carter, Olivia, 'The Honeyford Affair: Political and policy implications', in Barry Troyna (ed.), *Racial Inequality in Education* (London, 1987), pp. 44–58
French, Elizabeth, 'Parental involvement – an evolving process', *Multicultural Teaching*, 4:3 (1986), pp. 18–19
Freyer Stowasser, Barbara, 'The Turks in Germany: From sojourners to citizens', in Yvonne Yazbeck Haddad (ed.), *Muslims in the West: From Sojourners to Citizens* (Oxford, 2002), pp. 52–71
Friedman, Samantha and Rosenbaum, Emily, 'Nativity status and racial/ethnic differences in access to quality housing: Does home-ownership bring greater parity?', *Housing Policy Debate*, 15:4 (2004), pp. 865–901
Friedrichs, Jürgen, 'Ethnische Segregation', in Frank Kalter (ed.), 'Migration und Integration', *Kölner Zeitschrift für Soziologie und Sozialpsychologie*, 48 (2008), pp. 380–411
Friedrichs, Jürgen and Alpheis, Hannes, 'Housing segregation of immigrants in West Germany', in Elizabeth D. Huttman, Wim Blauw and Juliet Saltman (eds), *Urban Housing Segregation of Minorities in Western Europe and the United States* (Duke NC, 1991), pp. 116–44
Frouws, Bram and Buiskool, Bert-Jan, *Migrants to Work: Innovative Approaches towards Successful Integration of Third Country Migrants into the Labour Market: Final Report* (European Commission. Directorate-General for Employment, Social Affairs and Equal Opportunities) (Brussels, 2010)
Fuess, Albrecht, 'Islamic religious education in Western Europe: Models of integration and the German approach', *Journal of Muslim Minority Affairs*, 27:2 (2007), pp. 215–39
Gang, Ira N. and Zimmermann, Klaus F., 'Is child like parent? Educational attainment and ethnic origin', *The Journal of Human Resources*, 35:3 (2000), pp. 550–69

Gans, Paul, 'Intraurban migration of foreigners in Kiel since 1972. The case of the Turkish population', in Günther Glebe and John O'Loughlin (eds), *Foreign Minorities in Continental European Cities* (Wiesbaden, 1987), pp. 116–38

Garbaye, Romain, *Getting into Local Power: The Politics of Ethnic Minorities in British and French Cities* (Oxford, 2005)

Gardner, Rod, Karakaşoğlus, Yasemin and Luchtenberg, Sigrid, 'Islamophobia in the media: A response from multicultural education', *Intercultural Education*, 19:2 (2008), pp. 119–36

Gay, John Dennis, *The Geography of Religion in England* (London, 1971)

Geddes, Andrew, *The Politics of Migration and Immigration in Europe* (London, 2003)

Giersch, Herbert, Paqué, Karl-Heinz and Schmieding, Holger, *The Fading Miracle: Four Decades of Market Economy in Germany* (Cambridge, 1992)

Gilbert, David, 'Racial and religious discrimination: The inexorable relationship between schools and the individual', *Intercultural Education*, 15:3 (2004), pp. 253–66

Gillborn, David, 'Anti-racism: From policy to praxis', in Bob Moon, Sally Brown and Miriam Ben-Peretz (eds), *Routledge International Companion to Education* (London, 2000), pp. 476–88

Gillborn, David, *Racism and Education: Coincidence or Conspiracy?* (London, 2008)

Gillborn, David and Gipps, Caroline, *Recent Research on the Achievement of Ethnic Minority Pupils: OFSTED Reviews of Research* (London, 1996)

Gilliat-Ray, Sophie, *Muslims in Britain: An Introduction* (Cambridge, 2010)

Gilroy, Paul, *'There Ain't No Black in the Union Jack': The Cultural Politics of Race and Nation* (London, 2002)

Ginsburg, Norman, 'Racism and housing: Concepts and reality', in Peter Braham, Ali Rattansi and Richard Skellington (eds), *Racism and Antiracism: Inequalities, Opportunities and Policies* (London, 1992), pp. 109–32

Ginsburg, Norman and Watson, Sophie, 'Issues of race and gender facing housing policy', in Johnston Birchall (ed.), *Housing Policy in the 1990s* (London, 1992), pp. 140–62

Gitmez, Ali and Wilpert, Czarina, 'A micro-society or an ethnic community? Social organization and ethnicity amongst Turkish migrants in Berlin', in John Rex, Danièle Joly and Czarina Wilpert (eds), *Immigrant Associations in Europe* (Aldershot, 1987), pp. 86–125

Glebe, Günther, 'Housing and segregation of Turks in Germany', in Sule Özüekren and Ronald van Kempen (eds), *Turks in European Cities: Housing and Urban Segregation* (Utrecht, 1997), pp. 122–57

Glebe, Günther and Waldorf, Brigitte, 'Migration of guestworkers and Germans: Microlevel analysis of neighbourhood changes in Düsseldorf 1981–1983', in Günther Glebe and John O'Loughlin (eds), *Foreign Minorities in Continental European Cities* (Stuttgart, 1987), pp. 139–62

Göktürk, Deniz, Gramling, David and Kaes, Anton (eds), *Germany in Transit: Nation and Migration, 1955–2005* (Berkeley CA, 2007)

Goldberg, Andreas, 'Islam in Germany', in Shireen T. Hunter (ed.), *Islam, Europe's Second Religion: The New Social, Cultural, and Political Landscape* (Westport CT, 2002), pp. 29–50

Gorard, Stephen, Taylor, Chris and Fitz, John, *Schools, Markets and Choice Policies* (London, 2003)

Granato, Nadia and Kalter, Frank, 'Die Persistenz ethnischer Ungleichheit auf dem deutschen Arbeitsmarkt. Diskriminierung oder Unterinvestition in Humankapital?', *Kölner Zeitschrift für Soziologie und Sozialpsychologie*, 53:3 (2001), pp. 497–520

Green, Adrian and Pollard, A.J. (eds), *Regional Identities in North-East England, 1300–2000* (Woodbridge, 2007)

Green, Simon, *The Politics of Exclusion: Institutions and Immigration Policy in Contemporary Germany* (Manchester, 2004)

Green, Simon, 'Divergent traditions, converging responses: Immigration and integration policy in the UK and Germany', *German Politics*, 16:1 (2007), pp. 95–115

Grosvenor, Ian, *Assimilating Identities, Racism and Educational Policy in Post 1945 Britain* (London, 1997)

Guiraudon, Virginie and Joppke, Christian (eds), *Controlling a New Migration World* (New York, 2001)

Haberland, Hartmut and Skutnabb-Kangas, Tove, 'Political determinants of pragmatic and sociolinguistic choices', in Herman Parret, Marina Sbisà and Jef Verschueren (eds), *Possibilities and Limitations of Pragmatics* (Amsterdam, 1981), pp. 285–312

Hackett, Sarah E., 'The Asian of the north: Immigrant experiences and the importance of regional identity in Newcastle upon Tyne during the 1980s', *Northern History*, 46:2 (2009), pp. 293–311

Hackett, Sarah E., 'A learning curve: The education of immigrants in Newcastle upon Tyne and Bremen from the 1960s to the 1980s', in

Zvi Bekerman and Thomas Geisen (eds), *International Handbook of Migration, Minorities and Education – Understanding Cultural and Social Differences in Processes of Learning* (Dordrecht, 2011), pp. 349–64

Hackett, Sarah E., 'Peering around the "velvet curtain of culture": The employment and housing of Newcastle upon Tyne's Muslim immigrants, 1960s-1990s', in Gerald MacLean (ed.), *Britain and the Muslim World: Historical Perspectives* (Newcastle, 2011), pp. 222–37

Hackett, Sarah E., 'Integration im kommunalen Raum: Bremen und Newcastle upon Tyne im Vergleich', in Jochen Oltmer, Axel Kreienbrink and Carlos Sanz Díaz (eds), 'Das „Gastarbeiter" System. Arbeitsmigration und ihre Folgen in der Bundesrepublik Deutschland und Westeuropa', *Schriftenreihe der Vierteljahrshefte für Zeitgeschichte*, 104 (2012), pp. 247–59

Halliday, Fred, *Arabs in Exile: Yemeni Migrants in Urban Britain* (London, 1992)

Halliday, Fred, *Britain's First Muslims: Portrait of an Arab Community* (London, 2010)

Hanhörster, Heike, 'Whose neighbourhood is it? Ethnic diversity in urban spaces in Germany', *GeoJournal*, 51:4 (2001), pp. 329–38

Hansen, Randall, *Citizenship and Immigration in Post-war Britain: The Institutional Origins of a Multicultural Nation* (Oxford, 2000)

Haque, Zubaida, 'The ethnic minority "underachieving" group? Investigating the claims of 'underachievement' amongst Bangladeshi pupils in British secondary schools', *Race, Ethnicity and Education*, 3:2 (2000), pp. 145–68

Harrison, Malcolm and Davis, Cathy, *Housing, Social Policy and Difference: Disability, Ethnicity, Gender and Housing* (Bristol, 2001)

Häußermann, Hartmut and Siebel, Walter, *Soziale Integration und ethnische Schichtung – Zusammenhänge zwischen räumlicher und sozialer Integration* (Berlin, 2001)

Hawkes, Nicolas, *Immigrant Children in British Schools* (London, 1966)

Haydon, Graham (ed.), *Education for a Pluralist Society: Philosophical Perspectives on the Swann Report* (University of London Institute of Education, 1987)

Hearnden, Margaret and Sundaram, Vanita, 'Education for a diverse society: The multicultural classroom in the UK', in Julia Athena Spinthourakis, John Lalor and Wolfgang Berg (eds), *Cultural*

Diversity in the Classroom: A European Comparison (Wiesbaden, 2011), pp. 187–98

Heath, Anthony and Cheung, Sin Yi, *Ethnic Penalties in the Labour Market: Employers and Discrimination* (Leeds, 2006)

Heckmann, Friedrich and Schnapper, Dominique (eds), *The Integration of Immigrants in European Societies: National Differences and Trends of Convergence* (Stuttgart, 2003)

Heinrichs, Andreas, *Von Istanbul nach Gröpelingen – Alltag in der Lindenhofstraße: Fotoausstellung über die Einwanderung und das Leben in Bremen-Gröpelingen* (Kulturladen Gröpelingen, 1992)

Helicke, James, 'Turks in Germany: Muslim identity "between" states', in Yvonne Yazbeck Haddad and Jane I. Smith (eds), *Muslim Minorities in the West: Visible and Invisible* (Oxford, 2002), pp. 175–91

Henderson, Jeffrey and Karn, Valerie, *Race, Class and State Housing: Inequality and the Allocation of Public Housing in Britain* (Aldershot, 1987)

Henze, Jürgen, 'Muslim minorities and education in Germany – The case of Berlin', in Holger Daun and Geoffrey Walford (eds), *Educational Strategies among Muslims in the Context of Globalization: Some National Case Studies* (Leiden, 2004), pp. 233–6

Herbert, Joanna, *Negotiating Boundaries in the City: Migration, Ethnicity, and Gender in Britain* (Aldershot, 2008)

Herbert, Ulrich, *Geschichte der Ausländerbeschäftigung in Deutschland 1880 bis 1980. Saisonarbeiter, Zwangsarbeiter, Gastarbeiter* (Bonn, 1986)

Herbert, Ulrich, *A History of Foreign Labor in Germany, 1880–1980: Seasonal Workers/Forced Laborers/Guest Workers*, trans. William Temple (Ann Arbor, 1990)

Herbert, Ulrich and Hunn, Karin, 'Guest workers and policy on guest workers in the Federal Republic: From the beginning of recruitment in 1955 until its halt in 1973', in Hanna Schissler (ed.), *The Miracle Years: A Cultural History of West Germany, 1949–1968* (Princeton NJ, 2001), pp. 187–218

Hieronymus, Andreas, 'Muslim identity formations and learning environments', in Abdulkader Tayob, Inga Niehaus and Wolfram Weisse (eds), *Muslim Schools and Education in Europe and South Africa* (Münster, 2011), pp. 137–62

Hill, Arlette C., 'Democratic education in West Germany: The effects of the new minorities', *Comparative Education Review*, 31:2 (1987), pp. 273–87

Hillmann, Felicitas, 'A look at the "hidden side": Turkish women in Berlin's ethnic labour market', *International Journal of Urban and Regional Research*, 23:2 (1999), pp. 267–82

Hillmann, Felicitas, 'Gendered landscapes of ethnic economies: Turkish entrepreneurs in Berlin', in David H. Kaplan and Wei Li (eds), *Landscapes of the Ethnic Economy* (Lanham MD, 2006), pp. 97–109

Hoerder, Dirk, 'The traffic of emigration via Bremen/Bremerhaven: Merchants' interests, protective legislation, and migrants' experiences', *Journal of American Ethnic History*, 13:1 (1993), pp. 68–101

Hollifield, James F., *Immigrants, Markets, and States: The Political Economy of Postwar Europe* (Cambridge MA, 1992)

Holmes, Christopher, *A New Vision for Housing* (London, 2006)

Holmes, Colin, *John Bull's Island: Immigration and British Society, 1871–1971* (Basingstoke, 1988)

Holzner, Lutz, 'The myth of Turkish ghettoes: A geographical case of West German response towards a foreign minority', *Journal of Ethnic Studies*, 9:4 (1982), pp. 65–85

Hopkins, Peter and Gale, Richard (eds), *Muslims in Britain: Race, Place and Identities* (Edinburgh, 2009)

Human Rights Watch, *Racist Violence in the United Kingdom* (London, 1997)

Huntington, Samuel P., *The Clash of Civilizations and the Remaking of World Order* (New York, 1996)

Hussain, Serena, *Muslims on the Map: A National Survey of Social Trends in Britain* (London, 2008)

Huttman, Elizabeth D., 'Subsidized housing segregation in Western Europe: Stigma and segregation', in Elizabeth D. Huttman, Wim Blauw and Juliet Saltman (eds), *Urban Housing: Segregation of Minorities in Western Europe and the United States* (Durham NC, 1991), pp. 215–35

Interim Report of the Committee of Inquiry into the Education of Children from Ethnic Minority Groups, *West Indian Children in Our Schools, The Rampton Report* (London, 1981)

Ipsen, Detlev, 'Segregation, Mobilität und die Chancen auf dem Wohnungsmarkt: eine empirische Untersuchung in Mannheim', *Zeitschrift für Soziologie*, 10:3 (1981), pp. 256–72

Ireland, Patrick, *Becoming Europe: Immigration, Integration, and the Welfare State* (Pittsburgh PA, 2004)

Ishaq, Mohammed, Hussain, Asifa and Whittam, Geoff, 'Racism: A barrier to entry? Experiences of small ethnic minority retail businesses', *International Small Business Journal*, 28:4 (2010), pp. 362–77

Jackson, Pamela Irving and Doerschler, Peter, *Benchmarking Muslim Well-Being in Europe: Reducing Disparities and Polarizations* (Bristol, 2012)

Jackson, Peter, 'Paradoxes of Puerto Rican segregation in New York', in Ceri Peach, Vaughan Robinson and Susan Smith (eds), *Ethnic Segregation in Cities* (London, 1981), pp. 109–26

Jacobs, Brian D., *Black Politics and Urban Crisis in Britain* (Cambridge, 1986)

Jelinek, Milena M. and Brittan, Elaine M., 'Multiracial education 1. Inter-ethnic friendship patterns', *Educational Research*, 18:1 (1975), pp. 44–53

Jones, Trevor and Ram, Monder, 'Review article: Ethnic variations on the small firm labour process', *International Small Business Journal*, 28:2 (2010), pp. 163–73

Jones, Trevor, Barrett, Giles and McEvoy, David, 'Market potential as a decisive influence on the performance of ethnic minority business', in Jan Rath (ed.), *Immigrant Businesses: The Economic, Political and Social Environment* (Basingstoke, 2000), pp. 37–53

Joppke, Christian, *Immigration and the Nation-State: The United States, Germany, and Great Britain* (Oxford, 1999)

Joppke, Christian, *Veil: Mirror of Identity* (Cambridge, 2009)

Jozsa, Dan-Paul, 'Islam and education in Europe. With special reference to Austria, England, France, Germany and the Netherlands', in Robert Jackson, Siebren Miedema, Wolfram Weisse and Jean-Paul Willaime (eds), *Religion and Education in Europe: Developments, Contexts and Debates* (Münster, 2007), pp. 67–86

Julios, Christina, *Contemporary British Identity: English Language, Migrants, and Public Discourse* (Aldershot, 2008)

Kalka, Iris, 'Striking a bargain: Political radicalism in a middle-class London borough', in Pnina Werbner and Muhammad Anwar (eds), *Black and Ethnic Leaderships: The Cultural Dimensions of Political Action* (London, 1991), pp. 139–53

Kalter, Frank, 'Ethnische Kapitalien und der Arbeitsmarkterfolg Jugendlicher türkischer Herkunft', in Monika Wohlrab-Sahr and Levent Tezcan (eds), 'Konfliktfeld Islam in Europa', *Soziale Welt*, 17 (2007), pp. 393–418

Kalter, Frank, 'The second generation in the German labor market: Explaining the Turkish exception', in Richard Alba and Mary C.

Waters (eds), *The Next Generation: Immigrant Youth in a Comparative Perspective* (New York, 2011), pp. 166–84.

Kamp, Melanie, 'Prayer leader, counsellor, teacher, social worker, and public relations officer – on the roles and functions of imams in Germany', in Ala Al-Hamarneh and Jörn Thielmann (eds), *Islam and Muslims in Germany* (Leiden, 2008), pp. 133–60

Karakaşoğlu, Yasemin, 'Turkish cultural orientations in Germany and the role of Islam', in David Horrocks and Eva Kolinsky (eds), *Turkish Culture in German Society Today* (Oxford, 1996), pp. 157–79

Karakaşoğlu, Yasemin and Luchtenberg, Sigrid, 'Islamophobia in German educational settings: Actions and reactions', in Barry van Driel (ed.), *Confronting Islamophobia in Educational Practice* (Stoke on Trent, 2004), pp. 35–52

Karn, Valerie, 'The financing of owner-occupation and its impact on ethnic minorities', *Journal of Ethnic and Migration Studies*, 6:1/2 (1977), pp. 49–63

Karn, Valerie and Phillips, Deborah, 'Race and ethnicity in housing: A diversity of experience', in Tessa Blackstone, Bhikhu Parekh and Peter Sanders (eds), *Race Relations in Britain: A Developing Agenda* (London, 1998), pp. 129–58

Kasarda, John D., Friedrichs, Jürgen and Ehlers, Kay E., 'Urban industrial restructuring and minority problems in the US and Germany', in Malcolm Cross (ed.), *Ethnic Minorities and Industrial Change in Europe and North America* (Cambridge, 1992), pp. 250–75

Kastoryano, Riva, *Negotiating Identities: States and Immigrants in France and Germany*, trans. Barbara Harshav (Princeton NJ, 2002)

Kemper, Franz-Josef, 'Restructuring of housing and ethnic segregation: Recent developments in Berlin', *Urban Studies*, 35:10 (1998), pp. 1765–89

Kershen, Anne J., *Strangers, Aliens and Asians: Huguenots, Jews and Bangladeshis in Spitalfields 1660–2000* (London, 2005)

Khan, Saber and Jones, Adrian, *Somalis in Camden: Challenges Faced by an Emerging Community* (London, 2003)

Kibria, Nazli, *Muslims in Motion: Islam and National Identity in the Bangladeshi Diaspora* (London, 2011)

Kil, Wolfgang and Silver, Hilary, 'From Kreuzberg to Marzahn: New migrant communities in Berlin', *German Politics & Society*, 24:4 (2006), pp. 95–121

Kirp, David L., 'The vagaries of discrimination: Busing, policy, and law in Britain', *The School Review*, 87:3 (1979), pp. 269–94

Klausen, Jytte, *The Islamic Challenge: Politics and Religion in Western Europe* (Oxford, 2005)

Klopp, Brett, *German Multiculturalism: Immigrant Integration and the Transformation of Citizenship* (Westport CT, 2002)

Klusmeyer, Douglas B. and Papademetriou, Demetrios G., *Immigration Policy in the Federal Republic of Germany: Negotiating Membership and Remaking the Nation* (New York, 2009)

Knauf, Diethelm and Schröder, Helga (eds), *Fremde in Bremen – Auswanderer, Zuwanderer, Zwangsarbeiter* (Bremen, 1993)

Knott, Kim and Khokher, Sajda, 'Religious and ethnic identity among young Muslim women in Bradford', *Journal of Ethnic and Migration Studies*, 19:4 (1993), pp. 593–610

Knox, Elaine, '"Keep your feet still, Geordie hinnie": Women and work on Tyneside', in Robert Colls and Bill Lancaster (eds), *Geordies: Roots of Regionalism* (Newcastle, 2005), pp. 93–113

Kogan, Irena, 'A study of immigrants' employment careers in West Germany using the sequence analysis technique', *Social Science Research*, 36:2 (2007), pp. 491–511

Kolinsky, Eva, 'Non-German minorities in contemporary German society', in David Horrocks and Eva Kolinsky (eds), *Turkish Culture in German Society Today* (Oxford, 1996), pp. 71–111

Kontos, Maria, 'Self-employment policies and migrants' entrepreneurship in Germany', *Entrepreneurship and Regional Development*, 15:2 (2003), pp. 119–35

Kontos, Maria, 'Immigrant entrepreneurs in Germany', in Léo-Paul Dana (ed.), *Handbook of Research on Ethnic Minority Entrepreneurship: A Co-evolutionary View on Resource Management* (Cheltenham, 2007), pp. 445–63

Koslowski, Rey, 'European Union migration regimes, established and emergent', in Christian Joppke (ed.), *Challenge to the Nation-State: Immigration in Western Europe and the United States* (Oxford, 1998), pp. 153–88

Kristen, Cornelia, 'Ethnic differences in educational placement: The transition from primary to secondary schooling', *Mannheimer Zentrum für Europäische Sozialforschung Working Paper*, 32 (2000)

Kuepper, William, Lackey, G. Lynne and Swinerton, E. Nelson, *Ugandan Asians in Great Britain: Forced Migration and Social Absorption* (London, 1975)

Kürsat-Ahlers, Elçin, 'The Turkish minority in German society', in David Horrocks and Eva Kolinsky (eds), *Turkish Culture in German*

Society Today (Oxford, 1996), pp. 113–35

Lakey, Jane, 'Neighbourhoods and housing', in Tariq Modood *et al.* (eds), *Ethnic Minorities in Britain: Diversity and Disadvantage* (Policy Studies Institute, London, 1997), pp. 184–223

Lall, Marie and Gillborn, David, *Beyond a Colour Blind Approach: Addressing Black and Minority Ethnic Inclusion in the Education Strand of New Deal for Communities*, New Deal for Communities, The National Evaluation, 49 (Sheffield Hallam University, 2004)

Lashley, Horace and Pumfrey, Peter, 'Countering racism in British education', in Gajendra K. Verma and Peter D. Pumfrey (eds), *Cross-Curricular Contexts: Themes and Dimensions in Secondary Schools* (London, 1993), pp. 113–32

Laurence, Jonathan, *The Emancipation of Europe's Muslims: The State's Role in Minority Integration* (Princeton NJ, 2012)

Lawless, Richard, *From Ta'izz to Tyneside. An Arab Community in the North-East of England during the Early Twentieth Century* (Exeter, 1995)

Layton-Henry, Zig, *The Politics of Immigration: Immigration, 'Race' and 'Race' Relations in Post-war Britain* (Oxford, 1992)

Lee, Robert, 'Urban labor markets, in-migration, and demographic growth: Bremen, 1815–1914', *Journal of Interdisciplinary History*, 30:3 (1999), pp. 437–73

Lee, Robert, 'Configuring the region: Maritime trade and port-hinterland relations in Bremen, 1815–1914', *Urban History*, 32:2 (2005), pp. 247–87

Lee, Robert and Marschalck, Peter, 'The port-city legacy: Urban demographic change in the Hansestadt Bremen, 1815–1910', in Richard Lawton and Robert Lee (eds), *Population and Society in Western European Port-Cities c. 1650–1939* (Liverpool, 2002), pp. 252–69

Leiken, Robert S., *Europe's Angry Muslims: The Revolt of the Second Generation* (Oxford, 2012)

Leitner, Helga, 'Regulating migrants' lives: The dialectic of migrant labor and the contradictions of regulatory and integration policies in the Federal Republic of Germany', in G. Glebe and J. O'Loughlin (eds), *Foreign Minorities in Continental European Cities* (Stuttgart, 1987), pp. 71–89

Leohold, Volkmar, *Die Kämmeristen. Arbeitsleben auf der Bremer Woll-Kämmerei* (Hamburg, 1986)

Leslie, Derek, Lindley, Joanne and Thomas, Leighton, 'Decline and fall: Unemployment among Britain's non-white ethnic communities 1960–1999', *Journal of the Royal Statistical Society. Series A*

(Statistics in Society), 164:2 (2001), pp. 371–87

Leung, Constant, 'Integrating school-aged ESL learners into the mainstream curriculum', in Jim Cummins and Chris Davison (eds), *International Handbook of English Language Teaching* (Dordrecht, 2007), pp. 249–69

Levine, David and Wrightson, Keith, *The Making of an Industrial Society: Whickham, 1560–1765* (Oxford, 1991)

Lewis, Bernard, *Islam and the West* (Oxford, 1993)

Lewis, Philip, *Islamic Britain: Religion, Politics and Identity among British Muslims* (London, 2002)

Light, Ivan and Bonacich, Edna, *Immigrant Entrepreneurs: Koreans in Los Angeles, 1965–1982* (Berkeley CA, 1988)

Lindley, Joanne, 'Race or religion? The impact of religion on the employment and earnings of Britain's ethnic minorities', *Journal of Ethnic and Migration Studies*, 28:3 (2002), pp. 427–42

Little, Alan, Mabey, Christine and Whitaker, Graham, 'The education of immigrant pupils in Inner London primary schools', *Race & Class*, 9:4 (1968), pp. 439–52

Love, Anne-Marie and Kirby, Keith, *Racial Incidents in Council Housing: The Local Authority Response* (London, 1994)

Lucassen, Leo, *The Immigrant Threat: The Integration of Old and New Migrants in Western Europe since 1850* (Chicago, 2005)

Lucassen, Leo, 'Poles and Turks in the German Ruhr area: Similarities and differences', in Leo Lucassen, David Feldman and Jochen Oltmer (eds), *Paths of Integration: Migrants in Western Europe (1880–2004)* (Amsterdam, 2006), pp. 27–45

Lynch, James, *Multicultural Education: Principles and Practice* (London, 1986)

MacDonald, Ian, Bhavnani, Reena, Khan, Lily and John, Gus, *Murder in the Playground: The Report of the MacDonald Inquiry into Racism and Racial Violence in Manchester Schools* (London, 1989)

MacEwen, Martin, *Housing, Race and Law: The British Experience* (London, 1991)

Malheiros, Jorge, 'Indians in Lisbon: Ethnic entrepreneurship and the migration process', in Russell King and Richard Black (eds), *Southern Europe and the New Immigrations* (Brighton, 1997), pp. 93–112

Malik, Iftikhar H., *Islam and Modernity: Muslims in Europe and the United States* (London, 2004)

Mandel, Ruth, 'Turkish headscarves and the 'foreigner problem': Constructing difference through emblems of identity', *New German*

Critique, 46 (1989), pp. 27–46

Mandel, Ruth, 'A place of their own: Contesting spaces and defining places in Berlin's migrant community', in Barbara Daly Metcalf (ed.), *Making Muslim Space in North America and Europe* (Berkeley CA, 1996), pp. 147–66

Mandel, Ruth, *Cosmopolitan Anxieties: Turkish Challenges to Citizenship and Belonging in Germany* (Durham NC, 2008)

Manzer, Ronald, *Educational Regimes and Anglo-American Democracy* (Toronto, 2003)

Marschalck, Peter, *Inventar der Quellen zur Geschichte der Wanderung, besonders der Auswanderung, in bremer Archiven* (Bremen, 1986)

Martin, Philip L., *The Unfinished Story: Turkish Labour Migration to Western Europe, with Special Reference to the Federal Republic of Germany* (Geneva, 1991)

Martin, Philip L., 'Germany: Managing migration in the twenty-first century', in Wayne A. Cornelius, Philip L. Martin and James F. Hollifield (eds), *Controlling Immigration: A Global Perspective* (Stanford CA, 2004), pp. 221–53

May, Jon, Wills, Jane, Datta, Kavita, Evans, Yara, Herbert, Joanna and McIlwaine, Cathy, 'Keeping London working: Global cities, the British state, and London's new migrant division of labour', *Transactions of the Institute of British Geographers*, 32:2 (2007), pp. 151–67

McKay, David H. and Cox, Andrew W., *The Politics of Urban Change* (London, 1979)

McKay, Sandra Lee, *Agendas for Second Language Literacy* (Cambridge, 1993)

McLaughlin, Barry and Graf, Peter, 'Bilingual education in West Germany: Recent developments', *Comparative Education*, 21:3 (1985), pp. 241–55

Merkel, Janet, 'Ethnic diversity and the "creative city": The case of Berlin's creative industries', in Frank Eckardt and John Eade (eds), *Ethnically Diverse City* (Berlin, 2011), pp. 559–78

Metcalf, Hilary, Modood, Tariq and Virdee, Satnam, *Asian Self-Employment: The Interaction of Culture and Economics in England* (London, 1996)

Modood, Tariq, 'Employment', in Tariq Modood et al. (eds), *Ethnic Minorities in Britain: Diversity and Disadvantage* (Policy Studies Institute, London, 1997), pp. 83–149

Modood, Tariq, *Multicultural Politics: Racism, Ethnicity and Muslims in Britain* (Edinburgh, 2005)

Modood, Tariq and May, Stephen, 'Multiculturalism and education in Britain: An internally contested debate', *International Journal of Educational Research*, 35:3 (2001), pp. 305–17

Modood, Tariq, Triandafyllidou, Anna and Zapata-Barrero, Ricard (eds), *Multiculturalism, Muslims and Citizenship: A European Approach* (Abingdon, 2006)

Modood, Tariq, Berthoud, Richard, Lakey, Jane, Nazroo, James, Smith, Patten, Virdee, Satnam and Beishon, Sharon (eds), *Ethnic Minorities in Britain: Diversity and Disadvantage* (Policy Studies Institute, London, 1997)

Molokotos Liederman, Lina, 'Religious diversity in schools: The Muslim headscarf controversy and beyond', *Social Compass*, 47:3 (2000), pp. 367–81

Mould, Wim, 'No rainbow coalition on Tyneside', *Multicultural Teaching*, 4:3 (1986), pp. 9–12

Mühe, Nina, *Muslims in the EU: Cities Reports – Preliminary Research Report and Literature Survey Germany* (Budapest, 2007)

Mullard, Chris, 'Multiracial education in Britain: From assimilation to cultural pluralism', in John Tierney (ed.), *Race, Migration and Schooling* (London, 1982), pp. 120–33

Münz, Rainer and Ulrich, Ralf, 'Changing patterns of immigration to Germany, 1945–1995: Ethnic origins, demographic structure, future prospects', in Klaus J. Bade and Myron Weiner (eds), *Migration Past, Migration Future: Germany and the United States* (Oxford, 1997), pp. 65–119

Mushaben, Joyce Marie, 'Thinking globally, integrating locally: Gender, entrepreneurship and urban citizenship in Germany', *Citizenship Studies*, 10:2 (2006), pp. 203–27

Mushaben, Joyce Marie, *The Changing Faces of Citizenship: Integration and Mobilization among Ethnic Minorities in Germany* (Oxford, 2008)

Myers, Kevin and Grosvenor, Ian, 'Policy, equality and inequality: From the past to the future', in Dave Hill and Mike Cole (eds), *Schooling and Equality: Fact, Concept and Policy* (London, 2001), pp. 249–64

Nachmani, Amikam, *Europe and its Muslim Minorities: Aspects of Conflict, Attempts at Accord* (Brighton, 2009)

Nayak, Anoop, *Race, Place and Globalization: Youth Cultures in a Changing World* (Oxford, 2003)

Nayak, Anoop, 'Young people's geographies of racism and anti-racism:

The case of North East England', in Claire Dwyer and Caroline Bressey (eds), *New Geographies of Race and Racism* (Aldershot, 2008), pp. 269–82

Nielsen, Jørgen S., *Towards a European Islam: Migration, Minorities and Citizenship* (Basingstoke, 1999)

Nielsen, Jørgen S., *Muslims in Western Europe* (Edinburgh, 2004)

Nökel, Sigrid, 'Muslimische Frauen und öffentliche Räume: Jenseits des Kopftuchstreits', in Nilüfer Göle and Ludwig Ammann (eds), *Islam in Sicht. Der Auftritt von Muslimen im öffentlichen Raum* (Bielefeld, 2004), pp. 283–308

Northern Housing Associations Committee, *Race and Housing in the North East: A Joint Working Party Report from the North East Housing Associations Committee and the Community Relations Council of Tyne and Wear and Cleveland County in Response to the National Federation of Housing Associations' Report 'Race and Housing'* (1983)

O'Loughlin, John, 'Distribution and migration of foreigners in German cities', *Geographical Review*, 70:3 (1980), pp. 253–75

O'Loughlin, John, 'Chicago an der Ruhr or what? Explaining the location of immigrants in European cities', in Günther Glebe and John O'Loughlin (eds), *Foreign Minorities in Continental European Cities* (Stuttgart, 1987), pp. 52–70

Oomen-Welke, Ingelore and Schmitt, Guido, 'Teaching the mother tongue in Germany', in Witold Tulasiewicz and Anthony Adams (eds), *Teaching the Mother Tongue in a Multilingual Europe* (London, 1998), pp. 137–52

Open Society Institute, *Monitoring Minority Protection in the EU: The Situation of Muslims in the UK* (Budapest, 2002)

Özdamar, Tuncay, 'Hände weg von meiner Muttersprache', *Stimme*, 14:7–8 (2000), pp. 8–9

Özüekren, Sule and Ergoz-Karahan Ebru, 'Housing experiences of Turkish (im)migrants in Berlin and Istanbul: Internal differentiation and segregation', *Journal of Ethnic and Migration Studies*, 36:2 (2010), pp. 355–72

Panayi, Panikos, 'Middlesbrough 1961: A British race riot of the 1960s?', *Social History*, 16:2 (1991), pp. 139–53

Panayi, Panikos, *Ethnic Minorities in Nineteenth and Twentieth Century Germany: Jews, Gypsies, Poles, Turks and Others* (Harlow, 2000)

Panayi, Panikos, 'The evolution of multiculturalism in Britain and Germany: An historical survey', *Journal of Multilingual and*

Multicultural Development, 25:5–6 (2004), pp. 466–80

Panayi, Panikos, *Spicing up Britain: The Multicultural History of British Food* (London, 2008)

Panayi, Panikos, *An Immigration History of Britain: Multicultural Racism since 1800* (Harlow, 2010)

Panayotidis, Gregorios, *Griechen in Bremen. Bildung, Arbeit und soziale Integration einer ausländischen Bevölkerungsgruppe* (Münster, 2001)

Pankhania, Josna, *Liberating the National History Curriculum* (London, 1994)

Parekh, Bhikhu, 'European Liberalism and "The Muslim Question"', *International Institute for the Study of Islam in the Modern World*, 9 (2008)

Parker, John and Dugmore, Keith, *Colour and the Allocation of GLC Housing* (London, 1976)

Parker-Jenkins, Marie, 'Muslim matters: An examination of the educational needs of Muslim children in Britain', *American Journal of Islamic Social Sciences*, 9:3 (1992), pp. 351–69

Parsons, Craig A. and Smeeding, Timothy M. (eds), *Immigration and the Transformation of Europe* (Cambridge, 2006)

Paul, Kathleen, *Whitewashing Britain: Race and Citizenship in the Postwar Era* (Ithaca NY, 1997)

Pauly, Jr., Robert J., *Islam in Europe: Integration or Marginalization?* (Aldershot, 2004)

Peach, Ceri, *West Indian Migration to Britain: A Social Geography* (London, 1968)

Peach, Ceri, 'The Muslim population of Great Britain', *Ethnic and Racial Studies*, 13:3 (1990), pp. 414–19

Peach, Ceri, 'Does Britain have ghettos?', *Transactions of the Institute of British Geographers*, 21:1 (1996), pp. 216–35

Peach, Ceri, 'Pluralist and assimilationist models of ethnic settlement in London 1991', *Tijdschrift voor Economische en Sociale Geografie*, 88:2 (1997), pp. 120–34

Peach, Ceri, 'South Asian and Caribbean ethnic minority housing choice in Britain', *Urban Studies*, 35:10 (1998), pp. 1657–80

Peach, Ceri, 'Islam, ethnicity and South Asian religions in the London 2001 Census', *Transactions of the Institute of British Geographers*, 31:3 (2006), pp. 353–70

Peach, Ceri, 'Muslims in the 2001 Census of England and Wales: Gender and economic disadvantage', *Ethnic and Racial Studies*, 29:4 (2006), pp. 629–55

Pécoud, Antoine, '"Weltoffenheit schafft Jobs": Turkish entrepreneurship and multiculturalism in Berlin', *International Journal of Urban and Regional Research*, 26:3 (2002), pp. 494–507

Pécoud, Antoine, 'German-Turkish entrepreneurship and the economic dimension of multiculturalism', in Han Entzinger, Marco Martiniello and Catherine Wihtol de Wenden (eds), *Migration Between States and Markets* (Aldershot, 2004), pp. 119–29

Performance Innovation Unit, *Ethnic Minorities and the Labour Market: Interim Analytical Report* (London, 2002)

Petrie, Andrew, *Housing Needs of Black and Minority Ethnic Communities in the North East – A Scoping Exercise* (Huddersfield, 2005)

Phillips, Deborah, *Monitoring of the Experimental Allocation Scheme for GLC Properties in Tower Hamlets* (London, 1984)

Phillips, Deborah, 'What price equality? A report on the allocation of GLC housing in Tower Hamlets', *GLC Housing Research & Policy Report*, 9 (1986)

Phillips, Deborah, 'The rhetoric of anti-racism in public housing allocation', in Peter Jackson (ed.), *Race and Racism: Essays in Social Geography* (London, 1987), pp. 177–97

Phillips, Deborah, 'Black minority ethnic concentration, segregation and dispersal in Britain', *Urban Studies*, 35:10 (1998), pp. 1681–702

Phillips, Deborah, 'Parallel lives? Challenging discourses of British Muslim self-segregation', *Environment and Planning D: Society and Space*, 24:1 (2006), pp. 25–40

Phillips, Deborah, 'Minority ethnic segregation, integration and citizenship: A European perspective', *Journal of Ethnic and Migration Studies*, 36:2 (2010), pp. 209–25

Phillips, Deborah and Harrison, Malcolm, 'Constructing an integrated society: Historical lessons for tackling black and minority ethnic housing segregation in Britain', *Housing Studies*, 25:2 (2010), pp. 221–35

Phillips, Deborah, Davis, Cathy and Ratcliffe, Peter, 'British Asian narratives of urban space', *Transactions of the Institute of British Geographers*, 32:2 (2007), pp. 217–34

Phillips, Deborah, Simpson, Ludi and Ahmed, Sameera, 'Shifting geographies of minority ethnic settlement: Remaking communities in Oldham and Rochdale', in John Flint and David Robinson (eds), *Community Cohesion in Crisis? New Dimensions of Diversity and Difference* (Bristol, 2008), pp. 81–97

Pillai, Rachel, *Destination North East? Harnessing the Regional Potential of Migration* (London, 2006)
Power, Anne, Plöger, Jörg and Winkler, Astrid, *Phoenix Cities: The Fall and Rise of Great Industrial Cities* (Bristol, 2010)
Pralle, Elka, Hemmer, Eike and Isenberg, Hans-Georg, *Ausländerbeschäftigung auf der Klöckner-Hütte: Rekonstruktion betriebsgeschichtlicher und biografischer Aspekte* (Bremen, 1996)
Prenzel, Manfred, Baumert, Jürgen, Blum, Werner, Lehmann, Rainer, Leutner, Detlev, Neubrand, Michael, Pekrun, Reinhard, Rost, Jürgen and Schiefele, Ulrich (eds), *PISA 2003: Der zweite Vergleich der Länder in Deutschland – Was wissen und können Jugendliche?* (Münster, 2005)
Pütz, Robert, 'Transculturality as practice: Turkish entrepreneurs in Germany', in Ala Al-Hamarneh and Jörn Thielmann (eds), *Islam and Muslims in Germany* (Leiden, 2008), pp. 511–35
Qureshi, G.D., 'The Newcastle mosque and Muslim community centre', *Multicultural Teaching*, 4:3 (1986), pp. 34–5
Race, Richard, *Multiculturalism and Education* (London, 2011)
Rafiq, Mohammed, 'Ethnicity and enterprise: A comparison of Muslim and non-Muslim owned Asian businesses in Britain', *New Community*, 19:1 (1992), pp. 43–60
Ram, Monder, 'Enterprise support and ethnic minority firms', *Journal of Ethnic and Migration Studies*, 24:1 (1998), pp. 143–58
Ram, Monder and Smallbone, David, 'Ethnic minority business policy in the era of the small business service', *Environment and Planning C: Government and Policy*, 20:2 (2002), pp. 235–49
Ram, Monder, Abbas, Tahir, Sanghera, Balihar, Barlow, Gerald and Jones, Trevor, 'Making the link: Households and small business activity in a multi-ethnic context', *Community, Work and Family*, 4:3 (2001), pp. 327–48
Ramm, Gesa, Walter, Oliver, Heidemeier, Heike and Prenzel, Manfred, 'Soziokulturelle Herkunft und Migration im Ländervergleich', in Manfred Prenzel, Jürgen Baumert, Werner Blum, Rainer Lehmann, Detlev Leutner, Michael Neubrand, Reinhard Pekrun, Jürgen Rost and Ulrich Schiefele (eds), *PISA 2003: Der zweite Vergleich der Länder in Deutschland – Was wissen und können Jugendliche?* (Münster, 2005), pp. 269–98
Raoufi, Schole, 'The children of guest-workers in the Federal Republic of Germany: Maladjustment and its effects on academic performance', in Joti Bhatnagar (ed.), *Educating Immigrants* (London, 1981), pp. 113–36

Rasinger, Sebastian M., *Bengali-English in East London: A Study in Urban Multilingualism* (Bern, 2007)
Rassool, Naz, 'Language policies for a multicultural Britain', in Ruth Wodak and David Corson (eds), *Encyclopedia of Language and Education. Volume 1: Language Policy and Political Issues in Education* (Dordrecht, 1997), pp. 113–26
Ratcliffe, Peter, *Racism and Reaction: A Profile of Handsworth* (London, 1981)
Ratcliffe, Peter, *Race and Housing in Bradford: Addressing the Needs of the South Asian, African and Caribbean Communities* (Bradford, 1996)
Ratcliffe, Peter, '"Race", housing and the city', in Nick Jewson and Susanne MacGregor (eds), *Transforming Cities: Contested Governance and New Spatial Divisions* (London, 1997), pp. 87–99
Ratcliffe, Peter, 'Re-evaluating the links between "race" and residence', *Housing Studies*, 24:4 (2009), pp. 433–50
Rauch, Viola-Donata, 'More than an urban stage for conflict – the city's impact of self-representation of children of immigrants in Berlin', in Frank Eckardt and John Eade (eds), *Ethnically Diverse City* (Berlin, 2011), pp. 473–94
Renton, Dave, 'Hostility or welcome? Migration to the North East since 1945', *Papers in North Eastern History*, 15 (2006)
Renton, Dave, *Colour Blind? Race and Migration in North East England since 1945* (Sunderland, 2007)
Rex, John and Moore, Robert, *Race, Community and Conflict* (London, 1967)
Rex, John and Tomlinson, Sally, *Colonial Immigrants in a British City: A Class Analysis* (London, 1979)
Rex, John and Modood, Tariq, 'Muslim identity: Real or imagined? A discussion by John Rex and Tariq Modood', *Centre for the Study of Islam and Christian-Muslim Relations Papers*, 12 (Birmingham, 1994)
Rist, Ray C., *Guestworkers in Germany: The Prospects for Pluralism* (New York, 1978)
Rist, Ray C., 'On the education of guest-worker children in Germany: A comparative study of policies and programs in Bavaria and Berlin', *The School Review*, 87:3 (1979), pp. 242–68
Robbers, Gerhard, 'Germany', in Jorgen S. Nielsen, Samim Akgönül, Ahmet Alibašić, Brigitte Maréchal and Christian Moe (eds), *Yearbook of Muslims in Europe* (Leiden, 2009), pp. 141–50
Robinson, David, 'Missing the target? Discrimination and exclusion in

the allocation of social housing', in Peter Somerville and Andy Steele (eds), *'Race', Housing and Social Exclusion* (London, 2002), pp. 94–113

Robinson, David, Reeve, Kesia, Casey, Rionach and Goudie, Rosalind, *Minority Ethnic Residential Experiences and Requirements in the Bridging NewcastleGateshead Area* (Sheffield, 2007)

Robinson, Vaughan, 'Choice and constraint in Asian housing in Blackburn', *Journal of Ethnic and Migration Studies*, 7:3 (1979), pp. 390–6

Robinson, Vaughan, *Transients, Settlers and Refugees: Asians in Britain* (Oxford, 1986)

Röpke, Karin, 'Ergebnisse des Integrations-Konzeptes', *Stimme*, 14:3–4 (2003), pp. 12–13

Rose, Eliot, *Colour and Citizenship: A Report on British Race Relations* (London, 1969)

Rotte, Ursula, 'Education reform in Germany: Efforts and experiences in Bavaria after PISA 2000', in Ralph Rotte (ed.), *International Perspectives on Education Policy* (New York, 2006), pp. 105–26

Ruhs, Martin and Anderson, Bridget (eds), *Who Needs Migrant Workers? Labour Shortages, Immigration, and Public Policy* (Oxford, 2010)

Runnymede Trust, *Islamophobia: A Challenge for Us All: Report of the Runnymede Trust Commission on British Muslims and Islamophobia* (London, 1997)

Sachverständigenrat deutscher Stiftungen für Integration und Migration, *Wirtschaftliche Selbstständigkeit als Integrationsstrategie – eine Bestandsaufnahme der Strukturen der Integrationsförderung in Deutschland* (Berlin, 2010)

Sammet, Kornelia, 'Religion oder Kultur? Positionierungen zum Islam in Gruppendiskussionen über Moscheebauten', in Monika Wohlrab-Sahr and Levent Tezcan (eds), 'Konfliktfeld Islam in Europa', *Soziale Welt*, 17 (2007), pp. 179–198

Samra, Surinder K., 'Section 11 teaching: A new ball game', *Multicultural Teaching*, 4:3 (1986), pp. 20–3

Sarre, Philip, Phillips, Deborah and Skellington, Richard, *Ethnic Minority Housing: Explanations and Policies* (Aldershot, 1989)

Scarman, Lord, *The Brixton Disorders, 10–12th April 1981: Report of an Inquiry by the Rt. Hon. The Lord Scarman* (London, 1982)

Schain, Martin, *The Politics of Immigration in France, Britain, and the United States: A Comparative Study* (Basingstoke, 2008)

Schönwälder, Karen, *Einwanderung und ethnische Pluralität: politische*

Entscheidungen und öffentliche Debatten in Grossbritannien und der Bundesrepublik von den 1950er bis zu den 1970er Jahren (Essen, 2001)

Schönwälder, Karen, 'Zukunftsblindheit oder Steuerungsversagen? Zur Ausländerpolitik der Bundesregierungen der 1960er und frühen 1970er Jahre', in Jochen Oltmer (ed.), *Migration steuern und verwalten. Deutschland vom späten 19. Jahrhundert bis zur Gegenwart* (Göttingen, 2003), pp. 123–44

Schönwälder, Karen, 'West German society and foreigners in the 1960s', in Philipp Gassert and Alan E. Steinweis (eds), *Coping with the Nazi Past: West German Debates on Nazism and Generational Conflict, 1955–1975* (Oxford, 2006), pp. 113–27

Schönwälder, Karen and Söhn, Janina, 'Immigrant settlement structures in Germany: General patterns and urban levels of concentration of major groups', *Urban Studies*, 46:7 (2009), pp. 1439–60

Seidel-Pielen, Eberhard, *AUFGESPIEßT: Wie der Döner über die Deutschen kam* (Berlin, 1996)

Seifert, Wolfgang, 'Social and economic integration of foreigners in Germany', in Peter Schuck and Rainer Münz (eds), *Paths to Inclusion: The Integration of Migrants in the United States and Germany* (Oxford, 1998), pp. 83–114

Şen, Faruk, 'The economic, social and political impact of Turkish migration', in Sarah Spencer (ed.), *Immigration as an Economic Asset: The German Experience* (Stoke on Trent, 1994), pp. 93–104

Şen, Faruk, 'The historical situation of Turkish migrants in Germany', in Ahmed Al-Shahi and Richard Lawless (eds), *Middle East and North African Immigrants in Europe* (Abingdon, 2005), pp. 110–29

Şen, Faruk and Goldberg, Andreas, *Türken in Deutschland: Leben zwischen zwei Kulturen* (Munich, 1994)

Şen, Faruk and Goldberg, Andreas (eds), *Türken als Unternehmer. Eine Gesamtdarstellung und Ergebnisse neuerer Untersuchungen* (Opladen, 1996)

Shah, Naseem, 'A black perspective on current policy initiatives in the North East', *Multicultural Teaching*, 4:3 (1986), pp. 28–9

Shah, Saeeda, 'Educational leadership: An Islamic perspective', *British Educational Research Journal*, 32:3 (2006), pp. 363–85

Shah, Saeeda, 'Leading multi-ethnic schools: Adjustments in concepts and practices for engaging with diversity', *British Journal of Sociology of Education*, 29:5 (2008), pp. 523–36

Shaw, Alison, *Kinship and Continuity: Pakistani Families in Britain*

(Amsterdam, 2000)

Shore, Zachary, *Breeding Bin Ladens: America, Islam, and the Future of Europe* (Baltimore MD, 2006)

Siegert, Manuel, 'Schulische Bildung von Migranten in Deutschland', *Working Paper of the Bundesamt für Migration und Flüchtlinge*, 13 (Nuremberg, 2008)

Simpson, Ludi, 'Statistics of racial segregation: Measures, evidence and policy', *Urban Studies*, 41:3 (2004), pp. 661–81

Simpson, L., Purdam, K., Tajar, A., Fieldhouse, E., Gavalas, V., Tranmer, M., Pritchard, J. and Dorling, D., *Ethnic Minority Populations and the Labour Market: An Analysis of the 1991 and 2001 Census* (Leeds, 2006)

Smallbone, David, Ram, Monder and Deakins, David, 'Access to finance by ethnic minority entrepreneurs in the UK', in Léo-Paul Dana (ed.), *Handbook of Research on Ethnic Minority Entrepreneurship: A Co-evolutionary View on Resource Management* (Cheltenham, 2007), pp. 390–404

Smith, David J., *Racial Disadvantage in Britain: The PEP Report* (Harmondsworth, 1977)

Smith, David and Whalley, Anne, *Racial Minorities and Public Housing* (London, 1975)

Smith, Susan, *The Politics of 'Race' and Residence: Citizenship, Segregation and White Supremacy in Britain* (Cambridge, 1989)

Spencer, Ian, *British Immigration Policy since 1939: The Making of Multi-Racial Britain* (London, 1997)

Spencer, Sarah (ed.), *Immigration as an Economic Asset: The German Experience* (Stoke on Trent, 1994)

Spiess, C. Katharina, Büchel, Felix and Wagner, Gert G., 'Children's school placement in Germany: Does *Kindergarten* attendance matter?', *Early Childhood Research Quarterly*, 18:2 (2003), pp. 255–70

Srinivasan, Shaila, *The South Asian Petty Bourgeoisie in Britain: An Oxford Case Study* (Aldershot, 1995)

Stevenson, Patrick and Schanze, Livia, 'Language, migration and citizenship in Germany: Discourses on integration and belonging', in Guus Extra, Massimiliano Spotti and Piet van Avermaet (eds), *Language Testing, Migration and Citizenship* (London, 2009), pp. 87–106

Strom, Robert, Daniels, Susan, Wurster, Stanley, Betz, M. Austin, Graf, Peter and Jansen, Louise, 'A comparison of West German and guestworker parents' childrearing attitudes and expectations', in George

Kurian (ed.), *Parent-Child Interaction in Transition* (Westport CT, 1986), pp. 157–70

Supple, Carrie, 'Anti-racist teaching in the North East: A personal view', *Multicultural Teaching*, 4:3 (1986), pp. 16–17

Tabili, Laura, *Global Migrants, Local Culture: Natives and Newcomers in Provincial England, 1841–1939* (Basingstoke, 2011)

Tackey, Nii Djan, Casebourne, Jo, Aston, Jane, Ritchie, Helen, Sinclair, Alice, Tyers, Claire, Hurstfield, Jennifer, Willison, Rebecca, and Page, Rosie, *Barriers to Employment for Pakistanis and Bangladeshis in Britain* (Leeds, 2006)

Taylor, J.H., *The Half-Way Generation: A Study of Asian Youths in Newcastle upon Tyne* (Windsor, 1976)

Telang, Sudha D. (Newcastle upon Tyne City Planning Department), *The Coloured Immigrant in Newcastle upon Tyne* (Newcastle upon Tyne, 1967)

Tezcan, Levent, 'Kulturelle Identität und Konflikt: Zur Rolle politischer und religiöser Gruppen der türkischen Minderheitsbevölkerung', in Wilhelm Heitmeyer and Reimund Anhut (eds), *Bedrohte Stadtgesellschaft: Soziale Desintegrationsprozesse und ethnisch-kulturelle Konfliktkonstellationen* (Weinheim, 2000), pp. 401–48

The Commission on the Future of Multi-Ethnic Britain, *The Future of Multi-Ethnic Britain: The Parekh Report* (London, 2002)

The Guinness Trust, *The 2003/2004 Newcastle BME Housing Research Project* (Newcastle, 2004)

The Guinness Trust, *The 2003/2004 Newcastle New Deal for Communities BME Housing Research Project* (Newcastle, 2004)

The Office for National Statistics, *Ethnicity in the 1991 Census Volume 4, Employment, Education and Housing among the Ethnic Minority Populations of Britain* (London, 1997)

The Pew Global Attitudes Project, *Muslims in Europe: Economic Worries Top Concerns about Religious and Cultural Identity* (Washington DC, 2006)

Thompson, Linda, Fleming, Michael and Byram, Michael, 'Languages and language policy in Britain', in Michael Herriman and Barbara Burnaby (eds), *Language Policies in English-Dominant Countries: Six Case Studies* (Clevedon, 1996), pp. 99–121

Tibi, Bassam, 'Muslim migrants in Europe: Between Euro-Islam and ghettoization', in Nezar AlSayyad and Manuel Castells (eds), *Muslim Europe or Euro-Islam: Politics, Culture, and Citizenship in the Age of Globalization* (Lanham MD, 2002), pp. 31–52

Todd, Nigel, 'Black-on-Tyne: The black presence on Tyneside in the 1860s', *North-East Labour History Society*, 21 (1987), pp. 17–27

Tomlinson, Harry, 'International perspectives on education: The response of the mother country', in Carl A. Grant and Joy L. Lei (eds), *Global Constructions of Multicultural Education: Theories and Realities* (Mahwah NJ, 2001), pp. 313–30

Tomlinson, Sally, 'Race relations and the urban context', in Peter D. Pumpfrey and Gajendra K. Verma (eds), *Race Relations and Urban Education: Contexts and Promising Practices* (Basingstoke, 1990), pp. 13–22

Tomlinson, Sally, 'Teacher education for a multicultural Britain', in Maurice Craft (ed.), *Teacher Education in Plural Societies: An International Review* (London, 1996), pp. 27–44

Tomlinson, Sally, 'The education of migrants and minorities in Britain', in Sigrid Luchtenberg (ed.), *Migration, Education and Change* (Abingdon, 2004), pp. 86–102

Tomlinson, Sally, 'Race and education in Birmingham: Then and now', in Tahir Abbas and Frank Reeves (eds), *Immigration and Race Relations: Sociological Theory and John Rex* (London, 2007), pp. 159–74

Tomlinson, Sally, *Race and Education: Policy and Politics in Britain* (Maidenhead, 2008)

Tomlinson, Sally and Tomes, Hilary, *Ethnic Minorities in British Schools: A Review of the Literature, 1960–82* (London, 1983)

Triadafilopoulos, Triadafilos and Schönwälder, Karen, 'How the Federal Republic became an immigration country: Norms, politics and the failure of West Germany's guest worker system', *German Politics and Society*, 24:3 (2006), pp. 1–19

Triandafyllidou, Anna (ed.), *Muslims in 21st Century Europe: Structural and Cultural Perspectives* (London, 2010)

Troyna, Barry, '"Swann's song": The origins, ideology and implications of Education for All', *Journal of Education Policy*, 1:2 (1986), pp. 171–81

Troyna, Barry and Hatcher, Richard, 'Racist incidents in schools: A framework for analysis', in Dawn Gill, Barbara Mayor and Maud Blair (eds), *Racism and Education: Structures and Strategies* (London, 1992), pp. 187–207

Tyneside Campaign Against Racial Discrimination, *Colour Discrimination in Newcastle upon Tyne* (Newcastle, 1967)

Ulrich, Bernd, 'The senator's tale: The development of Bremen's bourgeoisie in the post-1945 era', *Social History*, 28:3 (2003), pp. 303–20 van Amersfoort, Hans and Cortie, Cees, 'Housing and population: Spatial mobility in twentieth-century Amsterdam', in Liza Nell and Jan Rath (eds), *Ethnic Amsterdam: Immigrants and Urban Change in the Twentieth Century* (Amsterdam, 2009), pp. 75–102

Varady, David, 'Muslim residential clustering and political radicalism', *Housing Studies*, 23:1 (2008), pp. 45–66

Verma, Gajendra K., 'Cultural diversity in primary schools: Its nature, extent and cross-curricular implications', in Gajendra K. Verma and Peter D. Pumpfrey (eds), *Cross Curricular Contexts, Themes and Dimensions in Primary Schools* (London, 1994), pp. 3–17

Verma, Gajendra K., 'Diversity and multicultural education: Cross-cutting issues and concepts', in Gajendra K. Verma, Christopher R. Bagley and Madan Mohan Jha (eds), *International Perspectives on Educational Diversity and Inclusion: Studies from America, Europe and India* (Abingdon, 2007), pp. 21–30

Verma, Gajendra K. (ed.), *Education for All: A Landmark in Pluralism* (Lewes, 1989)

Verma, Gajendra K. and Darby, Douglas, 'Immigrant policies and the education of immigrants in Britain', in Dr Pirkko Pitkänen, Devorah Kalekin-Fishman and Gajendra K. Verma (eds), *Education and Immigration: Settlement Policies and Current Challenges* (London, 2002), pp. 11–47

Verma, Gajendra K. and Pumpfrey, Peter David (eds), *Educational Attainments: Issues and Outcomes in Multicultural Education* (Lewes, 1988)

Verma, Gajendra, Zec, Paul and Skinner, George, *The Ethnic Crucible: Harmony and Hostility in Multi-Ethnic Schools* (Abingdon, 1994)

Vertovec, Steven and Peach, Ceri (eds), *Islam in Europe: The Politics of Religion and Community* (Basingstoke, 1997)

Visram, Rozina, *Asians in Britain: 400 Years of History* (London, 2002)

von Loeffelholz, Hans Dietrich, 'Social and labor market integration of ethnic minorities in Germany', in Martin Kahanec and Klaus F. Zimmermann (eds), *Ethnic Diversity in European Labor Markets: Challenges and Solutions* (Cheltenham, 2011), pp. 109–36

Waardenburg, Jacques, 'Diversity and unity of Islam in Europe: Some reflections', in Jamal Malik (ed.), *Muslims in Europe: From the Margin to the Centre* (Münster, 2004), pp. 21–34

Wade, Barrie and Souter, Pam, *Continuing to Think: The British Asian Girl: An Exploratory Study of the Influence of Culture upon a Group of British Asian Girls with Specific Reference to the Teaching of English* (Clevedon, 1992)

Waldorf, Brigitte S., 'Housing policy impacts on ethnic segregation patterns: Evidence from Düsseldorf, West Germany', *Urban Studies*, 27:5 (1990), pp. 637–52

Ward, Brian, 'A king in Newcastle: Martin Luther King, Jr. and British race relations, 1967–1968', *The Georgia Historical Quarterly*, 79:3 (1995), pp. 599–632

Ward, Robin, 'Economic development and ethnic business', in James Curran and Robert A. Blackburn (eds), *Paths of Enterprise: The Future of the Small Business* (London, 1991), pp. 51–67

Ward, Robin and Jenkins, Richard (eds), *Ethnic Communities in Business: Strategies for Economic Survival* (Cambridge, 1984)

Webster, Colin, 'England and Wales', in John Winterdyk and Georgios Antonopoulos (eds), *Racist Victimization: International Reflections and Perspectives* (Aldershot, 2008), pp. 67–88

Weiner, Myron, *The Global Migration Crisis: Challenge to States and to Human Rights* (New York, 1995)

Werbner, Pnina, 'From rags to riches: Manchester Pakistanis in the textile trade', *New Community*, 8:1–2 (1980), pp. 84–95

Werbner, Pnina, *The Migration Process: Capital, Gifts and Offerings among British Pakistanis* (Oxford, 1990)

Werbner, Pnina, 'Renewing an industrial past: British Pakistani entrepreneurship in Manchester', in Judith M. Brown and Rosemary Foot (eds), *Migration: The Asian Experience* (Basingstoke, 1994), pp. 104–30

Werbner, Pnina, 'What colour 'success'? Distorting value in studies of ethnic entrepreneurship', *Sociological Review*, 47:3 (1999), pp. 548–79

Werbner, Pnina, *Imagined Diasporas among Manchester's Muslims: The Public Performance of Pakistani Transnational Identity Politics* (Oxford, 2002)

Werbner, Pnina, 'South Asian entrepreneurship in Britain: A critique of the ethnic enclave economy debate', in Léo-Paul Dana (ed.), *Handbook of Research on Ethnic Minority Entrepreneurship: A Co-evolutionary View on Resource Management* (Cheltenham, 2007), pp. 375–89

Werbner, Pnina and Anwar, Muhammad (eds), *Black and Ethnic Leaderships: The Cultural Dimensions of Political Action* (London, 1991)

Wills, Jane, Datta, Kavita, Evans, Yara, Herbert, Joanna, May, Jon and McIlwaine, Cathy, *Global Cities at Work: New Migrant Divisions of Labour* (London, 2009)

Wilpert, Czarina, 'Children of foreign workers in the Federal Republic of Germany', *International Migration Review*, 11:4 (1977), pp. 473–85

Wilpert, Czarina, 'Germany: From workers to entrepreneurs', in Robert Kloosterman and Jan Rath (eds), *Immigrant Entrepreneurs: Venturing Abroad in the Age of Globalization* (Oxford, 2003), pp. 233–60

Wood, Martin, Hales, Jon, Purdon, Susan, Sejersen, Tanja and Hayllar, Oliver, *A Test for Racial Discrimination in Recruitment Practice in British Cities* (Leeds: Department for Work and Pensions, 2009)

Worbs, Susanne, 'The second generation in Germany: Between school and labor market', *International Migration Review*, 37:4 (2003), pp. 1011–38

Worthington, Ian, Ram, Monder and Jones, Trevor, 'Exploring corporate social responsibility in the U.K. Asian small business community', *Journal of Business Ethics*, 67:2 (2006), pp. 201–17

Yalçin-Heckmann, Lale, 'Negotiating identities: Media representations of different generations of Turkish migrants in Germany', in Deniz Kandiyoti and Ayşe Saktanber (eds), *Fragments of Culture: The Everyday of Modern Turkey* (London, 2002), pp. 308–21

Yilmaz, Hakan and Aykaç, Çağla E. (eds), *Perceptions of Islam in Europe: Culture, Identity and the Muslim 'Other'* (London, 2012)

Zentrum für Türkeistudien (ed.), *Nur der Wandel hat Bestand. Ausländische Selbständige in Deutschland* (Essen, 1995)

Zentrum für Türkeistudien, *Die Regionalen Transferstellen für ausländische Existenzgründer und Unternehmer in Nordrhein Westphalen. Ökonomische Daten der türkischen und ausländischen Selbständigen in NRW und Deutschland* (Essen, 1999)

Zentrum für Türkeistudien, *Türkische Unternehmer und das duale Ausbildungssystem: Empirische Untersuchung von Möglichkeiten der beruflichen Ausbildung in türkischen Betriebsstätten in Deutschland* (Münster, 1999)

Zentrum für Türkeistudien, *Türkische Unternehmer in Bremen und Bremerhaven. Eine Analyse ihrer Struktur, ihrer wirtschaftlichen Situation sowie ihrer Integration in das deutsche Wirtschaftsgefüge – Ergebnisse einer standardisierten telefonischen Befragung im Auftrag der Ausländerbeauftragten des Bundeslandes Bremen* (Essen, 2001)

Index

Afro-Caribbeans
  in Britain 44, 88, 149
  in Newcastle 115–17, 121
AG Weser 57, 69, 126–7, 129, 133
  see also shipbuilding
Alevis 24
Anatolia 25
Ansari, Humayun 7, 13, 21, 23, 35, 43–4, 49, 93, 96, 116, 149, 158–9, 166, 173, 185, 222, 225
Arabs 17–18, 42
  see also South Shields
asylum seekers and refugees
  in Bremen 137
  in Britain 13, 149, 171, 219
  in Germany 219
  in Newcastle 97–8
attacks
  on ethnic minorities in Newcastle 48–51, 109–10, 118–22
  on properties in Newcastle 111, 118–20, 122
  see also bullying; crime; graffiti; harassment; racism

attainment and success (educational)
  in Bremen 195, 208–9, 213–14, 217, 224
  in Britain 30, 153, 155–6
  in Germany 30, 155, 157, 188, 203
  in Newcastle 160, 166–8, 213–15, 217, 224
Aumund-Hammersbeck 133

Baden-Württemberg 61, 66, 68, 190
bankruptcy 79, 83
barrack accommodation in Bremen 14, 125, 129–31, 136
  houseboat 130
Bavaria 66, 154, 190, 193
Bengalis in Newcastle 98, 108–12, 117
Bentinck Estate 98, 108–11, 123–5
Benwell 108
Berlin 15, 33, 73, 91, 132, 154, 189–90, 193, 214, 217, 226
  Kreuzberg 126, 142

bilingual classes and children 153, 181–2, 186
  in Bremen 186
  in Germany 153
  in Newcastle 181–2
  see also mother-tongue languages; tuition
Birmingham 15, 40, 43, 55, 89, 167, 171, 184, 226
  Sparkbrook 89
Blockdiek 133, 141–2
Blumenthal 61, 133–4, 138–9, 141–2, 205–6
Böhrnsen, Jens 20
Bradford x, 15, 46, 88, 93, 170–1, 184–5, 217
Bremen-Vegesacker Fischerei-Gesellschaft 57, 129
Bremer Klausel 187, 211
Bremer Silberwarenfabrik 133
Bremer Vulkan 57, 64, 69, 129–31, 133
  see also shipbuilding
Bremer Woll-Kämmerei 57, 63, 129, 133
Bremerhaven 21, 23, 75–7
bullying 118
  at school 156
  at the workplace 63
  see also attacks; crime; graffiti; harassment; racism
Burglesum 61
businesses and businessmen 30, 33–7, 39–59, 71–84, 86, 93, 96, 102, 119, 135, 143, 147, 185, 216–17, 225
  see also entrepreneurialism and entrepreneurship; self-employment

Byker 50

Cameron, David x, 6, 55
Cardiff 17
Census 12, 22, 31, 40–1, 88, 93, 97–8, 107
Chinese 37, 44, 53, 72, 115–16
  Chinatown in Newcastle 52
citizenship 2, 12, 66, 73, 218–19
Cleveland 120
Cologne 91
concentration
  in education 161, 163–4, 166, 184, 194–5, 198–9, 205, 207, 214, 218
  in employment 29, 47, 83, 104
  in housing 88–9, 93, 101, 110, 126, 131, 133, 136, 138–42, 144–5, 147
  see also segregation
council or social housing
  in Bremen 126, 133, 135–7
  in Britain 88–9, 109
  in Germany 90
  in Newcastle 98–9, 101–2, 108, 110, 113–17, 123–4, 145
credit drapery 40–2, 45
  see also Jewish immigrants in Newcastle; peddlers; self-employment
crime 48, 51, 54, 56, 110, 118
  see also attacks; bullying; graffiti; harassment; racism
curriculum 160, 165, 170–1, 175–7, 187, 196, 211–12, 216

Das Viertel 126
Davies, Jon Gower 20, 42, 101–3, 125

diploma 186, 195, 201, 208, 214
discrimination 2, 11, 17–18, 28, 33–6, 39–40, 43, 56–7, 63–4, 76, 83, 86, 88–91, 94, 96–7, 100, 102–3, 105, 107, 113, 125, 127–8, 135–6, 145–6, 155–6, 166, 169–70, 172, 175, 193, 214, 218, 224, 227

Elswick 97, 100, 117, 119, 122
Empire Windrush 4
entrepreneurialism and entrepreneurship 31, 35–6, 39–41, 43–57, 70–5, 77–86, 97, 104, 106, 123, 143, 145, 162, 218
  see also businesses and businessmen; self-employment
ethnicity xi, 22–3, 42, 74, 89, 92–3, 96, 159

Fenham 97–8, 108, 123, 146, 178
festivals 23, 141, 187
Frankfurt 15, 132, 217

German Socio-Economic Panel (GSOEP) 13, 32, 34
ghettoes 126, 131–2, 139, 141
Glasgow 43, 51
Gosforth 98, 123, 134
graffiti 50–1, 108, 110–12, 119
  see also attacks; bullying; crime; harassment; racism
Greeks in Bremen 21, 189, 193–4, 197
Grohn 126, 133, 136, 141–2
Gröpelingen 126–8, 131, 133–4, 138–42, 146, 198, 205–7

guest-worker rotation system or principle 3, 6, 10, 27–9, 33, 60, 63, 65, 67, 150, 219, 221

Häfen 134, 141, 205
harassment 48–51, 54, 56, 83, 93, 99, 106, 108–12, 117–24, 146–7, 182–3, 213
  see also attacks; bullying; crime; graffiti; racism
heating in accommodation 109, 112, 130, 142
Heaton 50, 100, 108, 117, 122, 178
Hemelingen 132, 134, 138–9, 141–2, 205–6
Herbert, Ulrich 3, 5, 10, 28, 63, 65, 90, 128, 220–1, 225
Hessen 61, 67
Hinduism 31
Hinterhof Moscheen 131
  see also mosques
home or property ownership 18, 42, 57, 82, 87, 99–100, 102–4, 116, 142–3, 168, 224
  see also mortgages; owner-occupancy or owner-occupation
homework 186, 200–1, 203, 208, 214–15
Honeyford Affair 170
Huckelriede 141–2
Huddersfield 40

income 37, 45, 49, 75–6, 91, 99, 102, 109
  see also wages
Integrationswoche 20, 23, 187
internships 85

Iranians in Bremen 22, 137–8
Irish in the North East of England 17–18
Islamic extremism, fundamentalism or terrorism x, 6–7, 10
Islamophobia 157, 227
Italians in Bremen 61, 193–4

Jesmond 98, 100–1, 108, 117, 123, 134
Jews 43
   Jewish immigrants in Newcastle 41–3
   see also credit drapery; peddlers; self-employment

Kashmir 24
Kattenturm 133, 138
kindergarten 186, 191, 202–3, 208–10, 212, 215
Kindergeld 150, 194
Klöckner steel- and metal-works 57, 126, 129
Konzeption zur Integration der ausländischen Arbeitnehmer und ihrer Familienangehörigen im Lande Bremen 1979 19, 66–7, 69, 128, 135, 193–5, 202–5
Koschnick, Hans 65, 132, 196
Krefeld 154
Kulturladen 127

landlords 90, 92, 102, 131, 145
   ethnic minority landlords 40, 100, 103
Leicester 52, 184
Lesum 141–2
Lindenhof 126, 133, 136, 141

Liverpool 17, 55
London x, 4, 6, 35, 40–1, 43, 55, 88, 91–3, 112–13, 120, 162, 184, 217, 222
   Hackney 113–14
   Waltham Forest 120–1
Lucassen, Leo 4, 6, 8, 63, 132, 137, 190, 195, 201, 218, 222–3, 227–8
Lüssum-Bockhorn 133, 138

Manchester 43, 46, 55, 170, 184
Merkel, Angela x, 6
Micro-census 13, 32, 34, 72
Mitte 134, 138, 141–2, 205–6
Modood, Tariq 7, 23, 28, 34, 46, 116, 149, 223
Monkchester 50
Moorside 97, 117, 119, 122
Moroccans in Bremen 22, 137, 204
mortgages 98, 100–2
   see also home or property ownership; owner-occupancy or owner-occupation
mosques x, 8, 23, 25, 96, 118, 124, 130, 141, 143, 147, 160, 175, 185, 187, 213, 216–17
   see also *Hinterhof Moscheen*
mother-tongue languages 81, 153–5, 161, 170, 172–3, 175–8, 180, 182, 184–7, 190–1, 194–6, 200, 202–4, 208, 210–11, 213
   see also bilingual classes and children; tuition
multiculturalism x, 6, 9, 56, 123, 219–20, 222

Munich 132
  Ludwigsvorstadt 142

neighbourhoods 21, 23, 30, 45, 48–9, 87–8, 91–6, 99, 101, 107, 117–20, 122–8, 131, 133, 136, 138–48, 151, 185, 216–17, 221–2, 224
Neustadt 134, 138–9, 141–2, 198, 205–7
newsagents 50, 53
  see also shopkeepers; shops; stores
nursery school 178, 186

Ohlenhof 133, 141–2
Oldham 88
Osterholz 127–8, 134, 141–2, 205–6
Ostertor 126, 133
Östliche Vorstadt 134, 138, 198, 205–7
overcrowding 18, 88, 90, 92, 99, 102, 108–9, 114–16, 124, 130, 133, 137, 142, 146–7
owner-occupancy or owner-occupation 11, 87–90, 95, 98, 102, 105, 107, 109, 123–5, 142–3, 145–6, 217
  see also home or property ownership; mortgages

Panayi, Panikos xi, 2, 4, 9, 15, 18, 21, 56, 90, 149, 219
Parekh, Bhikhu 113, 223
  see also The Future of Multi-Ethnic Britain: The Parekh Report
parents 25, 29, 110, 151, 156–7, 161, 167–8, 170, 172–3, 179, 181–2, 193–6, 201, 203, 207–12, 214–15
Peach, Ceri xi, 4, 12, 31, 49, 89, 93, 104, 147, 223
peddlers 43
  see also credit drapery; Jewish immigrants in Newcastle; self-employment
Phillips, Deborah 12, 15, 87–9, 93, 110, 112–13, 116, 120, 122
PISA (Programme for International Student Assessment) 155, 188, 214
police 51, 106, 111–12, 119–22
Portuguese in Bremen 193–4
Powell, Enoch 16
primary schools or education 163–5, 176, 178, 181, 186, 189, 191, 198–9, 201, 204–7
  Buntentorsteinweg school 198
  Elswick Road Junior 164
  Halmerweg school 198, 207
  Kirchenallee school 198, 207
  Schule an der Schmidtstraße 20, 189, 198–202, 207
  Sonderschule 204
  Westgate Hill Infant School 164–5
  Westgate Hill Junior School 164–5
  West Jesmond Junior School 178
Punjab 24, 43

qualifications 30, 36, 156–7, 162, 171, 177, 180, 209, 213

Race Relations Act (1965) 3
Race Relations Act (1968) 3

Race Relations Act (1976) 3, 84, 105, 169
race riots 18, 106
racism 16, 35, 43, 51, 56, 60, 89, 102–3, 118, 122, 152, 155–6, 161–2, 169, 172–4, 185–6, 227
   see also attacks; bullying; crime; graffiti; harassment
Rampton Report 152, 169
regional patriotism or identity 11, 16, 226
   in Bremen 18–20
   in Newcastle 16–18, 42
religious education or instruction x, 158, 161, 170, 174, 185, 187, 211–13, 215–16
   confessional religious education 187
restaurant and catering trade 77, 83
restaurants 36–7, 43, 45–6, 53, 71, 86, 108
restaurant trade 20, 37
   see also takeaways
Reyrolles 38, 163
Rushdie Affair x, 6
Rye Hill 42, 102–3

Sandyford 50, 108, 176
Scarman Report 54, 105–6
Schönwälder, Karen 6, 9, 10, 59, 67, 87, 91, 132, 220–1, 227
Scotswood 49
seamen 1, 18
secondary schools or education 154, 164–5, 172, 176–7, 180–1, 186, 189, 194–5, 199, 209
   Gymnasium 186, 189, 194–5, 199, 204, 209, 214–15
   Hauptschule 189, 194–5, 198–9, 201–2, 204, 207, 209
   Heaton Manor 180–1
   Hemelinger Straße school 198
   Kornstraße school 198, 207
   Realschule 194–5, 199, 204, 209, 214
   Redewood school 180–1
   Rutherford school 178, 180–1
   Schule an der Schmidtstraße 20, 189, 198–202, 207
   Slatyford Comprehensive School 163, 165
   Sonderschule 204
   see also vocational training or education
segregation 11, 18, 20–1, 44, 87–8, 90–3, 95–6, 106, 110, 125, 130, 132, 136, 140, 146–7, 224
   self-segregation 93, 103, 166
   see also concentration
self-employment 11, 31, 33, 36, 40–5, 47–8, 53–4, 70–1, 73, 75–6, 78, 82, 84, 86, 106, 168, 224
   see also businesses and businessmen; credit drapery; entrepreneurialism and entrepreneurship; Jewish immigrants in Newcastle; peddlers
Sheffield 120–1
shipbuilding 16, 57–8, 62, 69, 126
   see also AG Weser; Bremer Vulkan
shipping 16, 18, 62
shopkeepers 41–2
   see also newsagents; shops; stores

shops 23, 37, 41–3, 45–6, 48–50, 52, 71, 86, 98, 102, 125, 127, 221
  see also newsagents; shopkeepers; stores
Sikhs 31
Sivas 25
South Asian bus crews in Newcastle 38–9
South Shields 17–18, 20–1, 41–2
Spanish in Bremen 61, 189, 193–4
Staatsarchiv Bremen xii, 63, 129
Ständige Konferenz der Kultusminister der Länder in der Bundesrepublik Deutschland or KMK 153–4, 189, 197, 202–3
Stimme 186
stores 25, 34, 37, 41, 50, 71, 143, 217
  see also newsagents; shopkeepers; shops
Sunnis 23–4
Swann Report 152, 169–70, 173–5, 177, 180, 184
Sylhet 24

takeaways 37, 45, 50, 53, 108
  see also restaurant and catering trade
Taylor, J.H. 20, 24, 39–43, 45, 101, 125, 166–8
teachers x, 150, 153, 156, 160–1, 166–7, 174, 176–9, 181, 186–7, 191, 195–6, 199–200, 202–3, 208
  ethnic minority teachers 163, 170, 174, 177, 186, 197–8, 200, 203, 208
  head teachers 165, 170, 183
  peripatetic teachers 176–7
Teesside 41
tenants 48, 93, 100, 103, 111, 116, 147, 168
Tenever 126–8, 133, 138, 140–2
The Future of Multi-Ethnic Britain: The Parekh Report 29, 46, 114, 161
  see also Parekh, Bhikhu
Tomlinson, Sally 7, 106, 149–50, 152–3, 155, 169–71
tuition
  English language 165
  German language 191–2, 195, 197, 199, 201, 204, 208
  see also bilingual classes and children; mother-tongue languages; *Vorbereitungsklassen*
Tunisians in Bremen 22, 137, 205
Tyneside 16–18, 20, 40–2, 161–2

underachievement (educational) 152, 155, 159, 167, 169–70, 186, 201, 214, 216
unemployment 19, 27–9, 31–3, 39, 44–5, 56–8, 67, 69–71, 75–6, 88–9, 126–7

Vahr 141–2, 205–6
Vegesack 61, 134, 136, 138–9, 205–6
vocational training or education 157, 186, 203, 208–9
Vorbereitungsklassen 153, 197, 207

wages 28, 30, 39, 63, 104, 224
  see also income

Walle 134
Wingrove 97, 117, 122
Woltmershausen 134

Yemenis 1, 20
Yugoslavians in Bremen 193–4, 197

Zentrum für Türkeistudien und Integrationsforschung 71–3, 75–8, 80–2, 86
zukunftsblind 10, 65
Zweites Deutsches Fernsehen (ZDF) 64